Neuroscience Meets Cybersecurity

Applying Brain Science to Enhance Digital Protection

Kritika

Apress®

Neuroscience Meets Cybersecurity: Applying Brain Science to Enhance Digital Protection

Kritika
Independent Researcher(Neuro-cybersecurity), New Delhi, Delhi, India

ISBN-13 (pbk): 979-8-8688-2182-0   ISBN-13 (electronic): 979-8-8688-2183-7
https://doi.org/10.1007/979-8-8688-2183-7

Managing Director, Apress Media LLC: Welmoed Spahr
Acquisitions Editor: Susan McDermott
Project Manager: Jessica Vakili

Distributed to the book trade worldwide by Springer Science+Business Media New York, 1 New York Plaza, New York, NY 10004. Phone 1-800-SPRINGER, fax (201) 348-4505, e-mail orders-ny@springer-sbm.com, or visit www.springeronline.com. Apress Media, LLC is a Delaware LLC and the sole member (owner) is Springer Science + Business Media Finance Inc (SSBM Finance Inc). SSBM Finance Inc is a **Delaware** corporation.

For information on translations, please e-mail booktranslations@springernature.com; for reprint, paperback, or audio rights, please e-mail bookpermissions@springernature.com.

Apress titles may be purchased in bulk for academic, corporate, or promotional use. eBook versions and licenses are also available for most titles. For more information, reference our Print and eBook Bulk Sales web page at http://www.apress.com/bulk-sales.

If disposing of this product, please recycle the paper

Table of Contents

About the Author xiii

About the Technical Reviewers xv

Acknowledgments xvii

Foreword xix

Chapter 1: Introduction – The Future of Cybersecurity and
Neuroscience 1

Neuroscience: An Unlikely Ally in Cybersecurity 6

Gaps in Today's Cyber Defense Models...11

    Static Authentication Processes and Slow Response Strategies 13

    User Cognitive States Neglect by Existing Detection Systems....................14

    Predicting and Preempting Human-Error-Induced Breaches 15

    Siloed Threat Intelligence and Outdated Regulatory Mechanisms...............16

    The Role of Neuroscience in Addressing Cybersecurity Gaps 17

Innovation Imperatives..19

    Beyond Enhancement: Redefining Cybersecurity Through Neuroscience.....20

    Building Neuro-Aware Security Systems..20

    Cognitive Training As a Core Component of Cybersecurity.........................22

    Neuro-Rights and the Policy Imperative 23

    Toward a Human-Centric Cybersecurity Paradigm..................................24

Key Takeaways..26

Chapter 2: The Neuroscience Behind Human Decision-Making..........27

Why This Chapter Matters? 30

The Neurobiology of Decision-Making 32

    Prefrontal Cortex (Executive Function and Risk Analysis) 33

    Amygdala (Threat Perception and Emotional Triggers).................35

    Anterior Cingulate Cortex (Conflict Resolution) 36

    Striatum and Dopaminergic Circuits: Habitual and Reward-Based Decisions 37

The Decision Loop: From Stimulus to Response 39

Application in Cyber Contexts: Brains on the Battlefield 49

Key Takeaways...56

Chapter 3: Behavioral Biometrics and Its Role in Security................59

Why Behavioral Biometrics Matters?..63

    It Is Not Safe to Rely Only on Passwords and Tokens.................63

    They Enable Continuous Authentication Beyond Login.................64

    User Experience Is Preserved, Not Compromised 64

    Adaptive Intelligence Enhances Resilience 64

    Insider Threat Detection Becomes Viable 65

Types of Behavioral Biometrics 67

    Keystroke Dynamics..68

    Mouse Movement Analysis 71

    Gait Recognition 73

    Touchscreen Gesture Recognition 74

    Voice Behavioral Biometrics...76

Neuroscientific Basis of Behavioral Biometrics 80

    Neural Basis of Habit Formation and Muscle Memory 81

    Role of Motor Cortex, Basal Ganglia, and Cerebellum in Patterned Movements...84

Influence of Cognitive Load and Emotional State on Behavioral Patterns 85

Brain-Behavior Correlations Supporting Biometric Stability 87

Challenges and Opportunities in Neuroscience-Informed Behavioral
Biometrics 88

Ethical, Legal, and Privacy Dimensions 90

Neuroethics of Unconscious Behavioral Profiling 91

Data Minimization and Consent in Neural-Informed Behavioral Data 94

Risk of Cognitive/Emotional Inference Beyond Intent 97

Future Outlook: Toward Neuroadaptive Biometric Ecosystems 100

AI + Neuroscience Convergence in Behavioral Authentication 100

Wearables and EEG-Informed Systems (Neuro-Biometrics) 102

Predictive Behavioral Analytics for Insider Threat Detection 104

Role of Personalized Neuroprofiles in Continuous Cybersecurity 106

Key Takeaways 108

**Chapter 4: How Brain–Computer Interfaces Will Transform
Cybersecurity?** **111**

Why the Chapter Matters? 113

Introduction to Brain–Computer Interfaces (BCIs) 115

Invasive BCIs 115

Semi-invasive BCIs: A Middle Ground 117

Non-invasive BCIs: The Most Practical 118

BCIs in Cybersecurity: Unlocking New Dimensions of Digital Defense 122

Platforms and Tools for Brain–Computer Interfaces in Cybersecurity 127

BCI Hardware Devices 128

Hybrid Multi-modal BCIs 132

Invasive and Research-Grade BCIs 136

Middleware and Signal Processing Frameworks 139

Decision Matrix 144

Security Risks and Ethical Implications 145

    Neuroprivacy and Brainprint Protection 147

    Consent, Autonomy, and Neural Data Reuse............................ 148

    Adversarial Vulnerability of BCI Authentication Systems............ 149

    Backdoor and Poisoning Threats in Neural Models 149

    Wireless Communication and BLE Risks 150

    Workplace Surveillance and Cognitive Coercion 151

    Psychological Impact on Agency and Intent............................. 151

    Data Retention and Lifespan of Neural Templates.................... 152

    Ethical Risks in Invasive BCI Applications 153

    Governance, Oversight, and Neuroethical Certification 153

Future Landscape: Toward a Cognitive Perimeter in Cybersecurity................. 155

Key Takeaways.. 158

Chapter 5: Neural Authentication: The Next Generation of Cyber Protection **161**

The Paradigm Shift from Static to Dynamic Identity............................. 162

    The Emergence of the Fourth Paradigm: "Something You Think" 164

    Neural Patterns As the Ultimate Biometric Frontier.................... 165

Why Neural Authentication Is Necessary 169

    Collapse of Traditional Authentication Models........................... 169

    Rise of Immersive and Neuro-Adaptive Systems 171

    Zero Trust Requires Continuous Verification............................. 172

    Human-Centric, Frictionless Security 173

    Defense Against Future Threats 174

Why This Chapter Matters?.. 175

Foundations of Neural Biometrics... 176

    The Neurophysiological Basis of Brainwave Identity................... 176

    Cognitive Stimuli and Identity Elicitation 187

Signal Acquisition and Preprocessing Pipelines 188

Machine Learning and Neural Pattern Classification 191

Limitations and Variability in Neural Biometrics 193

Comparisons with Behavioral and Multimodal Biometrics 195

Implementation Frameworks and Architecture 201

Signal Acquisition 201

Edge Processing Layer 203

Secure Communication Layer – Advanced Cryptographic Framework 205

Authentication Engine – Intelligent Decision-Making 206

Key Takeaways 208

Chapter 6: Enhancing Cyber Threat Detection with Neurotechnology...211

Why This Chapter Matters? 216

The Existential Threat Crisis 216

The Human–Machine Symbiosis Imperative 216

The Workforce Transformation Revolution 217

The Economic Transformation Imperative 217

The Strategic Future Imperative 218

Neurotechnology-Enhanced Threat Detection 218

Human Pattern Recognition Superiority 219

Limitations of Traditional Automated Systems 222

Neurotechnology Integration Approach 224

Cognitive Augmentation Systems 225

Hybrid Human–AI Detection Systems 228

Neuroplasticity and Adaptive Threat Detection 230

Continuous Improvement Mechanisms 232

Brainwave Patterns, Neuroimaging, and EEG Data for Threat Identification 234

EEG-Based Threat Recognition Systems 235

Advanced Neuroimaging Applications 241

Practical Implementation Frameworks.. 244

Signal Processing and Pattern Recognition 248

Ethical Considerations and Privacy Protection... 250

Neural Privacy and Data Security.. 250

Informed Consent and Analyst Rights 251

Key Takeaways... 252

Chapter 7: Exploring the Intersection of AI, Neuroscience, and Cybersecurity **255**

Why This Chapter Matters?.. 261

Establishes the Strategic Intersection That Will Develop the Future of Cybersecurity.. 261

Adds Another Level of Situational Intelligence: Neuro-Cognitive intelligence 261

Bridges the Gap Between Human-Centric Security and Autonomous Defense 262

Introduces Neuro-Inspired AI As a Frontier for Secure and Resilient Computing 262

Gives Practical Case Studies and Models of High-Risk Sectors.................. 263

The Rise of Hybrid Threat Landscapes... 263

Evolution Beyond Binary Attacks... 265

AI-Powered Adversarial Systems 267

The Neuroscience Advantage in Defense 269

Key Insights and Strategic Implications 276

AI-Enhanced Neural Detection Systems 278

Enterprise AI Security Platforms with Neural Integration Potential............ 278

Specialized Biometric and Authentication Systems 285

Security Orchestration and Analytics Platforms 291

Neural Interface Technologies 295

Ethical Framework for AI-Neural Security Convergence 298

Privacy-Preserving Neural Analytics.. 299

Neural Data AI Processing Ethics 301

Multi-domain Ethical Oversight 303

Cognitive Autonomy Preservation... 305

Key Takeaways.. 309

**Chapter 8: Ethical and Policy Considerations in Neuro-Integrated
Security 311**

Why This Chapter Matters? 312

Establishes the Moral Boundary of Next-Gen Security Systems 313

Fills a Critical Policy Vacuum in a Rapidly Evolving Field 314

Prepares the Industry for Real-World Risk Scenarios 314

Promotes Global Awareness of Emerging Human Rights 315

Provides the Ethical Compass for Future Innovation 315

The Neurotechnology Security Landscape.. 316

Non-invasive BCI Security Applications.. 317

Invasive Neural Implant Security Applications 320

The Consumer Neurotechnology Ecosystem 323

Emerging Hybrid Security Architectures.. 326

The Convergence Crisis: When Technical Capabilities Outpace Ethical
Frameworks 328

Why Governance Must Outpace Innovation?.. 332

Privacy in the Age of Neuro-Surveillance.. 335

Defining Neuroprivacy: Identity at the Neural Layer 336

The Neural Fingerprint Paradox... 337

The Risk of Involuntary Neurodata Collection 343

Current Regulatory Landscape and Critical Gaps 344

    Global Policy Comparison Matrix 344

The Neural Rights Imperative 347

    The Moment of Irreversible Decision 347

    Constitutional Protection As Minimum Standard 348

    The Democratic Governance Challenge 348

    Innovation Without Wisdom 349

    Path Forward 349

Key Takeaways 351

Chapter 9: The Role of Neurofeedback in Cybersecurity 355

Why This Chapter Matters? 356

Emerging Technology Landscape 359

Dual-Purpose Nature 360

Critical Infrastructure Protection 361

Human Factor Enhancement 363

Introduction to Neurofeedback in Cybersecurity 364

    Historical Development from Clinical Applications to Security Contexts 365

    Types of Neurofeedback: EEG, fMRI, fNIRS-Based Systems 366

    Real-time Brain State Monitoring and Modulation Capabilities 372

Neurofeedback As a Cybersecurity Enhancement Tool 380

Cognitive Enhancement for Security Professionals 381

    Attention and Focus Improvement 381

    Stress Management and Decision-Making 384

Biometric Authentication and Identity Verification 386

    Brainwave-Based Authentication Systems 386

    Continuous Authentication Monitoring 388

Threat Detection and Analysis Enhancement...390

    Analyst Performance Optimization 390

    Automated Threat Response Systems...392

The Role of Neurofeedback in Cybersecurity...394

    Strategic Implementation Framework..394

    Risk-Benefit Analysis and Future Outlook 395

    Strategic Recommendations 397

Key Takeaways...398

Chapter 10: The Future of Neuroscience-Driven Cybersecurity........403

State-of-the-Art: Where We Are Now 407

    Cognitive Biometrics..407

    Neuroadaptive Security Systems 408

    Neurobehavioral Analytics...409

    Barriers and Limitations 410

    Momentum and the Road Ahead 411

Visionary Frontiers: What the Next Decade May Bring...................................411

    Neural-Digital Twins: Simulating Human Risk Behavior 412

    AI-Neurofeedback Fusion: Predictive and Adaptive Security.....................413

    Neuro-security Fabrics: Cognitive-Aware Environments............................414

    Quantum Neuro-Cyber Interfaces..414

    Neuro-Augmented Cyber Facilities: A Hypothetical Scenario.....................415

Overcoming Critical Challenges 416

    Privacy and Neuro-Ethics 417

    Technological Hurdles 420

    Societal and Workforce Acceptance 421

Future Governance and Policy Frameworks 426

Global Neuro-Rights Charters..426

Standardizing Legal and Ethical Protocols 427

Cross-Border Challenges for Neural Data..429

The Cognitive Frontier: Reimagining Cybersecurity for the Neuro-Digital Age....430

Why the Mind Is the Next Cybersecurity Frontier? 430

Call to Action for Researchers, Policymakers, and Enterprises 432

Key Takeaways...433

Index...437

About the Author

Kritika is a dynamic and experienced interdisciplinary cybersecurity researcher whose groundbreaking work dives deep into the human side of digital risk and explores how our brains, behaviors, and biases shape the way we respond to cyber threats. What makes her work truly stand out is her unique interdisciplinary lens, centered on the rapidly evolving field of neuro-cybersecurity where the frontiers of the human brain and digital security intersect, investigating how cognitive vulnerabilities and neural processes shape cybersecurity behavior, exposing new risks and redefining resilience in the digital age. At the forefront of pioneering the intersection between neuroscience and cybersecurity, Kritika possesses an unparalleled perspective on the critical challenge of how the domain of cybersecurity must understand and adapt to human cognitive patterns, a fundamental requirement that traditional cybersecurity experts consistently overlook when implementing autonomous security solutions. With a substantial portfolio of having authored a number of publications and keynote engagements with her insights featured in top journals and thought leadership platforms such as ISACA, CXO DigitalPulse, CIOTech World an IGI Global, and like, her research isn't just about identifying problems but designing human-centered, ethically sound solutions for tomorrow's cybersecurity threats. Kritika's brilliance has been recognized globally from the Trailblazer Award in Security to the Young Engineer and Young Researcher Awards, cementing her position as a visionary leader in the evolution of cybersecurity.

About the Technical Reviewers

Lt. Col. Harkamal Sidhu(Retd.) is a veteran of the Indian Army and has done his MTech in Computers and IT. He has been trained for Cyber Security in Australia. He is Fellow of Australian Risk Policy Institute (ARPI), Canberra, Australia. He has National and International Certifications in Cyber Security to his name. He has been handling Design & Development of AI-Powered Cyber Security Projects with Programming Requirements in Python Language and Hardening of Cyber Defence Posture of Critical Info Infrastructure (CII).

He was posted as an Instructor (Cyber Security) at Military College of Telecommunication Engineering (MCTE), Mhow, M.P., India. He conducted Basic and Advanced Level Cyber Security Courses for BTech and MTech qualified officers. He got commendation cards for rendering excellent services for imparting cyber services abroad. He was pivotal to the establishment of the Centre of Excellence for Cyber Forensics for a leading Indian organization.

He has worked as an SME (Cyber Security) for the Government of India, after taking premature retirement from the Indian Army as Cyber Security Specialist, where he worked closely with many cyber organizations across the world. He represented the Government of India during Government 2 Government (G2G) talks at various countries.

At present, he is serving as the Vice President, Strategy & Operations (Cyber), of a private sector cyber security organization.

Lt. Gen. Dr. Rajesh Pant(Retd.) (PVSM, AVSM, VSM), PhD, Ex-National Cyber Security Coordinator, PMO, Government of India (2019–2023)) is an internationally recognized cybersecurity leader and former National Cyber Security Coordinator of India, where he oversaw national-level efforts to strengthen cyber resilience. Under his leadership, India's ranking in the UN Global Cybersecurity Index rose from 47 to 10.

A PhD in Information Security Metrics, he also holds degrees from IIT Kharagpur, Madras University, and Osmania University. During his 41-year career in the Army Signals Corps, he headed the Army's Cyber Training establishment and received three Presidential awards for distinguished service. He has also been honored with the IETE Baliga Memorial Award (2013), IIT Kharagpur's Distinguished Alumni Award (2023), and FSAI's Lifetime Achievement Award (2024).

He has represented India at leading global cybersecurity platforms, including the World Economic Forum, Global Cybersecurity Forum, QUAD dialogues, and Prague 5G Conclave, and led the resilience vertical of the Global Counter Ransomware Initiative.

With a never-say-die attitude, he currently serves as Chairman of the Cyber Security Association of India, Chairman of India Future Foundation, and Global Advisor to CyberPeace Organization. General Pant brings deep expertise at the intersection of global-, national-, enterprise-, and citizen-level cyber governance and security.

Acknowledgments

I would like to express my deepest gratitude to everyone who supported me throughout the journey of this book. An appreciation to the Apress team whose initiative and commitment made it possible to bring forth this interdisciplinary integration.

I am also grateful to *Lt. Gen. (Dr.) Rajesh Pant (Retd.)* and *Lt. Col. Harkamal Sidhu (Retd.)* for their thoughtful insights, expertise, guidance, and motivation that enriched the depth and clarity of this book.

I thank my family for their constant support and blessings.

Finally, I appreciate the readers and learners who will engage with this work and spark new ideas in their own exploration.

Foreword

In the 21st century, two frontiers define the contours of human progress, the mysteries of the brain and the complexities of cyberspace. Neuroscience, with its quest to decode cognition, perception, and decision-making, offers profound insights into how humans process information and respond to threats. Cybersecurity, with its relentless battle against evolving digital adversaries, seeks to protect the very infrastructure upon which modern society depends. This book lays the foundation for the emergence of this new interdisciplinary field termed Neuro-Cybersecurity.

The book explores how cybersecurity ultimately depends not only on technology, but on the biological limits and behavior of the human brain, arguing that every cyber incident, from phishing to system breaches, originates in the brain's decision-making circuits. It also explains how fatigue, cognitive overload, and emotional hijacking reduce accuracy, leading to errors. It is no wonder that the human still remains the weakest link in the cyber kill chain.

The work arrives at a critical juncture where the acceleration of AI-powered threats and the emergence of cognitive manipulation as a strategic tool demands to reconsider the fundamental approach to security. Understanding these cognitive vulnerabilities is no longer an academic exercise but a strategic imperative, systematically integrating neuroscientific principles with operational cybersecurity requirements.

As you turn these pages, prepare to journey across disciplines. The discussion on Behavioral Biometrics is extremely interesting as we examine how the patterns of type, swipe, walk, speak or mouse movement arise from deep neural processes that are impossible to fake. Ethical and legal concerns are adequately addressed and the author has also proposed frameworks for layered consent, neuro rights, and transparent AI governance.

There is no doubt that Brain Computer Interfaces are poised to revolutionize cybersecurity, and neural authentication will replace traditional models based on knowledge (passwords), possession (tokens), or inherence (biometrics). The neuroscience advantage provides unique benefits against sophisticated AI based attacks, and I compliment the author for her detailed research on this extremely important, timely, and relevant subject.

—Lt. General (Dr.) Rajesh Pant
Fmr National Cyber Security Coordinator of India (PMO)

## CHAPTER 1

Introduction – The Future of Cybersecurity and Neuroscience

Cyber risks have been increasing for several years now in terms of frequency and complexity of attacks. The average cost to companies globally of a breach of data in 2024 was \$4.88 million, which was 10% up on the previous year.[1] Phishing and compromised credentials are the dominant ways of starting breaches with both accounting for 16% and 15% breaches, respectively. These techniques offer the first exposure to more advanced attacks, including ransomware and Business Email Compromise (BEC) which constitutes approximately 6% of breaches, which cost on average \$4.89 million in each incident.[2]

One of the latest cybercrime trends is the fusion of technical hacks and psychological operations to produce a hybrid threat arena. Such cyberattacks not only exploit machines, but also influence and modify the choice of users making use of social engineering as the biggest tool for

---

[1] https://www.ibm.com/reports/data-breach
[2] https://hoxhunt.com/blog/business-email-compromise-statistics

© Kritika 2026
Kritika, *Neuroscience Meets Cybersecurity*, https://doi.org/10.1007/979-8-8688-2183-7_1

98% of cyberattacks. Over a period of time, cybercrime has added a new vector to the ever-enlarging cyber threat surface. Cyberattacks have greatly intensified because of the increased utilization of artificial intelligence (AI) in cybercrime. With AI, attackers can perform scalable, personalized campaigns that are very lucrative and very difficult to recognize. This shift forces a revolution in traditional cybersecurity methods, which are unable to keep up with these ever-evolving types of attacks.

Lapses made by individuals are becoming increasingly linked to cybersecurity events. Human errors of misconfiguration and falling for social engineering in 2024 are responsible for 68% of data breaches, which calls for an effective management of human behavior to play a greater role in security of cyberspace. In particular, cybersecurity professionals are facing a significant level of stress and burnout.

According to the 2024 ISACA State of Cybersecurity report, the weight of growing cyber threats is making 66% of cybersecurity practitioners feel further stressed than just half a decade ago.[3] Surging stressors include threat complexity (81%), funding constraints (45%), and employment and recruitment/retention challenges (45%). In Europe, work stress or burnout is reported by 73% of IT professionals who largely blame the demanding workloads and the short deadlines. Especially with the ever-changing nature of cyber threats and the limitations of traditional security systems, there is a dire need for new security measures to be formulated.

The application of neuroscientific principles in cybersecurity strategies provides encouraging opportunities. The analysis of the cognitive mechanisms of the brain helps organizations to design systems that can explicitly counteract the counteraction of misuse and cognitive errors. A good example is the use of behavioral biometrics such as keystroke dynamics and mouse movements to authenticate the use in real time by recognizing and performing the unique behavioral patterns of an

---

[3] https://www.isaca.org/resources/news-and-trends/newsletters/atisaca/2024/volume-19/stress-levels-on-the-rise-for-cybersecurity-professionals

individual's behavior. By connecting the brain with security systems using Brain–Computer Interfaces[4] (BCIs), it will be feasible to make real-time threat assessments and countermeasures, which will highly improve the overall cybersecurity.

In addition, the use of neuro-feedback during awareness and training can enhance cybersecurity professionals' capability and can further reduce the chances of being attacked by social engineering techniques like phishing and pretexting. Integral to that, as threats become increasingly complex, integrating neuroscience into cybersecurity measures means better and more personalized defenses.

More worrisome is the emergence of hybrid threats as cyberattacks' growing use is made to alter perceptions, sway people's thinking, and shake confidence in authority. These efforts combine with psychological influence, along with very targeted digital strategies. Actions such as joint misinformation activity prior to pivotal votes or hacking mental health applications to destroy societal well-being clearly illustrate this new threat.

Much of the credit for the growth of these hybrid operations goes to the sophisticated methods of psychological profiling, stimulated by oceans of behavioral data collected with the help of social media, search engines, and other wearable devices. According to a recent analysis by NATO's Strategic Communications Centre of Excellence, psychographic targeting has emerged as one of the primary approaches, which adversaries use to affect voter behavior in a covert manner. The co-mingling of cybercrime with cognitive manipulation is becoming more unsettling to democratic institutions and cohesive feelings on the societal plane.

Worse yet, the increasing marketization of cyberweapons accelerates this problem. The platforms providing for services such as Ransomware-as-a-Service (RaaS) and sellers of zero-day exploits have lowered bars for entry of new players, with the requirement of a comparatively low skill set. Cyber warfare is democratized, and it presents opportunities to those

---

[4]`https://builtin.com/hardware/brain-computer-interface-bci`

motivated by intent and who have limited financial resources. Each year, according to Check Point Software Technologies, over 60% of ransomware attacks used kits acquired from dark web marketplaces, complete with support and how-to guides.[5]

The roll-out of new technologies, including generative AI, quantum computing, and edge processing, substantially improves the already complicated cyber space. The amount of generative AI malware being developed by hackers for generating dynamic evasive threats that morph on the fly to evade detection is steadily rising. The infancy of quantum computing, however, brings disquieting dangers to the security of current encryption systems. On the other hand, edge computing ensures low latency; however, it magnifies cybersecurity risks, by placing data centers almost in proximity of endpoints, that are rarely protected.

The criticality lies in the lack of preparedness both in the public and private settings. Poor cybersecurity education, fragmented threat modeling and analysis, and failure to effectively govern all work against us in a quest to stay one step ahead of cyber risks. A Cybersecurity Workforce Study revealed by (ISC)2 2024 indicates that there will be an overall shortage of over 3.4 million cybersecurity experts worldwide[6] in 2024.

Firewalls and signature-based defenses are under increasing attack from adaptive malware, which may use generative AI to mimic normal behavior patterns. At the same time, the diplomacy of countries is becoming increasingly intensified in the digital sphere, leading to the creation of hotspots of cyber conflict. Cyberattacks (massive and destructive) have become more and more common throughout the system, and they have targeted infrastructure sectors like energy grids

---

[5] https://www.checkpoint.com/solutions/ransomware-protection/
[6] https://www.isc2.org/Insights/2024/09/Employers-Must-Act-Cybersecurity-Workforce-Growth-Stalls-as-Skills-Gaps-Widen

and healthcare systems, which are primary to human existence. In 2024, a giant cyberattack on American water treatment facilities caused temporary outages for millions while exposing the undervalued risks inherent in critical infrastructure systems.[7]

The spread of synthetic identities in digital ecosystem has further added complexity to the already existing threats. Based on the merging of real records and faked information, these identities have criminal objectives, such as financial fraud, espionage, and disinformation. According to new Federal Reserve data released in 2024, synthetic identity fraud is America's most rapidly honed financial crime with billions being reported lost annually.[8]

Hackers exploit psychological weak points, emotional vulnerabilities, and human being's attention boundaries to break through security or to steal useful information. There has been increasing sophistication in social engineering due to the use of AI-generated voice patterns that not only represent emotional expression but also capture and adapt to regional accents. Within this turbulent environment, dependency on traditional cyber security solutions may not be effective. Such transformation necessitates the adoption of a completely new setup that exploits the zenith of adaptive and flexible defensive mechanisms: the human way of thinking, the human brain.

Digital and cognitive environments are converging, and our protection of tomorrow's threats will require a growing reliance on knowledge of the intricacies of human cognition, perception, and behavior as well as technological innovation. The view presented earlier outlines that cyber

---

[7] https://www.ibm.com/think/news/cyberattack-on-american-water-warning-critical-infrastructure

[8] https://www.moodys.com/web/en/us/kyc/resources/insights/synthetic-identities-and-why-they-are-important-in-todays-digital-landscape

threats of 2025 (and beyond) are leveraging to include not only breaches in the digital world but also the frailty vested in human decision-making and actions: the brain. What has until now been treated as a niche field within cybersecurity is rapidly becoming the centerpiece of knowledge about and action in combatting contemporary cyber threats.

Neuroscience: An Unlikely Ally in Cybersecurity

It may appear that neuroscience and cybersecurity are two separate fields, one exploring the inner workings of the mind and the other protecting environments of data. Becoming aware of the functioning of the brain has become not only timely but instrumental, considering cybercriminals exploit human cognitive weaknesses (i.e., biases, distractions, and errors in judgment). Neuroscience provides access to the neural base of behavior, cognition, perception, and emotional regulation factors that have a strong effect on technological interaction.

In 2025, neuroscience developments have exposed the biology that causes errors in judgment of cyber threats. Research using fMRI and EEG demonstrates that mental exhaustion, anxiety, and data overload disrupt a person's ability to recognize phishing attempts and to follow security directions.[9] Frontiers in Human Neuroscience in 2023 pointed out that people have diminished vigilance in the context of cybersecurity when overloaded cognitively, especially on important tasks such as threat recognition and incident resolution.[10]

---

[9] Arisoy, C. (2023). *A Neurophysiological Exploration of Human Behavior in User-Centered Cybersecurity* (Doctoral dissertation).

[10] Guidetti, O. A., Speelman, C., & Bouhlas, P. (2023). A review of cyber vigilance tasks for network defense. *Frontiers in Neuroergonomics, 4*, 1104873.

Moreover, neuroscience has an important role to play in creating cognitive-aware cybersecurity interfaces that can adapt functionality in gear to how a user is thinking. Imagine an authentication system that is responsive if users are mentally overwhelmed and may hold off critical actions until they regain focus, or phishing defenses that leverage eye-tracking and real-time neural feedback? Experts from the McGovern Institute at MIT are creating adaptive security systems that adapt round the clock using neural markers of fatigue or confusion.

New frontiers in BCI and neural sensor technologies are expanding the horizon of applications like these. In highly protected environments, BCIs have confirmed the identity of the user through unique patterns from brainwaves, a biometric that could not be replicated or stolen. Meanwhile researchers study neurofeedback as a technique for training cybersecurity specialists to be on high alert in critical working conditions. Why is the US Department of Defense researching real-time neurofeedback in Security Operations Centers (SOCs) to support analysts in breaking through tiredness, reduce mistake, and maintain the situational awareness during long operations?

Understanding the neural mechanisms behind social engineering gives us a better feel for the true scale of this threat, which is universally considered to be hackers' most powerful instrument. Investigating cognitive processing associated with trust, authority, and risk allows researchers to figure out which brain functions are easiest to overload during social engineering endeavors. The insights can be used to enhance user experience with redesigned interfaces, improve education programs, and enhance the techniques in incident management that target and mitigate the errors – the most vulnerable part of cybersecurity.

The *Nature Human Behaviour* research proved that the functional connection between neural activity in the dorsolateral prefrontal cortex and personal vulnerability to misinformation is established, which leaves room for further development of efficient training alternatives.[11] Neuroscience also pinpoints important brain reactions that inform impulsive digital habits – such as choosing unsafe links or not using strong passwords. These behaviors are amenable to systematic modification over time with the help of focused neural training and improvement of inhibitory control. This approach has become popular in research on digital addiction and is being trailed in cybersecurity behavior change projects.

The use of neuroscience to examine and improve vulnerabilities caused by human actions as a discipline is becoming very important. What was considered secondary in previous efforts is now essential for developing human-centered and relevant security systems. Neural data is set to facilitate the transition of cyber defenses from action on known attacks to proactive security of systems from the behaviors which often incite breaches.

Using neurofeedback with neural authentication, scientists are studying potential ways these new technologies can help raise cognitive functioning in cybersecurity professionals. Neurofeedback real-time monitoring of the cerebrum activity gives the individual the capacity to get timely feedback that assists them in self-regulating their processes of cognition. Relying on DARPA-managed projects, the US Department of Defense is offering neurofeedback to SOC analyst training programs.[12] The aim is to reduce cognitive burden, enhance situation appreciation, and increase resistance to stress when confronted with prolonged operations. First-hand experiments require that trainees demonstrate pertinently enhanced control over multitasking, retention of memory, and quicker responses in stressful situations – which are essential skills in SOC

---

[11] Medaglia, J. D., Zurn, P., Sinnott-Armstrong, W., & Bassett, D. S. (2017). Mind control as a guide for the mind. *Nature Human Behaviour*, *1*(6), 0119.
[12] https://www.darpa.mil/research/programs/next-generation-nonsurgical-neurotechnology

analysts. Although reinforcing performance is critical, neuroscience is also necessary in clarifying the points that make individuals vulnerable to social engineering attacks.

Hacking human psychology to extract private information or unsafe procedures is usually the best way cyber thieves circumvent security systems. Neuroscientists are known to use brain imaging methods to study the neural circuits for trust, risk perception, and judgment to understand which people are predisposed to social engineering. Studies show that increased vulnerability to misinformation and disinformation is associated with reduced neural activity in the dorsolateral prefrontal cortex, which is one of the key areas for critical thinking and executive function.[13] This information could help develop training solutions that address neurological vulnerabilities directly, stepping out of the box of a person relying on superficial hints.

Moreover, by tracking the behavioral patterns, neuroscience will be able to reveal the underlying cognitive factors that make the individual vulnerable to online threats.[14] The most common risky behavior that people pursue online, such as clicking on suspicious links repeatedly, selecting weak passwords, or failure to update software, are often guided by innate cognitive biases. With interventions, neuroplasticity-boosting exercises, and behavioral priming techniques that include inhibitory control training the undesirable online behaviors can be transformed gradually. Similarly, such comparable methods have shown to work in clinical settings such as in substance abuse therapy and are under review regarding their use in cybersecurity behavior change efforts.

---

[13] Zhao, S., Wang, T., & Xiong, B. (2025). Neural correlates of conspiracy beliefs during information evaluation. *Scientific Reports*, *15*(1), 1–9.

[14] Naseem, S., Alhudhaif, A., Anwar, M., Qureshi, K. N., & Jeon, G. (2023). Artificial general intelligence-based rational behavior detection using cognitive correlates for tracking online harms. *Personal and Ubiquitous Computing*, *27*(1), 119–137.

Eye-tracking, including in integration with neural signals, has great promise in the identification of deception or hesitation in virtual communication.[15] From laboratory studies, scientists have combined pupilometry with EEG to detect occasions when users show uncertainty, confusion, or deception while using secure systems. The detected signals may trigger immediate automatic alerts, confirmation requests, or trigger the security protocols measure. Application possibilities are online banking fraud prevention and monitoring suspicious behavior among employees within corporate systems.

Nonetheless, embedding neural data in cybersecurity measures may create serious ethical dilemmas. Although monitoring brain activity provides promising enhancements to security, there are increasing concerns about mental privacy, need for consent, restriction of purpose and the prospect of cognitive surveillance. With the lines between cognitive enhancement and intrusive surveillance becoming increasingly indistinct, regulatory guidelines must evolve to protect what experts call "neuro rights" – rights of mental privacy, freedom to think and act on one's own, and refusal to data-driven manipulation.

Chile[16] has amended its constitution to provide for neuro rights whereas Spain has legislatively overseen the use of neurotechnology in the public and private spheres. Such a development means that cybersecurity and civil liberties will stand a greater degree of entanglement going forward that will require the collaboration of engineers, scientists, ethicists, and legal scholars, as well as human rights activists.

As such possibilities emerge, the integration of neuroscience in cybersecurity is a necessity to make an urgent need to keep up with technology. With an ever-widening digital horizon, exposure of the human

---

[15] Celniak, W., Słapczyńska, D., Pająk, A., Przybyło, J., & Augustyniak, P. (2023). Intelligent eye-tracker-based methods for detection of deception: A survey. *Electronics*, *12*(22), 4627.

[16] Porter, A. (2023). Neurorights: An Expansion of Life in Chile.

brain to cyberattacks is escalating, hence necessitating cyber protections to do likewise. Our next-generation systems should move from passive reaction to external threats to proactive evaluation and improvement of the cognitive health of its users.

Using those main points regarding neuroscience contributions to create adaptive and cognitive security practices earlier on, we move to the weaknesses of the present-day cybersecurity architecture. Along those lines, even though investment in the cybersecurity systems has gone up, there has not been an established decrease in the rate of breaches. This mismatch signals a critical problem that underlies the approach, most of today's cybersecurity systems tend to react after the attack (i.e., detected vulnerabilities) as opposed to working in advance. Such systems are based on deterministic principles, where they do not consider the subtleness of the human mind and behavior.

Gaps in Today's Cyber Defense Models

Conventionally, the use of passwords or biometrics does not handle changes in threat environments. Authentication systems usually cannot identify threats when users log in with legitimate credentials while under stress or mentally tired. Anomaly systems do not always identify concealed, stable operating threats or misinterpret normal activities as a risk due to the absence of proper context. The lack of understanding of an individual's state of cognition is most probably the greatest failure in a security system. The existing threat detection mechanisms do not allow the system to identify when a user is distracted, when they are emotionally predisposed to make bad decisions, or under cognitive overload – all but intensifying the risk of phishing, errors, or unwitting disclosure. In other words, current systems do not understand users as living, biologically different people with mutable mental capacities.

Although technical expertise is highly desired, the psychological preparation of cybersecurity experts is often overlooked in the training curricula. Cognitive fatigue suffered by staff in security operation centers, which is very common, prolongs responses and heightens the chance of oversight.[17] According to a survey in 2023 by ISACA, most security professionals already burn out early in their working lives, exposing latent areas of vulnerability that threatens national security as well as organizational health.[18] Interdisciplinary integration is also lacking. Although AI and machine learning have become popular, present development tends to disregard the principles of neuroscience. That results in AI tools being quite powerful in computational tasks but that are far from being able to mimic or complement the way human minds function.

Even though there has been significant improvement in the area of cybersecurity, existing measures against defense have proven to be inadequate when dealing with the complex and changing threats of today. Although significant strides have been made using innovations such as machine learning and AI in threat detection, traditional cybersecurity frameworks are still able to clearly demonstrate the inherent limitations.[19] The failure of these models to consider the human aspect of cybersecurity is most glaring because human error accounts for most security vulnerabilities. Also, existing cybersecurity models have no ability to foresee, prevent, or respond to the increasing hybrid threats, combining technical assault and psychological manipulation.

---

[17] Baruwal Chhetri, M., Tariq, S., Singh, R., Jalalvand, F., Paris, C., & Nepal, S. (2024). Towards human-ai teaming to mitigate alert fatigue in security operations centres. *ACM Transactions on Internet Technology*, *24*(3), 1–22.

[18] https://www.isaca.org/resources/news-and-trends/newsletters/atisaca/2023/volume-48/cybersecurity-and-burnout-the-cybersecurity-professionals-silent-enemy

[19] https://www.isaca.org/resources/isaca-journal/issues/2025/volume-1/a-neuroscience-perspective-on-ai-and-cybersecurity

Static Authentication Processes and Slow Response Strategies

Static authentication methods are the major failings in contemporary practices of cybersecurity. Even though measures like passwords or PIN entreaty or fingerprints or facial recognition are embraced widely, they do not consider the dynamic and variable human cognition that matters in the current cybersecurity situation.[20] There is a lot of individual cognitive variability such as distraction, fatigue, and emotional strain that often impede delivery of secure use of digital technology. Current authentication systems do not consider the shifting conditions of mental and emotional states of users. Such weakness is especially noticeable in such sensitive areas as financial transactions, medical systems, and government services, where authentication error may result in severe consequences.

Assuming the user gets momentarily distracted, that person might end up letting a cybercriminal through security measures. Because they concentrate on simple verification, standard security norms have difficulty detecting cases where the mental or emotional state of a true user has been compromised. Because these systems are static, however, they cannot follow the ever-changing threat landscape. With social engineering and SIM swapping and deepfake identity theft bypassing traditional security protocols, attackers are getting better at exploiting flaws in the authentication system. According to the 2024 IBM Security Intelligence Report, these attacks have increased by a worrying 25% in the past year, which has exposed the more careful probing of conventional authentication techniques.[21]

---

[20] Shree, R., & Kumar, V. (2024, January). Understanding the limitations of authentication protocols employed by existing information security models for networked applications. In *2024 International Conference on Optimization Computing and Wireless Communication (ICOCWC)* (pp. 1-7). IEEE.

[21] https://www.ibm.com/reports/threat-intelligence

User Cognitive States Neglect by Existing Detection Systems

Traditional cybersecurity models are quite weak in regard to overcoming the cognitive blinders found in human behavior. Currently, security systems mainly rely on anomaly detection algorithms used to analyze user behavior through anomalies for detection of threats. Though anomaly detection has been effective in a variety of cases, it does not allow for the psychological and cognitive factors influencing the user. The cognitive human issues including stress, cognitive overload, or emotional coercion, continually let slip through the net of modern detection mechanisms.

A striking example is the "alert fatigue" that cybersecurity specialists suffer from, which reduces workers to a state of relaxed alertness to the constant flow of warnings, thus making it harder to distinguish between false signals and actual threats. They may, therefore, overlook intolerable threats or just cause the routine activities to be marked as threats.

A report in 2023 that more than 70% of cybersecurity practitioners are burnt out, while close to 50% state that this hinders their ability to respond to incidents.[22] This problem does not lie in the workplace, where it affects the average user who might not be able to distinguish between a legitimate presence and a malicious one under mental strain. The fact that cognitive strain is not monitored in mechanisms of threat detection prevents many devastating breaches from becoming visible, or forces organizations to be in a state of vulnerability for long periods. In extreme pressure circumstances, such as during a major cyberattack/incursion, even security professionals may find it difficult to always maintain the required alertness. Consequently, the very mechanisms that are in place to thwart these threats are vulnerable to leaks due to cognitive flaws.

---

[22] https://media.isc2.org/-/media/Project/ISC2/Main/Media/documents/research/ISC2_Cybersecurity_Workforce_Study_2023.pdf

Predicting and Preempting Human-Error-Induced Breaches

Another great problem of modern cybersecurity is the lack of ability to detect and fix breaches caused by human error. Cybersecurity experts are also human and as such can make human mistakes and exhibit limitations. The most dangerous risk factor in most security architectures is user interaction. Reports from the InfoSecurity Magazine states that human error happens to be a contributing factor to about 95% of all cybersecurity incidents.[23] Ordinary problems such as clicking on phishing links, weak credentials, or mishandling private data are typically the foremost cause for large security incidents.

Human behavior is not a priority for existing cybersecurity measures and always gets relegated to backstage vis-à-vis technical measures. These models presume that as a cause of security breaches, the main sources of the issue are coding errors or hacking infiltration, while side-stepping the serious attack through users' actions that may reveal vulnerabilities. Existing cybersecurity frameworks are generally not as effective in analyzing than assessing imminent user mistakes or potential breakdowns. Hence, they are often reactive rather than being proactive, with focus on discovering and eliminating breaches. This issue is magnified by the lack of customized and tailor-made security solutions.

Traditional approaches impose one-size-fits-all rules to all clients in the hope that their behavior is stable and homogenous. This is because human actions are fluid and usually personal depending on prevailing circumstances. Take the example of a user who has recently suffered trauma, thereby risking an increase in their chances to fall prey to social

---

[23] https://www.infosecurity-magazine.com/news/data-breaches-human-error/

engineering or a worker, tired after a long day, who may make passwords less secure by leaving loopholes. Traditional models of cybersecurity do not take such special human factors into account, and thus, they fail to address the specific threats individual behavior will pose.

Siloed Threat Intelligence and Outdated Regulatory Mechanisms

The existing defense models are lacking because of the segmented approach adopted in dealing with threat intelligence and failure to align regulatory frameworks as cybersecurity threats evolve at a very fast rate.[24] Despite improving cooperative efforts between organizations and sectors, there is continued lack of information-sharing in various parts of the world. Sharing cyber threat intelligence is quite limited to particular organizations and governments, which creates serious voids in respect to collective use of information in relation to cybersecurity. Due to the lack of coordination, certain attacks that might be experienced by a single entity go unnoticed in other organizations or sectors, creating a patchwork of vulnerabilities.

Also, many existing regulations were established before the appearance of AI-based threats, which make them inadequate for contemporary complex cyber threats. Privacy regulations, data protection rules, and cybersecurity protocols were developed without considering the furious growth of cyber threats or the escalating power of AI and quantum computing. The regulatory environment has not yet built standards regarding neuro-rights or cognitive privacy which are on the verge of becoming focal points as neuroscience and AI progress in cybersecurity.

---

[24] Khan, O. U., Abdullah, S. M., Olajide, A. O., Sani, A. I., Faisal, S. M. W., Ogunola, A. A., & Lee, M. D. (2024). The Future of Cybersecurity: Leveraging Artificial Intelligence to Combat Evolving Threats and Enhance Digital Defense Strategies. *Journal of Computational Analysis and Applications, 33*(8).

Incompatibility of various threat intelligence makes it even harder with the lack of uniform cybersecurity laws from country to country. An example is that even though some areas advocate for strict data protection standards (like GDPR), many jurisdictions are more supportive of the interest of industry trading at the expense of harsher cybersecurity. A disparate position on cybersecurity internationally provides an opportunity to adversaries located in countries with lax regulations to target weaknesses in the systems.

The Role of Neuroscience in Addressing Cybersecurity Gaps

With the limitations of present models in mind, it is imperative that dynamic, psychologically inspired cybersecurity safeguards that can accommodate the cognitive and emotional defense weaknesses of users are created. The future of cybersecurity lies in the hands of neuroscience, which may transform the field by focusing on the human weakness that existent systems tend to ignore. By capitalizing on data on those reactions of the brain in cases of stress, fatigue, and cognitive overload, it is possible to develop cybersecurity systems that would take user behavior into consideration.[25]

Advances in neuroscience may change the face of new authentication processes that are sensitive to the cognitive fluctuations of a user. Little by little, leaving behind inflexible authentication approaches, these systems could analyze the signs such as EEG or movement of the eye to determine if the users are suffering cognitive overload, stress, or tiredness.

As a reaction to an alert about cognitive fatigue, the system can also put in extra security measures or delay the access of the user if the user

---

[25] Kritika, E. (2025). Ethical Frontiers: Navigating the Intersection of Neurotechnology and Cybersecurity. *Journal of Experimental Neurology*, 6(1), 21–25.

does not show high mental clarity. Due to that fact that these protocols address users' mental states and workloads, they will be much less sensitive to the changes in human error over time.

Cognitive training and neurofeedback interventions may help cybersecurity specialists lower stress-related burnout and enhance judgment in critical situations.[26] Exercising modern advances in neuroscience, businesses can develop training packages that will help increase cognitive resilience, reduce fatigue, and sharpen threat detection. The initiatives in neurofeedback, helped by the Department of Defense pilot programs, show how such technologies help improve operational performance.

Current cybersecurity defense models lack the capability to cater to the subtleties of human cognition and behavior that give rise to many of the security risks. These frameworks only focus in equal measure on technical remedies and do not consider the nuanced human factors or the high-level psychological tricks used by cyber adversaries. For managing this deficit, a dramatic change in strategy is required that leverages results from neuroscience, psychology, and AI to produce reactive, human-focused security solutions. Moreover, regulations in place do not even keep pace with neurological developments.

Although data protection and encryption attract much of the regulatory focus, neuro-rights, cognitive liberty, and mental privacy have not been paid much attention, although brain-monitoring technologies will be used primarily in security applications. To do that, the cybersecurity landscape needs to shift from device-based initiatives to a brain-aware strategy. For systems to produce dynamic, adaptive, real-time defenses, the intricacy of human cognition must be factored into upcoming designs.

---

[26] Kritika, E. (2025). Brainjacking: The Cybersecurity Nightmare of the Future.

Innovation Imperatives

Studying the current cybersecurity architectures, specifically their failure to incorporate delicate features of human cognition and psychological readiness, one can see that basic improvements are not enough. There is no doubt as to the necessity for a revolutionary leap in and of itself. In such a setting, neuroscience moves beyond enhancing cybersecurity; it redefines its very foundation. The intersection of neuroscience and cybersecurity is not a theory but a crucial catalyst for a greater cybersecurity. Adversarial methods of cyberattacks are becoming more complex and defense measures need to adapt to what is equally intelligent, future directed, and aware of human weaknesses.

To have effective cybersecurity, change in effort needs to occur from the protection of systems against the external threats to the internal vulnerabilities that exist within the users and individuals charged with the defense of the network. The only way of obtaining truly secure systems in the face of emerging threats is by having an amalgamation of cognitive, psychological, and technology-based views in our security strategies.[27]

In spite of impressive advances in technology, the very contemporary security mechanisms are facing difficulties keeping up with sophisticated, intelligent, and psyche-manipulation efforts of cyberattackers. When threats move away from exploiting technical weaknesses to influencing human psychology and choice, continuous small-tuning of security systems turns out to be untenable. To confront these challenges, we require a fundamental transformation to transform cybersecurity from a purely technical discipline to an interdisciplinary field with neuroscience at the center.

---

[27] Kritika, E. M. (2024). Neuroethical quandaries at the crossroads of cyberspace. *Scientific and Practical Cyber Security Journal, 8*(1), 57–63.

Beyond Enhancement: Redefining Cybersecurity Through Neuroscience

Neuroscience is more than a small step up to today's security models. It radically changes the profile and norms of cybersecurity. Cybersecurity's foundation should evolve out of a technical perspective to an understanding and utilization of the insights provided by the most recent neuroscience research.[28] From that new mindset, the conjunction of neuroscience and cybersecurity is no longer a theoretical game; it is a necessity for constructing robust digital infrastructures.

Because the techniques employed by adversaries are becoming more sophisticated, cybercriminals leverage software vulnerabilities as well as mental and emotional reactions of their intended victims. From very powerful fake videos meant to instill panic to phishing lures that impersonate authority and the flood of alerts in SOC operations, human elements are now at the center of the threats of the day. This highlights the necessity of defenses as sensitive to technology and human shortcomings as they are, with a harmonic defense against cyber threats. Here, neuroscience comes in handy in that it offers the card necessary to transform cybersecurity to a discipline that is responsive to human cognition.

Building Neuro-Aware Security Systems

Neuro-aware security systems' innovations are built on the systems' capacity to see, interpret, and adjust their behavior based on the mental states of their users. For instance, authentication methods watch brain activities, blink rate, rapid responses, or facial motions to determine one's mental health before granting access. They would be better than

---

[28] Kritika, M. (2024). Neuro-Driven Cybersecurity: Strengthening Digital Defense. *London Journal of Research In Computer Science and Technology, 24*(1), 17–26.

traditional biometric checks (examples of which include fingerprint or face scans) to record internal states such as stress, tiredness, inattentiveness, or pressure.

Imagine a digital guard that observes possible stress responses at login and requests an added check for reassurance. Imagine an application in which frequency or intensity of alerts may be adjusted in real time to coincide with the user's current cognitive state (tired or alert). The use of such technologies may decrease the rates of errors that would result in data breaching or stolen credentials when users are mentally compromised. Some of these security solutions are now beginning to become practical.

There are experimental systems' projects being carried out in academic and defense organizations. The Defense Advanced Research Projects Agency (DARPA), for instance, has backed its neurotechnology initiatives that revolve around enhancing soldier effectiveness and mental toughness, and some of this work is being transferred to cyber technology. Researchers are improving the tools used to gauge the cognitive workload and EEG-based threat models to make them fit properly in these security dashboard systems in real time.

Such systems will allow the integration of a "neurocognitive firewall" into the security infrastructure of these systems, that will allow the defenses to adjust in real time to the cognitive ability of the user. A neurocognitive firewall could be configured to automatically limit access to important materials when the user is very distracted or automatically notify directors if certain brain indications of coercion or distress are identified.

Cognitive Training As a Core Component of Cybersecurity

Alongside advances in circuitry are desperately needed changes regarding cybersecurity education and workforce training. However, traditionally, cybersecurity training has focused on teaching technical competencies, procedural comprehension, and standard operating procedures. Although such technical and procedural knowledge is essential, it leaves a lot to be desired in making professionals ready for the psychological and cognitive battles of current cyberattacks. The subsequent generation of cybersecurity training must incorporate cognitive neuroscience to generate practitioners ready to adapt fast, emotionally stable, and attuned to patterns under stress. This could include

- **Neurocognitive resilience programs**: Programs that make use of neurofeedback and techniques of stress inoculation to enhance the capacity to make sound judgments under pressure

- **Cognitive load management**: Teaching analysts the art of handling their cognitive bandwidth while in a state of heightened alert that is typical of security operations centers (SOCs)

- **Deception detection and pattern recognition**: Enhancing the ability of the brain to recognize abnormal patterns, which may assist the analysts to identify social engineering strategies correctly

- **Mindfulness and executive control training**: Creating plans for cognitive flexibility and resilient thinking to help users respond, instead of reacting to threats on a whim

Organizations such as the US Army Cyber Command and private companies with security capabilities are now exploring these approaches. Cybersecurity teams will soon be able to employ immersive simulations, virtual reality training, and immediate feedback to sharpen their skills.

Neuro-Rights and the Policy Imperative

A development in neurotechnology in the security topography requires the change of the current ethical and legal fields. Vector of mental sovereignty, or guaranteeing every individual's cognitive and emotional privacy, is now a burning issue. As digital privacy created greater legislative debates during the first part of the century, the same may happen to neuro-rights in subsequent years.

Several countries have begun to move ahead with initiatives. In 2021, Chile passed revolutionary legislation wherein they became the first country to constitutionalize neuro-rights by highlighting mental privacy, the concept of identity and the right to cognitive freedom. Spain and Brazil are also enhancing their own regulatory activity, and the United States and the European Union are holding legislative discussion orientated toward regulation of neurotechnology use in consumer as well as defense settings.

Cybersecurity practitioners need to ensure that organizations adopt the neuro-rights regulations on how cognitive data could be harvested, analyzed, and stored. Such data includes what is obtained from EEGs, emotion recognition technologies, and brain–computer interfaces (BCIs). Practitioners must deal with the trade-off between an increased security and both the preservation of the ethical norms and that of user's autonomy and integrity of mental processes.

Policymakers also have a role of regulating their potential to be used for good or harmful purposes by neurotechnologies. New inventions aimed at reinforcing cyber defenses can enhance safety, but they may be retooled for invasive monitoring or control, or psychological manipulation.

The process of innovation should not violate the basic human rights and for that innovation to take place, the construction of clear rules and international cooperation will be necessary.

Multidisciplinary Collaborations: A New Standard

As a result of vast transformation in cybersecurity ecosystem, there is a requirement for developing cross-domain expertise, as cybersecurity is no more constrained to the engineering sphere. This approach requires the marriage of ideas in neuroscience, psychology, ethics, AI, law, and policy to give birth to an ecosystem of collaboration. To overcome the current and future challenges, collective intelligence is all we need. We need to create interdisciplinary labs, innovation clusters, and policy forums where cybersecurity experts, neuroscientists, AI practitioners, and bioethicists and lawmakers can collaborate.

Such cooperative environments would support several objectives such as developing tools that are adapted to human needs, analyzing promising neuroethical risks, developing legal frameworks, and establishing universal standards for guaranteeing cognitive safety. Initiatives such as the OECD's Neurotechnology and Society initiative and the Brain Initiative of the IEEE are symbols of first steps in cross-sector cooperation. Thus, more synergy between different sectors is essential. In today's interconnected cyber world, there is real need to react as a collective, unified voice, the ramifications of individualistic responses can rapidly affect the entire ecosystem.

Toward a Human-Centric Cybersecurity Paradigm

The purpose of innovation lies in designing the system of cybersecurity that is dominated by the newest advances in technology and highly sensitive to human needs. When we integrate neuroscience into

24

cybersecurity strategy, we create a new arsenal informed to protect not only our data but the integrity of our minds and emotions.

Such a change will only be brought about with patience and perseverance. It depends on constant funding, consistent attempts at policymaking, ethics-guided strategy, and a change of cultural norms for us. But the urgency is clear. When cyber assaults penetrate our thinking and emotional processes, the demarcations between cyber and cognitive war fighting are imperceptible. Our protective systems must be able to keep up with risks that are emerging. We stand at a critical juncture in cybersecurity where such a fight to uphold the digital infrastructure is as contemporary as a defense of mental integrity. It is important for our future. It is an imperative.

Cyber protection in coming years might be built on the foundation of integrating neuroscience into the security infrastructure. For example, innovative systems could track the mental efforts of users or stress indicators before users are authenticated or cognitive firewalls remodulated their sensitivity level in response to the neurocognitive activity of the user.

Such innovations are already coming from research labs into real-world deployment. Examples of these systems are currently being experimented on and refined in institutions, the target of which is academic research and defense. There is the need for a basic revamp of cybersecurity training.

Traditional approaches focus on learning knowledge of how to respond in case of a breach – future cybersecurity should work toward creating cognitive training aimed at enhancing mental resilience, sharpening the users' ability to identify patterns during stress and safeguarding individuals from psychological manipulation. Policy is an inescapable feature of this domain.

With regard to increased prominence of neurotechnologies in security, the necessity in the updating of existing frameworks becomes evident to meet the demands of both mental sovereignty and ongoing development of emerging technologies. Presidents in some countries, like Chile and Spain, have tried to include neuro-rights in legislation. With both the United States and the European Union planning to do the same thing, it is important for practitioners and organizations to adjust. Ultimately, partnerships between specialists from various areas of activities should become the new standard. Combined in shared spaces, these diverse professionals, from security experts, to neuroscientists, to AI researchers, ethical researchers, and policymakers, can create spaces to build tools, to manage data ethically, and to create universal norms.

Key Takeaways

- Social engineering is a tool used for 98% of the cyberattacks that take place today.

- There has been an increase in the marketization of cyber weapons throughout dark web.

- Tracking behavioral patterns will reveal the underlying cognitive factors that make the individual vulnerable to online threats.

- Adversarial methods of cyberattacks are becoming more complex, and defense measures must adapt to what is equally intelligent, future-oriented, and aware of human weaknesses.

- New inventions aimed at reinforcing cyber defenses can enhance safety, but they may be retooled for invasive monitoring or control, or psychological manipulation.

## CHAPTER 2

The Neuroscience Behind Human Decision-Making

Cybersecurity operations move at extremely fast speeds; however, decisions only from human brains experience the limitations of biology. Algorithms function with exact precision, while people use their brain which is, ironically, closer to fragile, influenced by history, connected to our feelings and managed by several nerve, emotion, and thought processes. In each case of a breach, a compliance problem, or merging a threat, the common factor is human choices.[1] Although this is a key part of cybersecurity, it is also the element that is least understood and hardest to improve. This chapter looks at decision-making as a process performed by the brain, not just as a general habit. The theory maintains that figuring out how the brain works with cybersecurity matters isn't just for academics anymore, it's crucial for everyone's security. The fighting on the modern digital battlefield is now different. There exists a need to worry about the risks related to code, infrastructure, and the human mind. In many respects, the synapse is now a main area of vulnerability. In cyber

---

[1] Pollini, A., Callari, T. C., Tedeschi, A., Ruscio, D., Save, L., Chiarugi, F., & Guerri, D. (2022). Leveraging human factors in cybersecurity: an integrated methodological approach. *Cognition, Technology & Work*, *24*(2), 371–390.

defense, questions such as whether to escalate a suspicious alert are all decided by people on the frontline. Can a staff member fall for a phishing scam? Does an executive know how to separate a genuine threat from mere noisy discussions? They aren't only a matter of rules, they result from brain circuits, how much attention you give, memories already in place, emotional influences, and the situation. In SOCs, the people working there must process a huge amount of unclear data in very little time.[2] Such experience often leads to cognitive overload happening by design. What follows, due to mental resource constraints, are decisions that might appear strange, but are still considered okay under the circumstances. By seeing where and why the brain makes mistakes, we can remake our environments, tools, and rules to suit everyone and prevent errors.

For a long time, cybersecurity was strongly tied to technology – firewalls, endpoint detection, encryption, and intrusion detectors. However, what's become clear over the past decade is that any strong system is at risk from one careless human action. Even so, we treat computer code and network security with great care, yet not with the same attention to brain and mind. It is typically assumed in training programs that understanding something leads to doing what is secure. This may be incorrect. From a neuroscience viewpoint, attention only goes so far, memory needs to be completed from fragments, and feelings and company both play major roles in guiding our choices. Simply put, security cues are handled differently than the mind is thought to handle them in policies. Most cyber strategies are lacking not extra technology but a deeper understanding of the brain and mental processes that make up the human firewall. Fire drills make sure everyone practices winning escape habits repeatedly. Most of the trainings in cybersecurity are dependent on slides as compared to simulations in other fields. This gap can only be closed when we realize that the brain encodes risk, recalls related

---

[2] https://www.cynet.com/incident-response/what-is-a-soc-10-core-functions-and-6-key-challenges/

memories, and chooses what it should do, all affected by the neural areas such as the prefrontal cortex, amygdala, and basal ganglia. They are not just myths. They are regions where risk judgments, repeated behaviors, and rules of thumb in making choices all meet. It is no longer considered an experimental field when neuroscience is combined with cybersecurity. It is becoming vital for building cyber strength, considering that attackers are currently interested in influencing our minds as much as getting around security. Using phishing to exploit feelings and social engineering with attentional issues, adversaries are already using what we know about how the brain operates.[3] We have to ask: will defenders respond in the same way? At this point, most cyber defense models focus on technology and view people as potential, unpredictable threats. However, this strategy is no longer valid, remains overly simplified, and may be lacking substance. People are not simply vehicles for risk, they are neurological systems that must cope with uncertainty, tiredness, social effects, and mental biases. Instead of designing cybersecurity only from the head, we should start taking the brain into account. As a result, there is a need to use cognitive neuroscience at every stage of our security practices for reasons such as

- Making alert systems that follow how the brain imparts attention, rather than annoying it by providing too much stressful information

- Customizing education to utilize both the way memories are and strong emotions are formed

- Developing systems that correct tendencies to make common mistakes in thinking

- Relying on neuroadaptive systems that pick up on analyst tiredness or too much workload as it happens

---

[3] Siddiqi, M. A., Pak, W., & Siddiqi, M. A. (2022). A study on the psychology of social engineering-based cyberattacks and existing countermeasures. *Applied Sciences*, *12*(12), 6042.

What happens in industries is not just hypothetical. Prototypes are already being used in operations such as cybersecurity for the military and building tools for brain interfaces. This chapter leads into the discussion of that important shift.

Why This Chapter Matters?

This chapter matters for much more than academic study. It helps build the brain-related knowledge needed to consider cybersecurity from the perspective of people's minds. Several key propositions support this framework such as

- Brains are just as important to attack as whole systems in many attacks. Nowadays, the biggest risk comes from using the brain, not just by finding exploitable software. Phishing messages activate the amygdala faster than the prefrontal cortex is able to consider reason. Deepfakes make use of unique recognition features of a face.[4] Misinformation uses the natural tendency of humans to confirm things they already believe. The idea here is to trick the system into going around, not through, cognitive functions, not to fool it with powerful computing.

- The brain doesn't always make rational decisions, but it tends to make the same mistakes: People are not the reason cybersecurity fails just because they cannot always make rational decisions. They are risks because people's brains make decisions that vary with their

---

[4]Sharma, S. K., AlEnizi, A., Kumar, M., Alfarraj, O., & Alowaidi, M. (2024). Detection of real-time deep fakes and face forgery in video conferencing employing generative adversarial networks. Heliyon, 10(17).

experience, react emotionally, and are influenced by biases. We can trace, study, and improve these patterns using tools from neuroscience.

- Neural systems can't help but produce errors, but we can manage them: In neuroscience, we learn that slips, lapses, and tired decisions occur when our brains are pushed too far or work on the same thing for a long time. Instead of penalizing mistakes, systems have to identify, predict, and divert when people experience cognitive issues. We must learn how these styles of thinking develop both at the synapse and in the brain as a whole.

- We should focus on reducing cognitive load during design, rather than only assuming it is due to people's shortcomings: Expertise is not always the problem, sometimes analysts fail simply because their brains are not capable of what their analysis tools require of them. Alerts, dashboards, and policy documents should be designed as cognitive spaces that aid or interfere with making good decisions.

- Having cognitive bias is actually a result of our brains functioning economically: Biases are formed because our brain wants to do things efficiently, not correctly. It falls back on heuristics when conditions are uncertain or things happen fast. However, since most heuristics developed through evolution, they can work against people in cyberspace. Being able to spot common biases in cybersecurity situations enables us to create better solutions.

- Proactive anticipation vis-à-vis reactive approach: In the same way AI studies threat actions, neuroscience examines how humans react. Neurocognitive explanations for attention, fatigue, the influence of emotional relevance, and bias can help us predict issues with security decisions. So, neuroscience-based interventions in real time can help people live better by coping with day-to-day activities in an efficient manner.

The chapter proposes that it is the brain and not the network that must now be defended. Users, analysts, and leaders make daily decisions that are grounded in brain functions which can be observed, represented, and shaped. It's now clear that cybersecurity involves elements of neuroscience, not just technology. We cannot fully improve human elements in cybersecurity until we look at the brain, where every perception, judgment and behavior begin. Next, we delve into the internal workings of the brain that direct both our caution and our risks.

The Neurobiology of Decision-Making

Learning how the brain decides on courses of action is key to creating resilient neuro-security strategies. When milliseconds play a big role and everyone is watching for deception, making a choice is really a brain activity. This section looks into the complicated ways the brain shapes our decisions when we are under duress, doubt, or digital effects, as shown in Figure 2-1.

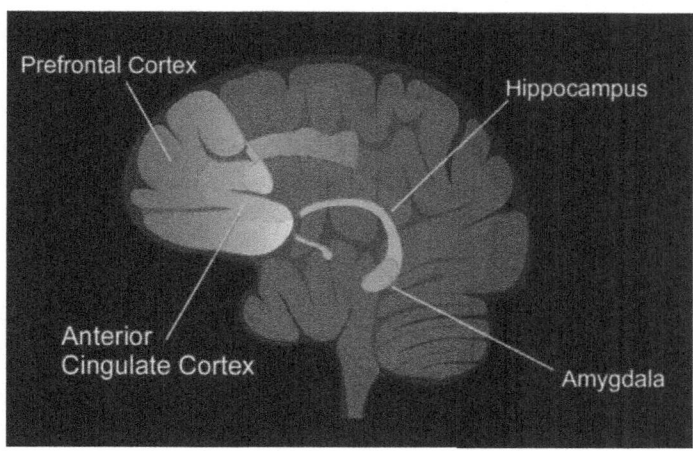

Figure 2-1. *Key Components of the Brain*

Prefrontal Cortex (Executive Function and Risk Analysis)

The PFC,[5] which is situated in the front of the brain, handles executive functions which determine how able we are to organize our plans, manage emotions, see what may follow in the future, and decide actions that fit with society's codes. It combines sensory perceptions, memories, and our emotions to form a strategy that fits the situation. Trusting a system prompt to cybersecurity specialists has to be evaluated by their PFC which helps draw on their training and prevents acting before considering the risk. When the pressure pertaining to or the fatigue in an operation is high as in most cyber operations, the performance of the PFC may diminish, leading to errors or rushed choices.

---

[5] Kolk, S. M., & Rakic, P. (2022). Development of prefrontal cortex. *Neuropsychopharmacology, 47*(1), 41–57.

Greater workloads and constant attention in a Security Operations Center (SOC)[6] may overburden the brain and stop the PFC from picking out the most important risks. This matter becomes most urgent during a zero-day or ransomware attack, as having to estimate risks without complete knowledge is required very quickly. Furthermore, the PFC must be able to use ethics and review future consequences which come into play when deciding whether to stop phishing attacks and when to shut down a network under attack. Unlocking the potential of adaptive computer interfaces for those under stress is now explored through using EEG-based monitoring in neuro-cybersecurity.[7] By adding neuro-awareness to cyber operations, we may avoid executive fatigue-related security breaches and change how we help top leaders.

Besides making judgments in different situations, the prefrontal cortex (PFC) helps people think about what is right or wrong during serious cyber incidents. If analysts have to choose between shutting down a suspicious computer which might cause data loss or continuing to monitor, the PFC supports them in considering the consequences over time instead of choosing the first option. Researchers now believe that being in uncertain danger for a long time can lower the PFC's involvement and encourage the use of lazy decision habits instead of careful reasoning. Due to this, it becomes important for SOCs (Security Operations Centers) to use structured decision tools, like cognitive dashboards or playbooks, that will help improve executive control and reduce depending on worn-out neural paths.

---

[6] Basta, A., Basta, N., Anwar, W., & Essar, M. I. (2024). *Open-source Security Operations Center (SOC): A Complete Guide to Establishing, Managing, and Maintaining a Modern SOC*. John Wiley & Sons.

[7] Kritika, M. (2024). A comprehensive study on navigating neuroethics in Cyberspace. *AI and Ethics*, 1–8.

Amygdala (Threat Perception and Emotional Triggers)

Deep in the temporal lobes, you will find the amygdala[8] which looks like two almonds next to one another. It helps a lot with detecting and processing fear, anxiety, and signals of danger in our environment. Experts say the amygdala becomes especially significant whenever someone views a fake account warning or a time-sensitive phishing message online. Sometimes, the speed of threat detection can take over your slower, more logical thinking. As a result, people can learn to navigate websites too quickly for their guard to spring into action.

Since the amygdala's job is to respond to risks fast, not think things through, attackers can mislead this part of our brain with relative ease in cyberattacks. These scams use the shortcut in our minds to rush us by stating things like "You Are Suspended!" or "Someone Tried to Login from an Unknown Place!" These signals cruise past your mind's reasoning and prompt sudden impulses in you. Affective neuroscientists have discovered that strong emotions can weaken the involvement of the prefrontal cortex in thinking and decision-making.[9] Making user interfaces less alarming and warnings less emotional may lessen the risk of your brain not paying proper attention. Additionally, adding emotional training to user courses can make individuals more emotionally tough and aware of security when they are under pressure.

Moreover, the amygdala looks for threats of fear as well as signs of shame, being rejected or losing face in social life. Cybercriminals now often write emails that suggest something wrong at work, causing not just

---

[8] Shackman, A. J., Grogans, S. E., & Fox, A. S. (2024). Fear, anxiety and the functional architecture of the human central extended amygdala. *Nature Reviews Neuroscience*, 25(8), 587–588.

[9] Orji, L. C., & Ita, U. A. (2024). AMYGDALA HIJACK: CONTEMPORARY INSIGHTS INTO CAUSES, CORRELATES AND CONSEQUENCES. *Midwifery*, 7(3), 102–111.

panic but unease as well. It is tricky to see conscious attacks on social perceptions, as they elude logical thinking easily. If sentimental language is picked up by mail filters, the system could send warnings to users as an early way to help them guard against trickery. This filtering approach is aware that emotional manipulation can be as powerful when it affects the brain as when it involves tricky language.

Anterior Cingulate Cortex (Conflict Resolution)

The ACC is found at the connection between emotional and cognitive processes.[10] It makes sure to notice when an online platform turns out differently from what it promised. The ACC identifies internal conflicts and helps by focusing our mental resources to do something about them. The function is much like anomaly detection in cybersecurity, highlighting when data is not what it should be. If researchers and ACCs operate efficiently, internal conflicts are quickly and correctly handled by a trained user.

Spotting cognitive dissonance is a very important job of the ACC because it happens when our expectations don't fit with our experience. A user may experience this if they get an email from a trusted colleague that doesn't quite feel right or if a usual login portal seeks details that seem odd. At these times, the ACC gets involved by noticing possible flaws and inviting a closer look. Scans with functional MRI reveal that individuals who have higher ACC activity during conflict circumstances usually report seeing fake emails and pause when dealing with suspicious transactions.[11] However, when routine, exhaustion or disinterest dull the system, people are more likely to ignore concerns. Defining alerts to fit what typical users

---

[10] Alejandro, R. J., & Holroyd, C. B. (2024). Hierarchical control over foraging behavior by anterior cingulate cortex. *Neuroscience & Biobehavioral Reviews*, 105623.

[11] Singh, T. (2025). Cybersecurity, Psychology and People Hacking.

expect and offering appropriate reminders based on unusual activity can help people decide more accurately in real time.

The brain is now thought to use the ACC to detect possible problems before they happen. Cybersecurity experts use this function when they must detect dangers using data that is not clear or unfinished. When the audit trail indicates movement between systems, but no obvious sign of attack, the ACC makes security professionals more aware of subtle things to spot. AI that warns analysts only when something is suspicious, following specific predictive criteria, works well with the ACC's goal of being ahead of potential threats. Playing games with rewards for noticing conflicts on time can enhance how parallel ACC processes work over a period.

Striatum and Dopaminergic Circuits: Habitual and Reward-Based Decisions

Together with the dopaminergic system, the striatum, which is subcortical, helps control learning that results from getting rewards and forming habits.[12] When users accomplish things such as responding to notifications or making digital payments, their brain's dopamine levels rise and teach them to repeat those actions. Attackers may use cyber threats by exposing us repeatedly to reward-likes stimuli (for example, special deals) that can lead us to act without thinking. With time, people's automatic instincts harden, lessening their need to think and making them easier to manipulate.

---

[12] Manto, M., Adamaszek, M., Apps, R., Carlson, E., Guarque-Chabrera, J., Heleven, E., ... & Yamashiro, K. (2024). Consensus Paper: Cerebellum and Reward. The Cerebellum, 23(5), 2169–2192.

The striatum plays a big role in tasks that happen fast[13] such as clicking ads, getting discounts, or interacting with game elements. It's for this reason that lots of social engineering scams look like e-commerce specials or loyalty programs. Runs of dopaminergic reinforcement allow us to form routines that may be used to influence our actions. In this way, someone habitually accepting daily system updates could click "Yes" on a fake prompt when exposed to malware. This principle is very useful in cybersecurity behavior modeling: discovering the types of rewards that drive user actions makes it easier to come up with effective methods to protect against them. We must develop secure habits with encouragement and simulate attack situations inside a secure environment so users become better prepared. Eye-trackers and wearable devices collecting bio-signals are becoming new ways to observe if users' habits or actions are guided by attention or instinct.

Essentially, the striatum makes it possible for skills in cybersecurity to become automated. If analysts frequently do incident triage, threat hunting, or forensic reviews, these complex tasks can be turned into simple habits. On the positive side, such practices make the network more efficient, but on the other side, hackers aware of the practices may develop threats that will pass through normal security scans. For example, such malware could be found disguised or obfuscated within files that mimic these popular formats used mostly at certain times. Therefore, to avoid using the dopamine pathways to forecast, it is important to have variable responsibilities, to move analysts among related jobs and to alternate work schedules, all of which affect and disrupt routine predictability in the brain. Table 2-1 illustrates the various neural structures and their corresponding state of art in the context of cybersecurity operations.

---

[13] Khalil, R., & Brüne, M. (2025). Adaptive Decision-Making "Fast" and "Slow": A Model of Creative Thinking. *European Journal of Neuroscience, 61*(5), e70024.

Table 2-1. *Neural Structures and Their Functions in Cybersecurity Contexts*

Brain region	Function	Cybersecurity relevance
Prefrontal Cortex	Rational decision-making, planning	Evaluating risks, policy development, incident response
Amygdala	Threat detection, emotion	Response to phishing, urgency cues
Anterior Cingulate Cortex	Conflict monitoring, attention switching	Spotting anomalies, warning legitimacy assessment
Striatum	Habit formation, reward learning	Repeated user behavior, training reinforcement

The Decision Loop: From Stimulus to Response

Cybersecurity always starts when something happens such as a strange email, a network message that seems out of place, or an alert that appears prompting swift action. They go into a system that includes both brain and mental activity. As a result, key actions that kick in to shape the data into a behavioral output are described in steps which may lead to actions, lack of actions, or errors. The process brings together seeing, feeling, thinking, weighing emotions, and controlling chemicals, finally resulting in making a decision. Figure 2-2 illustrates how the following mechanisms takes place when a decision has to be considered evolving the stimulus to the final response state.

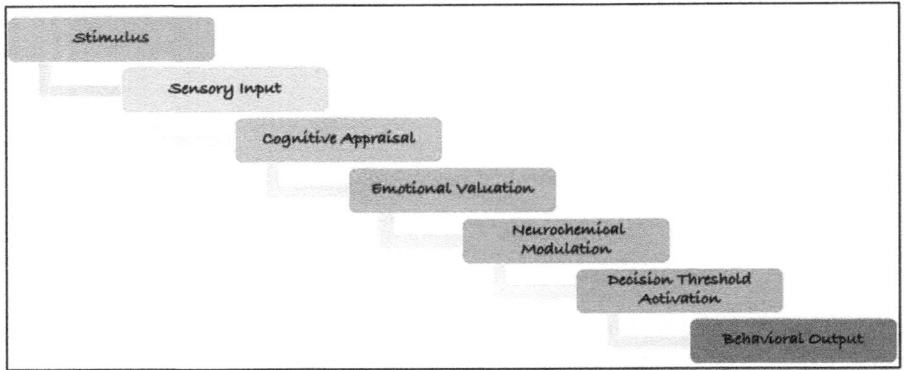

Figure 2-2. *The Decision Loop Process*

Stimulus: Stimuli that relate to cybersecurity may come from outsiders (like an email hack) or internally from someone's past experience.[14] As a result, primary sensory areas in the brain occipital, temporal, or the somatosensory section detect and start processing the first wave of neural activity, as shown in Figure 2-3. At first, the brain has to process the event and find its location. To grab attention, cyberattackers make the messages pop out with flashing text, bold colors, or timers. It ensures that the brain only processes information that seems important. Sensory details that do not matter are ignored, while notable or powerful feelings come to the front of attention. A headline with the word **"urgent"** can more easily reach a person's attention because it connects to our prehistoric warning system for danger. Again, a stimulus activates memory pathways in the hippocampus, enabling users to tell real alerts apart from fake events because they can associate them with past experiences.[15] If the stimulus

---

[14] Burda, P. (2024). Let the weakest link fail, but gracefully: understanding tailored phishing and measures against it.

[15] KRITIKA, E. (2025). A Neuroscience Perspective on AI and Cybersecurity. *ISACA Journal*, (1).

is effective, it often leads a user to become a victim of fraud. As a result, the way the stimulus is built serves as the starting point for interaction between humans and cyber systems.

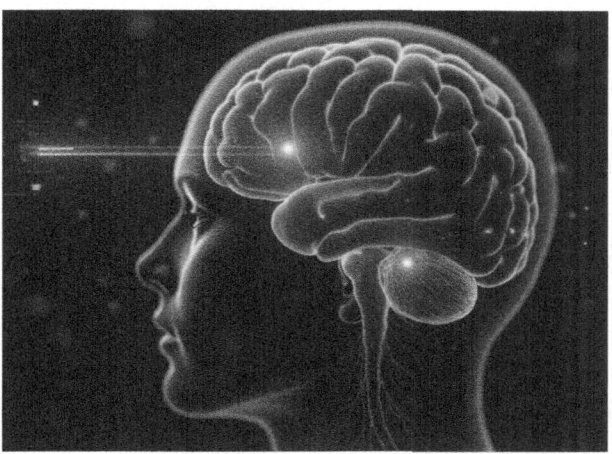

Figure 2-3. *Stimulus Response to Request*

Beyond visual salience, the situation also has a big influence on how our brain deals with the stimulus, in addition to how much we can notice it. A notice about some task at work might be overlooked, but as soon as there is a major system outage, that same signal is given priority. Thanks to the reticular formation, the brain adds context to perception by interacting with the limbic system and judging when an event should be noticed. Psychologists find that certain warning signals can confuse the brain by making it think there's impending danger.[16] Because of these tricks, readers pay less attention to aspects that urgently need to be verified. Cybersecurity training needs to create situations that make people feel nervous or pressured to toughen their reactions based on

---

[16] Harris, L. T. (2025). The Who of Social Psychology: The Challenges of Humans Studying Human Behavior. The handbook of social psychology. Situational Press. https://doi. org/10.70400/NYKH3013.

use-case scenarios. In addition, every person responds differently to stimuli because of things like their history, how anxious they are, and what they are skilled at. A newcomer can overlook a small issue, but a skilled person's brain can pick up threats through regular comparisons of what happens to what is expected. Helping people watch and learn through simulation programs may teach them better ways to keep only important cybersecurity information from being blocked.

Sensory Input: When a stimulus is detected, the sensory receptors convert it into sensory input to send to the main processing parts of the brain. During urgent decisions in the cyber world, it means looking at signifiers in emails or on websites and listening to alarms from security systems. The primary sensory areas[17] pick up the information first, then move it to association areas for the right interpretation. During moments of digital rush, this phase is essential within cybersecurity. Being overloaded with too much information at this point may make it harder to judge things when signals are not easy to understand. The thalamus works as the brain's switchboard, making sure threatening or rewarding signals are rushed to the amygdala and prefrontal cortex. Unfortunately, having good sensory fidelity doesn't mean perception is accurate. Usually, when people make mistakes, it is because they are unaware of information or they misread what they notice. A security analyst going through lots of logs may not notice a big issue because it appears ordinary. So, software should be designed to highlight important signals and mute the less important ones for users.

A skill that people might not realize affects accuracy during brain activity is metacognition. Those with cybersecurity training go beyond reading data, they review their own input to confirm reliability.[18] Having

---

[17] Bagur, S., Bourg, J., Kempf, A., Tarpin, T., Bergaoui, K., Guo, Y., ... & Bathellier, B. (2025). A spatial code for temporal information is necessary for efficient sensory learning. *Science Advances*, *11*(2), eadr6214.

[18] https://www.sentinelone.com/cybersecurity-101/cybersecurity/cybersecurity-training

our internal check boosts our decision strength, especially when we are unsure what to do. Reflective work, using feedback and mindfulness exercises can all help improve metacognition and level of confidence. Experts can also find it difficult to identify unusual attack types because they depend too much on tactics they are used to facing. Here, being flexible with how you think is very important. Because of this capacity, linked to the medial prefrontal cortex, it's possible to modify our beliefs when we receive conflicting evidence. Without using it, analysts may not pay attention to things that appear unusual in statistical models. It's worth noting the role of mental simulation as well. As soon as users wonder, "If I click this link, what might happen next?" they activate part of the brain that tells them to be careful. Inviting children to practice problem scenarios ahead of time can decrease their tendency to act without thinking. Cognitive appraisal, then, involves exploring the unknown when incidents occur, varying confidence levels and testing and predicting the outcomes before acting.

Cognitive Appraisal: Now, the PFC in the brain takes charge. Cognitive appraisal[19] deals with the process of reviewing what something means for you, the results it may have, and how you might react. The brain looks at information we receive through our senses, matches it against our previous experiences and expectations, and figures out if it's ordinary, unusual, or dangerous. As an example, a knowledgeable analyst can see right away that something is wrong with a phishing email since experience is coded in the dorsolateral prefrontal cortex[20] (dlPFC). Using working memory, the ACC in the brain monitors the struggle between different

---

[19] Nguyen, L. T., Dang, T. Q., & Duc, D. T. V. (2025). The dark sides of AI advertising: the integration of cognitive appraisal theory and information quality theory. *Social Science Computer Review, 43*(2), 397–424.

[20] Gong, W., Zhao, H., Wei, Z., Feng, T., & Feng, P. (2025). The functional connectivity between the dorsolateral prefrontal cortex and the medial prefrontal cortex underlying the association between self-control and delay discounting. Brain Structure and Function, 230(5), 1–16.

interpretations. When a user is presented with an official-looking login screen on a page they would not expect, the system raises the need for additional checks. The process of making decisions can now be influenced by thinking like availability heuristics ("Because I've seen it before, it has to be proper") or optimism bias ("It won't really happen to me"). Similar mistakes can lead to major risks in cybersecurity and mistakes following protocol. Because cyber threats are becoming more advanced, it is important for cognitive appraisal to keep up. That's why training and practicing that eliminates fake phishing should not stop.

Emotional Valuation: At this point, affective neuroscience takes a leading role. The amygdala considers if the information coming in is dangerous, neutral, or pleasant. The insula in the brain helps people feel what their body is experiencing, while the PFC works together with rational thoughts to understand feelings. Attackers can trigger a rush of stress, fear, or a chance for benefits to take advantage of this system within cybersecurity. When you receive an email like "Your account has been compromised **click here right away!**" you are more likely to panic and react quickly, not giving yourself time to think.[21] Such a hard-wired defense evolved to help animals survive, not to cope with the Internet. The judgment a person assigns to their emotions can push them toward quick decisions or reflective ones. Too much activation of feelings in high pressure places like SOCs can cause burnout, alertness gone too far, or the loss of rational judgment (amygdala hijack). On the other hand, overworking your team can result in complacency, a trait that's dangerous as threats adapt. Cybersecurity professionals should be taught through affective resilience to focus and calm their minds so they respond well to cyber threats.

---

[21] Conrad, C. D., Aziz, J. R., Henneberry, J. M., & Newman, A. J. (2022). Do emotions influence safe browsing? Toward an electroencephalography marker of affective responses to cybersecurity notifications. *Frontiers in Neuroscience*, *16*, 922960.

How people around us affect our feelings can often increase the intensity of our neural responses. In some cases, noticing that plenty of people share the same error can add to your embarrassment, raising the level of brain activity. In part, this loop is established through the ventromedial prefrontal cortex and reflects how emotions can spread digital influence widely. There are times when emotions aren't just felt but instead predicted, people envision how bad they would feel if they didn't pay attention and something negative happened. Risk behavior is shaped by this process before we have even started to weigh the risks. They achieve this by adding small touches of empathy or FOMO in their messages, knowing they will cause people to predict their own emotions. Having a high EQ is essential in their work. Those with strong emotional intelligence can control their inner state and keep their judgment clear during pressure situations. Learning to recognize and manage your emotions using practices such as biofeedback or guided breathing may help this part of your brain. Basically, emotional valuation requires us to understand, predict, and handle emotions. Having the right emotional balance enables You to decide logically which helps avoid foolish or impulsive actions that can spoil an entire operation.

Neurochemical Modulation: When we make decisions, neurochemicals are the ones working behind the scenes. At this moment, the actions of neurotransmitters such as dopamine, serotonin, norepinephrine, and cortisol greatly influence our decisions.[22] For example, dopamine helps predict rewards and assists users in choosing behavior that they found rewarding before. Serotonin plays a role in deciding how cautious we are and norepinephrine governs our arousal and vigilance. A good feedback system can help raise dopamine levels and encourage people to keep up good security practices. In addition, ongoing

---

[22] Sarmiento, L. F., da Cunha, P. L., Tabares, S., Tafet, G., & Gouveia Jr, A. (2024). Decision-making under stress: A psychological and neurobiological integrative model. *Brain, Behavior, & Immunity-Health*, *38*, 100766.

stress faced by cybersecurity experts leads to higher levels of cortisol which reduces the ability of the prefrontal cortex and causes them to favor instant protection above long-term planning. Additionally, changes in neurochemical levels may be behind daily differences in our decisions. Being right about a danger one day and wrong about it the next might not have anything to do with skill, but with how tired, moody, or what they have eaten. Because of this, it is possible that future cyber defense tools will include neuroadaptive interfaces that notice when a person is getting tired or stressed and improve the working environment for high-stakes decisions.

Our neurochemistry is greatly affected by our body's sleeping and waking cycles and deep sleep. If you don't get enough sleep, your body will decrease serotonin and increase norepinephrine, resulting in poor judgments and stronger feelings.[23] Night shift staff in cybersecurity often find that their mental balance can prevent them from acting or thinking clearly. We should also focus on our diet. Neurotransmitters in your brain are made with the help of omega-3 fatty acids, B-vitamins, and keeping yourself hydrated. Very few companies consider this in their operations, but cognitive nutrition programs could be added to future strategies for better cyber resilience. Researchers are beginning to see the influence of oxytocin on team-working and choice-making. When trust and shared ambitions exist in a SOC team, oxytocin rises and encourages people to remain watchful together. In addition, neuromodulators respond to outside influences. Some wearable gadgets are being developed to release small amounts of dopamine or cortisol which could keep people focused more easily throughout the day. In the future, these neuroenhancement systems could be added to analyst workstations. Neurochemical modulation is not just something that happens automatically, it responds

---

[23] Afradi, A., Tarahomi Ardakani, H., Mousaee, S., Malekpour, O., & Ramezanzadeh, A. (2025). The Neurochemical Basis of Emotions: Bridging Psychology and Chemistry. *International Journal of New Chemistry*, *12*(5), 1013–1028.

to our experiences and quickly acts on how risk is perceived and how the brain adapts to stressful, rewarding situations in the digital world.

Decision Threshold Activation: This is known as the **"Go/No-Go"** gate.[24] After the brain appraises, feels emotion, and processes the situation, it decides whether to act or stay still. They integrate signals from the cortex and decide if the accumulated influence from the cortex requires an action. This technique has similarities to Drift Diffusion Models (DDMs) that psychologists apply to decide between choices when information is uncertain. Context causes thresholds to change, they are not always the same. When situations are very dangerous, teams may decide to act rapidly rather than ensure everything is correct (such as incident response teams). On the other hand, in forensic cases, the requirement for action is increased because efforts must be accurate and supported by law. Surprisingly, decision thresholds can also be trained. Spending a lot of time practicing the same kind of threat helps security professionals react and decide more effectively. Still, if you set low thresholds for all, you may increase false positives and lead to people becoming tired of alerts. The ability to match sensitivity duly giving impetus to criticality, with the right answer turning our attention to the main question: Does the user click, report, ignore it, or transfer it?

Although these thresholds determine when an action should happen, their settings can change in real time. Under high pressure for time, thresholds are often automatically lowered which is called "deadline-induced urgency" by psychologists. As a result, decisions may be made quickly and before important verification is complete. In contrast, when people are accountable to each other, for example, in a group online activity, staff tend to hold back unless they feel accepted. Another thing to look at is how confident you are about the result. People make decisions more quickly when they have confidence in a situation, which at times

---

[24] Stine, G. M., Trautmann, E. M., Jeurissen, D., & Shadlen, M. N. (2023). A neural mechanism for terminating decisions. *Neuron, 111*(16), 2601–2613.

leads to incorrect decisions. As a result, some may start to depend only on automated tools or what they already know. Therefore, adaptive interfaces may add signs of uncertainty or a reminder to pause before allowing the user to take an important action. In the brain, the basal ganglia influence these levels, mainly by way of the subthalamic nucleus. Repeating tasks in time-sensitive environments may help people revise their thresholds. Carrying out simulated activities that can fall in the middle of distinct black-and-white cases is more effective than just passing/failing a drill. Ideally, adjusting decision thresholds depends on task complexity, the environment and how someone feels a place where neuroadaptive cybersecurity programs could improve things a lot.

Behavioral Output: The loop reaches its end when your actions or lack of action make themselves known. Examples of outputs are clicking on a link, reporting suspicious email, locking your system down, or doing nothing. Following action selection by the motor cortex which was based on earlier readings, the associated muscles are fired and feedback loops set up to record the results. What skills we display plays an essential role in forming new neural connections. Through the use of error prediction signals, especially from the dopaminergic midbrain, the brain can alter how synapses act, improving future choices by using reinforcement learning. When something good comes out of the action (such as avoiding a danger), dopamine makes it more likely that you will do that again. Should this occur, the brain changes its expectations, slowing down or redirecting the associated circuit. Informing about a risk can set off a chain reaction: staff are notified, emergency plans are put in place, and audits start. Because of this, behavior provides personal information and also gives a systemic message. By looking at the final decision stage, we realize that investing in stimulus design, training, and stress management upstream can enhance how well decisions are made in cyber defense.

After completing an action, a person's behavior comprises how they tell or comprehend their story of what took place. Feedback loops initiated by this narration in the default mode network (DMN) may affect our future behavior during similar threats. If a person clicks a phishing link and encounters no risk, the brain could see that as permitted which might lead the user to take more such risks. In the same way, when something punishes or educates, the brain restores these regions to previous levels. In this situation, feedback is very important. When the system alerts us when we find a phishing attempt, it encourages us to keep using the system and avoid threats. Good cyber behavior also tends to become common when team members imitate each other through mirroring. So, organizational culture serves as the framework for standard behavioral practices. After making a decision, individuals who continue to check that their choice was correct involve the dorsal anterior cingulate cortex and make learning easier. When learners take a moment to review outcomes, rather than rush to the next step, the information strikes deep and stays longer. Outputs from behavior such as keystrokes and click activity, can be used as data, helping AI evolve and learn about a user's behavior alongside their brain.

Learning about how decisions occur at the neural level is not the end of the story. The major benefit of this knowledge is using it to link biology with what happens in cyber environments. No matter if you're defending your business, managing potential executive risks, or crafting a phishing email, everything you do follows the same decision loop. We should now look at how these neural patterns show up in cybersecurity, whether for the blue or the black hat side and all others.

Application in Cyber Contexts: Brains on the Battlefield

We see the effects of neurobiology in real actions of users, defenders, and attackers. Every cyber actor takes advantage of how the brain processes information, whether they know it or not. Getting to know the neural basis for decisions is just the start. The most important aspect of this knowledge is in seeing how biological processes affect actual online actions. Any time you work in cybersecurity to defend, oversee, or execute tasks, your brain is following the same basic chain of steps. We will now see how these neural patterns appear in the cyber environment from defenders to attackers and all others.

Security Professionals: Strategic Cognition Under Pressure: Cybersecurity professionals work in environments that require immediate and key decisions on a regular basis. Part of a pilot's job in the prefrontal cortex is to manage mental workload, organize controllers' messages and understand what is happening at any moment. During real-time incident response, ACC helps the brain decide what should be considered a threat and what is not. Even so, conditions like chronic stress, extreme tiredness and fatigue from constant alertness can negatively impact the PFC and lead to security professionals missing things or acting late. In Security Operations Centers, neuroergonomics[25] is more important now. For example:

- Such dashboards can modify their interface and simplify them as required by the operator's workload (for example, IBM QRadar Advisor with Watson provides this function).

- When you use contextual AI, such as in Microsoft Sentinel, you reduce the noise of alerts by addressing the risks in order of priority.

- Stress-monitoring wearables, along with other biofeedback, are used by SOC managers to address possible burnout.

- Practicing via entertaining threat simulations widens your brain's ability to learn by challenging it with events that mimic real security threats.

---

[25] Paletta, L. Advances in Neuroergonomics and Cognitive Engineering.

- Thanks to eye-tracking and attention alertness, these systems automatically provide updates to maintain users' attention during a long shift.

Protecting systems and safeguarding those who defend them are two important benefits of these technologies.

End Users: Emotional Triggers and Errors: The end user is always the easiest target in cyberattacks, since the majority of threats come from playing on human emotions rather than software issues.[26] Emotional hijacking in phishing is where these emails push your buttons by using fear, urgency, or the promise of a reward ("You've won an iPhone!"). Studies using brain imaging show that this kind of stimuli lowers the user's ability to make good judgments and activates the limbic system, so they end up making fast actions and submitting the form. Today, many cybersecurity training programs are designed to appeal to a person's emotions.

- Leveraging the thoughtful interlude provided by platforms like KnowBe4, which prepares users to stop for a moment and think, leads to more ACC engagement.

- By using dopamine-driven feedback, behavioral reinforcement rewards good choices such as prompting with nudges.

- Using sentiment scoring, as a diagnostic tool, companies can find unsuitable behavior by examining the mood of their conversations.

---

[26] Kritika, E. (2025). Ethical Frontiers: Navigating the Intersection of Neurotechnology and Cybersecurity. *Journal of Experimental Neurology*, 6(1), 21–25.

- Having a real-time emotional AI assistant, people can see red flags in suspicious language and be reminded to pause and reconsider (like the feature tone detector from Grammarly used with security overlays).

- Training through well-told stories can help the brain hold on to what is learned for longer, since stories trigger empathy and emotional memories.

The goal of today's training is not to give knowledge, but to transform the way individuals feel when responding to threats matching cyber defenses with their brain's feeling systems.

Cyber Adversaries: Neuroscience as a Weapon: Those who aim to mislead others have learned the brain's predictable patterns to help make their lies work more often. In neuro-phishing, attackers make emails that appeal to the brain's instincts and emotions to make a recipient more likely to act.[27] When marketers use "exclusive language," they fire up the dopaminergic system in our brains. Using fearful statements, however, causes the amygdala to kick in and hinders clear judgment. In addition, social engineering has become a highly developed way to trick people's brains such as

- Deepfake videos work on our brains through mirror neurons and the fusiform face area to pretend to be trusted, often fooling people.

- Impersonating someone authoritative in a phone call is easy, since voice spoofing makes people more trusting of the caller's voice.

---

[27] Stoian-Karadeli, A., & Daniel-Gabriel, D. I. N. U. (2023). Securing the Mind: The Emerging Landscape of Cognitive Warfare. *Redefining Community in Intercultural Context*, 26.

- Having audio, video, and text techniques at once in misinformation tricks the PFC and causes individuals to make spontaneous decisions.

- Dark UX editing interfaces in a way that puts the most suspicious buttons in expected places so users do dangerous actions without thinking.

- By spam-flooding or changing the security alerts, cognitive overload attacks use up the ACC's small amount of processing power in order to hide genuine threats.

Today's hackers are breaking through firewalls and also going after the mental barriers of security. The next stage is for defenses to help prevent attacks by preparing users' minds rather than just hardening our systems.

Executive Decision-Making: The Neuroscience of Cyber Policy and Strategy: When making cybersecurity policy, planning investments and creating crisis plans at the C-suite level, managers rely on the dlPFC and PFC which support long-term thinking, flexible planning solutions, and coordination between related teams. Risk, reward, and social impact are used by these regions to help make major choices. While under stress, such as during ransomware talks or telling the public about a data breach, emotions can make you make mistakes. Executives sometimes become overly emotional or delay revealing information when they're worried about their reputation. Thanks to neurocybersecurity,[28] employers have a better chance of making well-thought-out decisions.

- Fictional cases that help prepare decision-makers in high-pressure scenarios involving how the brain and nerves work (for example, cyber incident tabletop exercises).

---

[28] Kritika, M. (2024). Neuro-Driven Cybersecurity: Strengthening Digital Defense. *London Journal of Research In Computer Science and Technology*, *24*(1), 17–26.

- Cognitive load-modeling instruments to see when executives may choose options that are not the best decisions.

- Apps and websites offering decision support should not overload your mind with too many options.

- Before making a decision, pre-mortem neuroethics analyzes the morality and brain function of various strategies.

- Visualizing data in executive dashboards to suit how people choose to look at it (analytic or narrative).

Thanks to these techniques, top leaders can use logical thinking and neuroscience for effective cybersecurity planning.

Insider Threats: Neurocognitive Red Flags: Threats happen, both intentionally and by accident, when people in charge of security change how they make decisions.[29] The difference is due to changes in dopamine, dysregulation of emotions, or poor self-monitoring from the front part of the brain. Cognitive neuroscience helps understand how the brain alerts us to risky decisions early in life as listed below:

- Examples of digital behavioral biometrics such as abnormal typing habits or strange movements on a device, may show signs of uneven thoughts or feelings.

- Employee conversations are observed by affective computing systems which can indicate if someone is becoming stressed or unhappy ahead of time.

- Workplace neurofeedback programs guide employees to handle excess emotions and control their impulses.

---

[29] Voss, E. (2023). *Insider Threat: A Case Study, Recognizing the Early Warnings Signs by Humans* (Doctoral dissertation, Northcentral University).

- By comparing a person's ongoing behavior with their normal behaviors, predictive neuro-analytics can identify any unusual activity that might suggest insider risk.

- Signs of attention fatigue, measured by eye movements or interactions, can show when a person is losing focus before there is an error.

Changing the perspective on insider risk to one based on neurocognitive science, organizations can address issues early and help individuals rather than only through observed tactics.

Neuroadaptive Security Systems: Real-Time Brain-Informed Defenses: We should now focus on making cybersecurity adaptive, based on what users are experiencing mentally and emotionally during their computer use.[30] Based on your mental stress, tiredness, and level of concentration, these systems manage authentication and access rights, as well as alert features, for your comfort. Some examples of using brain inspired concepts are

- With BCI in authentication, EEG patterns verify login, so no one can get in under pressure.

- When attention of the user seems to drift, Adaptive Phishing Filters increase the number of alerts and reminders.

- Such systems are intended to notify users when decision fatigue occurs and may require several steps to carry out important actions.

---

[30] Albarrak, A. M. (2024). Integration of Cybersecurity, Usability, and Human-Computer Interaction for Securing Energy Management Systems. *Sustainability (2071-1050)*, *16*(18).

- Gaze tracking, heart rate control and micro-expression analysis are used in real time for risk and deception risk assessment.

- User interfaces that automatically become either easier or more complicated depending on the user's cognitive processing right now.

Due to these changes, security can now recognize and help improve a person's mental state online, making it proactive, fitting and aware of the brain.

Key Takeaways

- **Making decisions is not only an intellectual activity, it's also influenced by the brain**: How people choose in cyber environments depends on the way these four key brain areas communicate with one another. To successfully predict and manage behavior in cybersecurity, knowing this architecture is important.

- **It Turns Out That Cybersecurity Begins With the Mind as Much as With the Machines**: Whether a SOC worker scans alerts or a person falls for a phishing trick, it is brain circuits that mostly decide the results, not merely computer systems. So, cyber resilience should take into account neurocognitive resilience.

- **The Decision Loop Helps Us Foresee What a Cyber Attacker Might Do**: Understanding the steps from action to risk evaluation, to emotion and then reaction or restraint lets cybersecurity experts predict issues in human decisions, mainly when stress or time pressure is high.

- **It's Possible to Either Use or Defend Against Cognitive Biases and Habit**: Getting exposed to a problem over and over or experiencing high emotion in email attacks make use of things we always do with little thought. Nevertheless, these same brain routes can be adjusted to guard against being influenced by neuroscience-based interventions.

- **The Way Someone Responds to Cyber Problems Relies on Their Neurotype and the Surrounding Environment**: Brains are different in the ways they respond. Feeling fatigued, exhausted, different in the way the brain works or extremely stressed can make it more difficult for someone to make accurate decisions. Such systems must be able to react to these considerations.

- **The Brains of People Are Already Under Attack by Our Adversaries Thanks to Neuroscience**: Experienced attackers rely on turning your attention, emotional response, and feelings of trust to stop your logical mind from working. The main attacks in the field of neuro-offensive strategies are social engineering and deepfakes.

- **The Future of Security Is Neuroadaptive Security**: The next area to explore is combining EEG, HRV, and other brain and body signals into systems that can automatically respond to the user's mental and emotional cues. Security becomes truly scalable when it is built on an understanding of minds.

- **How People Learn and Use Your System Should Be in Harmony with How Their Brains Work**: Raising awareness in the workplace usually is not enough. All defense locations should use simulations, biofeedback tools, and cognitively ergonomic interfaces to make sure decisions are taken effectively under pressure.

- **Everyone from Different Backgrounds Must Work Together**: Experts in the fields of neuroscience, cybersecurity, design, and policy should come together. Treating each area of neuro-cybersecurity on its own will only support the attackers' exploitation.

- **From Finding Out the Probability of Accidents to Predicting Them**: Applying neuroscience makes it possible to predict risks from errors by humans, colleagues, and abnormal patterns in behavior, helping prevent cyberattacks.

CHAPTER 3

Behavioral Biometrics and Its Role in Security

The use of AI is making both hackers and security experts more efficient with tighter security and encrypted messages, cyberattackers are choosing to target us – *"the people,"* often known as the weakest link, achieved by influencing someone's behavior and taking over control of their digital information without them realizing. Currently, authentication mainly relies on passwords (something you know, i.e., Type 1 authentication), hardware tokens (something you have, i.e., Type 2 authentication) and biometrics, like fingerprints and facial recognition (something you are, i.e., Type 3 authentication), but all of these only function at the moment they are used. Once they allow access, they do not typically keep an eye on what happens next, creating a loophole in what happens after a successful login. This fact demonstrates the weakness underlying the typical approach to validating user identities like passwords, security keys, and even your fingerprints or retina to recover your account just once at the moment we tend to log in, compromising the company's resources and information to get hold on confidential information access. Behavioral biometrics is a fast-developing field dedicated to checking that someone is who they claim to be over the course of their use of a system. This raises the need for the change in direction to focus more on moving from trusting static credentials to using authentication based on user actions described by

© Kritika 2026
Kritika, *Neuroscience Meets Cybersecurity*, https://doi.org/10.1007/979-8-8688-2183-7_3

the term *"**behavioral biometrics**."*[1] The digital security community is now noticing that how a person behaves is usually a better way of identifying them than their knowledge or belongings adapting to conditions generally built around a person's thinking and moving patterns. Not only is this the change about technology, but also about principles. This technology replaces securing the device boundary with a deeper attention to the regular, recurring actions of an individual when using a device or application. It's not about comparing the password anymore, the systems simply ask: Does this seem like our user?

These systems track characteristics that are not chosen by the person, including typing, clicking rhythm, pressure in swiping, steps, and how someone uses a computer while thinking owing to their origin in complex brain processes affected by feelings and thought, predicting them is nearly impossible as it is unique to every individual. The type of movements recorded by biometrics like typing and finger swipe begin with the brain's processing as a result of the brain's order to be regulated by cognition, mood, and muscle memory, guiding their actions through a personalized series of signals sent throughout the body.[2] This lag between pressing a key and the computer reacting is determined by our brain, our mindset, stress level, fatigue, and level of concentration, causing the behavior to change giving behavioral biometrics a strong advantage against imitation or fake versions rendering the need of relying on machine learning and adaptive systems becoming necessary. While behavioral biometrics as a term has been studied in history, the true potential of it lies in the real-world applications with recent advancements in critical infrastructure sectors such as financial

---

[1] Singh, J. P., Jain, S., Arora, S., & Singh, U. P. (2021). A survey of behavioral biometric gait recognition: Current success and future perspectives. *Archives of Computational Methods in Engineering, 28*, 107–148.

[2] Yousefi, F., & Kolivand, H. (2024). Brain signals as a new biometric authentication method using brain-computer interface. In *Encyclopedia of Computer Graphics and Games* (pp. 228–241). Cham: Springer International Publishing.

and banking institutions, healthcare services, government operations, education, telecommunication, etc., the systems offering a powerful set of tools enhancing security with passive and continuous authentication without compromising user experience.

By processing high-speed data and using pattern recognition, it has become invariably possible to regularly verify user identification as in the case of online banking fraud used by one of the leading banks in Asia. In businesses, detecting unusual ways that files are accessed or located can identify insider threats immediately. Allowing the use of this type of application follows a larger pattern, and MFBA (multi-factor biometric authentication)[3] is seen as an additional trait such as "something you do" element, together with the previously used "something you know" (passwords) and "something you are" (fingerprints, facial images) along with traditional password or fingerprint methods of security safety along with monitoring unusual behavior, as a result of which it not only helps in identity verification at login but at every point of session being in use. Therefore, a need to study how behavioral biometrics and traditional authentication can be combined and gain from these partnerships. Among their strong advantages, behavioral biometrics can be integrated with standard verification methods rather than making users change their old security methods, behavioral patterns simply reinforce them by adding another quiet and automatic security step.

As an example, let's consider a system that uses multiple levels of authentication.

- They use a password (that they know) to log onto the system.

---

[3] Mohammed, A. H. Y., Dziyauddin, R. A., & Latiff, L. A. (2023). Current multi-factor of authentication: Approaches, requirements, attacks and challenges. *International Journal of Advanced Computer Science and Applications*, *14*(1).

- The device is opened by the person's fingerprint (something they are).

- Patterns of their keypresses and mouse clicks are watched at all times (this is already being done).

- Location of user at time of access.

- Time of access.

With this system, the impersonation is an extremely costly affair for attackers who must have the access to the credentials along with complementing the complex and varied expressions that are unique for every individual. Yet, though this way helps with security, it still brings some problems. Assessing the readiness of behavioral biometrics to be used regularly requires looking at what they achieve against what they lack now. The modern digital scene, with many mobile devices, employees working remotely, a bring-your-own-device culture, and highly personal online experiences, calls for security that is as flexible and well-suited as the dangers it wants to stop.[4] By using behavioral biometrics, systems can tell if the user on the screen is really authorized, regardless of whether the login details are accurate. With such passive authentication, people's security increases and they no longer have to rely on obvious verification methods to access what they need.

---

[4] Kritika. (2024). Arduousness in Technological Aspects of Remote Work, in H. Chandan (Ed.), Impact of Teleworking and Remote Work on Business: Productivity, Retention, Advancement, and Bottom Line (pp. 151–177). IGI Global. https://doi.org/10.4018/979-8-3693-1314-5.ch007

Why Behavioral Biometrics Matters?[5]

With cyber threats increasing at a faster rate than our security against them, traditional methods are unable to keep up. Passwords might be figured out by someone else. You can lose your tokens by losing your account or by them being stolen. Methods like fingerprints or facial scans once thought to be unassailable can now be fraudulently replicated or faked. Then, what cannot be imitated, is always there and can never be fully taken away, remains personal? The solution is found in behavior. Digital identities and the way threats are detected are being greatly affected by behavioral biometrics such as how we type, swipe, walk, or talk.[6] Unlike other systems, behavioral biometrics stay active, change with our patterns, and are linked to our daily use of technology. They use continuous subtle monitoring, so they do not disturb the user like extra steps but immediately notice anything suspicious.

It Is Not Safe to Rely Only on Passwords and Tokens

The data states that 74% of all security breaches are due to mistakes by humans or their accounts being compromised. Since passwords are often used more than once, they can be taken or copied by attackers and MFA methods such as SMS tokens and approvals through apps can be exploited. On the other hand, behavioral biometrics monitor activity all the time and check for unusual actions in addition to confirming a person's identity, allowing protection even if their usual login details have been taken.

---

[5] Papaioannou, M., Mantas, G., Panaousis, E. M., Essop, A., Rodriguez, J., & Sucasas, V. (2023, June). Behavioral biometrics for mobile user authentication: benefits and limitations. In *2023 IFIP Networking Conference (IFIP Networking)* (pp. 1–6). IEEE.

[6] Nachiar, T. S., Priya, T. S., Hemalatha, P. R., & Anchitaalagammai, J. V. (2022). Human Behavioral Identifiers: A Detailed Discussion. In *Object Detection with Deep Learning Models* (pp. 237–252). Chapman and Hall/CRC.

They Enable Continuous Authentication Beyond Login

Such methods check users at the beginning and fade afterwards. When access is approved, the system thinks the user is legitimate until they log out or the session times out. Because of how ardent cyber threats are now, this traditional model can't withstand attacks like session hijacking or privilege escalation. The behavior of users during a session is closely observed by behavioral biometrics which alarm about changes, make times users re-prove who they are, or end sessions when needed. This is most important in challenging jobs, mainly in financial, healthcare, and defense settings.

User Experience Is Preserved, Not Compromised

Having good cybersecurity is sometimes thought of as adding an extra step that can be inconvenient. Behavioral biometrics do not require users to take any action or become aware of the technology which is different. Unlike asking for a password, a fingerprint scan, or an OTP code, behavioral systems do not need something from the user to verify themselves. They quietly study and check how individuals behave with each other in the moment. There are no interruptions, fewer tired users, and a much lower chance of lost transactions, which is useful for applications like e-banking and online shopping.

Adaptive Intelligence Enhances Resilience

Since behavior changes, typing, walking, and talking can all be influenced by tiredness, an injury, and mood. Even though this could be a drawback, new behavioral biometric technology learns and changes as time goes on to tell them apart. Because they adapt over time, biometric traits are stronger than static templates used in physiological biometrics which deteriorate.

Insider Threat Detection Becomes Viable

For cybersecurity experts, one major problem is spotting nefarious actions from those who are given proper access to the system such as insiders. Threats to databases can be intentional, like exfiltrating data or accidental, like a database not being set up properly. In both cases, it is very hard for perimeter or login security alone to catch these threats. Thanks to behavioral biometrics, unusual activities by a user are flagged, even if their access data is still valid. When you add behavioral analytics and user risk profiling to it, this process becomes very effective.

For better clarity, people should note that behavioral biometrics, unlike physiological biometrics, cover technologies like facial recognition, iris scans, and fingerprint readers. As passport control and smartphone locks rely on physiological traits, their fixed and easily spoofed features make them only useful for single, instant checks of trust. It's common for them to need both advanced instruments and a critical amount of computing capacity which are not easy to build or acquire. On the other hand, behavioral biometrics find identity information through the way users use computers and other electronic devices. By using existing parts such as keyboards, microphones, and accelerometers, these patterns are detected passively, so they can be implemented in massive numbers without major financial cost. Also, as users change, behavioral biometrics can adapt, making it a reliable choice for ongoing user study and analysis. Both the functions and the ideas behind the two biometric paradigms are uniquely different. Instead of identifying someone by physical features, behavior biometrics, see if their behavior is usual for them. This move from unchanging to adaptive realness is what makes behavioral biometrics a major part of modern cybersecurity. Table 3-1 provides the contrast between the two types of biometrics, namely, physiological and behavioral based on certain list of parameters.

Table 3-1. *Comparative Analysis of Physiological vs. Behavioral Biometrics*[7]

Parameter	Physiological biometrics	Behavioral biometrics
Definition	Uses physical traits for identity verification	Uses behavioral patterns to identify and authenticate users
Nature of Data	Static and rarely changes over time	Dynamic; varies with context, time, and user state
Examples	Fingerprints, iris, face, palm vein	Keystroke dynamics, gait, voice patterns, mouse movements
Authentication mode	One-time or event-based (e.g., fingerprint scan)	Continuous, session-based, and contextual
User engagement	Requires active participation (e.g., placing finger on scanner)	Typically passive and operates in the background
Sensor requirements	Requires specialized hardware (scanners, cameras)	Can use standard device interfaces (keyboard, microphone, etc.)
Spoof resistance	Moderate; can be spoofed with high-quality reproductions	High; behavioral traits are difficult to mimic accurately
Adaptability	Low; templates are fixed post-enrolment	High; evolves and adapts with user behavior over time
Accuracy	High under controlled conditions	Moderate to high; affected by environmental and emotional factors

(continued)

---

[7] Abdulrahman, S. A., & Alhayani, B. (2023). A comprehensive survey on the biometric systems based on physiological and behavioural characteristics. *Materials Today: Proceedings, 80*, 2642–2646.

Table 3-1. (*continued*)

Parameter	Physiological biometrics	Behavioral biometrics
Real-time detection capability	Limited; mainly at login	Strong; capable of real-time anomaly detection
Applications	Border control, smartphone unlock, employee verification	Fraud detection, continuous authentication, insider threat alerts

The chapter now shifts its focus to a detailed study of the main types of behavioral biometrics, all demonstrating how patterns of human behavior help create strong digital identifiers. We analyze the basic reasons behind why these traits are hard to copy, the most important areas they are used in, and the specific approaches needed for their success. For each group, we search for major tools and platforms that make use of these aspects in different cybersecurity fields such as companies and home users. Apart from describing how each modality works, we consider its strengths, weaknesses, and effects on what is right and wrong. Afterward, we check how behavioral data can be introduced to standard authentication systems to contribute to better security architectures in the years to come.

Types of Behavioral Biometrics

Since cybersecurity risks keep changing and become more advanced, it is harder for traditional authentication methods such as passwords and biometrics, to protect our data. Thieves can still copy or guess a password and advanced technology may allow them to spoof or replicate fingerprints or faces. In these days, behavioral biometrics are used widely to check if someone is authorized by reviewing the specific types of behaviors they use with computers and on the Internet. Behavioral biometrics look at what users do instead of focusing on their physical traits. Since these behaviors such as typing, using a mouse, walking, or touching a touch screen are based on detailed neural and mental processes that vary person to person, it is very hard to copy them.[8] The main benefit is that behavioral biometrics keep checking identity during use, rather than just confirming it once when you log in, so suspicious or unauthorized actions can be noticed in the moment.

It includes a look at the main types of behavioral biometrics that have been put into practice in cybersecurity and authentication. For all types, we will explain the main idea, how it works, and actual uses. After that, we will analyze what works and what doesn't about their use and see how each technology behaves in different settings, desktop, mobile, or access control. We will also look at popular biometrics tools, open source or commercial, and test their functionality, how laborious their implementation is and what their main purposes are. This section aims to give both cybersecurity experts and researchers the right understanding to pick and adopt the most suitable behavioral biometric tools for their security setup and environment.

Keystroke Dynamics[9]

Keystroke dynamics looks at the different timing and style of someone's keystrokes. Keypress durations (dwell time), the latency between pressing each key (flight time), the speed of typing, amount of errors, and general typing rhythm are some of the metrics considered. Some advanced

---

[8] Biele, C. (2022). Human movements in human-computer interaction (HCI).

[9] Shadman, R., Wahab, A. A., Manno, M., Lukaszewski, M., Hou, D., & Hussain, F. (2023). Keystroke dynamics: Concepts, techniques, and applications. *ACM Computing Surveys.*

techniques look at both digraphs (two-key combinations) and trigraphs (three-key sequences) to gain more insight into a person's traits and actions. Table 3-2 provides the comparative analysis of different keystroke dynamics tools on the basis of three parameters such as strengths, weaknesses and application use.

Advantages:

- Keep track of individuals by capturing the keyboard patterns naturally, so additional tools and tasks for the user may not be required.

- It is easy to deploy because its setup involves software solely, so no additional hardware is needed.

- **Careful observation throughout**: Makes sure the session is safe from being hijacked all the way through.

Limitations:

- **User condition changes**: Typing speed may not match what the user really wants to say, especially when the user is stressed, tired, injured, or upset, which can lead to false errors.

- Different keyboards or keypads can make data collection inconsistent which complicates reliable authentication.

- **Vulnerability to skilled mimicry**: If an attacker knows how a user types, they could successfully mimic the typing patterns

Table 3-2. *Comparative Tools Table for Keystroke Dynamics*

Tool name	Description	Strengths	Weaknesses	Typical use case
TypingDNA[10]	AI-driven keystroke biometrics	Easy API, supports multiple languages, GDPR-compliant	Requires network connectivity for cloud-based analytics	Web and enterprise authentication
BehavioSec[11]	Behavioral profiling platform	Strong anomaly detection, enterprise-grade analytics	High cost, complex integration	Banking and high-security sectors
KeyTrak[12]	Lightweight keystroke plugin	Open-source, minimal resource use	Limited commercial support	Academic research, lightweight deployments
BioCatch[13]	Combines typing with cognitive biometrics	Multi-vector analysis, high accuracy	Complex deployment and tuning	Fraud detection in finance and e-commerce
Sequentum[14]	Customizable logging tool	Highly flexible, scriptable	Requires technical expertise	Research, customized solutions

---

[10] https://www.typingdna.com/

[11] https://risk.lexisnexis.com/products/behaviosec

[12] https://www.keytrak.com/

[13] https://www.biocatch.com/

[14] https://www.sequentum.com/

Mouse Movement Analysis[15]

Mouse movement biometrics observe how a person handles the cursor, checking their cursor speed, acceleration, movement consistency, response to clicks, and path taken. Because such behaviors are hard to copy or often unintentional, they are useful signs of the real user behind the account. Table 3-3 provides the comparative analysis of different mouse movement tools on the basis of three parameters such as strengths, weaknesses and application use.

Advantages:

- **Automatic and always on**: Any time a user uses the mouse, security literature can record information without extra request from the person using the computer.

- **Tracing automated scripts or bots**: Bots often move the mouse in a predictable way and this aspect can help find fraud in websites.

- **Can be used in addition to other biometrics**: Adding keystroke dynamics makes it possible for multi-modal behavioral identification.

Limitations:

- Mouse sensitivity, DPI settings and different input devices can cause issues due to variability.

- How simple or complex the task is or how the user feels, can make their behavior unreliable for the system.

- Does not work well on smartphones or tablets that do not have a mouse.

---

[15] Yamauchi, T., & Wang, K. (2025). Reading Moods by Mouse-Cursor Tracking: Representational Similarity Analysis. *IEEE Transactions on Affective Computing*.

Table 3-3. *Comparative Tools Table for Mouse Movement Analysis*

Tool name	Description	Strengths	Weaknesses	Typical use case
MouseTracker[16]	Real-time tracking of mouse movements to analyze cognitive decision-making	– High temporal resolution – Integrated suite: Runner, Designer, Analyzer – Stimuli flexibility (images, text, audio) – Computes curvature, speed, trajectory deviation	– Requires structured experimental design – Best suited for controlled lab environments	Studying cognitive conflict – Psychological research – Human–computer interaction
EpiAnalytics[17]	Advanced behavioral mouse tracking	Rich analytics and session recording	Complex interface	Fraud detection and user profiling
RealEye[18]	Combined eye and mouse tracking	Integrates webcam-based eye tracking for enhanced profiles	Requires webcam for full features	Remote usability testing and behavioral research

---

[16] https://www.mousetracker.org/about

[17] https://www.jdpower.com/business/epianalytics

[18] https://www.realeye.io/

Gait Recognition[19]

To recognize someone by gait, observation is made of a person's walking motion and data is recorded about their stride length, cadence, the angles of their joints and body sway. Handling this is possible with video monitoring, sensors attached to people or motion-recording technology. Table 3-4 provides the comparative analysis of different gait recognition tools on the basis of three parameters such as strengths, weaknesses and application use.

Advantages:

- **It is obvious**: Because gait is controlled by complex nerves and muscles, it cannot be easily copied or disguised.

- Unlike fingerprints or scans from the face, gait can be picked up without the person even having to take part.

- **Used in physical security**: Mostly involved in controlling who goes in and out, observing places and monitoring to spot individuals.

Limitations:

- Sensitive terrain, wrong footwear, possible injuries or carrying things can change how a person walks and effect their accuracy.

- **Cost and difficulty of hardware**: The sensors or cameras used for accurate gait recognition are often very expensive and complicated.

- There are ethical and legal problems with having cameras always on in public.

---

[19] Amogha, B., & Deshpande, R. (2023, February). A review on behavioural biometric GAIT recognition. In *Proceedings of 3rd International Conference on Recent Trends in Machine Learning, IoT, Smart Cities and Applications: ICMISC 2022* (pp. 89-97). Singapore: Springer Nature Singapore.

Table 3-4. *Comparative Tools Table for Gait Recognition*

Tool name	Description	Strengths	Weaknesses	Typical use case
SmarTrack API[20]	Real-time gait pattern analysis	Real-time, compatible with CCTV	High setup cost	Public safety, access control
OpenGait[21]	Open-source gait recognition framework	Academic-grade algorithms	Limited commercial support	Research and prototype systems
Vicon Motion Systems[22]	3D gait motion capture hardware	Highest accuracy in lab settings	Non-portable, expensive	Biomechanics research, security labs

Touchscreen Gesture Recognition[23]

When using touchscreen gesture biometrics, how hard users tap, how quickly they swipe, the shapes and actions of gestures, and scrolling behavior is reviewed. They result in behavioral patterns that are unique to how each user uses the device. Table 3-5 provides the comparative analysis of different touch screen gesture recognition tools on the basis of three parameters such as strengths, weaknesses and application use.

Advantages:

- **Optimized for mobile platforms**: Poor experiences can result if people use text-based passwords to authenticate on mobile which is why gesture authentication is smoother.

---

[20] https://www.smartrack.com/lander
[21] https://github.com/ShiqiYu/OpenGait
[22] https://www.vicon.com/
[23] Guarino, A., Malandrino, D., Zaccagnino, R., Capo, C., & Lettieri, N. (2023). Touchscreen gestures as images. A transfer learning approach for soft biometric traits recognition. *Expert Systems with Applications, 219,* 119614.

- **User-friendly**: Usually unobtrusive and fit in smoothly with the way users handle the system.

- **Combines well with other modalities**: It can work together with other techniques: Gesture biometrics and voice or facial biometrics can be used together for a greater level of authentication.

Limitations:

- **Device variability**: Screen sensitivity, size, and the type of hardware used can result in inconsistent data.

- **Spoofing risk**: A risk exists when advanced emulators or gesture generators are used by themselves and not with extra security measures.

- **Behavioral changes**: Temporary issues may appear when an injury or change in habit is involved.

Table 3-5. *Comparative Tools Table for Touch Screen Gesture Recognition*

Tool name	Description	Strengths	Weaknesses	Typical use case
Zighra[24]	Continuous mobile authentication	AI-powered, seamless UX	Requires licensing	Mobile banking, app security
iMotions[25]	Multi-modal biometric platform	Combines touch, eye, facial data	Expensive	High-security enterprise
Sensory Inc.[26]	Embedded gesture recognition	Fast, device-native processing	Limited customizability	IoT and mobile device security

[24] https://zighra.com/
[25] https://imotions.com/
[26] https://www.sensory.com/

Voice Behavioral Biometrics[27]

Voice behavioral biometrics analyzes the tone, rhythm, accent, speed and emotion in a person's speech. BotSpeechov uses both the sound of speaking and natural actions while speaking to verify identity. Table 3-6 provides the comparative analysis of different voice behavioral biometrics tools on the basis of three parameters such as strengths, weaknesses and application use.

Advantages:

- **A natural interface**: Voice makes authentication simple and easy, especially when you are not touching things.

- By using remote verification, you can verify access by using a phone call or a voice assistant even if you're not present.

- Can be paired with voice command systems to allow for extra control features.

Limitations:

- Health conditions, loud surroundings, or poor recordings can change a person's work performance.

- Vulnerable to voice sounds fakes (deepfakes): Improvements in creating fake voices using AI means we need better precautions against these attacks.

- Privacy and consent are concerns when it comes to using voice monitoring all the time.

---

[27] Wells, A., & Usman, A. B. (2023). Trust and voice biometrics authentication for internet of things. *International Journal of Information Security and Privacy (IJISP)*, *17*(1), 1–28.

Table 3-6. *Comparative Tools Table for Voice Behavioral Biometrics*

Tool name	Description	Strengths	Weaknesses	Typical use case
Nuance Gatekeeper[28]	AI-powered voice biometrics	Strong anti-spoofing, scalable	Costly	Call center and banking security
IDLive Voice[29]	– AI-based clone detection (no need for user interaction) – Works with existing voice biometrics – No user friction or liveness prompts – Lightweight integration via SDK or API	High accuracy in detecting voice deepfakes – Frictionless experience for end-users – Real-time detection capabilities	– Limited transparency on model architecture – Requires high-quality voice input for best performance	Preventing voice spoofing in call centers – Secure voice-based identity verification – Financial fraud prevention

(continued)

---

[28] https://www.nuance.com/content/dam/nuance/en_uk/collateral/ enterprise/data-sheet/ds-nuance-gatekeeper-en
[29] https://www.idrnd.ai/

Table 3-6. (*continued*)

Tool name	Description	Strengths	Weaknesses	Typical use case
Veridas[30]	– Anti-spoofing AI – Real-time verification – Cross-platform compatibility – Text-independent authentication – Language-independent system	– Fast and frictionless – No enrollment barrier – Highly accurate and secure – Easily integrates with systems	– Sensitive to noise in live environments – Internet connection required – Data privacy concerns – Device and mic quality dependency	– Banking and fintech – Healthcare – Customer support – Telecommunications
Core Security[31]	– Voiceprint identification – Active learning algorithms – Real-time fraud detection – Integration with core password	– Enhanced security – Cost reduction – User convenience – Scalability	– Environmental sensitivity – Voice variability – Privacy concerns – Susceptible to spoofing	– Financial services – Healthcare – Telecommunications

With behavioral biometrics, the way identity check is understood and performed in cybersecurity changes radically. In contrast to traditional and physical biometrics, behavioral traits are always changing, respond to situations, and keep going. They are tailored to face insider threats, social engineering attacks, and Advanced Persistent Threats (APTs), situations where traditional static credentials might not work. In this section,

---

[30] https://veridas.com/en/voice-biometric-authentication/
[31] https://www.coresecurity.com/products/core-password/voice-biometrics-authentication

we look at five standard behavioral biometric techniques: keystroke, mouse movement, gait recognition, touchscreen gestures, and voice biometrics. They all identify particular traits in a user's actions which provides another way to analyze and confirm their behavior. When examining their functions, the situations in which they work best and the tools involved, it is obvious that no one behavioral biometric works best in every situation. Fusion of diverse behavioral traits maybe considered as an important strategy, reducing risk in several layers. Even so, although behavioral biometrics can provide many positive features, they still have challenges like instability in stressful situations, the fact that they are tied to hardware and possible spoofing and dangers to data security. For this reason, deployment choices must take into account both technical aspects and ethics, user agreement, and the law. After exploring how many types of behavioral biometrics work, it becomes important to study the biological reasons behind their implementation and distinctiveness. Table 3-7 provides the comparative analysis of different biometric traits on the basis of parameters such as core features it covers, key advantages and limitations and the environment where it works the best.

Table 3-7. *Summary of the Types of Biometric Traits*

Biometric trait	Core features	Key advantages	Key limitations	Best suited environments
Keystroke dynamics	Typing speed, dwell time, flight time, error rate	Passive, low cost, continuous authentication	Affected by fatigue/emotion; mimicable with data	Web login systems, secure enterprise desktops
Mouse movement	Trajectory patterns, velocity, acceleration, click timing	Strong bot detection, low friction, passive monitoring	Hardware/ device variability; less effective on touchscreens	Fraud detection, bot filtering, e-commerce

(*continued*)

Table 3-7. (*continued*)

Biometric trait	Core features	Key advantages	Key limitations	Best suited environments
Gait recognition	Stride length, cadence, body sway, joint dynamics	Distinctive, non-contact, covert detection	Sensitive to injury/ environment; high hardware cost	Physical access control, surveillance systems
Touchscreen gestures	Swipe speed, pressure, gesture angles, tap dynamics	Mobile-native, seamless UX, non-intrusive	Hardware variability; emulator spoofing risk	Mobile banking, app authentication, wearable devices
Voice behavioral	Pitch, rhythm, cadence, accent, stress tone	Natural modality, dual physical-behavioral component	Noise sensitivity; spoofable with deepfakes	Call centers, smart assistants, telecom security

Neuroscientific Basis of Behavioral Biometrics

Behavioral biometrics connect what we see people do to the mental processes and brain functions that cause it. In order to develop systems that remain stable and secure, we must know the brain systems that affect habit formation, control of movements and changes in behavior. Here, we investigate how the brain and mind shape what people (and machines) do, allowing such patterns to work well in cybersecurity. Motor behaviors result from synaptic alterations, the functioning of specific brain circuits, and the formation of memories. Recognizing how the brain works in relation to behavior makes it clear why parameters like typing rhythm, gait, and using a touchscreen are both reliable and unique.

Neural Basis of Habit Formation and Muscle Memory

In behavioral biometrics, the idea of habit is very important. People act consistently while typing or swiping a password because those routines come from previous practice. As a result of habit formation, behaviors become more fluent and less effortful as certain neurons respond differently.

Neuroanatomy of Habit Formation

Habits are key to the way behavioral biometrics works. Because passwords are typed or swiped many times, this helps people perform them in a repeatable way. When a habit develops, the act goes from being controlled to being done automatically, made possible by particular changes in the brain. Habitual behaviors engage a network of brain structures:

- **Basal Ganglia**[32]: The basal ganglia, most importantly the dorsolateral striatum, is the key to forming habits from habits from repeated movements. It combines data from the body, instructions for movement and reward signals, then uses repetition to form procedural memory. A great deal of research shows that as actions become habitual, the striatal circuits in the brain begin to have a bigger part in them.

---

[32] Rocha, G. S., Freire, M. A., Britto, A. M., Paiva, K. M., Oliveira, R. F., Fonseca, I. A., ... & Cavalcanti, J. R. (2023). Basal ganglia for beginners: the basic concepts you need to know and their role in movement control. *Frontiers in Systems Neuroscience, 17*, 1242929.

- **Prefrontal Cortex**: The dorsolateral part of the Prefrontal Cortex (PFC) is responsible for goal-oriented behavior, as it plans actions and checks for errors. Continued repetition causes PFC to be less active and the basal ganglia to handle behavior, so the task becomes automatic.

- **Motor Cortex**: Learned motor programs are perfectly executed by the primary motor cortex (M1) and the premotor regions.

- **Cerebellum**: The cerebellum helps to make movements smoother and timed, which helps people repeat their skills.

Cellular and Molecular Mechanisms

Habit formation is underpinned by synaptic plasticity.

- Changes in Long-Term Potentiation (LTP) and Long-Term Depression (LTD) inside corticostriatal synapses help to record habitual patterns of behavior.

- Reward prediction errors are signaled by dopaminergic projections from the substantia nigra pars compacta which aids the reinforcement learning process in the basal ganglia.

As a result of these processes working together, motor engrams are formed which enable the brain to control complicated actions with little need for attention.

From Deliberate Actions to Automatic Habits

Changing from using a goal to using a habit means the brain must change the way it organizes itself. At the beginning, early learning needs executive control as well as monitoring our thoughts, and later on, most of the control shifts to the striatum and areas involved in body movement.

Because of this handover, the system delivers quick and steady results which are key for trusted behavioral biometrics. Key to this discussion, the maintenance of these motor patterns by networks of neurons makes specific types of behavior stay the same, which in turn supports more accurate biometric recognition. The way people's brain structures and synaptic activity differ plays a major role in shaping each user's movements.

Muscle Memory: Encoding Complex Motor Programs

Muscle memory is when our muscles are able to repeat patterns of motion, since they have been learned and stored as motor programs. Such motor programs are arranged in layers within the cortex and subcortex which helps quick and uniform action. For illustration, manually typing a password activates learned finger patterns saved as motor programs in M1 and helps the timing and accuracy of our typing by relying on brain networks that include the cerebellum. The same kind of motor programs, when used for typing, keeps the distance and timing between keystrokes consistent and easy to measure. Table 3-8 provides the primary function of key brain regions along with their role in behavioral biometrics traits.

Table 3-8. *Key Brain Regions and Their Role in Habitual Behavior*

Brain region	Primary function	Role in behavioral biometrics
Basal ganglia	Procedural learning and habit formation	Automates repetitive motor actions
Prefrontal cortex	Executive function and cognitive control	Oversees early learning and error correction
Primary motor cortex	Execution of voluntary motor commands	Drives movement patterns (e.g., typing)
Cerebellum	Motor coordination and timing	Refines movement precision and rhythm

Role of Motor Cortex, Basal Ganglia, and Cerebellum in Patterned Movements

Motor actions such as typing, swiping on a touchscreen, and walking use well-planned brain codes that make movements similar each time. Different body parts in the primary motor cortex (M1) are arranged in a unique way, making sure only those body parts are responsible for precise movements.[33] The mapping performed in this way supports the distinct character of each person while performing motor activities. These areas in the brain are necessary for planning and arranging these movements. The striatum, globus pallidus, and substantia nigra in the basal ganglia are important for initiating and improving motor commands. Fluid and goal-driven actions happen because the basal ganglia help with a desired movement and stop distracting action. In addition, the movement produced by the Cerebellum adjusts actions in real time to correct any deviations and make sure all movements are in sync. The nervous system watches and adjusts movements to changes in posture, weight, and the world around you. To put it another way, each person's motor actions such as timing, pressure, or trajectory, while typing or swiping, are represented by their unique neuromotor pattern. With BehavioSec and BioCatch, these small signals are traced and used to generate a digital identity profile. Table 3-9 provides various neural traits linked to particular behavioral biometric trait and the particular function they perform.

---

[33] Bhattacharjee, S., Kashyap, R., Abualait, T., Annabel Chen, S. H., Yoo, W. K., & Bashir, S. (2021). The role of primary motor cortex: more than movement execution. *Journal of motor behavior*, *53*(2), 258–274.

Table 3-9. *Neuroanatomical Correlates of Common Behavioral Biometrics*

Biometric modality	Primary neural correlate	Function
Keystroke dynamics	Motor cortex, basal ganglia	Finger sequencing, motor timing, and inhibition
Gait recognition	Cerebellum, basal ganglia	Rhythmic coordination, balance, stride modulation
Mouse movement	Premotor cortex, SMA	Directional targeting, path prediction
Touchscreen Swiping	SMA, sensory-motor cortex	Gesture pattern encoding and muscle memory

With these neuromechanisms, specific motor patterns still show up for each individual, no matter the type of device being used. For this reason, when used with neuroscience, behavioral biometrics can ensure smooth ongoing authentication with fewer chances of someone trying to spoof or replicate someone's behavior.

Influence of Cognitive Load and Emotional State on Behavioral Patterns[34]

Although behavioral biometrics rely on actions a user does without thinking, they can still be altered by the person's moods and thoughts. When people are involved in dynamic real-world situations, they normally experience significant strain on their mental abilities such as doing several tasks at once, getting tired of making decisions, or finding

---

[34] Skulmowski, A., & Xu, K. M. (2022). Understanding cognitive load in digital and online learning: A new perspective on extraneous cognitive load. *Educational psychology review*, *34*(1), 171–196.

it difficult to focus. When these conditions develop, the DLPFC and ACC are activated to give more attention to steering the task and noticing mistakes. Temporarily, the reallocation leads to less effectiveness of the M1, premotor areas, and basal ganglia motor circuits which disrupts how efficiently people move and carry out tasks.

Implications for Behavioral Biometrics

- Most traditional biometric systems only look at behavior patterns that do not change. Sometimes, these profiles result in missed diagnoses when a person is going through a lot of mental or emotional stress.

- Improved systems are expected to include adjustable psychology models that consider changes in the physiological state. A good example is NeuroID which uses small interruptions while filling out forms to separate those telling the truth during stress from those lying.

- With the help of neural-inspired algorithms, another top market leader, TypingDNA, updates how it assigns importance to different unconventional features depending on the user's fatigue and stress.

- In the future, medical technology might measure vital signs using accessories and link changes in health and behavior.

The use of neural adaptability in biometrics keeps mistakes from happening, which improves the system's accuracy and user confidence.

Brain-Behavior Correlations Supporting Biometric Stability

The firmness of behavioral biometrics comes from brain-level processes that are constant through different moments in life. Going through the same steps in behavior strengthens links in the brain, allowing signals to travel more effortlessly with time. With neural reinforcement, the brain relies less on the frontal cortex and more on automated basal ganglia, helping movements stay the same when mental functions are not normal. Furthermore, the parietal cortex and SMA tie in all incoming sensory signals with motor movement information.[35] With this loop, the system is able to adjust for tiredness, minor lapses, or changes in devices, while sustaining user-specific actions such as writing pressure or speed of scrolling. As the adjustments happen in the background, they make a person's behavior recurrent which is beneficial for authentication. Also, keeping behavior stable in the brain requires neuroplastic stability. We may teach our brain new tricks, but changing how a person normally types or uses gestures is hard if we do not retrain them extensively. Because of how the brain works, traits in behavior do not change much even as time goes on. Table 3-10 provides how neural activity works on repetitive behavior over a span of days along with the reliability relevance.

Table 3-10. *Timeline of Neural Consolidation for Repetitive Behavior*

Time period	Neural activity	Biometric relevance
0–1 day	Cortical planning dominant	Unstable behavioral output
1–7 days	Subcortical transition begins	Increasing reliability
7+ days	Basal ganglia dominant	Highly stable biometrics

---

[35] Passarelli, L., Gamberini, M., & Fattori, P. (2021). The superior parietal lobule of primates: a sensory-motor hub for interaction with the environment. *Journal of integrative neuroscience, 20*(1), 157–171.

Companies like Biocatch and TypingDNA uses this long-term capability by setting up baseline behaviors that change slowly with time, helping to maintain security as users improve.

Challenges and Opportunities in Neuroscience-Informed Behavioral Biometrics

While behavioral biometrics are becoming more sophisticated and informed by neuroscience, they encounter two interesting concerns: numerous opportunities together with major hurdles in scientific, technical, and ethical areas. It is important to understand these things when designing systems that are both strong and welcoming to everyone.

Core Issues

Neuro-Behavioral Variability: Behavioral changes are unavoidable in healthy people because of neurophysiological shifts. Changes in circadian rhythms, lack of sleep, emotions, using caffeine or medicine, temperature, or lighting can have an effect on a person's sensorimotor abilities. Changes in temperature, humidity, and pressure may cause reaction time, hand steadiness, and decision skills to vary which interrupts the stability of biometric measurements.

Neurodiversity and Inclusivity: There are many areas and functions in our brain. Because of Parkinson's disease, Autism Spectrum Disorder (ASD), Attention Deficit Hyperactivity Disorder (ADHD), or stroke, certain people may have unique ways of sensing and moving. Commonly, traditional models in behavioral biometrics identify such actions as suspicious because they do not have enough data about different neural patterns. This means we should include everyone in biometric data and ensure models fit for neurodivergent people do not reduce the security of the system.

Challenges Caused by Sensors and Hardware: It is important to record signals in high-quality ways to notice the many tiny movements in how a person behaves. Although much of today's commercial devices are portable, they typically have sensors not precise enough to gauge fine movements like finger pressure, tremors, or latency changes. Because of this, using AI in real-world situations can be less accurate in environments that are either constrained or using legacy technology.

Changes in Psychological Tasks and Behavioral Aging: Motor habits evolve over the course of a lifetime because of injury, getting older, training, or not using them and it is known as biometric drift. A person with a wrist fracture or learning to type on a different interface may continue to show signs of these changes for a long time. Due to this, fixed patterns for behavior may be outdated over time and we should therefore rely on changeable baseline settings that take account of neural plasticity.

Emerging Opportunities

Building BCI Technology into Devices: Now that non-invasive EEG headband systems (such as Emotiv and NextMind) are gaining popularity, they make it possible for biometrics to work more closely with neural data. They could check how a person responds and what they are thinking, thereby using both intent and action for verification.

Neuroadaptive Biometric Systems: They adjust their settings automatically in response to a person's mood or thinking, detected by devices on the body or within the room. If a person appears hesitant or shaky while logging in due to stress, the system will understand it and recognize it as valid rather than flagging it for investigation.

Context-Aware and Longitudinal Models: Applying neuroscience to behavioral biometrics allows for seeing common actions over time and marking them with context for all types of devices and situations. When looking at swipe behavior, users on a smartphone may differ from users on a tablet, yet both types of usage tend to have the same fundamental features. AI can watch the changes and build personalized and reliable identity records based on what users share.

Personalized Neural Signatures: Thanks to recent advances, it is now possible to link the details of someone's behavior to each person's unique brain function. As a result, profiles can be drawn for individuals which assists in detecting more fraudulent activity and better finding the originators of threats. With AI involved, these signatures can help identify dangers almost instantly despite any changes in behavior.

Although it is difficult to apply behavioral biometrics due to the way brains are always changing, these complications also make way for new inventions. When more is known about cognition and the motor systems of the brain, behavioral authentication techniques can both improve accuracy and become more aware of human actions, making identity verification closer to smooth and simple.

Ethical, Legal, and Privacy Dimensions

Behavioral biometrics based on neuroscience raise serious ethical and legal issues because they can assess and interpret thought processes, feelings, and things we don't notice. While technology can now protect us and make things more customized, the same advancements can go beyond what is acceptable in independence, choice, and brain privacy. It covers three important fields: ethical aspects of unconscious behavior profiling, the use of basic data, and the risks of guessing someone's mental state or mood. The table lists out important ethical risks and ways to deal with them.

Neuroethics of Unconscious Behavioral Profiling

The behaviors linked to neuroscience based biometrics analysis is inaccessible to our consciousness and occur below the level of deliberate thinking. Delicate motions, fast response times, and very small eye movements give indications of stress, being attentive, losing focus, and even if someone is lying. As a result, there is a dilemma because the strength of these systems depends on picking out information individuals are unaware they are broadcasting. Whereas people can choose and alter passwords or PINs, hidden and unconscious movements of the body are not under their control.[36] It causes major concerns regarding mental privacy. A United Nations Special Rapporteur pointed out that "mental surveillance" is a growing factor in digital ethics. Whenever systems guess a user's identity, emotion, or intention using subconscious mental activities, they reduce an individual's independence to mere predictions. In some cases, a person doesn't even realize that the device is collecting and interpreting this kind of data. As an illustration, a firm called NeuroID looks at how a user moves the mouse and after delaying clicks in order to differentiate between stress, dishonesty, and a blatant lie. Even though it works against fraud, this method can make the mistakes of predictive profiling possible in hiring, insurance, or policing.

---

[36] Kritika, E. (2025). Brainjacking: The Cybersecurity Nightmare of the Future.

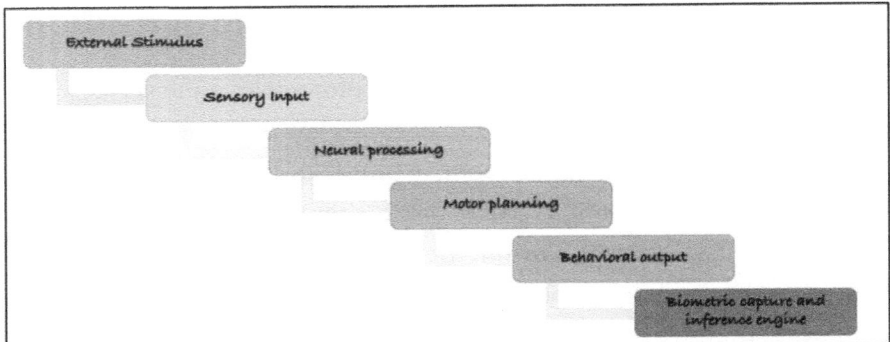

Figure 3-1. *Neural Pathways of Behavioural Biometrics*

The flowchart, as shown in Figure 3-1, explains the neuro-behavioral process by which stimuli are turned into familiar behavioral patterns used for biometrics. A stimulus is shown first which can be an icon, a spoken prompt, or a touch. The eyes or ears detect the signal after it is exposed. They then send it on to the thalamus, the main relay station in the brain. The thalamus separates the incoming sensory information and sends it to parts of the brain responsible for a more thorough review. Visual input goes to the primary visual cortex, while inputs with emotional importance may activate the amygdala which manages feeling and arousal.

At this point, areas in the cortex called "neural interpretation layers" review both what and where the stimulus is. Recall that the amygdala and insula handle our emotions and play a role in adjusting brain activity in downstream areas responsible for motor operations. The prefrontal cortex brings together these mental and emotional assessments and sees to it that our attention, intentions, and decisions are well coordinated. When actions such as typing a password or moving the mouse are demanded, the basal ganglia and motor cortex help with the detailed planning of such movements. The basal ganglia begin and guide movement, while the cerebellum makes sure the movements are carried out correctly and happen on time.

The neuro-motor planning leads to movement, resulting in unique physical traits such as typing rhythm, how we apply pressure with the mouse or finger, the way we move the mouse, or how long we fix our gaze in one place. These signals are identified behind the scenes by what are known as behavioral biometric systems in user interfaces. Usually, the user does not realize that such simple activities are closely monitored and analyzed. After that, AI-driven inference engines work on these signals, searching for recurring patterns and relating them to past neuro-behavioral profiles. Such systems may discover information about one's identity, how they feel, how attentive they are or even spot signs of deception or mental tiredness. Moving from seeing to acting to understanding with AI happens very quickly and people can often remain unaware of what's taking place, revealing the thoughts involuntarily. It shows that there must be clear ways to give consent, transparency in algorithms, and safeguards for mental privacy. Without these protections, anyone could use information from your movements and actions to identify you or influence you based on your traits, which might not be what you wanted.

Ethics for unconscious profiling should cover the following areas:

- It should be clear what kind of information is being used and how it is used behind the scenes.

- How intelligible AI explanations are.

- Right to refuse being put into any specific behavior group.

- Data collections that focus on neurodiversity.

- People should give different forms of consent for each aspect of behavioral inference.

Ethical neuroscience ought to be integrated into the main design approach so people's unconscious minds are never wrongly used in the name of security.

Data Minimization and Consent in Neural-Informed Behavioral Data

The practice of gathering required and insufficient data for neuroscience-based biometrics becomes much more complicated.[37] Certain things can be detected from behavior such as feelings, sleepiness, or the beginning stages of some neurological illnesses. So, a little amount of behavioral information can be enough for analyzing beyond the declared purpose. Normally, the notion of consent in digital environments is no longer ethical. Many people don't realize how much a simple mouse click or swipe can show about them. Even worse, they frequently accept broad service terms that talk about behavioral data in difficult legal language. Nowadays, people may not realize how much of their data is collected and processed every time they work or use certain apps. There are serious concerns when it comes to neural-informed behavioral data such as

- Would users need to give consent every time a new usage of data is made (e.g., going through their identity or inferring emotions)?

- Over Time – The way people behave keeps changing and is considered long-term information. For how long should neural behavioral maps stay active without being updated?

---

[37] Moutinho, L., & Cerf, M. (2024). The Future of Neuroscience and Biometrics in Business. *Biometrics and Neuroscience Research in Business and Management: Advances and Applications*, 333.

- Privacy – Can insurance companies or law enforcement purchase the information I give? How are these companies overseen?

- Deletability – Can innate mental and brain traits be detached from our actions by deleting a profile?

GDPR Article 9 puts biometric and health data under the category of "special," so that consent to their sharing must be clearly given. At the same time, a lot of neural behaviors can't be simply defined by this provision, leaving us confused about how to apply the law.

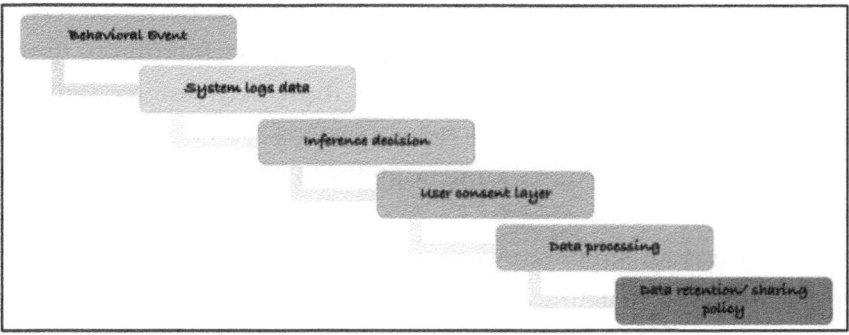

Figure 3-2. *Consent Layers in Neural Behavioural Data Processing*

The Consent Layers in Neural Behavioral Data Processing, as shown in Figure 3-2, outlines the process from initial user action to behavioral finding and long-term care of data. The initialization of a behavioral event comes when a user performs an activity such as a mouse click, swipe, an eye movement, or hits a key on the keyboard. Although these seem ordinary, they carry key messages about planning movements, emotions, and the mind. At first, the user may not know that the AI is watching for unconscious movements that can be analyzed. Soon after, the system gathers and saves these kinds of data, including specific things like the tempo of typing, where the cursor goes and how often a user blows, mostly without the person noticing. All logs are dated and set up to be understood by algorithms.

When capture is done, the data makes its way to the inference layer to allow AI and neuro-symbolic processing to analyze more complex patterns. Using the system, the user's details or condition (such as biometric authentication, stress, or confusing behavior) could be detected. People often make these assumptions without set limits, which makes everyday actions reveal a lot about what the user thinks and feels. The next important point is about consent. At this step, the system confirms whether permission for processing data exists, how that permission is given (such as in terms of service, clicking on interface buttons, or users deciding), and whether the user can change those permissions. Sadly, this approach causes problems for today's systems which allow for sloppy decisions without giving users proper options to influence how things are handled.

With a user's agreement (or consent proxy), the system carries out processing and structures the information, ultimately allowing for personalization, detecting fraud, and use in user modeling. Since these profiles tend to persist, they depend on interpretation and can be misunderstood or used in different ways in the future. The last step in this process is data retention and sharing, which defines the length of storage, the individuals and groups that get the data, and what systems keep track of it. Some questions that need answering are concerning deletion rights, access logs held by federated services, and meeting current regulations. At this point, the biggest dangers arise due to AI decisions in hiring, insurance, and law enforcement. Because of the complexity in this process, this flowchart points to the clear need for layered consent, neuro-rights protection, and transparent data management in fields that combine cognition and computing.

A framework is needed that is based on ethics, provides complete transparency, and holds people accountable to support neuroscientific findings. In the first place, having detailed options for collecting data allows users to make informed choices. They ought to help users make quick decisions to allow or prevent certain levels of privacy like identity check, mood sensing, or mind analysis rather than simply letting the AI take control. Secondly, different policies should be developed to store behavioral biometric data, depending on how sensitive its neurocognitive impact is. Similarly, the data about your actions related to logging in should not remain stored for long periods, but ones that reveal your mood or mental state should be either hidden or cleared out very quickly to prevent them from being misused or exploited. System architecture should include these policies and they must be audited frequently. Also, charters that guarantee people's basic neuro-rights must be enforced by law. Such laws need to ensure that a person's cognitive liberty, privacy, and mental integrity are protected.

Based on Chile's Neuro-Rights in the Constitution and OECD's ethics approaches on neurotechnology, organizations should make sure that involuntary mental monitoring, discrimination using confirmed traits, and permanent cognitive tracking do not occur. Also, the compliance of neuro-rights needs to be compatible worldwide so that there are no gaps in monitoring data ethics. When these aspects are applied together, neural-behavioral biometrics changes from a secret method of observation to a system where individuals are included and morals are respected.

Risk of Cognitive/Emotional Inference Beyond Intent

Using knowledge from neuroscience, systems can now recognize signs of confusion, when someone is attentive or tired and also emotions such as anxiety and frustration. Even though it improves user personalization and spotting anomalies, the power to reach beyond what users share with the app is a downside. The biggest ethical risk is that the system interprets sharing a certain way, even though the user intended something else. Sometimes, a person just logs into their banking app, yet the system might check their emotional health, risks taken, or if they have any memory problems without informing them. This means that artificial intelligence has far-reaching effects such as

- Many of these emotionally vulnerable users are picked out and shown exploitative ads through behavioral advertising.

- Through algorithmic policing, people could be found susceptible to sudden emotions or mental changes without being formally accused.

- If typing-related cognitive changes are found, insurers may reject your claim or require you to pay greater premiums.

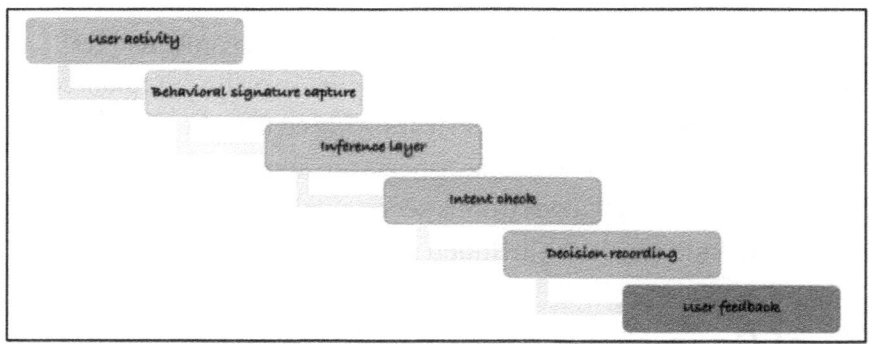

Figure 3-3. *Unintended Inferences from Routine Behavioral Data: A Cognitive Risk Map*

This flowchart, as shown in Figure 3-3, is a full and responsible process for working with neural-based behavioral data, especially in situations where someone's activity, for example, joining a video call, can reveal a lot about them. The first step, called User Activity, sets things in motion by starting to collect information when a video meeting is joined. During this part of the conversation, Step 2 collects faint biometric details from eye blinks, voice tone and pitch, nodding of head, and facial expressions. Even though these signals are connected to the user's thoughts and feelings, they usually happen unconsciously. Step 3 involves Inference Layer and contains advanced AI that interprets the raw data as an emotional reaction or mental state, for example, stress, attention, tiredness, or deception. It does not automatically turn words into emotions, but uses neural networks and strong baselines to understand and guess how the user feels. It is especially important to include Step 4: Intent Check in this architecture from an ethical standpoint. At this step, the system checks that the user has allowed this level of activity. It clarifies that saying yes to vague terms, like in the case of online services, is passive, but an active informed consent happens when someone knowingly lets technology use their thoughts or feelings for that particular reason. When the consent is confirmed, Step 5: Decision Recording sorts the identified data. According to how sensitive the data is and the user's preferences, the information may be safely stored, examined by auditors, sent to the appropriate people, or simply arranged for removal. Finally, as Step 6 explains, at times when feedback is ready, users get summaries of what was learned about them.

To experts in neuro-ethics, this can be seen as breaking the boundaries of physical privacy by using biometric involving main factors such as

- Creating restrictions on what can be inferred in neural-biometric systems.

- Audit trails should be used for every conclusion drawn from criminal investigation.

- Requiring that scientific studies of behavioral-cognitive findings be valid and reproducible.

- A ledger of why and when a person's mental state was assessed using AI would be useful to users.

Highlighting the framework's layers, proper treatment of neural-informed data should include moral judgment, legal consent, and control by the user throughout all processes. Still, as cybersecurity shifts from reactive security to proactive thinking, the situation is evolving much faster now. We are moving toward not just improved ethics but a major change that makes cybersecurity as flexible, clever, and confident as the human brain.

Future Outlook: Toward Neuroadaptive Biometric Ecosystems

The convergence of AI and neuroscience in the digital age is helping us shift to neuroadaptive biometrics system. Such systems aim to offer an adaptive, strong, and highly individual layer of protection by relying on both users' actions and how their brains carry them out.

AI + Neuroscience Convergence in Behavioral Authentication

AI systems can detect subtle actions such as brief halts while typing, changes in how people walk, or the speed of moving the cursor on the screen. Bringing in neuroscience theories of thinking and movement, we can create a new approach where authentications are guided by neuroscience, take the situation into account, and respond to changing situations. For this reason, behavioral authentication systems can improve and update their recognition over time based on a user's emotions. As an illustration, a neuroadaptive engine has the ability to sense that a user's typing is slowed by lack of sleep or tension and varies its security methods instead of wrongly suspecting the user of unauthorized activity.

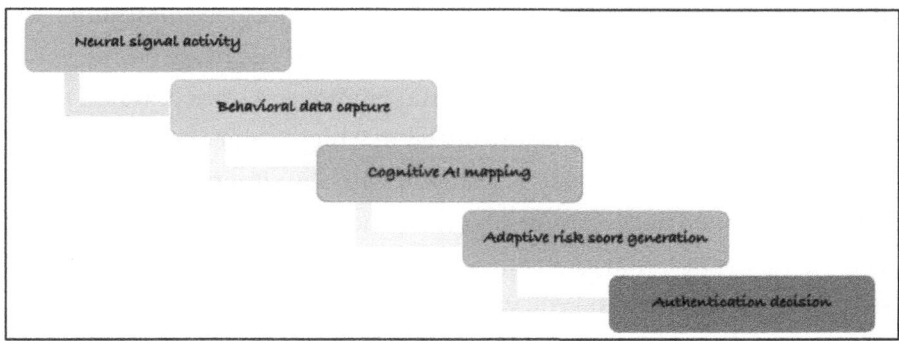

Figure 3-4. *Convergence Model of AI and Neuroscience for Behavioral Authentication*

The illustration in Figure 3-4 shows that the new wave of behavioral authentication systems relies on the combination of neuroscience and artificial intelligence. At the first stage, Neural Signal Input collects the behavioral information and physical changes during activity such as movements, speed, emotions, and mental attention of users. Because traditional sensors do not register neural activity, these signals are found instead in obvious behaviors such as typing patterns, mouse movements, and eye fixation. Arriving at the Behavioral Data Capture layer, where information about user input from phones, webcams, keyboards, and wearables is gathered as it happens. At this stage, the scientific foundation of the system is formed and records are kept for time, pressure, or how hard the task is. Technological innovation really starts when AI models, mainly deep learning and Bayesian models, use behavior research to associate it with neuroscience principles, including learning events in the cerebellum and how the prefrontal cortex controls attention. At this step, the system analyzes cognitive states or departures from standard neural-behavioral patterns.

Once everything is mapped, the system proceeds to creating an adaptive risk score. Differential is set dynamically considering the situation, patient's history, and the state of the brain, rather than staying at the same-as-usual thresholds. The system could forgive small shifts in behavior if a user is tired late at night. It may also see hasty typing as a clue that someone else might be using the employee's device. When the system reaches the Authentication Decision which is not chosen only as pass/fail. Therefore, the choice is changed with the situation: allowing full access, very limited access, requiring a second step to authenticate or even checking the user's behavior again. The major breakthrough is that the system keeps improving in sync with the brain and actions of every user, lowering false positives and picking out unusual, suspicious behaviors in real time.

They are predicted to improve overall security, decrease any hassles for users and resist attempts at making fake identities. At the same time, they need ethical approaches to prevent the invasion of mental privacy when finding behavioral data.

Wearables and EEG-Informed Systems (Neuro-Biometrics)

New technology in the form of EEG headbands and smartwatches is becoming small and powerful enough to measure brain signals right away. They increase the use of behavioral biometrics by including information about brainwave frequency, heart rate, and skin moisture acquired directly from the body. As an example, continuous authentication systems can make use of brain signals to track a user's level of thinking, emotions, or alertness which supports authentication without an active input. By using these insights, a SOC might instantly modify the amount of access a user has or the rules for issuing alerts.

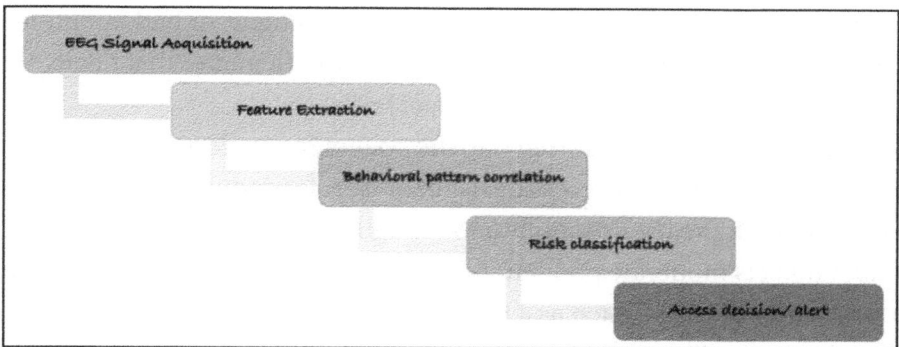

Figure 3-5. *Neuro-Biometric Authentication via EEG Wearables*

EEG-based neuro-biometric authentication, as shown in Figure 3-5, first captures physiological signals using smart devices such as EEG headbands, smartwatches, or AR glasses. EEG machines monitor the brain's electrical signals in various brainwave ranges and each range signifies a unique mental or emotional state. At the same time, sensory inputs measure factors like your heart rate fluctuation, skin response, rate of breathing, and the widening of your pupils. When the rich dataset is formed, the next step is to look at the signals, clean them up, and describe them with presentable measures such as an attention index, level of focus, emotional state or stress level. These features show in real time how a user's mind and emotions are changing. Post-extraction, the system goes into correlating these features to previously set benchmarks for user behavior. As people interact many times, these baselines develop over the years and define standard behaviors in tasks like working on one job, juggling duties and dealing with difficult situations. Abnormal stress or changes in how attentive a person is can indicate that they are starting to behave differently. The next step is to analyze the patient's data using AI that matches the current profile with expected patterns. Typically, machine learning or Bayesian methods are used by these algorithms to give a risk score for unauthorized access, mental fatigue, or bad intentions. Most cases are sorted into low (it is safe), medium (a matter that needs confirmation), or high (a potential danger) risk levels.

With this information sorted out, the system moves forward to the finishing stage where an access decision or alert is produced. Gaining access is easy if the user's actions and thoughts remain as usual. If the system detects moderate poor attention, it may make you provide an extra form of authentication such as a biometric scan or password. Should suspicious signs like possible deception or coercion occur, these are detected, security alerts are raised and the person is denied access?. Most advanced systems run this whole process constantly, protecting the user even after they have signed in. Thus, security systems can learn to respond to what actions users take and also to their changing mental and physical states. They help us discover ways that are smarter than a single entry of password or OTP and move us to systems where the presence of the same person is checked all the time.

Predictive Behavioral Analytics for Insider Threat Detection

Behavioral analysis, combined with neuroscience, can greatly increase our ability to identify and stop insider threats. Traditional models depend on old methods and logs which fail to pick up on intention, pressure points, or mental exhaustion, things that commonly lead to bad behavior from inside the organization. AI uses behavioral biometrics to analyze small habits in users' actions such as spending more time looking at the same thing, failing to log in multiple times, or suddenly typing quicker, thus identifying when users may become vulnerable, burned out, or have the intention to take sensitive data.

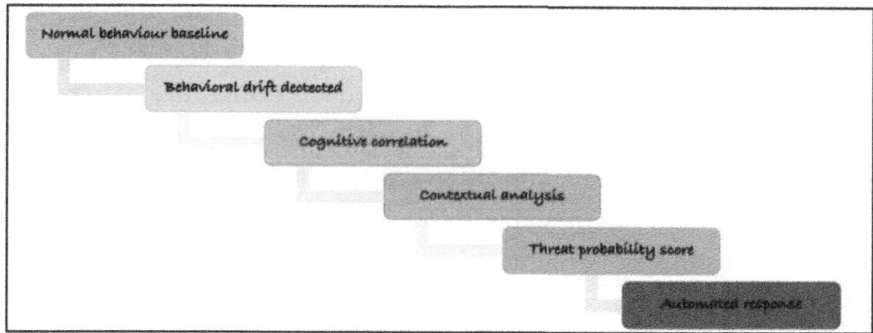

Figure 3-6. *Predictive Neuro-Behavioral Threat Model*

Figure 3-6 shows the operational steps of a predictive neuro-behavioral threat model for identifying and reducing insider risks through the combined use of behavior analytics and neurocognitive understanding. Normal Behavioral Baseline is formed by consistently tracking and understanding the user's way of walking, doing tasks, managing emotions, and interacting. This tells us what "normal" looks like for the person, depending on the circumstances they face. Whenever changes from the normal pattern are noticed, the system notes a Behavioral Drift Detected event. Some examples may include typing much faster, switching between tasks more often, moving the mouse randomly, or changing how someone looks around the screen, all things that are easy to ignore in typical monitoring. After that, Cognitive Correlation analyzes the results using neuroscience models to decide whether there is evidence of fatigue, emotional changes, mental workload problems, or unintentional actions. By way of example, when someone doesn't blink much or maintains a steady stare, it could be a sign of intense focus or pressure and slow typing may be an indication of confusion or misleading intentions. After that, AI models study Contextual Analysis which takes into account time, who the user is, the task type, the user's access level, and where and when the user is working (e.g., remotely or within a set deadline). Applying this method, we can identify both real and false threats by taking the person's situation into account. As a result of this enhanced dataset, the system computes a Threat Probability Score which covers both unusual behavior and how likely it is that the actor has genuine malicious or compromising intentions. This result is shared with the Automated Response layer which can do a variety of things in real time: for example, boost monitoring, challenge with stronger authentication, alert a person, or block access to critical systems.

Role of Personalized Neuroprofiles in Continuous Cybersecurity

In the future, neuroadaptive security will rely on making personalized neuroprofiles that outline what a person does, feels, and moves like while in different brain states. As people's lifestyles, minds, or ways of interacting evolve, their profiles are modified accordingly.

These observations can result in certain mental health disorders such as

- **Adaptive Access Control** lets access be granted or denied, depending on anyone's current mental condition.

- The neural correlates prompts the user to take rest or log out when the brains are prone to the response of tiredness.

- **Just-in-Time Risk Prediction**: Detecting signs of risky behavior or being easy targets for phishing due to people's temporary emotion.

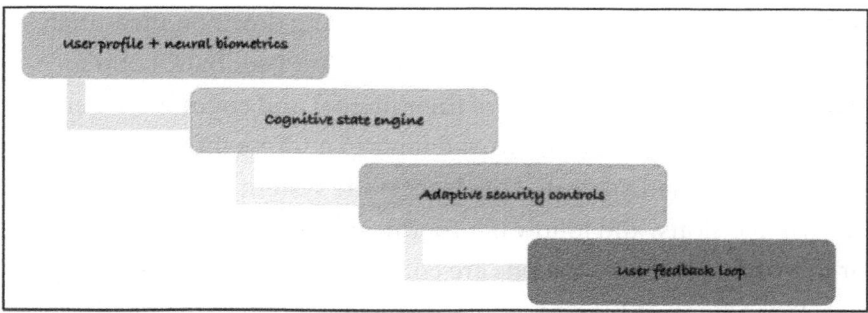

Figure 3-7. *Personalized Neuroprofile Integration in Enterprise Security*

The illustration in Figure 3-7 that combines personal information and neural features supports the system, allowing it to always grow stronger in protecting against cybercrime. It all starts with User Profile + Neural Biometrics, a storage of how an individual habitually acts, thinks, feels, and shows certain neurological patterns, built up from information gathered by devices or interactivity logs. This kind of data includes both steady identity characteristics and instant and temporary changes in mental activity, alertness, tiredness, or levels of stress. Next, the data is sent to the Cognitive State Engine, an AI system that uses inputs from the brain and actions to generate instant readings of a person's emotions and thoughts. Applied brain science concepts like neural oscillation patterns and heart rate variability in addition to behavior consistency are used to recognize and describe a user's mental state based on their own mental profile. Because of this, the system can discover when there are changes that could indicate a mental strain, being distracted, or a security problem.

The insights from the cognitive intelligence lead the Adaptive Security Controls, which in turn ensure real-time changes in authentication, what users can access, and other session settings. When these expressive cues are identified by the Cognitive State Engine, the system can close sensitive avenues, require an extra level of reauthentication or remind the user to rest. Being flexible in malware detection helps maintain security and makes the user's experience better by cutting down on meaningless delays in work. In the end, the system uses a User Feedback Loop to give users details about the state of their mental and cognitive security, notices about changes in policies and tools to address those changes. The result of this mechanism is that users trust the system more, can make their own decisions, and follow neuroethical guidelines by receiving clear information. All these steps are connected and create a security system that adjusts to human differences while fulfilling the needs of cybersecurity in a business.

They detect unusual behavior immediately, with very few errors, by putting behavioral patterns into their neurocognitive framework. At the same time, they raise issues about invasion of privacy and psychological analysis which demand strict rules and clear ways of running government.

It is not enough for leaders and technologists to adopt technologies alone; they must also predict ethical issues, cooperate across fields and allow technologies to support the dignity of people's minds. When building these systems, we should always respect mental privacy, include people from different neurotypes, and follow rules like GDPR and laws for neuro-rights. When AI and neuroscience are linked in cybersecurity, the goal is to understand the person using the system, protect them without notice, and build security that is as flexible as the brain.

Key Takeaways

- With behavioral biometrics, user authentication depends on their actions and unique habits, not only their identity or secret knowledge. Differential traits have a neurological foundation, are always changing, and cannot be easily replicated, keeping threats like the theft of credentials, hijacking a session, and social engineering far from us.

- The main part of the chapter is devoted to carefully studying five types of biometrics (keystroke dynamics, mouse movement, gait recognition, touchscreen gestures, and voice biometrics) and discussing their foundations, possible uses, popular tools, and limitations. It provides useful tables that describe the appropriate use of different biometrics in computer banking and mobile device situations and argues for using different biometric approaches for better safety.

- The reason why behavioral biometrics are unique and stable is due to the nervous system's areas involved in training habits, muscle memory, and emotional and mental functions. Areas in the brain like the basal ganglia, cerebellum, and motor cortex are responsible for keeping track of how well things occur, but elements such as stress, tiredness, or some forms of mental diversity may cause changes. Thanks to these studies, we can now differentiate normal actions from suspicious sending and they support using round-the-clock monitoring to advance cognitive-aware authentication.

- Multi-factor authentication (MFA) works best when behavioral biometrics are included as valuable features and not just used by themselves. When these measures are implemented, they continuously verify the user's identity, monitor them during the session, and permit real-time checks for risks. This connection is demonstrated by offering a layered model for authentication and cases from fintech and critical infrastructure areas.

- The way behavioral biometrics work leads to major ethical problems related to how we give consent, the use of private mental information, and profiling people's minds. The chapter introduces a strong governance system that includes images and tables to control unconscious inference, consent levels, inclusion of neurodiversity, and decision reversal. It points out that shielding users' mental privacy is a duty both from a legal and ethical standpoint in neuroscience-related security.

- In the future, combining AI and neuroscience will result in biometric ecosystems that make authentication flexible, personal, and adapt according to our thought processes. Thanks to EEG wearables, cognitive state engines and personalized neuroprofiles, cybersecurity can detect the user's emotional and mental state and act quickly to prevent breaches related to tiredness, pressure, or suspicious actions. It brings a change from focusing on security after a threat to focusing on digital trust before one appears.

## CHAPTER 4

How Brain–Computer Interfaces Will Transform Cybersecurity?

Imagine that in future you would need none of those usual security measures to access your bank account. Really, it's your individual brain activity that acts as your identity and moves you around the Internet. You just need to think "allow" to enter and any illegal entry is immediately noticed due to how your brain responds. This isn't just a theoretical possibility; it will soon happen due to Brain–Computer Interfaces (BCIs) eminently changing cybersecurity.

Cybersecurity is ever-evolving. In earlier years, organizations mainly used things like passwords, tokens, biometric checks, and multi-layer firewalls to keep those trying to attack out but with the threats growing smarter and traditional security lines blurring due to many devices sharing information, the old ways to protect are outdated. Brain–computer interfaces (BCIs) make it possible to merge the brain, which controls human intent, with security systems in a new way. It shows a move from traditional defenses to a security approach based on a person's thought processes. The electrical signals of brain neurons are recognized by BCIs

Kritika, *Neuroscience Meets Cybersecurity*, https://doi.org/10.1007/979-8-8688-2183-7_4

which turn thoughts into actions without someone moving. Originally made for helping people with paralysis regain their motor skills, BCI technology has quickly become more developed. BCI is now being studied and developed for consumer electronics, game usage, and cybersecurity because of recent progress in neural signal gathering, machine learning, and neurotechnology. With their ability to read a person's unique brain activity, BCIs provide almost perfect security because it is hard to copy or steal such data.

At this point, this evolution becomes extremely important. The number of devices linked to cyberspace has increased and this has increased the attack surface. According to Statista,[1] by the year 2025, the number of IoT devices used globally will be over 75 billion, which may give way to a lot more intrusions and data breaches. Today, traditional methods of authentication, such as passwords and biometrics, are becoming more exposed to brute force, phishing, and ever-evolving fingerprint and facial recognition spoofing. NIST[2] points out that currently available biometric systems are still limited in their ability to meet the new security needs involving privacy and blocking fraudulent attempts. Besides assuring authentication, BCIs might revolutionize how we detect threats. Quite often, cyberattacks takes place in most cases either due to social engineering tactics, undue trust in insiders, or mistakes made due to a lot being on employees' minds. Neural information provided by BCIs enables security teams and systems to detect feelings of stress or dishonesty in real time, so they can respond early to avoid incidents. This way of integrating the brain and cognitive processes forms the basis of moving from reactive to anticipatory cybersecurity. BCIs in cybersecurity reflect the move from traditional, one-layer cybersecurity approaches to protection methods

---

[1] https://www.statista.com/statistics/471264/iot-number-of-connected-devices-worldwide

[2] https://pages.nist.gov/800-63-3/sp800-63b.html

that react and use data coming from humans. At the same time, making this shift brings new obstacles. Neural data is highly personal and private, someone accessing or messing with it could lead to far greater harms than seen with most data leaks. We must build robust rules and regulations as well as technical solutions for neuro-cybersecurity.

Why the Chapter Matters?

- **Revolutionizing Access Control to include Identity Verification Through Neuro-Authentication**: Traditional ways of proving one's identity such as passwords, PINs, and fingerprints are increasingly being attacked by phishing, impersonation, and theft. Brain–Computer Interfaces make it possible to authenticate people with their distinct brain patterns which are hard to fake or take away. This makes it much safer to verify identity since the chances of compromising credentials are lower and strong defense is given as digital environments become more complex.

- **Enhancing Real-Time Threat Detection by Monitoring Cognitive States**: Efforts to exploit fatigue, stress, and deception often call for using social engineering or having some insiders help attackers. With BCIs, constant monitoring of indicators in the brain lets cybersecurity systems act right away if someone exhibits suspicious behavior. Proactive integration of neurofeedback helps cybersecurity prevent breaches, reducing the need for reactive measures.

- **Addressing the Expanding Attack Surface in a Hyperconnected World**: There are now many more accessible points in digital networks because of the rise of IoT and smart gadgets. By 2025, there are projected to be over 75 billion IoT devices on the global network which means attackers could target more systems. BCIs provide extra security to hyperconnected systems by letting human brains help in crafting security policies.

- **Navigating Ethical and Privacy Challenges of Neural Data Security**: Thoughts, emotions, and intentions are very clearly reflected by the signals in the brain. Unlike regular personal information, neural data is considered very private and could be exploited by others. The importance of strong ethics, data privacy, and rules to oversee neural data is highlighted by this chapter to avoid neuro-cybersecurity making people lose their essential human rights or mental health protections.

- **Guiding the Transition Toward Neuro-Integrated Cybersecurity Frameworks**: Cybersecurity is moving from focusing only on a network's perimeter to using data from and about its users and operations. Knowing how BCIs are involved in this process matters a lot to those in cybersecurity, neuroscience, and policy aspects.

The chapter focuses on how BCIs are already changing cybersecurity, their benefits in securing systems using human thinking, and the tough issues they face. Since cybersecurity is transforming, we must understand how signals in the brain affect cyber defense to make better safeguards in the future.

Introduction to Brain–Computer Interfaces (BCIs)

The human brain is the most complex and only known computational system whose formation acts in a billion neural signals per second, which determines thought, perception, and behavior. Historically, in order to be able to use these signals in communicating with external devices partook indirect channels of interactivity and manifestation of the use of speech, spastic signals, or muscle motion. This dynamics is changing with the advent of Brain–Computer Interfaces (BCIs) that allows direct communication of the brain with an external system and not having to use conventional neuromuscular pathways. BCIs read and decipher mixed signals of brain activity and convert them into meaningful commands that can be read by a machine. BCIs were originally designed to help patients with severe motor disabilities, as they accomplish this by enabling them to command wheelchairs, robotic limbs, or computers but soon became a multidimensional field that intertwined neuroscience, artificial intelligence, information processing, and security. Table 4-1 provides the comparative analysis of different types of BCI devices, namely, invasive BCIs, Semi-invasive BCIs and non-invasive BCIs devices based on list of parameters.

Invasive BCIs

Invasive BCIs are placed directly into the brain tissue, also called the motor cortex, or any other desired part.[3] They record the most signal fidelity and spatial resolution and data in single neurons or small populations

---

[3] Zhao, Z. P., Nie, C., Jiang, C. T., Cao, S. H., Tian, K. X., Yu, S., & Gu, J. W. (2023). Modulating brain activity with invasive brain–computer interface: a narrative review. *Brain sciences*, *13*(1), 134.

of neurons, since they exploit apertures between the skull and other biological barriers.

How They Work?

Microelectrode arrays (such as the Utah array) are implanted in cortical tissue and will measure electrical potentials produced by or in individual neurons. The invasive brain computer interface devices offers grinding and accurate information about the neural processes, and thus, complex intentions, fine motor movements, or even speech patterns can be decoded.

Advantages

- **High spatial-temporal resolution**: They are able to sense microvolts with a millisecond accuracy.

- **Our rich neural information**: Can perform very complex control with a great deal of accuracy (e.g., the movements of a robotic arm or a cursor).

- The prospect of secured neural so-called tokens in cybersecurity since they are unique in their own way.

Challenges

- **Surcharges**: Risk of infection, inflammation, and damage to nerves.

- **Minimal stability**: Scars may reduce the performance of electrodes in the long term.

- **Ethical and regulatory problems**: Owing to their errant character, they can only be used outside the medical or experimental environments.

Semi-invasive BCIs: A Middle Ground

The semi-invasive BCIs strike a balance between signal fidelity and a less complex surgery.[4] They do not penetrate the brain tissue; they can measure the activity of the brain by putting electrodes on the surface or close to the brain surface like that of Electrocorticography (ECoG) or vascular stentrodes (devices inserted into blood vessels near the brain).

How They Work?

ECoG electrodes are applied to dura mater (the outermost membrane of the brain) right under the skull. They respond to grouped electrical activity of many neurons as opposed to nerve cells. Likewise, stentrodes are inserted in cortical blood vessels as a way of reading brain signals without the need to go through an open brain process.

Advantages

- **Regarding the quality of the signal**: Has better signal-to-noise ratio (SNR) than non-invasive EEG.

- **Safe to use Compared to wholly invasive implants**: No invading cortical tissue.

- **Stable at extended periods of time**: They can be used in long-term monitoring.

---

[4] Wang, Y., Jiang, C., & Li, C. (2025). A Review of Brain-Computer Interface Technologies: Signal Acquisition Methods and Interaction Paradigms. *arXiv preprint arXiv:2503.16471.*

Challenges

- **Still needs operation**: It is less intrusive but it still needs medical treatment.

- **Moderate price and complexity of regulation**: It will not be deployed at scale yet.

Non-invasive BCIs: The Most Practical

The now most ubiquitous non-invasive BCIs are mostly used in research as well as in consumer and emerging cybersecurity applications.[5] They are able to capture information about the activity of the nerves without making an operation, usually encompassing sensors on the scalp or portable devices.

Electroencephalography (EEG)

EEG[6] is a measurement of electrical signal associated with the scalp at a high sensitivity in time (milliseconds). It records important brainwaves – alpha, beta, theta, and gamma but also specific potentials in a particular event such as P300 (authentication). EEGs such as OpenBCI or Emotiv are inexpensive and portable and are easily deployed.

---

[5] Schroder, T., Sirbu, R., Park, S., Morley, J., Street, S., & Floridi, L. (2025). Cyber Risks to Next-Gen Brain-Computer Interfaces: Analysis and Recommendations. *Neuroethics*, *18*(2), 34.

[6] Marino, M., & Mantini, D. (2024). Human brain imaging with high-density electroencephalography: Techniques and applications. *The Journal of Physiology*.

Functional Near-Infrared Spectroscopy (fNIRS)[7]

fNIRS quantifies alteration in the blood oxygenation value in the cortex which is an indication of brain activation. Although it has a superior spatial resolution compared to EEG, it has slower temporal dynamics (seconds).

Magnetoencephalography (MEG) and fMRI[8]

These provide high spatial resolution; however, they are costly, bulky, and not usable on a day-to-day basis and this makes them inappropriate for use in cybersecurity outside the lab.

Advantages

- **Safe and non-invasive**: No recuperation or danger of surgery

- **Scalable and economical**: Can be deployed in consumer type system or in enterprise systems

---

[7] Dans, P. W., Foglia, S. D., & Nelson, A. J. (2021). Data processing in functional near-infrared spectroscopy (fNIRS) motor control research. *Brain Sciences*, *11*(5), 606.

[8] Pagani, M., Gutierrez-Barragan, D., de Guzman, A. E., Xu, T., & Gozzi, A. (2023). Mapping and comparing fMRI connectivity networks across species. *Communications Biology*, *6*(1), 1238.

Table 4-1. *Comparative Analysis of Types of BCIs*

Parameter	Invasive BCIs	Semi-invasive BCIs	Non-invasive BCIs
Signal source	Implanted microelectrodes directly in cortical tissue	Electrodes placed on cortical surface or within blood vessels	Scalp-based sensors (EEG, fNIRS, MEG)
Spatial resolution	Very high (single-neuron or small neuronal clusters)	High (regional cortical signals)	Low (broad cortical areas)
Temporal resolution	Millisecond-level	Millisecond-level	Millisecond (EEG) to seconds (fNIRS)
Signal fidelity (SNR)	Very high	High	Moderate to low
Latency	Extremely low (<10 ms)	Low (~10–50 ms)	Low for EEG (~100 ms); higher for fNIRS (>2s)
Surgical requirements	Requires open-brain surgery	Minimally invasive (endovascular or subdural)	None
Risk factors	Infection, scar tissue, biofouling, rejection	Infection (less severe), limited longevity	Minimal to none

Longevity/stability	Limited (months to years)	Better than fully invasive (years)	Unlimited use (external only)
Practicality	Low (research/clinical only)	Medium (pilot clinical trials)	High (consumer and research-ready)
Data complexity	Very detailed (microvolt-scale neuronal data)	Rich cortical data	Less detailed, more noise/artifacts
Cost	Very high (surgical + hospital costs)	High	Low to medium
Deployment context	Clinical neuroprosthetics, ultimate secure ID	Advanced rehab, experimental secure systems	Cognitive monitoring, authentication, fatigue detection
Examples	Utah Array, NeuroPort	ECoG grids, Synchron Stentrode	EEG caps (OpenBCI, Emotiv), fNIRS headbands
Cybersecurity use cases	High-assurance brainprint tokens, direct neural intent	Mid-tier secure authentication, neural biometrics	Real-time mental state monitoring, continuous neural authentication

BCIs in Cybersecurity: Unlocking New Dimensions of Digital Defense

With cyber threats variably escalating in advancement, humans constituting the elements of security, namely, security analyst personnel, administrators, end users, are considered as the weakest lightning rods but, simultaneously, the first line of guarding securities against a hacker or a potential hacker. However, the cognitive state of theirs, being tired, focused, or distracted, is likely to be the deciding factor, either promotion or prevention of an intrusion. The process of interaction between human minds and digital systems can be transformed through the realization of bidirectional communication that is achieved through Brain–Computer Interfaces (BCIs). The outcome is intent-driven control, adaptive trust, and biometric accuracy as they all are founded on neuroscience.

Neural Authentication[9]: Brainprints As the Ultimate

Brainprints Unique structures in brain responses create an impossible to forge biometric, one connected with what you think. P300 event-related potential (ERP), which is a subconscious neural spike, that appears 250 to 500 ms P300-stimulus visibility, constitutes a robust signature to recognize the users. It works in the following way:

- A P300 authentication system presents stimuli (e.g., images or letters).

- A P300 ERP is identified by EEG sensors when a subject is identifying a target item.

- The machine learning models prove the authenticity of the pattern against an enrolled brainprint.

---

[9] Rathi, N., Singla, R., & Tiwari, S. (2022). Towards a role-based authentication system based on SSVEP-P300 hybrid brain–computer interfacing. *Behaviour & Information Technology*, *41*(15), 3301–3317.

The reasons why it is secure:

- The brain-prints are very tough to spoof or forge. Contrary to the ability to replay or steal the data of the fingers, iris (static biometrics), it is impossible due to the live dynamic qualities of neural response.

- Experimental studies show authentication accuracy of P300 schemes of greater than 90%.

- The systems installed in IAM settings are capable of conducting authentication both passively and repetitively, and this allows real-time identity verification.

Example:

MDPI researchers have developed an SVM-based BCI simulator that uses the P300 to perform channel attack tracking using fake P300 signal classes, reaching 99.996% accuracy in detecting channel attacks.[10]

Cognitive State Monitoring: Safeguarding the Human Firewall

Mental weariness, cognitive burden, or distraction are common situations where errors in SOCs take place. Real-time monitoring using BCI-based systems, such as EEG and/or fNIRS, can provide the opportunity to preserve the integrity of the system with respect to the relevant cognitive states. EEG activity shows measurably altered alpha (8–12 Hz) and theta (4–7 Hz) EEG frequencies during fatigue or diminished attention

---

[10] Mezzina, G., Annese, V. F., & De Venuto, D. (2021). A cybersecure P300-based brain-to-computer interface against noise-based and fake P300 cyberattacks. *Sensors*, *21*(24), 8280.

and fNIRS presents additional information on the state of oxygenated hemoglobin (HbO) levels in the prefrontal cortex that corresponds to mental strain. Compound systems are about ~80–88% accurate at identifying cognitive load when compared to single-modality system. These systems can adapt dynamically: they can suppress less urgent alerts when overloaded, switch this or that monitoring role, or use neurofeedback to decrease stress. War and aircraft research has been proven effective in the real application under high stakes environment where they are directly applicable to cybersecurity operations.

Example: Fatigue detection by using EEG has been used in operational environments. An example of this application is the Bitbrain system that has provided comprehensive, live vehicle fleet/industrial control fatigue monitoring in real time in an effort to further increase safety on the roads in the event an operator is exceeding their fatigue levels and may give in to dangerously driving just before a breakdown occurs. Hybrid EEG-fNIRS systems were also implemented in aviation: they were used to monitor pilot workload and attention during pilot flight simulations and could detect >80–88% with high accuracy in noisy conditions. Applying to cybersecurity, this technology has the potential to advise SOC interfaces to adjust the priorities of alerts dynamically depending on the mental state of the analysts.

Intent-Based Access Control: Turning Thoughts into Authorization

BCIs allow mentally specified intention to be turned into a type of authentication – motor imagination (e.g., imagining moving a limb) creates distinct EEGs. Chained with such imagined commands, one can form so-called mental passphrases, in which the deep learning models decode access actions. CNN-LSTM and MECASA-based deep learning models have obtained up to 93 and 77-93% accuracy in motor-imagery tasks, respectively. They allow absolute hands-free, tamper-proof accesses, suitable in a high-security system like critical infrastructure. One can provide additional levels of safety, for example, revocation in the middle of the session once duress is detected by measuring the related stress-related neural markers. The thought process of a database administrator granting high-level access can take minutes, and in the future, it is the BCI that will verify the identity of the person and whether they are in a sane state of mind, and nothing more.

Example: Authentication on motor imagery is progressing at a fast rate. In the authentication of imagined movements, researchers applying CNN-LSTM-based systems got 77–93 accuracy levels using portable EEGs to decode the intended movements to detect authentication. Nexstem AI released an open-source motor imagery brain–computer interface framework that can be used to control devices with intentional thoughts: first conceived to be used by assistive technologies, it is currently being tested to authorize safe login procedures. Though immature, such systems are already being put to the confidential test in defense and secure agency trials to prove out the premise of hands-free, thought-based access.

Neurosecurity: Defending the Neural Attack Surface

While **Brain–Computer Interfaces (BCIs)** offer resilient security parameters, they also introduce completely new, and probably serious risks. The **neural data** they handle is extremely private and sensitive as it may expose internal functioning. Attackers could exploit this vulnerable information to steal your private **mental states** or secretly bypass authentication. Studies demonstrate machine learning-based BCI authentication is susceptible to both poisoning as well as adversarial attacks, where input features are disguised to result in misclassification. Also, EEG gadgets utilizing the Bluetooth-based technology, such as Muse and Emotiv, are vulnerable to the MITM or caverta attack as they might open access to the neural material without a user acknowledging it. Such architectures like Argus and Pseudo-Random Channel Mixing prove secure communication channels and signal health validations are in place, with more than 99.99% sensitive signal tampering detection. Such controls are there to secure confidentiality, integrity, and availability of the neural systems, and they lead to the dawn of neurosecurity.

Example: Recent MDPI study showed that attenuating signals to hack through channels by tampering could break P300 authentication a scenario that led to the design of anomaly detection algorithms such as Pseudo-Random Channel Mixing to identify hackers and thwart them with the success rate of 99.99%. More so, another study published in Nature Communications proposed wireless ear-EEG devices with secured communications and encryption needs under dry electrodes, in which fatigue would be monitored reliably with protection against accessing transmissions with highly personal neural information. These projects can be used to indicate the formation of neurosecurity architectures in parallel with BCI powers.

Hybrid BCIs: Synergizing EEG and fNIRS for Robust Defense

The limitations of each modality are EEG or fNIRS. EEG provides fast temporal feedback but spatial poor resolution, whereas fNIRS has spatial accuracy but slow feed. Hybrid EEGfNIRS systems integrate them, providing performance that is robust, with accuracies of classification that are usually above 90%. The improvement in the workload classification is 2–8% over single modalities in others. Such systems are used in cybersecurity through recording real-time P300 authentication in brainprints as they monitor their cognitive conditions. The two-channel defense is exponentially making it hard for adversarial interferences, thus needing both fNIRS and EEG manipulation in combination which increases the attacker threshold. With the evolution of wearable technology, the hybrid BCIs are now useful and unrivalled in mission-critical applications in neuro-cybers.

Example: Hybrid fNIRS-EEG systems have already served real world application in the high-demand circumstances. A hybrid fatigue-monitoring study has been found to attain more than 90% accuracy even in driver simulations with small multi-channel systems. The other study was able to attain 91% accuracy in motor imagery undertakings only with four EEG channels with fNIRS signals in operative conditions. Such results demonstrate the practicability and robustness of hybrid BCIs, and so they are quite appropriate to multifactor authentication and cognitive alerting cybersecurity practitioners like SOC analysts and security engineers.

Platforms and Tools for Brain–Computer Interfaces in Cybersecurity

BCIs do not work in vacuums. There is an ecology of hardware devices, signal-processing code, and integration pipelines that connect raw neural signals to cybersecurity systems. When it comes to neuro-cybersecurity, it is essential to use the right tools as security applications require high-level signal fidelity, trigger in real time, and need integration with already established Zero Trust and IAM (Identity and Access Management) services. Evolving wearable EEG and hybrid (EEG + fNIRS) technology and open-source/commercial BCI middleware have opened BCIs to cybersecurity R&D over the past five years (20202024). OpenBCI Cyton, Emotiv Epoc+, and Galea non-invasive EEG headsets are already used to study brainprints (cognitive biometrics) and motor imagery mental passphrases and to monitor cognitive workload of SOC analysts. The latter are now supplemented by general purpose middleware platforms such as the BCI2000, EEGLAB, and OpenViBE, which makes real-time extraction of ERP (Event-Related Potential) and detection of fatigue, and classification of intent possible, which are key components in any form of neural authentication or mental state driven access control.

In addition to hardware and signal processing, it is also essential to integrate into the cybersecurity stack. Such an example is LabStreamingLayer (LSL) that aligns multiple behavioral/biometric signals with neural data, so they can easily merge with SIEM (Security Information and Event Management) systems. Due to this incorporation, adaptive security policies can be achieved, for example, withdrawal of privileges when cognitive duress was identified or dynamic alert-load based on operator fatigue. With the evolution of cybersecurity evolving to proactive, cognitive-aware defense models, knowledge of these tools and platforms will be necessary. Here, we discuss important BCI hardware, middleware platform, hybrid systems, and their application, in particular, to cybersecurity applications, as well as present real-life pilots, datasets that demonstrate their feasibility.

BCI Hardware Devices

Non-invasive BCI Devices

The most usable form of BCIs to cybersecurity today is the non-invasive ones since they would not involve any surgical operations and could be easily implemented in any enterprise setting due to speed. The EEGs used to work on these sorts of devices utilize sensors attached to the scalp and detect electrical actions without infiltrating the skin. They are perfect for low-cost research, SOC analyst observation, cognitive workload measurement, and even neural identification prototypes on ERP. They have usually moderate to high signal fidelity without requiring a certain level of usability in a less controlled environment. They are also the most common entry into piloting neurocybersecurity applications because they are portable and fairly low-cost. Table 4-2 provides the comparative analysis of different non-invasive BCI devices on the parameters such as key features available, time to setup required, use cases in cybersecurity context, the suitable environments along with strengths and limitations.

Table 4-2. *Comparative Non-Invasive BCI Devices*

Device	Key features	Setup time	Cybersecurity use cases	Best for	Pros	Cons
OpenBCI Cyton/Daisy[11]	8–16 channels EEG, 24-bit ADC, BLE wireless, expandable with Daisy module	10–15 mins (gel electrodes)	P300 cognitive authentication, motor imagery passphrases, SOC fatigue monitoring	Research labs, low-cost prototyping	– Affordable & open-source – Good EEG signal quality – Compatible with BCI2000, EEGLAB, OpenViBE	– Needs gel (messy) – Moderate learning curve
Emotiv Epoc+ / Epoc X[12]	14-channel EEG, wireless, saline sensors, enterprise SDK	5–10 mins	SOC analyst stress/fatigue detection, insider threat risk analytics	Enterprise pilots, security ops centers	– Faster setup than gel EEG – Enterprise-ready SDK	– Higher cost than OpenBC – Limited customization

(continued)

[11] https://docs.openbci.com/Cyton/CytonSpecs/
[12] https://www.emotiv.com/products/epoc-x

Table 4-2. (*continued*)

NeuroSky MindWave[13]	1-channel EEG, dry sensor, attention/meditation metrics	<5 mins	Training and phishing awareness, basic engagement tracking	Awareness programs, education	– Very affordable – Plug-and-play	– Very low signal resolution – Not secure for authentication
Muse S/ Muse 2[14]	4-channel EEG headband, focus/meditation tracking	<5 mins	Basic SOC engagement tracking, phishing simulation fatigue	Awareness and stress monitoring	– Portable and simple – Affordable consumer-grade	– Limited channels – Not suitable for security-critical tasks
Cognionics Quick-20[15]	20-channel dry EEG, no gel needed, research-grade	~5 mins	ERP-based authentication, mobile SOC pilots	Rapid enterprise deployments	– Fast setup – Good balance between quality and usability	– More expensive than OpenBCI – Slightly less accurate than gel EEG

[13] https://store.neurosky.com/pages/mindwave

[14] https://choosemuse.com/

[15] https://www.cgxsystems.com/

Decision Matrix

The most frequently used BCIs in cybersecurity research and pilots are non-invasive ones since they do not involve surgery and are portable and do not have a high price. Figure 4-1 provides the internal chip board used in various non-invasive headset devices. along with various devices available for commercial use.

- The real research-grade alternative is OpenBCI Cyton/Daisy. It channels 8 16 with Texas Instruments ADS1299 (documented spec in OpenBCI Docs) and offers satisfactory EEG signal quality when used in P300 brainprints and motor-imaging-based authentication models. Its disadvantage is the gel electrode preparation (~1015 minutes) and the slightly increased calibration requirements by the user.

- Emotiv Epoc+ is more suitable in the case of piloting in an enterprise to use when quicker setup (510 minutes) and a commercial SDK are required. It has been applied in projects and pilots of SOC fatigue monitoring, as well as studies of cognitive workloads (verified by Frontiers in Human Neuroscience, 2021). It is priced at about $850–1,200 and thus more costly than OpenBCI but more user-friendly for non-technical groups.

- With a 5-minute assembly time, dry electrode design, Cognionics Quick-20 is decent when it is time to make a rapid deployment, but still good enough to produce results on a research-grade level. It is more expensive ($3,000–5,000); however, eliminates the inconvenience of gel preparation.

- In use for training and awareness programs, the NeuroSky MindWave or Muse headbands can be sufficient on engagement measuring but not good on authentication because of single or low-channel

131

EEG with low level resolution. They require no more than 5 minutes to set up and cost less than $300 which makes them a perfect fit for low-risk purposes such as phishing awareness simulations.

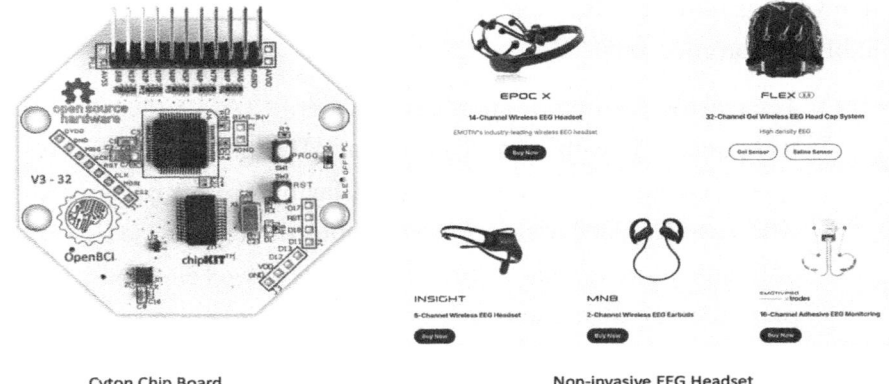

Cyton Chip Board   Non-invasive EEG Headset

Figure 4-1. *Left: Cyton Chip Board, Right: Non-invasive Headset*

Hybrid Multi-modal BCIs

Hybrid BCIs integrate EEG with other sensing modalities to leverage fNIRS (functional near-infrared spectroscopy), electrodermal activity (EDA), and eye tracking. Such a multi-level procedure is a more complete cognitive picture, so they are suitable in the context of high-security applications where mental state recognition and brainprint authentication have to go hand in hand. These products are particularly suited to use in defense, critical infrastructure, industrial SOCs where operator fitness and mental resilience are as vital to know as proof of identity. Although hybrid BCIs allow slightly better accuracy and spoof resistance, they are more time-consuming as well as expensive to recoup. Table 4-3 provides the comparative analysis of different hybrid BCI devices on the parameters such as key features available, time to setup required, use cases in cybersecurity context, the suitable environments along with strengths and limitations.

Table 4-3. *Comparative Hybrid BCI Devices*

Device	Key features	Setup time	Cybersecurity use cases	Best for	Pros	Cons
Galea Hybrid[16]	EEG + fNIRS + eye-tracking + facial EMG + EDA in one headset	15–20 mins	Dual authentication (brainprint + physiological states), advanced SOC readiness monitoring	Defense-grade security, critical infrastructure	– Multi-signal fusion – Future-proof neurotech platform	– Expensive – Complex calibration
Bitbrain EEG/fNIRS Platform[17]	Hybrid EEG + fNIRS with cognitive workload analytics	~20 mins	Industrial SOC fatigue detection, operator workload mapping	Industrial and energy sector cybersecurity	– Accurate workload tracking – Enterprise-grade solutions	– Costly – Less portable

(continued)

---

[16] https://galea.co/
[17] https://www.bitbrain.com/

Table 4-3. (*continued*)

Device	Key features	Setup time	Cybersecurity use cases	Best for	Pros	Cons
Artinis Brite23[18]	Wearable fNIRS for mental workload measurement	~20 mins	Team-based SOC readiness tracking, high-security workforce monitoring	Defense and critical operations	– Measures oxygenation + EEG	– Limited to research pilots
Kernel Flow	fNIRS brain imaging, prefrontal workload measurement	~20 mins	Cognitive workload + hybrid authentication research	Future defense-grade authentication	– Advanced cognitive state analysis – Suitable for team monitoring	– Extremely expensive – Not yet widely deployed

[18]https://www.artinis.com/brite-frontal

Decision Matrix

Hybrid BCIs combine EEG with fNIRS, eye-tracking, and physiological signals, providing multi-factor neural verification, at the expense of increased costs and complexity. Figure 4-2 demonstrates the three hybrid headsets, namely, Galea hybrid headset, kernel hybrid headset and water based EEG headset.

- In case MTF and DoD levels of cognitive protection are the goal, Galea Hybrid is a curious item. It also combines EEG, fNIRS, EDA, and EMG, which makes it suitable when it comes to having two-factor authentication and/or monitoring of SOC preparedness responses in a critical infrastructure or military setting. Setup, however, is more complicated (15–20 min) and much more expensive ($5,000–$8,000).

- To reduce industrial SOC errors and cognitive workload mapping, Bitbrain EEG/fNIRS offer enterprise-level solutions to the task of detecting operator fatigue within industrial cybersecurity applications. It provides dry or semi-dry electrodes, although it is time-consuming (~20 minutes) and cost-effective to deploy.

- When monitoring of cognitive monitoring is required at the team level (e.g., when monitoring several SOC analysts in parallel), Artinis Brite23 and Kernel Flow can provide prefrontal oxygenation data, which can be utilized to monitor cognitive readiness when stakes are high. But these are highly advanced research tools, prohibitively costly, and not yet adopted in the field of production security.

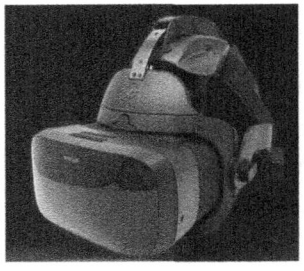  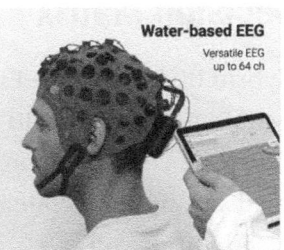

Galea Hybrid Headset   Kernel Hybrid Headset   Water based Hybrid Headset

Figure 4-2. *Left: Galea Hybrid Headset, Center: Kernel Hybrid Headset, Right: Water-Based EEG Headset*

Invasive and Research-Grade BCIs

These invasive and high-density research-grade BCIs provide extremely high-fidelity brain data, but are not practical in more general cybersecurity applications due to cost, complexity, and in the case of implants, the surgical risks. They are normally found in research labs (academic or defense) to generate gold standard ERP authentication data sets or to investigate next-generation cognitive security paradigms. Although they are presenting the future promise of extremely safe neural authentication, they are still mostly experimental toward cybersecurity in non-niche military and medical settings. Table 4-4 provides the comparative analysis of different invasive BCI devices on the parameters such as key features available, time to setup required, use cases in cybersecurity context, the suitable environments along with strengths and limitations.

Table 4-4. Comparative Invasive BCI Devices

Device	Key features	Setup time	Cybersecurity use cases	Best for	Pros	Cons
BioSemi ActiveThree[19]	Lab-grade 32–64+ channel EEG with gel electrodes, ultra-high fidelity	~30+ mins	High-fidelity ERP authentication dataset creation, research validation	Advanced academic research labs	– Gold standard ERP accuracy – Highly reliable	– Very expensive – Impractical for field deployment
g.tec g.Nautilus[20]	High-density wireless EEG, clinical research-grade	~30 mins	Advanced authentication research, hybrid ERP-fNIRS testing	Neuroscience and security R&D labs	– High channel count – Clinical-grade	– Expensive – Complex

(continued)

---

[19] https://www.biosemi.com/products.htm

[20] https://www.gtec.at/

Table 4-4. (*continued*)

Device	Key features	Setup time	Cybersecurity use cases	Best for	Pros	Cons
Neuralink (experimental)[21]	Fully invasive implantable interface	Surgical implant	Long-term potential for brain-controlled authentication in ultra-secure contexts	Future defense/ military applications	– Direct brain signal access – Highest fidelity	– Invasive surgery – Not viable for enterprise use

[21] https://neuralink.com/

Decision Matrix

BCIs with invasive connections and high population research grade give the best neural information and are too complex and impractical except in academic and military research labs.

- BioSemi ActiveThree is the most reliable system when it comes to gold-standard ERP authentication datasets. It offers 32 64+ channels of ultra-high fidelity EEG but needs more than 30 minutes to prepare using a gel-based system and exceeds US$20,000, it is not suited to field use.

- In the wireless high-density EEG research, g.tec g.Nautilus has lower weight, clinical-quality equipment, high signal fidelity and yet expensive and complex to operate in cybersecurity aspects.

- About what yet-to-be experimental use could result in the authentication of thought, Neuralink, an invasive implantable BCI, hypothetically enables secure thought-controlled systems, but its surgical implantation process and ethical considerations will make it inapplicable in enterprise cybersecurity in the near future.

Middleware and Signal Processing Frameworks

Recording brain signals using an EEG or fNIRS device covers one half of the neuro-cybersecurity math. Raw neural data are noisy and high-dimensional and susceptible to artifacts caused by eye movements or muscle motion or outside electromagnetic effects. In the absence of strong signal processing and classification structures, the security events cannot be derived out of these signals: typical examples are identifying a user by their brainprint, identifying cognitive stress in SOC analysts, or authentication via mental passphrase. At this point, middleware and signal processing structures are necessary. Table 4-5 provides the comparative analysis of different middleware and signal processing frameworks on the parameters such as core capabilities, use cases in cybersecurity context, the best stage to use the devices, the suitable environments along with strengths and limitations. They

- Obtain signals in real-time of EEG/fNIRS equipment

- Filter noise and obtain features (e.g., P300 peaks, motor imagery patterns, spectral power)

- Labeling of cognitive states (attention, fatigue, recognition of a secret stimulus)

- Streamed the data into the security processes such as IAM (Identity and Access Management), SIEM (Security Information and Event Management), or adaptive Zero Trust frameworks

At the far end of the digital infrastructure, middleware mediates the digital infrastructure with the human neural interface. For example:

- P300 authentication A P300 authentication scheme is an authentication mechanism in which middleware identifies the recognition response of a brain to a secret signal, and authenticates identity.

- In adaptive SOC monitoring, middleware fuses the EEG + fNIRS with system telemetry to dynamically load balance the workload of analysts or exaggerate alerts upon cognitive fatigue detection.

BCI2000, EEGLAB, OpenViBE, and LabStreamingLayer (LSL) are the most widely used middlewares in the neuro-cybersecurity research projects and pilots. They perform one particular operation in the pipeline: acquiring signals, extracting their features, classifying and merging with other external security solutions.

Table 4-5. *Comparative Middleware and Signal Processing Frameworks*

Middleware/Tool	Core capabilities	Cybersecurity relevance	Typical usage stage	Best for	Pros	Cons
BCI2000[22]	Real-time EEG acquisition, filtering, ERP (P300/SSVEP) detection, integrates with machine learning classifiers	Enables real-time cognitive authentication (P300 brainprints) and mental passphrase workflows	Operational and pilot deployments	Defense and research labs needing real-time ERP authentication	– Proven in DARPA pilots – Modular and open source – Supports multiple BCI devices	– Requires steep technical setup – Less user-friendly

(continued)

[22] https://www.bci2000.org/mediawiki/index.php/Main_Page

Table 4-5. (*continued*)

Middleware/ Tool	Core capabilities	Cybersecurity relevance	Typical usage stage	Best for	Pros	Cons
EEGLAB[23]	MATLAB-based advanced EEG analysis suite: ICA (artifact removal), time-frequency decomposition, ERP averaging	Supports brainprint template generation, dataset creation, and model training for continuous authentication	Research and model development stage	Building authentication templates and workload models	– Powerful signal cleaning tools – Large research community – Flexible offline + real-time options	– Needs MATLAB license – Requires expertise in signal analysis

[23] https://sccn.ucsd.edu/eeglab/

			Prototyping stage			
OpenViBE[24]	Visual pipeline designer for EEG classification (ERP and motor imagery), online feedback, supports many BCI devices	Ideal for prototyping mental passphrase authentication systems (motor imagery secure logins)	Prototyping stage	Quick proof-of-concept neural login systems	– Easy visual workflow design – Fast prototyping – Works with OpenBCI/Emotiv	– Not enterprise-hardened – Limited scalability
LabStreaming Layer (LSL)[25]	Real-time synchronization of multi-modal biosignals (EEG, fNIRS, eye-tracking, HRV) with system telemetry	Enables fusion of neural + behavioral + security events, powering adaptive Zero Trust SOC models	Advanced enterprise pilots	High-security SOC readiness and insider threat monitoring	– Multi-signal integration – Works well with hybrid BCIs – Compatible with SIEM pipelines	– Needs additional classifiers – Only handles synchronization

[24] https://openvibe.inria.fr/
[25] https://labstreaminglayer.readthedocs.io/

Decision Matrix

Choosing BCI middleware to start with neuro-cybersecurity, the deployment life cycle you may be in (research, prototyping, operational pilots, enterprise integration), and the degree of real-time processing that is required.

- **For real-time authentication and defense pilots ➤ Choose BCI2000**: A notable example is BCI2000 processing of live EEG ERPs, which occurred within DARPA Targeted Neuroplasticity Training (TNT) in order to enhance analyst decision-making. It is used in P300 pilots of authentication system whereby the ability of the user to identify a secret image produces a verifiable neural signature. However, it only works with technical knowledge on how to handle it and should be well calibrated.

- **To create authentication templates and dataset in building ➤ EEGLAB**: EEGLAB is the software of choice when artifact subtraction (ICA), ERP average, and spectral analysis are to be performed. By way of example, EEGLAB was applied in MDPI Sensors 2022 EEG-authentication experiments where raw signal outputs of an OpenBCI were cleaned before feeding into neural classifiers to produce brainprints used in workstation logins.

- **To give a quick prototype of neural login workflows**: The visual workflow designer of OpenViBE is optimal to use with motor imagery mental passphrases (e.g., imagine moving your right hand to log in). It is usually found within university research labs used to verify proof-of-concept authentication though not to be implemented with an enterprise.

- **To monitor and adaptive Zero Trust with multiple signals (SOC) ➤ LabStreamingLayer (LSL):** According to the pilots under hybrid EEG + fNIRS SOC readiness, LSL-associated neural data with SIEM event logs to automatically revise the sensitivity of alert loads to analysts. It does not classify signals on its own and rather serves as a glue between neurodata and security telemetry.

Security Risks and Ethical Implications

Innovations in the form of Brain–Computer Interfaces (BCIs) are set to become one of the most reliable technologies to transform cybersecurity. BCIs allow cognitive authentication, persistent user verification, and even intent-based access control by interfacing directly with neural signals representing an unironclad defense against all forms of typical authentication credential theft, phishing, or social engineering. BCIs have the potential to detect potential fatigue and stress among individual analysts in Security Operations Centers (SOCs) to minimize human error and inappropriate responses in critical situations. Defense agencies are already testing P300 brainprint logins, the use of mental passphrases and a hybrid EEG and fNIRS login to classified environments. Technically, this eliminates the rift between human cognition and machine trust, which makes cyber defense proactive instead of reactive. Nevertheless, this is an unprecedented level of integration of neuroscience in cybersecurity that also reveals deep security, privacy, and ethical issues. In contrast to a password or fingerprints, neural information can provide much more than an identity; it can be used to divulge an individual emotion, motive, or personal recognition choices. Brainprint templates are irreversible in case of hacking and thus leave open vulnerabilities. Furthermore, BCI-based systems present novel vulnerabilities: the system can be fooled by the adversarial EEG-based attacks, the Bluetooth-based BCI device is hijackable mid-flight, and the poorly regulated neural data flow can be exploited by malicious agents or even employers.

In addition to the technical context, BCIs violate essential human rights and ethics. Neuroprivacy or the right to mental sovereignty has become the focal point of discussions of how the stored and retrieved brainwaves data can be employed. Neuro-rights laws have been proposed by governments such as Chile, and legislators in the United States have started investigating consumer neurotech companies with regard to untransparent data policies. However at a global scale, there is still a disorganized and ill-equipped regulatory infrastructure responding to the neuro-surveillance of the workplace, coercion, and flocced margins of agency that BCIs would allow. Therefore, although BCIs may revolutionize cybersecurity by rendering it human-centric, intent-driven, such novel technologies also pose significant risks to privacy, consent, adversarial susceptibility, data regulation, and psychological independence. Providing the basis to design responsible, resilient architectures of cybersecurity using BCI, this section outlines ten security risks as shown in Figure 4-3 maps the security risks and ethical implications of using BCI-based cybersecurity, including neuroprivacy and adversarial attacks to regulatory gaps and governance challenges.

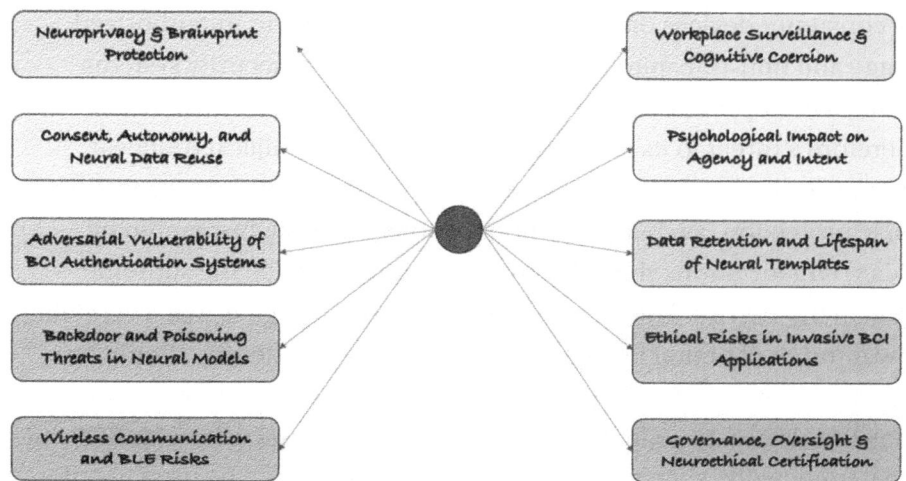

Figure 4-3. *Security Risks and Ethical Implications*

Neuroprivacy and Brainprint Protection

The core difference between conventional and BCI-based authentication system is a shift in the meaning of credentials: instead of using a password, one uses a brainprint (e.g., P300 ERP response). Brainprints also contain highly personal data and the degree of concern about privacy is also high, the user can reveal sensitive information about their emotional or cognitive processes without their knowledge. These data are not secured by conventional data privacy laws. As an example, the FTC[26] and the US Senate[27] have advocated safeguarding against neural data harvested

---

[26] https://www.commerce.senate.gov/2025/4/cantwell-schumer-markey-call-on-ftc-to-protect-consumers-neural-data

[27] https://www.theverge.com/policy/657202/ftc-letter-senators-neurotech-companies-brain-computer-interface

by consumer devices on the basis of dangers related to unauthorized usage and non-transparency. The problem in cybersecurity systems is that a brainprint template may be stashed or sent somewhere and therefore a threat to its abuse should it be stolen or hijacked since it cannot conveniently be revoked as a password. It must have proper life cycle protection (such as encryption, anonymization, ownership by users) Organizations should consider brainprints to be the supreme level of biometrics. The idea behind privacy-by-design is that a verifiably low number of neural features needed to verify the identity should be gathered; the raw EEG/FbIRS signals should not ever be written outside the edge device. In order to achieve trustable cybersecurity with BCI, any legal framework, such as NeuroRights[28] in Chile, would be used to enforce brain-data consent and ownership so that no brain–computer interface signals are re-purposed or resold.

Consent, Autonomy, and Neural Data Reuse

In conventional cybersecurity, subscribers agree and are willing to allow their footprints to be entered into the record. But what is neuronal data that the users might not understand what biometric signals in the brain are being stored and used over and over again. Research indicates that traditional informed consent forms are not sufficient to collect longitudinal brain records, particularly, where that information may be reprocessed applying novel ML methods or integrated in behavioral biometric telemetry.[29] The requirement of cognitive autonomy is dynamic

---

[28] https://fpf.org/blog/privacy-and-the-rise-of-neurorights-in-latin-america

[29] Farahany, N. A. (2023). *The battle for your brain: defending the right to think freely in the age of neurotechnology*. St. Martin's Press.

or renewable consent. When used in BCI-enabled SOC, workers also need to be informed that their brain signals may be transmitted to SIEM or IAM, and that they must have the right to opt out, or anonymize their record.

Adversarial Vulnerability of BCI Authentication Systems

Models of machine learning applied to EEG signals can be particularly sensitive to perturbation. It has been found that even noise measured at a level that is imperceptible adds into the time-series of EEG can misclassify or fail this one silently in brainprint authentication models. As an example, an adversarial perturbation attack might cause a P300 classifier to accept an imposter as an authorized user or cause a denial-of-service by causing a stream of false negative judgments.[30] These weaknesses are critical in high-security settings that want to implement BCI-based MFA. Defense systems have to include adversarial testing and strong model-standardization techniques such as adversarial training, randomized stimulus presentation and anomaly detection in classification. Devoid of these safeguards, BCI-based authentication would be easier to exploit as compared with traditional biometrics.

Backdoor and Poisoning Threats in Neural Models

Adversarial backdoor research demonstrates that an adversary may add trigger patterns to training data that later lead to misclassification, allowing an adversary to create a poisoned brainprint model that misclassifies

---

[30] Martínez Beltrán, E. T., Quiles Pérez, M., López Bernal, S., Huertas Celdran, A., & Martínez Pérez, G. (2022). Noise-based cyberattacks generating fake P300 waves in brain–computer interfaces. *Cluster Computing, 25*(1), 33–48.

only when an adversary-encoded trigger pattern is present. This would be the case where a model is trained as a backdoor that would allow a rogue insider or state entity access depending on scenarios with BCI authentication when the backdoor has been engineered during training to allow an insider or state with a backdoor access to authenticate with a specific mental imagery sequence that is not visible to regular users.[31] This danger is especially harmful to teams of SOC development or pipelines that are open source. The mitigation plan involves: secure enclaves in model training, training data provenance, and regular model integrity checking to identify tampering.

Wireless Communication and BLE Risks

Non-invasive BCIs use Bluetooth Low Energy (BLE) to transmit data concerning EEG/fNIRS to processing systems.[32] BLE is also susceptible to attacks, such as BlueBorne and replay injection, as well as man-in-the-middle hacks Such weaknesses present shims through which an attacker can intercept raw neural signals and change them on a route to middleware(e.g., BCI2000 or OpenViBE) or inject fake EEG patterns to circumvent an authentication attempt or create false epochs.[33] This is why encryption of BLE and verification of firmware is necessary.[34] Neural

---

[31] Meng, L., Jiang, X., Chen, X., Liu, W., Luo, H., & Wu, D. (2024). Adversarial filtering based evasion and backdoor attacks to EEG-based brain-computer interfaces. *Information Fusion*, *107*, 102316.

[32] Tarkhani, Z., Qendro, L., Brown, M. O. C., Hill, O., Mascolo, C., & Madhavapeddy, A. (2022). Enhancing the security & privacy of wearable brain-computer interfaces. *arXiv preprint arXiv:2201.07711*.

[33] https://www.bitbrain.com/blog/cybersecurity-brain-computer-interface

[34] https://bastille.net/protecting-from-ble-data-exfiltration-attacks-with-bastille-networks

telemetry channel should not be a weak point of the security structure; secure pairing, device whitelisting, network segmentation, and signal integrity signing are required to make the circle complete.

Workplace Surveillance and Cognitive Coercion

The monitoring systems currently offered by BCI vendors are focused on continuous tracking of cognitive states (attention, fatigue, stress) and can easily lead to the surveillance of the employees – data may be used to pressure or coerce users based on the analytics or neural performance data.[35] Alternatively, an example of fatigue metrics as an automatic control condition by the SOCs would be to reroute alerts or downgrade privileges without prior consent, creating a psychological or performance pressure. Limitations to such use by system designers must be codified, cognitive data may not be employed as a punishment, but it can only be applied to support (e.g., in triaging alert tasks).[36] It can be prevented by transparent policy, opt-in consent, anonymizing data, and the independent control that can assist in avoiding abuse and safeguard mental privacy.

Psychological Impact on Agency and Intent

Introducing transformative BCI use, such as thought-controlled access authorizations or mental passphrases, confuses the introspector with the intent of the user. In the case of systems carrying out actions on the basis of neural commands, there can arise dilemmas as to who should be held responsible in the event of incorrect or harmful acts, namely,

---

[35] Muhl, E., & Andorno, R. (2023). Neurosurveillance in the workplace: do employers have the right to monitor employees' minds?. *Frontiers in Human Dynamics*, 5, 1245619.
[36] https://arxiv.org/abs/2303.07242

the user (who requested the act) or the system (which mis-identified the act). Ethical[37] aspect comprises user agency, so-called free will, and accountability design. Certain mental commanding procedures, failsafe protocols, post-authorship confirmation screens/data, and audit trails are needed to maintain clarity during BCI-controlled control.[38]

Data Retention and Lifespan of Neural Templates

Neural biometric templates, unlike PINs or passwords, may be valid at permanent intervals. In the case of a brainprint model, in the event of a breach (or even being reverse-engineered), the so-called simple reset is non-existent.[39] This persistence is the reason why template storage policies are essential, raw EEG data must never be stored longer than their direct use, templates should be revocable and revocable similarly to a cryptographic token,[40] and they should be handled by secure enclaves. The threat of permanent compromise can be avoided using secure hardware modules to store encrypted templates, audit logs recording access, and re-enrollment procedures that periodically renew the enrollment credentials.

---

[37] Kritika, M. (2025). A comprehensive study on navigating neuroethics in Cyberspace. *AI and Ethics*, 5(1), 93–100.

[38] Davidoff, E. J. (2020). Agency and accountability: ethical considerations for brain-computer interfaces. *The Rutgers journal of bioethics*, 11, 9.

[39] Wang, M., Wang, S., & Hu, J. (2022). Cancellable template design for privacy-preserving EEG biometric authentication systems. *IEEE Transactions on Information Forensics and Security*, 17, 3350–3364.

[40] Pradel, G., & Mitchell, C. (2021). Privacy-preserving biometric matching using homomorphic encryption. *arXiv preprint arXiv:2111.12372*.

Ethical Risks in Invasive BCI Applications

Although not paramount to recent non-invasive cyber pilots, the ethical complexity of implantable BCIs, such as Neuralink or Stentrode, cannot be ignored. Implants add risks of surgery, possible new personality, uncertainty of the neutrality of the device, and a legal haze. Were cybersecurity systems to ever implement implant authentication, then policies need to be defined on the rights of consent, reprogrammability, the right of removal as well as mental health. Such structures should comply with any new laws on neuro-rights and medical device legislation before invasive BCIs may be thought to be feasible even in access control.

Governance, Oversight, and Neuroethical Certification

Cybersecurity systems using BCI ought to go through neuroethical certification, external control, and auditing, considering the sensitivity of neural data. Like those in the privacy laws such as GDPR, companies that implement such systems are required to possess an audit trail, the review of third party on the information collected, a retention restriction, and a user complaint system. The push to have misuse blocked by outside authority as with the NeuroRights Bill in Chile, or demands by US legislators to have the FTC regulate neurotechnologies is an indication of where the perceived personhood of neurotechnologies lies. In the absence of adequate supervision, the BCI-enhanced cybersecurity poses the threat to public confidence and liabilities to organizations.

The ability of Brain–Computer Interfaces to re-establish the understanding of cybersecurity in its core, moving it away from unchanging credentials and reactive defensive techniques to dynamic, cognition-based trust systems. They also offer what, until now, no other technology ever could – persistent, intent-aware authentication, collaborative human-machine interaction that is unrestricted in kind, and real-time adaptive defense technologies that adapt to the mental well-being of the operator. Brainprints and P300 responses and the measurement of the level of cognition at work, are already shown to have the potential to enhance the digital security of Defense, critical as well as high security enterprise settings, far more than in the current biometrics business. But this technological break cannot go without a price. It is a high-risk trend: BCIs present a new and highly personal attack surface, with consequences of a breach being essentially catastrophic since there is no possibility of altering one neural template like it may be with a password. They even face the risk to turn the workplace into a sphere of total neuro-surveillance, with labile mental states being quantified under control. The assumption, then, that neural signals are secure is challenged by adversarial vulnerabilities such as perturbations, data poisoning, wireless hijacks. Worse still, there are the ethical concerns, such as the corrosion of mental freedom, semi-autonomous agency when machines behave based on brain activity, and the desire of totalitarian possible use of neurodata.

Compared to technical solutions, the road ahead requires more than just that. Human autonomy cannot be guaranteed solely by means of encryption and adversarial robust models. The construction of neuro-cybersecurity has to be erected under privacy-by-design, strict governance, dynamic consent, and enforceable neuro-rights that place the brain as the final sphere of personal sovereignty. International policies, equivalent with GDPR but involving neural data, are a matter of urgency. This has to be a combination of two things, innovation, and ethics, without a combination of the two, BCIs will be a device of coercion rather than liberation. BCIs cannot be considered utopian or dystopian, rather, they are transformative in just about every sense because of our responsibility in ensuring that they are used in a responsible manner as this will determine their usefulness in matters relating to cybersecurity. When carefully conceived, they will seal the security chasm between man and machine; when hastily constructed without guardrails, they will crack the most massive privacy fault line in human history.

Future Landscape: Toward a Cognitive Perimeter in Cybersecurity

With the development of brain–computer interfaces (BCIs) and cybersecurity, we will soon reach the tipping point where the psychological phenomena themselves are the limit of trust, not the behavior or the trace. BCIs in future will not be relegated to experimental security frameworks such as authentication systems but will become a part and parcel of operational security topologies and will spawn in the process the development of a decentralized neural identity model, or BCI-ID. Such systems providing biometric authentication, which use the brainprint as a base EEG, are inherently dynamic and extremely difficult to replicate due to their nature, with authentication rates over 96% achievable under five seconds of data being reported in Frontiers in Neuroscience (2022). With advancement in edge-computing devices and the reduction in latency of brain-signal processing, it is safe to say that true-time brainprint verification will be used in military grade networks, key infrastructure control panels, and zero-trust enterprise systems. At the same time, a distributed cognition-aware defense infrastructure will be done on cloud-integrated BCI platforms. Other companies are also already developing neurotech ecosystems on a cloud scale, such as Neurable and Kernel, where the attention, stress, and intentions of the operators are tracked and assessed as they occur in real time to adjust workload, prompt assistance, or intervene before they occur. Within cybersecurity, this could translate into the possibility that Security Operations Centers (SOCs) integrate a BCI dashboard into a task reallocation process which dynamically reassesses task assignments as analysts in those Security Operations

Centers become more or less cognitively-loaded or into the capability of tracked high-stress signals indicating the onset of decision fatigue at the time of incident response. Also, with further changes in the BCIs being more intent-responsive and sensing the emotional state, neuro-adaptive interfaces will progress, giving control over access privileges to be given or denied in real-time depending on the preparedness or stability of the user. The Next-Generation Nerve Interfaces project by DARPA (2023) has shown that systems based on motor-imagery, can be used to administer an order with high reliability, and there is potential that secure access systems will use a mental passphrase or recognition response of users rather than an input by keyboard. Nonetheless, such developments cannot be considered separately to the appearance of new dangers and ethical issues. The malicious attacks like brainprint spoofing, signal interference, and intercepting of neurodata through Bluetooth are still noteworthy, and with the growing number of consumer grade BCIs broadcasting to cloud platforms with less secure encryption requirements. These threats require the next generation of cyber-defensive protocols, the ones that can verify the integrity of the neural streams, analyze the adversarial noise, and encrypt brainwave telemetry both at rest and on the move. Along with it, the development of policy frameworks to protect neuro privacy and agency is equally imperative. The first-in-the-world NeuroRights bill adopted in Chile in 2021 has brought impetus to a widespread acceptance of cognitive liberty as a human right, and the IEEE P2731 and P7000 standards series are in the early stages of creating both ethical and technical standards of neurodata regulatory governance. The future, hence, is two-dimensional: on the one hand, the BCIs will allow cognitive firewalls, know-intent systems, and the symbiosis between human and machine when it comes to the security of the cyberspace; on the other, however, the BCIs will compel society to reexamine the definition of such concepts as privacy, consent and sovereignty over their minds in the era of the digital world. A responsible race toward developing these systems (or any system in any field, considering other horizons, as well) to be a source of resilience only, or a source of control, will depend on technical innovation paired with ethical foresight.

This chapter is bold in its scope, proposing brain–computer interfaces (BCIs) as the future of cybersecurity, arguing we should change the use of credentials and move toward intent-based as well as neurobiological-based authentication. Although the argument presented in this chapter is progressive and thoroughly based on similar examples, such as OpenBCI and BCI2000 application in DARPA, it sometimes exaggerates the applicability of the technology in the real-world scenario. EEG still suffers the same limitations in non-invasive systems with noise, between-run variability, and system calibration that is far better understood than necessary in academic applications but could be a critical part of an applicative system.

The innovative, but technically immature vision is a possibility of BCIs integration with Zero Trust and SIEM platforms. The current security systems do not have the ability to absorb and utilize cognitive data and feasible APIs of BCI-SIEM are mainly theoretical. Furthermore, in regard to the ethical issues, especially with respect to consent, ownership of neural data and privacy of thoughts, there is room to treat these with more considering aspects. As an example, can workers have rights during the monitoring of their cognitive states in the Security Operations Centers? This creates some basic neuroethical questions that require well-defined legal precedents and international policy agreement. Irrespective of these shortcomings, the chapter does an excellent job of bringing out the convergence of the fields of cybersecurity and neuroscience, to look at how disruptive the power of real-time cognitive feedback, dynamic authentication and the ability to recognize intent may be. It provides a powerful premise to reconsider the digital identity and human-system interaction within the vicinity of high-security domain. The breakthroughs in technology, however, will not be sufficient to achieve success, which will require bolstering with scalable deployment models, industry standards, and socio-legal preparedness. As is, this chapter presents an exciting conceptual jump – it is promising, but is limited by serious practical and ethical limitations.

Key Takeaways

- BCIs make the paradigm shift in cybersecurity; they provide intent-based verification and continuous user-state observation in real time, which traditional biometrics could not support, BCIs bypass brain signals and directly infer secure control actions, often changing access decisions with each signal readout and playing spoofing.

- The chapter categorizes the BCI systems into invasive, semi-invasive, and non-invasive systems with a greater focus and application in the field of cybersecurity on the non-invasive one such as EEG and fNIRS on the grounds of safety, low cost, and the ability of such a system to obtain the intent of mind without going under the knife.

- OpenBCI, Emotiv Epoc+, and NeuroSky, among other hardware platforms, and middleware such as BCI2000, EEGLAB and OpenViBE, allow one to robustly monitor a brain and filter the signals, as well as design cognitive biometrics, and bring the prototyping of secure authentication frameworks at scale.

- BCI-based cognitive authentication uses brainprints or mental passphrases based on distinguishing brain responses, exemplified by P300 event-related potentials and motor imagery, the latest such brainprinting

providing a technique of identity verification
that cannot be externally observed, replayed, or
biometrically forged with anything close to complete
fidelity.

- With EEG providing continual feedback on status of
  mental states, such as attention, stress, and fatigue,
  dynamic evaluation of human operators and associated
  readiness and reliability can be mapped and adaptive
  protection measures such as access suspension,
  workload redistribution, or decision input can be
  enforced in SOC settings.

- BCI streams can be effectively integrated with Zero
  Trust infrastructures and security solutions like SIEM
  (Security Information and Event Management) and
  IAM (Identity and Access Management), but currently
  must be made operationally viable by standardizing
  the signal pipelines, APIs, and low-latency responsive
  systems.

- Field trials on BCI-based identity models and operator
  state profiling in high-security locations like defense,
  financial systems, and most importantly, critical
  infrastructure protection have already been tested in
  case studies based on DARPA neuroplasticity training
  programs and scholarly prototypes through OpenBCI
  achievements.

- BCI security threats to cognitive authentication have
  already articulated the need to deploy encrypted neural
  pipelines, anti-spoofing algorithmic solutions, and
  physical- and device-hardening, even in real-world
  cognitive authentication applications.

- This is because ethical and legal issues about brainwave data custody involve issues of cognitive privacy, consent, neural profiling, and how our mental conditions are likely to be abused and thus triggering calls to implement neuro-rights laws such as the constitutional revision of 2021 in Chile and universal principles on the protection of mental data.

- Their vision of the future consists in a vision of decentralized BCI authentication systems (BCI-ID), brain-cloud interconnection to achieve safe cognitive decision-making, and EEG-fNIRS solutions embedded in the daily security system, assuming that the ethical, technological, and legal frameworks are progressing in parallel.

CHAPTER 5

Neural Authentication: The Next Generation of Cyber Protection

"In the war for identity, the mind is the last unspoofable fortress."

We find ourselves in an age where digital identity is being erased under the pressure of technologically complex growth that is exponentially expanding. They have changed the very concept of risk and trust on the Internet, combining ubiquitous connectivity, hyper-personalized artificial intelligence, and multi-vector cyber-attacks. A password used to be enough to establish the identity of a user. Even multifactor authentication systems, that involve the use of SMS codes in addition to authenticator apps and even biometrics are failing to provide adequate protection against an ever-increasing arsenal of cyber adversaries today. Deepfakes generate faces in an uncanny valley sort of way, phishing attacks can work at scale on human cognitive biases, and adversarial AI can generate behavioral patterns that are indistinguishable from the real. In a world which is ever evolving, neural authentication is a radical solution not a new incremental improvement but a new paradigm to protect the identity which is the very foundational stone of digital trust gets vulnerable.

© Kritika 2026
Kritika, *Neuroscience Meets Cybersecurity*, https://doi.org/10.1007/979-8-8688-2183-7_5

The Paradigm Shift from Static to Dynamic Identity

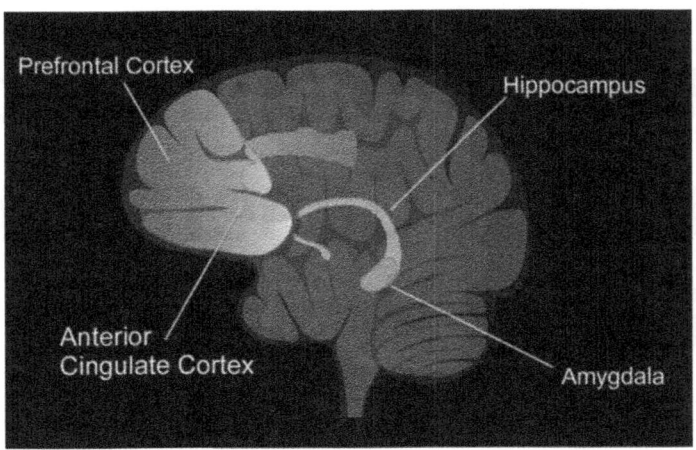

Figure 5-1. *The Paradigm Shift from the Trinity Model to the Evolution of the Fourth Paradigm*

Digital authentication has been developing in a foreseeable pattern, developing in successive paradigms that mirror technological development and the increasing sophistication of cybercrime. Figure 5-1 illustrates the paradigm shift to the evolution of fourth paradigm "something you think".[1] This trajectory can be conceptualized in terms of the classical authentication model on which decades of security design has been based:

> **Something You Know (Knowledge Factors):**
> The oldest and most popular kind of digital authentication is the use of passwords, PINs, security questions, and passphrases. These

---

[1] Pahuja, S., & Goel, N. (2024). Multimodal biometric authentication: A review. *AI Communications, 37*(4), 525–547. https://doi.org/10.3233/aic-220247

knowledge-based systems were highly dominant during the early Internet era and they were easy and universal. Nevertheless, as opposed to conventional security credentials which rely on what you know (e.g., a password) or what you are carrying (e.g., a key card), biometric authentication relies on who you are as its key credential, thus illustrating the inherent limitation of knowledge-based solutions.

Something You Have (Possession Factors): Hardware tokens, smart cards, mobile phones, and authenticator applications are the second wave of evolution. These physical or device-based credentials provided an additional physical security that did not require relying on human memory and mental weaknesses. This example of smartphone-based two-factor authentication is a successful example of the use of this paradigm.

Something You Are (Inherence Factors): The third evolutionary phase was physical biometrics, such as fingerprints, face recognition, iris scanning, voice patterns, and so forth. Biometric authentication involves verifying that a person is who they claim to be by examining physical aspects of a person, such as facial features, a scan of the iris or fingerprint before permitting them to access sensitive information or systems. Such a paradigm promised us unforgeable, ever-present credentials that were based on biological uniqueness.

The Emergence of the Fourth Paradigm: "Something You Think"

Neural authentication is a paradigm shift, a fourth factor, Something You Think.[2] This cognitive aspect of identity verification works[3] with a few revolutionary principles:

Dynamic Cognitive Patterns: In contrast to the fixed biometrics, neural patterns capture the current states of cognition, mental processes, and thoughts in real time. These patterns are dynamic in nature and vary with attention, emotional state, and conscious intent.

Temporal Authenticity: Brainwave patterns can provide not only the identity verification but the temporal authentication of cognitive presence. Not only can the authentication system identify who you are but it can also identify that you are currently actively thinking.

Intentional Authentication: It is possible to use conscious cognitive tasks to perform neural authentication, thus making authentication an active mental task and not a passive physical measurement. The users are capable of authenticating themselves by thinking or by doing mental calculations or by reacting to cognitive stimuli.

---

[2] Durgaraju, S. (2024). AI-Driven Adaptive Authentication for Multi-Modal Biometric Systems. *Journal of Electrical Systems*, *17*(1), 75–88. https://doi.org/10.52783/jes.6643

[3] Kritika, E. (2025). Brainjacking: The Cybersecurity Nightmare of the Future.

Contextual Adaptation: Neural patterns are environmentally sensitive and psychologically adaptive in nature, which render them extremely challenging to anticipate, re-experience, or produce in an artificial way without being consciously involved.

Neural Patterns As the Ultimate Biometric Frontier

Neural authentication is referred to as the ultimate biometric frontier[4] because it is the only system with the next generation of security benefits and biological limitations:

Non-Replicability: Fingerprints[5] are liftable, faces can be deep faked, voices can be synthesized, but the production of certain types of neural patterns is too conscious to be done passively and outside a living brain. The patterns of electrical activity produced by neural firing cannot be simply duplicated without the involvement of neurons, consciousness, and active thinking.

Continuous Liveness Detection: In the superior architecture of neural authentication, liveness detection is one of the key parameters. This

---

[4] Abdul-Al, M., Kyeremeh, G. K., Qahwaji, R., Ali, N. T., & Abd-Alhameed, R. A. (2024). The evolution of biometric authentication: A deep dive into multi-modal facial recognition: A review case study. *IEEE Access*.

[5] Yu, Y., Xue, J., Li, X., Lin, D., Liu, W., & Niu, Q. (2023). A Review of Fingerprint Sensors: Mechanism, Characteristics, and Applications. *Micromachines*, *14*(6), 1253. https://doi.org/10.3390/mi14061253

is certainly not a minor component as far as integrity is concerned, it is the cornerstone, for it relies upon the vital current of EEG signals. In traditional biometrics, there exist presentation attacks artificially reproduced biological attributes. However, in liveness detection, EEG signals are active neural firing patterns which cannot be maintained without conscious engagement.

Multi-Dimensional Uniqueness: Neural signatures are built based on time (when responses occur), spectral (frequency properties), spatial (topographic distribution) and cognitive (task specific responses) dimensions, forming a multi-dimensional identity space that is exponentially more complex compared to biometric templates.

Adaptive Complexity: The neural authentication can utilize more advanced cognitive functions, more time complexity, or multi-modal cognitive loads as challenges change, giving it an intrinsic adaptive complexity.

Neural authentication, instead of using external characteristics (such as fingerprints or tokens) or knowledge-based elements (such as passwords), utilizes the brainwave patterns of an individual as the identifying mark of personality.[6] These neural messages are internal, live, and determined by the individuated mix of cognitive and affective wiring of the brain. Since they are generated in the living brain and vary

---

[6] Aldayel, M., Alsedairy, N., Al-Nafjan, A., & Alsenan, S. (2024). Systematic review of brain-computer interface-based user authentication system: Trends, challenges, and directions. *IEEE Access, 12,* 96848–96861.

in a dynamic way with mental state, they are almost impossible to steal, forge, or replicate. Such re-conceptualization of identity in terms of neurophysiology is not a luxury of theoretical speculation. It is a matter of convenience. Following the democratization of the tools of digital deception and the transition of threat actors into cognitively aware opponents, security needs to transform into a form that is intrinsically human and biologically based. Neural authentication offers such an anchor, a type of authentication that is continuous, context-aware, and most importantly, by design impossible to spoof. But it is not merely exclusion of unauthorized users it is also about making sure that the entity on the other side of the interaction is truly human, cognitively present, and mentally alert. Neural authentication is therefore set to become a pillar in the design of robust identity systems over the next few decades.

Neural authentication is an advanced and developing form of identity authentication that uses the distinct electrical exercise of the brain of a person as a biometric credential. Such brainwave patterns, which can be measured mainly non-invasively via electroencephalography (EEG), represent a mixture of genetic neuroanatomy and the lifetime experiences that incessantly rewire neural networks.[7] Neural signals are not fixated like more conventional biometric identifiers like facial structure or fingerprint, they are dynamic, highly personalized, contextualized, emotional, cognitive, and even intentional. In a neural authentication procedure, the user can be presented with certain cognitive or sensory stimuli which are expected to elicit brain responses that can be differentiated. The most eminent of them are the Event-Related Potentials (ERPs), specifically the P300 component of it which is a measurable brainwave response,

---

[7] Alahaideb, L., Al-Nafjan, A., Aljumah, H., & Aldayel, M. (2025). Brain–Computer Interface for EEG-Based Authentication: Advancements and Practical Implications. *Sensors*, *25*(16), 4946.

happening roughly 300 milliseconds[8] after the recognition of a familiar stimulus. This cue is steady within any one person, but varies enough among individuals to be a strong indicator of identity.

The difference between neural authentication and the conventional systems is that the former is laid down on the basis of four principal tenets:

- **Uniqueness**: No two people have exactly the same neurophysiological reaction to the stimuli, and thus, every EEG signature is unique.

- **Liveness Detection**: Since EEG is a real-time measurement of neural activity, presence and consciousness liveness check are a part of the authentication procedure.

- **Non-replicability**: The neural responses are not easily replicated or played back, unless the user participates actively and consciously, and therefore substantial resistance to a spoofing or replay attack is achieved.

- **Contextual Adaptation**: As brainwaves vary with mental task, mood, attention, and environment, they are highly impossible to statically clone or predict.

There are a few forms in which neural authentication can be implemented:

- **Resting-State EEG:** A baseline of the spontaneous brain activity when the user is resting.

- **Stimulus-Induced ERPs**: These are responses to familiar, emotionally significant, or task-relevant stimuli as an individualized key.

---

[8] Di Mambro, A. (2025). Beyond brainwaves: exploring emotions, identity, and motor imagery through EEG-based BCI.

- **Multimodal Biometric Fusion**: Fusing brain signals with other biometrics (face data) or behavioral (e.g., keystroke rhythm) or ocular tracking data to increase robustness.

Such modalities render neural authentication applicable not only to one-time verification but also to continuous authentication, an important feature in scenarios where there is a need to continually monitor that an individual is who they claims to be. The model does not statically grant access to systems or data, but dynamically regulates access in real time based upon the continuous validation of brain activity, providing security and session integrity in real time.

Why Neural Authentication Is Necessary

In a world where legitimacy of online identity is continually being attacked, conventional methods of authentications are fast becoming irrelevant. Whether it is an exponential growth of credential stuffing and MFA bypass methods or the emergence of identity spoofing with the use of AI, the necessity of an entirely new paradigm has never been more apparent. Neural authentication represents not a mere science-fictional convenience of the future but a welcome and long overdue replacement of a security paradigm which is already reeling under the consequences of its own assumptions. So, without further ado, let us dive into the top five reasons that make neural authentication a necessity in the modern cyber environment, and in the world that is quickly becoming the tomorrow.

Collapse of Traditional Authentication Models

The breach of the old authentication models has become a fatal weakness. Passwords and passcodes are everywhere, but the effectiveness of passwords is frighteningly low and that is why it is considered as the poorest form of authentication. The breach of the old authentication models has become a fatal weakness. Passwords are everywhere, but the effectiveness of passwords is frighteningly low. According to the Verizon 2024 Data Breach Investigations Report, stolen credentials account for 77% of Basic Web Application Attacks,[9] with approximately 88% of breaches involving the use of stolen credentials in some capacity. With the introduction of Multi-Factor Authentication (MFA) as an additional line of defense, the adversaries have not fallen behind. Table 5-1 presents the various authentication mechanisms present in the current security landscape.

Table 5-1. *Current Authentication Security Landscape*

Authentication category	Market adoption	Known vulnerabilities	Verified incident rate	Regulatory status
Knowledge-based (Passwords)	Universal	Credential theft, reuse	77–88% of breaches	Being phased out
SMS-based MFA	Declining	SIM swapping, SS7	FBI/CISA advisory issued	Not recommended
App-based MFA	95% of MFA users	MFA fatigue, social engineering	Limited public data	Recommended
Hardware tokens	Enterprise-focused	Physical theft, social engineering	<5% reported incidents	Highly recommended
Biometric systems	Growing consumer adoption	Template spoofing, privacy concerns	Limited breach disclosure	Mixed regulatory response

---

[9] https://blog.1password.com/verizon-data-breach-report-2024-analysis

With the introduction of multi-factor authentication (MFA) as an additional line of defense, the adversaries have not fallen behind. New strategies, such as MFA fatigue attacks, SIM swapping, or impersonation with the use of deepfakes, routinely bypass security measures that were previously dependable. Even biometrics, which is usually billed as the gold standard in authentication, is no longer tamper proof. It is possible to lift fingerprints and reproduce them with the help of 3D printing and can be further tweaked to produce high false alarms. Deepfake audio can fool voice authentication. What adds even more risk is that, unlike a password, which you can change after it has been stolen, a biometric template becomes an unchangeable weak point once it has been stolen. Neural authentication eliminates these issues directly. As opposed to physical traits, brainwave patterns are intrinsically dynamic they change slightly with mental state and cannot be cloned in a static way. They also necessarily involve the conscious presence of the user, so there are no risks of being controlled remotely. This guarantees degree of liveness detection and behavioral coupling that cannot be rivaled by other systems.

Rise of Immersive and Neuro-Adaptive Systems

With the boundaries getting blurred between the digital and cognitive environment, immersive technologies are creating a revolution in human–computer interaction. Biosensing hardware (such as VR/AR headsets, Brain–Computer Interfaces (BCIs), and neurogaming platforms) is becoming accustomed to being incorporated into daily digital interactions.[10] This change is spearheaded by Apple with its Vision Pro, by Meta with its neural wristband project, and startups such as NextMind.

---

[10] Wen, D., Fan, Y., Hsu, S. H., Xu, J., Zhou, Y., Tao, J., ... & Li, F. (2021). Combining brain–computer interface and virtual reality for rehabilitation in neurological diseases: A narrative review. *Annals of physical and rehabilitation medicine*, *64*(1), 101404.

These technologies present a novel concept of integrated, passive, and persistent opportunity of identity verification. Devices with EEG can measure brainwave patterns non-intrusively. As an illustration, in a VR-based medical consultation or a virtual board meeting, in the background, the users may be constantly authenticated, and the system may identify abnormalities or possible violations on the fly. The introduction of this context-aware, non-obstructive model of verification fundamentally changes the understandings of what it is to be authenticated in immersive digital environments. Neural authentication does not become an add-on in such neuro-adaptive environments, rather it becomes inconspicuous to the system architecture. It makes sure that the user who is dealing with the system is not just an authorized user but is also present mentally and cognitively.

Zero Trust Requires Continuous Verification

The newest cybersecurity gold standard is Zero Trust Architecture (ZTA),[11] which runs on the principle: "Never trust, always verify." Nonetheless, numerous current implementations continue to depend on intermittent or perimeter-based verification schemes that create large security vulnerabilities after access is provided. Neural authentication is Zero Trust compatible as it performs continuous biological authentication. Instead of validating a user just upon logging in, neural systems allow presence, cognitive involvement, and behavioral consistency during the session to be evaluated on an ongoing basis, which at times become unacceptable to users, being annoying.

---

[11] Ahmadi, S. (2024). Zero trust architecture in cloud networks: Application, challenges and future opportunities. *Ahmadi, S. (2024). Zero Trust Architecture in Cloud Networks: Application, Challenges and Future Opportunities. Journal of Engineering Research and Reports, 26*(2), 215–228.

Applications are in

- **Defense and Intelligence**: Ensuring that operatives using classified systems are mentally present during the session.

- **Finance**: High value transactions can be secured by protecting against a session hijack even in the middle of an interaction.

- **Healthcare**: Authenticating the identity of remote clinicians accessing sensitive patient data to avoid misattribution or fraud.

Such a context-aware, dynamic verification model can go a long way toward patching security loopholes and making life much harder with attackers.

Human-Centric, Frictionless Security

The users of today require security that is effective as well as invisible. Authentication workflows that are dominated by friction are subject to human error, create security fatigue, and frequently prompt users to take risks by using shortcuts or reusing passwords.[12] Neural authentication brings a human-based model that makes security consistent with how people behave. Authentication using EEG can be completed in the background passive mode, with no active participation required beyond putting on a compatible device.[13] That, in turn, makes it especially well-suited in the scenarios, in which the ability to work without interruptions

---

[12] Doty, S. (2025). *Exploring Human Error: Comparing Intention and Action in US Healthcare Startups*. Capitol Technology University.

[13] Samal, P., & Hashmi, M. F. (2024). Role of machine learning and deep learning techniques in EEG-based BCI emotion recognition system: a review. *Artificial Intelligence Review*, 57(3), 50.

is of high importance, for example, in high-stakes simulations, live diagnostics, or high-paced financial trading settings. In addition, neural authentication leads to privacy-by-design. Many neural authentication models are decentralized, opposed to cloud-based biometric systems that store identity data on central servers. The neural templates are computed and compared locally on the client-side, which minimizes the risk of the mass data breach and regulatory risks.

Defense Against Future Threats

In a future filled with intelligent opponents, AI-based social engineering bots, deepfake-enhanced cognitive infiltrators, and real-time behavioral mimics, the weakness of fixed identity elements become painfully apparent. Psychological intrusion or machine level identity spoofing cannot be easily detected by the traditional security models. In this environment, neural authentication is a bio-cyber defense mechanism that appears.[14] It is anchored in the single thing that the current AI is incapable of imitating the presence of consciousness, locked into the biological context. EEG signatures provide identity authentication similar to their physical counterparts but, in addition to that, they provide a measure of cognitive conditions that include stress, attention, and intent which adds richness and redundancy to the security layer. The next generation is multimodal fusion. Neural signals, when used in conjunction with other modalities, including gaze tracking, behavioral biometrics, and physiological signals such as heart rate variability, form an ecosystem of defense that is orders of magnitudes more difficult to spoof. This multi-layered, neurobiologically based model is the most promising new horizon of identity assurance in a world where we are on the verge of post-truth existences.

---

[14] Anjum, N., Alshahrani, H., Shaikh, A., Kiran, M., Raz, S., & Alam, A. (2025). Cyber-Biosecurity Challenges in Next-Generation Sequencing: A Comprehensive Analysis of Emerging Threat Vectors. *IEEE Access*.

Why This Chapter Matters?

In a world that has gone digital with unremitting discontinuity, the future of cybersecurity does not lie in making slight adjustments to aging structures. It depends on thinking radically, not making minor modifications to obsolete structures. Neural authentication is one of the biggest changes in the sphere of identity verification to date, and its ramifications must be familiar to the contemporary cyber security specialist. This chapter is important since it captures the core of identity crisis that the digital world is suffering today. The important factors are

- **Strategic Vision of the Future of Identity Verification**: Neural authentication is not a futuristic idea, it is already being rolled out in industries such as defense, fintech, and neurogaming. Senior cybersecurity executives need to be on top of things by being knowledgeable of its architecture, advantages, and dangers.

- **Neuroscience and Cybersecurity**: The chapter is a unique combination of two historically divided fields. It exposes readers to a more interdisciplinary and hence innovative way of thinking by explaining the possibilities of using neurophysiological data to fuel cyber defense.

- **Ethical and Regulatory Awareness**: As one of the most sensitive types of personal data, neural data raise concerns on the ethical, legal, and psychological aspects of using the brain as a credential, which compliance leaders, policymakers, and risk officers should also know.

- **Fighting AI-Era Attacks**: As attacks become cognitive, personalized and AI-enhanced, the only way to strongly proceed is through biologically verifiable technologies such as neural authentication. It is one of the skills that contemporary CSOs and CISOs need to have regarding its defensive potential.

Since, at this point, we have defined what neural authentication is, why it is needed so urgently, and why this chapter is a key to the future of identity security, it is time to address the biological foundation on which this paradigm rests. To get a real idea of how reliable it is and what are its limitations, it is vital to unravel the neuroscientific concepts and biometric background that makes neural authentication not only possible, but incredibly solid. What ensues is an investigation into the process of brainwaves being turned into identity signals, and how cognitive science is slowly transforming cybersecurity at the most basic level.

Foundations of Neural Biometrics
The Neurophysiological Basis of Brainwave Identity

The neural authentication technology is all about the science of brainwaves; these are patterns of electrical activity caused by neurons firing in the brain. These are patterns that are measured using electroencephalography (EEG) and reflect a real-time picture of what is going on inside the brain, with regard to sensory perception up to higher-level thinking. The most common non-invasive reason of recording these signals is EEG, which has a millisecond level temporal resolution, which is relevant to identity recognition. There are five important frequency bands of brainwave activity[15]:

- **Delta (0.5 4 Hz):** Delta activity is usually related to deep sleep and the unconsciousness process.

- **Theta (4 -8 Hz):** This is associated with drowsiness, daydreaming, and meditation.

- **Alpha (8 -13 Hz):** Refers to relaxed wakefulness and is greatest when the eyes are closed.

- **Beta (1330 Hz):** Indicates engaged thinking, problem solving, and concentration.

- **Gamma (>30 Hz):** Gamma is linked to the high-level cognitive processes, such as perception and memory binding.

Every person has a unique spectral fingerprint within these bands which is adjusted by several factors like brain anatomy, cortical thickness, synaptic density, and functional connectivity. Such differences between individuals leave a neural signature that, in a controlled condition, is consistent enough to be adopted as a biometric identifier. Event-Related Potential (ERP) is one of the most vital phenomena used in neural authentication. ERPs are brain responses that are time-locked to definite stimuli and are tremendously helpful in quantifying the brain recognition of familiar or meaningful occurrences, of which P300 wave is a positive deflection that takes place in about 300 milliseconds when a known stimulus has been recognized. It can be thought of as a cognitive "aha" moment, a reliable occurrence once the brain perceives an input that is

---

[15] Allegretta, R. A., Rovelli, K., & Balconi, M. (2024, July). The role of emotion regulation and awareness in psychosocial stress: an EEG-psychometric correlational study. In *Healthcare* (Vol. 12, No. 15, p. 1491). MDPI.

personally relevant or anticipated. Authentication based on P300 needs advanced signal processing to carry out the practical implementation. The below code shows the way of scraping the authentication-based features of an ERP system with industry-standard tools.

Phase 1. Environment Setup and Dependencies

```
import mne
import numpy as np
from scipy import signal
from sklearn.preprocessing import StandardScaler
import matplotlib.pyplot as plt

# Configuration
SAMPLING_RATE = 256 # Hz, typical for authentication systems
ERP_WINDOW = (-0.2, 0.8) # Pre-stimulus to post-stimulus window
P300_WINDOW = (0.25, 0.45) # P300 component typical
latency range
```

Phase 2. Core Authentication Feature Extractor Class Encapsulates all ERP processing methods for neural authentication

```
class ERPAuthenticationFeatures:

    def __init__(self, sfreq=256):

        self.sfreq = sfreq
        self.scaler = StandardScaler()
        print(f"ERP Authentication Features initialized with
        {sfreq} Hz sampling")
```

```python
def get_system_info(self):
    """Return system configuration for verification"""
    return {
        'sampling_frequency': self.sfreq,
        'erp_window': ERP_WINDOW,
        'p300_window': P300_WINDOW
    }
```

Phase 3. Data Preprocessing Pipeline Implements standard ERP preprocessing steps with authentication-specific optimizations

```python
def load_and_preprocess(self, raw_data, events, event_id):

    print("Starting ERP preprocessing pipeline...")

    # Create working copy to preserve original data
    raw_filtered = raw_data.copy()

    # Apply bandpass filter optimized for ERP components
    # 0.1-30 Hz captures P300 while removing drift and high-
    frequency noise
    raw_filtered.filter(0.1, 30., fir_design='firwin',
    verbose=False)
    print("Applied 0.1-30 Hz bandpass filter")

    # Create epochs around stimulus events
    epochs = mne.Epochs(raw_filtered, events, event_id,
                        tmin=ERP_WINDOW[0], tmax=ERP_WINDOW[1],
                        baseline=(None, 0), preload=True,
                        reject=dict(eeg=100e-6), verbose=False)

    print(f"Created {len(epochs)} epochs for analysis")
    print(f"Artifact rejection threshold: 100 µV")

    return epochs
```

```python
# Add method to class
ERPAuthenticationFeatures.load_and_preprocess = load_and_
preprocess
```

Phase 4. P300 Component Analysis Focuses on the P300 ERP component – key to neural authentication

```python
def extract_p300_features(self, epochs, target_
condition='target'):
    print(f"Extracting P300 features from '{target_condition}'
    condition...")

    # Select epochs containing familiar stimuli (targets)
    target_epochs = epochs[target_condition]
    print(f"Processing {len(target_epochs)} target trials")

    # Average across trials to obtain clean ERP
    evoked = target_epochs.average()

    # Define P300 time window indices
    p300_start = int((P300_WINDOW[0] - ERP_WINDOW[0]) *
    self.sfreq)
    p300_end = int((P300_WINDOW[1] - ERP_WINDOW[0]) *
    self.sfreq)

    # Extract data within P300 latency window
    p300_data = evoked.data[:, p300_start:p300_end]
    n_channels = p300_data.shape[0]

    print(f"P300 analysis window: {P300_WINDOW[0]*1000:.0f}-
    {P300_WINDOW[1]*1000:.0f} ms")
    print(f"Analyzing {n_channels} EEG channels")

    # Initialize feature dictionary
    features = {}
```

```python
# Peak amplitude features (key authentication
discriminator)
features['p300_peak_amplitude'] = np.max(p300_data, axis=1)
peak_indices = np.argmax(p300_data, axis=1)
features['p300_peak_latency'] = (peak_indices / self.sfreq)
+ P300_WINDOW[0]

# Topographic distribution features
# Assumes standard 10-20 electrode placement
if n_channels >= 6:
    features['frontal_p300'] = np.mean(p300_data[:3, :])
    # Frontal electrodes
    features['parietal_p300'] = np.mean(p300_data[-3:, :])
    # Parietal electrodes
    features['fronto_parietal_ratio'] = features['frontal_
    p300'] / features['parietal_p300']

# Area under curve (reflects overall P300 magnitude)
features['p300_auc'] = np.trapz(np.abs(p300_data), axis=1)

# Peak-to-peak amplitude (additional discriminative
feature)
features['p300_peak_to_peak'] = (np.max(p300_data,
axis=1) -
                                np.min(p300_data, axis=1))

print(f"Extracted {len(features)} P300 feature types")
print(f"Peak amplitude range: {features['p300_peak_
amplitude'].min():.2e} to    {features['p300_peak_
amplitude'].max():.2e} V")

return features, evoked
```

```python
# Add method to class
ERPAuthenticationFeatures.extract_p300_features = extract_p300_
features
```

Phase 5. Spectral Power Analysis Extracts frequency-domain features complementing time-domain ERP analysis

```python
def extract_spectral_features(self, epochs):
    print("Computing spectral features for authentication...")

    # Compute power spectral density using multitaper method
    # Provides robust frequency domain analysis
    psds, freqs = mne.time_frequency.psd_multitaper(epochs,
                                    fmin=1, fmax=40,
                                    n_jobs=1, verbose=False)

    print(f"Computed PSD for {len(freqs)} frequency bins")

    # Define standard EEG frequency bands for authentication
    bands = {
        'delta': (1, 4),    # Deep sleep, unconscious
        processing
        'theta': (4, 8),    # Drowsiness, meditation, memory
        'alpha': (8, 13),   # Relaxed wakefulness, eyes closed
        'beta': (13, 30),   # Active thinking, concentration
        'gamma': (30, 40)   # High-level cognitive binding
    }

    band_powers = {}
    for band_name, (fmin, fmax) in bands.items():
        # Create frequency mask for current band
        freq_mask = (freqs >= fmin) & (freqs <= fmax)
        freq_count = np.sum(freq_mask)
```

```
    # Calculate mean power within frequency band
    band_powers[band_name] = np.mean(psds[:, :, freq_
    mask], axis=2)

    print(f"{band_name.capitalize()} band ({fmin}-{fmax}
    Hz): {freq_count} frequency bins")

print(f"Extracted spectral features across {len(bands)}
frequency bands")

return band_powers, psds, freqs
# Add method to class
ERPAuthenticationFeatures.extract_spectral_features = extract_
spectral_features
```

Phase 6. Feature Vector Construction Combines time and frequency domain features into unified authentication signatures

```
def create_authentication_vector(self, erp_features, spectral_
features):

    print("Constructing unified authentication feature
    vector...")

    feature_vector = []
    feature_names = []

    # Add time-domain ERP features
    erp_feature_types = ['p300_peak_amplitude', 'p300_peak_
    latency', 'p300_auc', 'p300_peak_to_peak']

    for feature_type in erp_feature_types:
        if feature_type in erp_features:
            if isinstance(erp_features[feature_type],
            np.ndarray):
```

```python
            # Multi-channel features
            feature_vector.extend(erp_
            features[feature_type])
            feature_names.extend([f"{feature_type}_ch{i}"
            for i in range(len(erp_features[feature_
            type]))])
        else:
            # Single-value features
            feature_vector.append(erp_
            features[feature_type])
            feature_names.append(feature_type)

# Add topographic ERP features if available
topo_features = ['frontal_p300', 'parietal_p300',
'fronto_parietal_ratio']
for feature_type in topo_features:
    if feature_type in erp_features:
        feature_vector.append(erp_features[feature_type])
        feature_names.append(feature_type)

# Add frequency-domain spectral features
band_order = ['delta', 'theta', 'alpha', 'beta', 'gamma']
for band in band_order:
    if band in spectral_features:
        # Average across epochs, include all channels
        band_data = np.mean(spectral_features[band],
        axis=0)  # Average across epochs
        feature_vector.extend(band_data)
        feature_names.extend([f"{band}_power_ch{i}" for i
        in range(len(band_data))])
```

```
# Convert to numpy array and normalize
feature_vector = np.array(feature_vector)

# Apply standardization for consistent feature scaling
feature_vector_normalized = self.scaler.fit_
transform(feature_vector.reshape(-1, 1)).flatten()

print(f"Authentication vector constructed: {len(feature_
vector)} dimensions")
print(f"ERP features: {sum(1 for name in feature_names if
'p300' in name)}")
print(f"Spectral features: {sum(1 for name in feature_names
if 'power' in name)}")
print(f"Feature vector range: [{feature_vector_normalized.
min():.3f}, {feature_vector_normalized.max():.3f}]")

return feature_vector_normalized, feature_names
```

```
# Add method to class
ERPAuthenticationFeatures.create_authentication_vector =
create_authentication_vector
```

The computational basis of the neural response to authentication features is achieved through this implementation framework that fills the gap between the theory of neurophysiology and practical biometric systems.

There are other ERPs that are explored to be used in identity verification like the N400 (associated with semantic processing) and the Mismatch Negativity (MMN) (used to show deviation detection).[16] These ERPs show that even during unconscious or passive states, the brain shows

---

[16] Liang, Q., Chen, Z., Tang, X., & Wang, X. (2025). Applications of event-related potentials in Alzheimer's disease: a systematic review and analysis. *Frontiers in Aging Neuroscience, 17,* 1513049.

detectable patterns which vary individual to individual. Not only that, studies indicate that topographic publication of these signals, in which they take place on the scalp, differs tremendously across people. Genetic and developmental issues modify this variation and therefore it becomes hard to have two individuals who, in reaction to similar stimuli, produce the same ERP profiles.[17] Besides the stimulus driven responses, resting state EEG has also been found to be an effective authentication tool. In the condition of the relaxed brain with no definite mental task, it nevertheless continued to generate a rich fabric of spontaneous activity that has been variously described as the neural baseline of the individual. These features are consistent over days and even weeks, particularly in the alpha and beta bands, and may serve as passive indicators of identity that do not need user effort. In general, the neurophysiology of identity consists in a convergence of three major dimensions:

- **Spectral properties:** Frequency band power, frequency band distribution.

- **Temporal dynamics**: Timing and sequence of brainwave response to stimuli.

- **Topographic patterns**: Topographic patterns are the spatial arrangements of neural activity across regions of the scalp.

It is the combination of these elements that create a brain print, a complex, dynamic, and highly personal identifier that is based upon the biology of the brain.

---

[17] Smith, M. R., Berry-Kravis, E., Thaliath, A., Isenstein, E. L., Durkin, A. R., Foss-Feig, J., ... & Ethridge, L. E. (2025). Phenotypic variation in neural sensory processing by deletion size, age, and sex in Phelan-McDermid syndrome. *Journal of Neurodevelopmental Disorders*, *17*(1), 51.

Cognitive Stimuli and Identity Elicitation

Although resting-state EEG measures the natural activity of the brain, neural authentication is much stronger and more precise when certain cognitive stimuli can trigger certain and measurable neural responses.[18] This is the technique which is based on the fact that our brain perceives familiar, meaningful or emotional stimuli (compared to unknown or neutral stimuli). This principle, when used together with EEG, is what allows creating very personal brainwave responses. Neural authentication Cognitive stimuli may be grouped into two broad categories:

- **Passive stimuli**: They do not need active participation of the user. Such things include display of pictures, audios, or words that are personally relevant or are known to the user.

- **Active stimuli**: These include mental arithmetic, spatial rotation, or recalling information and need the active processing of the user.

Perhaps the most studied stimulus-based authentication paradigm is the so-called oddball paradigm, where a rare (target) stimulus occurs in a sequence of frequent (non-target) stimuli. A measurable P300 ERP is elicited when the user is aware of the target (e.g., a known face or name). It is hard to fake this kind of response since it involves actual recognition and conscious awareness. The other is the use of visual or hearing signals that are personalized. As an example, one can be proposed to answer mentally to a series of pictures relating to one's personal life (family, favorite places, objects, and so on), which can evoke highly encoded neural processes. The structure of the stimuli is also very crucial in the provoking of similar reactions. The personalization increases the intensity and precision of the

---

[18] Fidas, C. A., & Lyras, D. (2023). A review of EEG-based user authentication: trends and future research directions. IEEE Access, 11, 22917–22934.

ERP whereas neutral or irrelevant stimulus can lead to weak or unclear response. Besides, some cognitive processes, including selective attention and working memory, enhance the idiosyncrasy of these responses by playing a significant role in shaping the individual's brain-processing strategies leading to responses that are unique to each individual and help strengthen the authenticity of the same stimulus. The idea behind involving cognitive stimuli in neural authentication is to get a conjunction involving biological particularity and psychological specificity. The two encoding processes cause the authentication system to be not only a challenge of who you are but also what you know and how you think. This is especially applicable in continuous authentication, where a user can be subjected to mild stimuli periodically when interacting with a system, and their brain responses in real-time can be relied upon to verify their authenticity.

Signal Acquisition and Preprocessing Pipelines

Every neural authentication mechanism has a winning or losing potential that is dependent on the accuracy and integrity of the signal acquisition and preprocessing pipeline. Although brainwave data carries a plethora of identity-relevant information, it is also highly noisy and prone to all sorts of artifacts, including muscular activities and eye blinking, as well as electrical noise in the environment. Thus, the reliability of subsequent processing, feature extraction, and lastly the process of classification is dependent on the quality of input signal.

EEG Hardware: Wet vs. Dry Electrodes

EEG equipment is of two principal types, namely, wet and dry electrodes.[19] Wet electrodes are characterized by a conductive gel placed between the electrode and the scalp, and the fidelity of the signal is high and low impedance. The systems have gained a lot of popularity in clinical and research settings because they are reliable. They do need to be set up, which is quite time-consuming, need trained personnel, and can prove uncomfortable to the person using them. Dry electrodes, on the other hand, where no gel is needed and the setup process and user comfort is improved. The development of the materials sciences and sensors has enhanced them considerably, which makes them potentially applicable in the real world, where they can be used in mobile authentication, games, or VR-enabled systems.[20] Dry electrodes, however, usually have a greater impedance and are more prone to noise. Consumer devices such as the Muse headband or Emotiv Insight have the adequate resolution to perform simple cognition and authentication steps. Research-grade systems (e.g., BioSemi, g.tec) have more channels, more effective shielding, and are more portable and costly as well as customizable.

Preprocessing Techniques

After obtaining signals, they should be subjected to strict preprocessing pipeline to remove noise and artifacts. Important measures are

---

[19] Ke, Y. (2024, September). Current Study on Dry and Wet Electrodes in the Field of Non-Invasive Brain-Computer Interface. In *2024 International Conference on Mechanics, Electronics Engineering and Automation (ICMEEA 2024)* (pp. 665–674). Atlantis Press.

[20] Nwagu, C., AlSlaity, A., & Orji, R. (2023). EEG-based brain-computer interactions in immersive virtual and augmented reality: A systematic review. *Proceedings of the ACM on Human-Computer Interaction, 7*(EICS), 1–33.

- Band-pass filtering of interest frequencies (normally 0.5145 Hz).

- Removal of power line noise (50 or 60 Hz) by means of notch filtering.

- Rejection of artifacts that include blinks, facial movements, tenseness of muscle movements (discarding the parts of the video).

- Independent Component Analysis (ICA) can be used to delink and eliminate such source artifacts as eye blinks or heartbeat noise.

All of these steps of preprocessing aid in the achievement of this end, guaranteeing that the signal that remains is genuinely a brain signal and not a mixture of physiological and environmental noise.

Signal Segmentation and Feature Extraction

EEG data will be cleaned and then segmented into what is called epochs, which are usually 1–2 seconds in duration, and usually centered around stimuli events. Authentication models work with these epochs as the units of analysis. Relevant characteristics are taken out of every epoch in order to describe the brain activity of the user.

Features types:

- **Temporal characteristics**: Peak latency, waveform shape and signal variability

- Spectral aspects such as power spectral density and band-power

- Time-frequency descriptors that are calculated on wavelet transforms or short-time Fourier transforms

- Topographical features that take account of the spatial distribution of activity on the scalp

It is a step that usually defines the effectiveness of the whole system. The selected features should be consistent between two or more sessions, very personalized and noise-insensitive. Acquisition and Pre-processing pipeline forms the infrastructure backbone to the neural biometric systems. Authorizations performance may be substantially impaired by poor signal quality or non-proper filtering. Conversely, a properly tuned set of pipelines, notably those complemented with real-time artifact removal and dynamic filtering, can allow scalable robust identity recognition.

Machine Learning and Neural Pattern Classification

Having acquired uncluttered and well-organized data, the next difficulty is finding a way of classifying the patterns of the brain that have been extracted. It is at this point that machine learning (ML) provides the computational foundation of converting raw neural features to practical identity decisions.

Algorithms for Brainwave Classification

In neural authentication, some ML algorithms are employed for brainwave classification:

- **Support Vector Machines (SVM)**: Works well on high features spaces; does not overfit the data.

- **Linear discriminant Analysis (LDA)**: Easy to implement, computationally efficient, and surprisingly effective.

- **Random Forests**: Appropriate when nonlinear associations are of importance and when one wishes to deal with heterogeneous feature types.

- **Neural Networks**: Neural networks can automatically learn feature hierarchies in the raw data, for example, Convolutional Neural Networks (CNNs) and Recurrent Neural Networks (RNNs).

Although computationally expensive, deep learning models have demonstrated welcome success in learning complex EEG time and spatial patterns. CNNs are good at spatial correlations of input variables (e.g., scalp topography), and RNNs are good at sequential input data (e.g., time series of brainwaves).

Validation and Training

They are usually trained on individually designed sets of data whereby a baseline of current brain patterns is created against each user. The most common method is supervised learning, whereby labels on classes inform the reception of a signal either by the alleged user or not. Dropout, cross-validation, and regularization methods are used to prevent overfitting and increase generalization. The authentication systems should also be able to perform real-time inference, thus necessitating the need to have models which can trade in accuracy with computational speed. Learning in increments (i.e., updating the model after the model is periodically augmented with new data) is also an upcoming practice.

Real-Time vs. Offline Authentication

The possibilities of an offline authentication mean that EEG data are processed in a batch, and may be used in a research or training application. Real-time authentication, however, requires fast signal acquisition, process, and decisions, which typically must occur in a matter of milliseconds. The key equipment to this environment is low-latency pipelines, edge computing, and efficient ML models.

Evaluation Metrics

The performance is gauged by normative biometric measures:

- FAR: This is the possibility of an unauthorized user being falsely accepted.

- **False Rejection Rate (FRR)**: The likelihood that a genuine user is falsely rejected.

- **Equal Error Rate (EER)**: Where FAR and FRR are equal, this is sometimes taken as a yardstick.

- **Area Under Curve (AUC)**: Available as review of the discrimination capabilities of the model between genuine and impostor samples.

A well defined system has low EER (<5%) and high AUC (>0.9) even under conditions of mild noise and inter-session variance.

Limitations and Variability in Neural Biometrics

Although promising, there are a number of limitations to neural biometrics that should be thoroughly dealt with before its mass use. These are listed below.

Physiological and Cognitive variability

Neural signals are not easily immune to such internal factors as fatigue, stress, medication, caffeine consumption, or even mood. They can affect brainwaves' properties through these variables, causing authentication errors. Patients with neurodiversity (e.g., ADHD, autism) can have different than average EEG patterns, casting a doubt on the universal applicability of the models.

Inter-Session and Inter-Day variability

Another problem with EEG-based systems is session-to-session and day-to-day consistency. Signal shifts can be caused by slight differences of electrode location, head motion, or the impedance of the scalp. In addition, reproducibility is further hampered by context sensitivity and circaseptic rhythms of mental states.

Hardware and Environmental constraints

Artifacts may be due to external noise (e.g., electromagnetic interference), physical movement, or temperature changes. EEG gadgets that are consumer grade can also have unreliable sample rate or a poor shield that results in data that is of low quality.

Mitigation Strategies

A number of approaches can lessen such limits:

- **Adaptive calibration**: Systems which scroll the users baseline on a regular basis to cope with signal drift

- **Multimodal fusion**: Required to enhance the robustness and add EEG parameters to some other biometrics like facial recognition, keystroke dynamics, etc.

- **Transfer learning**: Using pretrained models and fine-tuning them to the new users

- **Signal normalization**: Using statistical methods to minimize session-to-session variability

Comparisons with Behavioral and Multimodal Biometrics

Although neural authentication is the edge of the identity verification, one should put it in perspective of the other biometric modalities, particularly, the behavioral biometrics and the multimodal systems that integrate various factors. Behavioral biometrics use the fact that people type, swipe, walk, and interact in other ways with digital systems in a unique manner. Their beauty lies in the fact that they are usually passive, continuous, and do not need any additional hardware to work besides the current devices. Nonetheless, behavioral traits are subject to familiarization and environment because they may change significantly in response to fatigue, stress, or in the context of the device. Neural biometrics, on the other hand, is based on physiology signals that are produced by the brain. They are also more resistant to spoofing by their very nature, since they take conscious cognitive presence, and cannot be easily externalized. However, they also present some challenges: EEG equipment remains rather obtrusive, calibration is not an easy task, and the quality of the signals is dependent on movement and electrode positioning.

The most promising one is multimodal biometrics, in which neural signals are combined with behavioral or conventional biometrics (e.g., facial recognition, keystroke dynamics). It has been experimentally demonstrated that multimodal systems can attain considerably broader and greater accuracy and robustness compared to a single modality. As an illustration, EEG and keystroke dynamics have demonstrated a result of 99%-authentication in controlled conditions, and EEG hybrid with dynamic signature verification demonstrated similar scores with low false acceptance. These findings demonstrate the effect of mitigating weaknesses by the fusion of behavioral traits, and neural data gives usability and continuity as well as spoof-resistance and cognitive liveness, respectively. The following Table 5-2 summarizes the comparison features of behavioral, neural, and multimodal biometrics in terms of accuracy, robustness, usability, privacy, and deployment capabilities.

Table 5-2. *Comparative Analysis of Behavioral, Neural, and Multimodal Biometrics*

Feature/Metric	Behavioral biometrics (e.g., keystroke, gait, touch-dynamics)	Neural biometrics (e.g., EEG, brainwave-based)	Multimodal biometrics (behavioral + neural/ other)
Definition/ modality	Patterns in user behavior: How one types, moves, interacts, gestures	Physiological brain signals; EEG captures unique neural patterns.	Fusion of two or more modalities (neural + behavioral or neural + physiological, etc.) to combine strengths.
Typical accuracy/ performance	Varies by behavior type, environment; for example, 80–90+% in favorable settings for keystroke or touch dynamics. (Some behavioral schemes reported ~82% in "touch + movement" schemes)	Accuracy is promising but sensitive to noise, electrode quality, physiological state. In some studies, neural alone has lower robustness unless in controlled settings. (Exact figures depend on the EEG setup.)	Higher accuracy generally than either alone; for example, EEG + keystroke dynamics system reached 99.80% identification and 99.68% authentication in generalized settings. Another: EEG + dynamic signature achieved ~98.78% identification, with false acceptance/ forgery metrics (FAR ~3.75%, HTER ~1.87%) when combined.

(*continued*)

Table 5-2. (*continued*)

Feature/Metric	Behavioral biometrics (e.g., keystroke, gait, touch-dynamics)	Neural biometrics (e.g., EEG, brainwave-based)	Multimodal biometrics (behavioral + neural/ other)
Robustness to spoofing/ attacks	Moderate. Behavioral can be spoofed or mimicked if attacker studies behavior; but harder than static biometric (fingerprint). Still, possible via imitation.	Higher in many cases, because neural signals are harder to mimic, require internal brain activity; but vulnerable to signal artifacts, environmental noise, user physiological/ psychological variability.	Best among the three: If one modality is compromised or noisy, the other can compensate. Multimodal combinations have shown resilience to impersonation or forgery in experiments.
Continuity of authentication	Good: Behavioral is naturally continuous (typing, touch, gait while user is interacting)	Possible but more challenging: neural authentication often requires dedicated measurement periods or stimuli; continuous EEG is possible but more resource-intensive and susceptible to fatigue and signal drift.	Combines behavior's continuity with neural's strength; some multimodal setups have continuous/near continuous monitoring, depending on hardware. Improves session integrity.

(*continued*)

Table 5-2. (*continued*)

Feature/Metric	Behavioral biometrics (e.g., keystroke, gait, touch-dynamics)	Neural biometrics (e.g., EEG, brainwave-based)	Multimodal biometrics (behavioral + neural/ other)
User convenience and intrusiveness	Generally high. Most behavioral methods can be passive (e.g., mouse/touch patterns) and unobtrusive. Requires no special external hardware beyond what users already have (smartphones, wearables) in many cases.	Lower convenience. Users need EEG sensors, electrode placement, calibration, possible discomfort. Intrusiveness and hardware cost are higher.	Mixed. More hardware + complexity required; but if designed well, can keep inconvenience moderate (e.g., using lightweight EEG, passive signature/touch behavior). Trade-off vs. security.
Sensitivity to environmental/ physiological variation	Behavior changes with mood, fatigue, device changes, context (e.g., typing on phone vs. laptop). Variability can degrade performance.	Very sensitive: Signal quality depends on electrode contact, head movement, ambient noise, user mental state (stress, fatigue, emotional state).	Better ability to tolerate variability since one modality may be robust when the other is degraded. But fusion methods must be carefully designed to handle missing/noisy data.

(*continued*)

Table 5-2. (*continued*)

Feature/Metric	Behavioral biometrics (e.g., keystroke, gait, touch-dynamics)	Neural biometrics (e.g., EEG, brainwave-based)	Multimodal biometrics (behavioral + neural/ other)
Hardware/ resource requirements	Low to moderate: Sensors already in devices (touch screens, accelerometers, etc.), low computational cost for many behavioral features.	Higher: EEG acquisition hardware, many channels, high sampling rates, signal-processing pipelines; more computational load, more stringent conditions.	Highest: Combining feature extraction and processing for both modalities, synchronization, fusion, handling mismatch in sample rates, etc. Demands more from system architecture and energy.
Privacy/ethical risk	Lower risk than physiological or neural in many respects: behavior data is less directly tied to mind/body; easier for user to understand and consent. But concerns of profiling, behavioral tracking.	Higher risk: Neural data can reveal more intimate information (mental state, emotional state), harder to anonymize, irreversible nature. Must consider user consent, data ownership tightly.	Aggregated risk: Ccombination of modalities adds more data; needs strong privacy protections. But multimodal systems can also allow modular privacy (if one modality kept local).

(*continued*)

Table 5-2. (*continued*)

Feature/Metric	Behavioral biometrics (e.g., keystroke, gait, touch-dynamics)	Neural biometrics (e.g., EEG, brainwave-based)	Multimodal biometrics (behavioral + neural/ other)
Use cases best suited	Continuous authentication during sessions (e.g., for web services), fraud detection, device unlocking, monitoring insider threat, adaptive access control.	High-security settings (military, critical infrastructure), contexts where static biometrics are insufficient, scenarios where physiological proof desired.	Environments needing both high assurance + good UX: financial systems, health data, identity verification, critical system access where multiple factors needed.
Latency/ response time	Usually low: Behavioral features can be extracted quickly; small delays acceptable.	Can be higher: Need signal collection, preprocessing, perhaps stimulus-evoked responses, artifact cleaning.	Depends on design; fusion adds overhead, though with careful engineering latency can be acceptable.

Although the benefits of neural authentication are unmatched by security systems in history, its use is better understood when contrasted with other paradigms of biometrics like behavioral biometrics and multimodal systems. This comparative viewpoint brings out the special strengths as well as the aspects in which fusion can perform better.

Implementation Frameworks and Architecture

Neural authentication implemented in practice needs a strong architectural framework that meets both technical and operational needs as shown in Figure 5-2. The current neural authentication systems are based on layered architecture design method that guarantees scalability, security, and reliability in various deployment requirements.

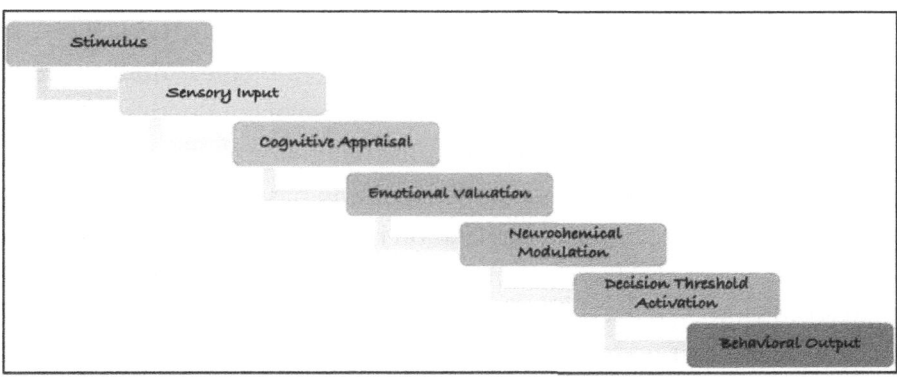

Figure 5-2. *The Neural Authentication System Architecture*

Signal Acquisition

The signal acquisition step is the most critical part of neural authentication where brain electric activity can be recorded with enough fidelity to obtain credible biometric attributes. This stage involves the choice of hardware, the arrangement of electrodes, signal conditioning, and digitization as demonstrated in Figure 5-3. Neurophysiological signal features are delta (0.5–4Hz) that reflects deep sleep and unconsciousness, theta (4–8Hz) that reflects drowsiness, alpha (8–13Hz) that reflects relaxed wakefulness, beta (13–30Hz) that reflects active thought, concentration, problem solving,

and gamma (30–100Hz) that reflects high-order cognitive binding and perception. The most pertinent signals are in 0.1–45 Hz range, which has to be properly anti-
aliased and sampled rate to be authenticated.

Neural authentication EEG amplifiers in modern applications have to comply with a high level of technical requirements, such as sampling rate (frequency), bandwidth, resolution, input range, input referred noise, and Common Mode Rejection Ratio (CMRR). Dynamic range, input impedance, thermal noise, gain accuracy, channel isolation, and multi-channel architecture are also important parameters that are critical to performance. The characteristics of electrode technologies and interface features are wet electrode technology with the use of conductive gel to ensure the best signal quality, dry electrode technology with the latest materials and design that does not use a gel, and passive dry electrode technology. The sampling and digitization rates should be more than twice the rate of interest, and the minimum rates should be 512 Hz to cover a signal bandwidth of 0–45 Hz and recommended 1024 Hz to oversample by a margin. The advantages of wet electrode systems include good signal fidelity and low noise floor, constant impedance properties over the first few hours, broad bandwidth across the entire range EEG frequencies, clinical performance, and regulatory. They, however, have shortcomings, including setup time, gel degradation, potential skin irritation, and not a mobile or continuous monitor.

Edge Processing Layer

The dual task of conversion and recording of signals at processing layer makes it critical and therefore it is required to be under strict real-time constraint and delivers an optimal balance between computational efficiency and signal fidelity. The current neural authentication systems use standard hardware abstraction layer to allow various types of EEG devices. This includes

- **Clinical grade**: 256-64 channel EEG arrays with wet electrodes (e.g., BioSemi ActiveTwo, g.tec g.HIamp)

- **Consumer devices**: 4–14 channel dry electrode headsets (e.g., Emotiv EPOC X, Muse S)

- **Hybrid systems**: Gel-free semi-dry electrodes of clinical-quality signal

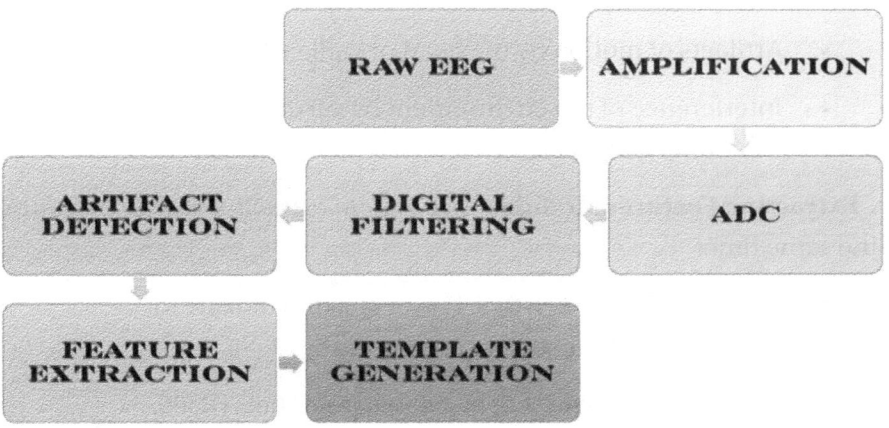

Figure 5-3. *Signal Processing Pipeline*

The edge processing enforces some of the crucial functions:

Adaptive Filtering Engine: It is in contrast to the fixed filters; adaptive systems modify the filter parameters in accordance to the real-time signal quality measurement. This includes

- Starting with 0.1–50 Hz range with adaptive cutoffs

- Automated notch filtering which identifies and eliminates power line interference

- Automatic quality electrode monitoring and adaptive impedance monitoring

Real-time Artifact Rejection: Artifact real-time detection by machine learning algorithms that are able to detect and eliminate artifacts:

- ICA eye blinks, saccades as ocular artifacts

- Artifacts of muscular clenching of the jaws, facial expressions

- Artifacts of motion by the head or cable motion

- Interference of the environment by surrounding electronic gadgets

Extracting Features Modules: The system extracts a variety of features at the same time:

- **Spectral characteristics**: Power spectral density in delta, theta, alpha, beta, and gamma

- **Temporal features**: Event-related potentials (P300, N400, MMN) with an accurate latency

- **Spatial factors**: Patterns of topographic distributions and inter-electrode connection

- **Measures of entropy**: Sample entropy, approximate entropy, and permutation entropy of complexity analysis

Secure Communication Layer – Advanced Cryptographic Framework

The secure communication layer features the best cryptography protocols that are tailored toward the protection of biometric templates. This layer solves some unique challenges that neural data pose like high dimensionality and temporal sensitivity.

Biometric Cryptosystems: The neural templates are transformed with the fuzzy extractor and secure skeletons that are authenticated and retain privacy. The system implements

- **Homomorphic encryption**: It is used to provide computation on encrypted neural templates without their decryption.

- **Secure multi-party computation**: In the protocol, neural patterns are not disclosed to individual parties, even though distributed authentication is possible.

- **Differential privacy**: Adds noise-neural features based on inference attacks.

Communication Protocols: The system uses numerous layers of security:

- **Transport Layer Security(TLS) 1.3**: CA t-perfect forward secrecy, t-perfect certificate transparency

- **Application layer Encryption**: AES-256-GCM Rotating Encryption Keys

- **Integrity of messages**: HMAC-SHA-254 with time validation to avoid a replay attack

Template Protection Standards: Adherence to international standards of biometric templates protection such as

- **International Organization Standards**: ISO/IEC 24745 (Biometric information protection)

- NIST SP 800-76-2 (Biometric data specification to personal identity verification)

- IEEE 2857 (Privacy engineering biometrics)

Authentication Engine – Intelligent Decision-Making

The authentication engine is the computational core of the neural authentication system which uses advanced machine learning algorithms and decision-making models.

Multi-model Architecture: Several specialized models interacting with each other are deployed within the system which include

- **Registration algorithms**: Develop effective baseline neural features at user registration.

- **Verification models**: Do one-to-one checking to access control.

- **Model Identification models**: One-to-many matching with user identification with large databases.

- **Constant authentication models**: Trace current neural activities of the session security.

Deep Learning Models:

- **Convolutional Neural Networks (CNNs)**: Process topography in EEG.

- **Recurrent Neural Networks (RNNs/LSTMs)**: Model elements of time variation in neural signals.

- **Transformer internals**: Model brain patterns of long-range dependence.

- **Graph Neural Networks**: Find patterns of connectivity between the brain parts.

Ensemble Methods: The Ensemble methods use multiple models in order to make authentication decisions based on

- Model-confidence based weighted voting

- Uncertainty quantification by Bayesian model averaging

- Online model selection by signal quality indicators

Adaptive Learning Framework: The system is in a continuous improvement by

- **Online learning**: Algorithms accommodate the neural pattern changes of users at a slow pace.

- **Transfer learning**: Take advantage of what similar users know in order to be more accurate.

- **Meta-learning**: Master effective methods of learning that are new to you.

- **Federated learning**: Enhance user-wise models without intrusion to privacy.

Also, user-specific thresholds and dynamically weighted features designed based on real-time quality measurements may further lower the error rates. Although neural biometrics might be a disruptive technology to identity assurance, that domain should still be developed to handle the real-world variability, issues of privacy, and the ethics behind it. The next horizon is the hybrid models which integrate neural data with the contextual awareness, the cybersecurity paradigm that has more resilience and is more humanistic.

Key Takeaways

- Radical Authentication Models Digital security as a possession (token) followed by biometrics then a fourth model, neural authentication (brainwave pattern).

- It uses electroencephalography (EEG) signals, which are dynamic real-time states of the cognitive process and they are almost impossible to spoof or replicate.

- It has four tenets, namely, uniqueness, liveness detection, non-replicability, and contextual adaptation of brain signals.

- Unlike fingerprints or facial information, brainwave patterns are dynamic and conscious-dependent, which ensures that there is constant authentication and renders the replay or theft of the brainwave patterns impossible.

- With Zero Trust architecture in their blood and MFA/ biometrics downfall on the attack by AI, neural authentication delivers cognitive presence and data integrity during defense, finance, and medical practices.

- The reliability depends upon EEG acquisition, preprocessing (filtering, artifact rejection), segmentation, and feature extraction of the temporal, spectral, and spatial domains.

- Machine Learning to Classify SVM, LDA, Random Forests, CNNs, RNNs, and Transformers are exploited to learn how to predict the authentication decision based on the brainwave features, in terms of accuracy versus computation cost.

- Implementation Architecture A layered architecture consists of signal acquisition hardware (wet/dry electrodes), signal edge processing with adaptive filtering, cryptographic protection, machine learning-based authentication engines, and federated/online learning to achieve continual adaptation.

- The variability can be caused by fatigue, stress, change of electrode, hardware quality, environmental noise, etc. Mitigations are adaptive calibration and multimodal fusion and transfer learning.

- Neural authentication is set to be the final biometric frontier, which will be crucial in mitigating neural-based cognitive attacks, as well as ethical and regulatory concerns about neural data privacy.

CHAPTER 6

Enhancing Cyber Threat Detection with Neurotechnology

"Over the several seconds you have been reading this sentence, your mind has received thousands of neural messages, identified dozens of regularities, and it will have made hundreds of unconscious decisions, humanity has perhaps its most advanced and most expensive threat recognition system, and that has finally been taken out against cyber-criminals."

The world of cybersecurity is at a point of inflection that it has never been before. Our experience with the arms race between the protectors and the attackers spans more than 30 years, with the defensive strategies always being a step farther behind the new approaches of the attackers. Traditional cybersecurity frameworks, which are based on the premises of signature-based detection, behavioral analysis, and rule-based response systems, have hit their theoretical and practical boundaries. The stark truth facing the modern cybersecurity practitioner is that these standard methods should not only be inadequate, but are essentially unable to respond to the manipulative, dynamic, and increasingly automated threat surfaces that typify modern cyber warfare. APTs, zero-day attacks, and machine-learning automated offense plans have indicated fundamental weaknesses in our current defense paradigm that cannot be solved

© Kritika 2026
Kritika, *Neuroscience Meets Cybersecurity*, https://doi.org/10.1007/979-8-8688-2183-7_6

through minor improvements over the use of existing technologies.[1] Such advanced patterns of attack act within the ill-defined regions between recognized trends and normal behavioral thresholds, taking advantage of the intelligence gaps in computation-based security detection mechanisms. What we get is an environment of cybersecurity where threat actors can enjoy continuous access to critical infrastructure over months or years, where zero-day exploits spread silently around global networks, and where security operations centers are deluged with false positive alerts as actual attack propagation fails to come to attention.

That has been the context of protective incompetence, and the neurotechnology does not represent simply another weapon in the cybersecurity arsenal, yet it represents the revising of a zero-assumption on just how human cognitive capacity may be blended with artificial intelligences, yielding actual super-heroic defenses against threats that operate.[2] The most complex information-processing system that the world of science has seen is the human brain, developed over a million years of evolution to be efficient at recognizing patterns, analyzing the context, handling intuitive decision-making when facing uncertainty and yet operate efficiently under stressful conditions like fear and uncertainty. The human brain is a massively parallel processor whose networks of neurons estimated to number around 86 billion with more than 100 trillion synaptic connections among them and thus capable of identifying anomalies, recognizing patterns, and making contextual judgments that are otherwise beyond reach of the most sophisticated contemporary artificial intelligence software.[3]

---

[1] Fahad, M., Airf, H., Kumar, A., & Hussain, H. K. (2023). Securing against apts: Advancements in detection and mitigation. *BIN: Bulletin Of Informatics*, *1*(2).

[2] Kritika, E. (2025). Ethical Frontiers: Navigating the Intersection of Neurotechnology and Cybersecurity. *Journal of Experimental Neurology*, *6*(1), 21-25.

[3] Shankar, S., Pan, Y., Jiang, H., Liu, Z., Darbandi, M. R., Lorenzo, A., ... & Liu, T. (2025). Bridging Brains and Machines: A Unified Frontier in Neuroscience, Artificial Intelligence, and Neuromorphic Systems. *arXiv preprint arXiv:2507.10722.*

The unique ability of human brains to notice thinly veiled sets of data that fall below the algorithmic identification threshold is what makes this neurological advantage most applicable to the context of cybersecurity. Intuitive pattern recognition is one of the things that can only be acquired over years of experience by the best cybersecurity analysts, who learn how to recognize the indicators of a threat by means of mechanisms that often occur below the radar of conscious thought. Such professionals tend to explain their threat perception as some type of gut feeling or that something is off which is indicative of actual neurological processes wherein a threat is identified such as rapid pattern matching, situational analysis, and threat analysis taking place at levels of complexity and speed that current AI is not able to handle.

The innovation symbolized by neural enhanced cybersecurity rests on the potential to detect, measure, and model these unconscious cognitive procedures toward implementation as part of operative threat filters. With medicinal electroencephalography (EEG), functional magnetic resonance imaging (fMRI), magnetoencephalography (MEG), and near-infrared spectroscopy (NIRS), we are now able to follow the neural signatures of expert threat recognition moment-to-moment. These types of neuroimaging technologies identify specific neural patterns of activity when expert analysts are presented with actual threats and offer objective metrics of cognitive confidence, areas of concentration and pattern recognition confidence. The change that this will entail can hardly be undersold. It is the first in the history of cybersecurity that human expertise, which has been elusive, difficult to quantify, and operationalize, can be scripted in a manner that augments and complements artificial intelligence systems instead of competing with them. These Neural-enhanced systems establish actual human–machine symbiosis in which the processing speed and scalability of AI are complemented by the contextual understanding and superhuman-ness of human thought in terms of pattern recognition. The given integration will combat the inherent drawbacks of both solely human and solely automated methods of cybersecurity.

The early experience of DARPA with the Cognitive Technology Threat Warning System (CT2WS) shows strong grounds to suggest the feasibility and practicality of neural-enhanced threat detection.[4] The CT2WS system enabled these performance enhancements in ways that initially appeared to have been inconceivable before monitoring the brain signals of observers, using EEG caps, and measuring brain responses when observers described that they detected a threat, they simultaneously reduced the time it takes to detect a threat and cut the percentage of false positives by 300% and 85%, respectively. From the above findings it can be concluded that neural augmentation can independently address two issues that would conventionally be assumed to be mutually exclusive – enhanced speed and increased accuracy. Many more implications lie well beyond the feeling of better detection figures. Neural-enhanced systems would detect patterns of threat making them easier to neutralize at the initial steps of an attack process where defensive measures are most effective and possible harm is minimized. This has enabled organizations to have cognitive early warning systems that respond faster than the human reaction time, yet with human-level accuracy in recognizing the patterns/patterns of human perception because these systems capture subconscious signals of the recognition of threat that happen 200–400 milliseconds before the conscious mind is aware of it.

In addition to this, neural enhancement is improving on the very important issue of analyst fatigue and cognitive overload that has become epidemic in security operations centers across the globe. Neural-enhanced systems can optimize human performance using a combination of real-time feedback, workload distribution management, and optimal analytical performance through constant assessment of neural state such as attention levels, stress measures, and cognitive load indicators. This potential grants security operations the novel ability to change the paradigm of high-stress, reactive systems into a proactive, streamlined, and complementary system

---

[4] https://newatlas.com/tag-team-threat-recognition-technology/24208/

that nurtures instead of overworks human capacities. The intersection of cybersecurity and neurotechnology also creates completely novel threat intelligence and attack attribution horizons. Varied types of cyberattacks induce differentiable neural patterns in trained analysts when exposed to them, offering new ways of characterizing threats and locating attack vectors. With this kind of analysis of the neural signatures of certain types of threats, we will be able to build more advanced classification systems that can integrate human and machine learning into a unified effort and provide far more inclusive sets of threat models that can dynamically adapt themselves to new patterns of attacks that might appear. At this critical point in the cybersecurity realm, the issue is not that neural enhancement will develop into a game-changer in cyber defense, but whether organizations will realize its revolutionary potential early enough to create long-term competitive advantages over their fellow cyberattackers, who equally keep reinventing them at an unprecedented rate. These case studies, technical frameworks, and implementation guidance in this chapter give cybersecurity professionals the knowledge and resources they need to take advantage of the neural enhancement technologies that are already providing demonstrable benefits in government, military, commercial, and academic settings.

This chapter is more than a discussion of new technology, this is a blueprint, a roadmap of a future imperative where human intellect and the capabilities of artificial intelligence merge together to enable defensive solutions that are, at last, competitive and more advanced than threats posed in the modern world of cybersecurity.

Why This Chapter Matters?

The Existential Threat Crisis

Today, cybersecurity defenses are insufficient, with zero-day exploits going unrecognized up to 287 days and APTs successfully enduring over a year and a half. It is the principle of cognitive superiority introduced in the chapter that emphasizes the unrivaled ability of the human brain to recognize patterns and quickly identify potential danger. By combining the cognition of man with the machine, the CT2WS system implemented by DARPA showed a 300% increment in the rate at which it detects and an 85% decline in false positives. EEG monitoring also creates the possibility of subconscious threat identification that can be detected as far as 400 milliseconds prior to when awareness can be established. The neural-enhanced model in this respect introduces a paradigm shift in cybersecurity since it allows detection that can be both quicker and more effective as compared to using traditional algorithmic systems exclusively.

The Human–Machine Symbiosis Imperative

A crisis occurs in Security Operations Centers where analysts have allotted 80% of their time on false positives and, at the same time, real threats remain undetected. This relates to an erroneous division between machine and human processing. The neural confidence weighting principle as described here allows the real human–machine symbiosis through the utilization of EEG signals (P300, N400, gamma bursts) to measure human confidence and improve AI-decision-making dynamically. This strategy has caused significant returns 43% increase in threat detection in the field of finance, 89% decrease in the number of cyber incidents in healthcare, and decreased burnout. Cognitive load monitoring using EEG also makes workload more optimal and keeps analysts performing throughout long threat response activities.

The Workforce Transformation Revolution

The issue of the cybersecurity skills shortage is a severe weakness with more than 3.5 million open jobs worldwide and traditional training not advancing recognizing patterns to master level. In this chapter, the neuroplasticity-based training is presented where the learning capacity of the brain that processes feedback is utilized to speed up the acquisition of skills via the brain. Research of 12 universities reveals an increment of 45% in the threat recognition when utilizing this technique as compared to traditional training. Monitoring neural responses in the context of simulating increases the ability of the training systems to adapt to the cognitive profile of the individual learner so as to reinforce strengths and strengthen weaknesses. Offering an objective, standardized measure of expertise, neural-based assessments can help an organization assemble top-notch teams that can learn and deliver over a short period of time and achieve a sustainable defensive separation.

The Economic Transformation Imperative

Neural-augmented cybersecurity systems transform ROI by delivering a tangible and measurable business value as seen in superior threat-detection rates, cost-saving, and analyst productivity. One of the world's largest investment banks avoided fraud of $2.3 million and 43% burnout in 24 months, resulting in 89% reduction in the number of medical device incidents, zero patient safety concerns, and complete compliance; healthcare deployments generated tangible paybacks in 18 months. These systems can enable real-time monitoring of performance, and thus as an organization, it can move resources around to maximize its organizational structures. Neural enhancement early adopters incur the benefit of short-term operating benefit in addition to longer-range strategic benefits as the technology becomes a standard in the cybersecurity segment.

The Strategic Future Imperative

Defense must keep up with the latest tactics of the digital world where cyber threats develop essentially through automation of the computer world and the speed of the machines in execution of the attacks. Fusion between neural-AI represents a paradigm in which artificial intelligence is synergistically combined with the uniquely human superior cognitive traits and capacity in areas such as judgment in context, intuition, and creative problem-solving. Combinations of multi-modal neuroimaging (EEG, fMRI, MEG, NIRS) enable organizations to create expert threat-detection processes, models, and develop next-generation adaptive security systems. These hybrid architectures expand on the possibilities of today which allow quick, smart reactions to threats before they have even been conceived. Beneficiaries of the early adaptor stage are not only optimizing existing workflows, they are laying the path to future-proof cybersecurity measures that will ultimately determine survival and dominance in the impending epoch of cyber warfare.

Neurotechnology-Enhanced Threat Detection

The underlying assumption behind the technology of neural-enhanced cybersecurity corporately hinges on an advanced postulation of human cognitive excellence in dealing with pattern recognition and contextual analysis. Though artificial intelligence mechanisms are particularly good at handling large amounts of structured data and discovering pre-determined patterns, human brain is uniquely equipped with abilities that have not been replicated in a computational system. Such mental benefits are intensified especially in cybersecurity where danger frequently takes the form of minute abnormalities, context-related inconsistencies, and trends that appear at the boundary among a number of information areas.

Human Pattern Recognition Superiority

Contextual Understanding and Semantic Processing

The power of human analysts to identify aberrant patterns in highly complex, multi-dimensional environments that can only be overwhelmed using traditional algorithmic methods is nothing short of remarkable. This is due to the hierarchical architecture of brain processing, in that sensory information is successively abstracted using layers of cortex to obtain rich contextual representations of information. In the context of applying to cybersecurity, it means being able to detect the presence of threat indicators that can present themselves as being benign when isolated but develop meaning in broader operational contexts. The human mind is able to process the meaning and the purpose behind the observed behavior through the realization of the semantic capabilities of the human function rather than categorize the surface characteristics through catalogue.[5] Such semantic awareness enables professionals to distinguish between valid administrative tasks and adversarial reconnaissance, detect possible social engineering attacks being presented as ordinary communications, and detect the attack preparation that may traverse different systems and time zones. The cognitive foundation of brain capability in continuing and controlling semantics associations of thousands of ideas at a time is impossible to reproduce by any actual AI systems.

Intuitive Threat Assessment and Subconscious Processing

The most notable part of human threat detection is perhaps in subconscious processing, whereby trained analysts have developed abilities to recognize without conscious knowledge by using intuitive recognition skills.

---

[5] Geeraerts, D. (2021). Cognitive semantics. In *The Routledge handbook of cognitive linguistics* (pp. 19–29). Routledge.

Neuroimaging[6] research has shown that skilled cybersecurity analysts have different neural responses to real threats wherein the activation patterns are observed 200–400 milliseconds before the conscious awareness of severely threatening events.[7] The subconscious threat detection is an example of expertise that is accrued over the years through exposure to varied attack patterns, forming neural networks with the ability to distinguish threat signatures by performing extensive signatures quickly, within a parallel processing of many indicators. Intuitive assessment process combines use of information across several sensory and cognitive channels, which forms cohesive threat assessments involving technical data, behavioral data, context in environmental, and prior knowledge. This combination takes place by means of the default mode network in the brain that considers later processing of security-pertinent information despite the conscious attention being directed in another interest. Expert analysts frequently report feeling things in their gut or saying something does not seem right-that are valid descriptions of actual neurological activity involving comparing rapid referencing of what they are looking at-or hearing/using large amounts of patterns that have already been catalogued in long-term storage.

Adaptive Learning and Dynamic Pattern Recognition

Human cognitive systems are extremely flexible to adjust to new threat patterns and changing methodologies of attacks.[8] In contrast to rule-based systems which have been designed to update manually as new threat signatures emerge, the human brain constantly updates its pattern recognition capability as a result of experience and feedback. This is by

---

[6] https://arxiv.org/html/2502.08025

[7] Kritika Er. Ethical Frontiers: Navigating the Intersection of Neurotechnology and Cybersecurity. J Exp Neurol. 2025;6(1):21–25.

[8] Andrade, R. O., & Yoo, S. G. (2019). Cognitive security: A comprehensive study of cognitive science in cybersecurity. *Journal of Information Security and Applications*, *48*, 102352.

adaptation learning through neuroplasticity, which involves connection-building of the neural pathways linked to positive threat detection and the disconnection to false detection or the failure to detect.[9] The adaptive learning system engulfs a varying period of time that extends to short-term action modification in dealing with a threatening situation to the long-term strategic transformation of recognition structures that respond to the threat. Experienced analysts build more advanced pattern recognition skills as they progress through their careers, being trained to look out for thought-provoking nuances that amateur analysts may overlook but also learning to become immune to the usual false tip-off mechanisms.

Cross-Domain Knowledge Transfer

The capability of human cognition to process and convey knowledge and recognition patterns across attack vectors and threat domains is one of the most potent features of human cognition in cybersecurity-related scenarios.[10] Professional forensic investigators may leverage insight gained in malware analysis to assist in network intrusion detection, and gain insight into social engineering inquiries to better protect their email, and draw experience in inquiry to pinpoint weaknesses in their physical security to strengthen their digital forensics. It is a form of cross-domain transfer, produced by the brain recognizing patterns and relationships that transcend a particular technical implementation.

---

[9] Zeine, F., Jafari, N., Nami, M., & Blum, K. (2024). Awareness integration theory A Psychological and genetic path to self-directed Neuroplasticity. *Health Sciences Review*, *11*, 100169.

[10] Andrade, R. O., Fuertes, W., Cazares, M., Ortiz-Garcés, I., & Navas, G. (2022). An exploratory study of cognitive sciences applied to cybersecurity. *Electronics*, *11*(11), 1692.

Limitations of Traditional Automated Systems

False Positive Epidemic and Alert Fatigue

In conventional cybersecurity, the false positive rate of the systems has been a continuing problem, which lowers the performance efficiency and drains the number of analysts it takes to handle it. The false positive epidemic leads to alert fatigue[11] that results in the analysts being desensitized to warnings and possibly missing the presence of an actual threat that has gotten lost amidst the irrelevancy of millions of other notifications. The source of the high proportion of false positives is the strict and acontextual application of algorithmic detection systems. The conventional security tools make measurements of singular events or actions with reference to pre-established thresholds without taking hold of wider contextual considerations which human analysts inherently use when making judgments.[12] An automated network with an unknown IP Address connection would generate an alarm but a human analyzer would instinctively know that it is a software-update traffic because the determining factors are the time of day and the set of characteristics of the destination IP addresses and patterns.

Zero-Day Detection Impossibility

Probably the biggest shortcoming of signature based systems and behavioral analysis systems is their inherent inability to sniff out any truly new attack vectors. In actuality, by definition, zero-day exploits work using vulnerabilities that have not yet been cataloged and use attack vectors that

---

[11] https://www.securitymagazine.com/articles/97260-one-fifth-of-cybersecurity-alerts-are-false-positives
[12] https://mmrjournal.biomedcentral.com/articles/10.1186/s40779-023-00502-7

have not yet been observed.[13] The signature-based traditional systems are incapable of detecting an attack that does not have a history, therefore exposing the organizations to the most insidious and serious ones. Advanced persistent threats represent such a limitation, as they commonly utilize zero-day exploits along with living-off-the-land strategies, which abuse legitimate system tools in order to perform malicious actions. Such attacks are able to persist months, or even years, concealing their presence entirely to any conventional detection mechanisms. The dwell time of APTs averages more than 200 days, in which attackers[14] have time to exfiltrate sensitive data, introduce backdoors, and set up destructive payload prior to automated security mechanisms having even the slightest idea of their presence.

Context Blindness and Environmental Isolation

The problem of automation of cybersecurity is called context blindness because the assessment of a security event is done without regard to surrounding factors, environmental factors, organizational context, or operational imperatives, which may have great impact on threat determination.[15] An attempted log in at 3 AM could be very suspicious to the majority of the organizations, but it would be entirely normal to an organization that equates to global 24-hour operations. In the same vein, massive data transfers which would point toward possible exfiltration in most situations could be common when performing scheduled backup or system migrations. Such an environmental seclusion does not allow automated systems to gain the contextual awareness that human expert

---

[13] Neupane, A., Saxena, N., Maximo, J. O., & Kana, R. (2016). Neural markers of cybersecurity: An fMRI study of phishing and malware warnings. *IEEE Transactions on information forensics and security*, *11*(9), 1970-1983.

[14] https://mmrjournal.biomedcentral.com/articles/10.1186/s40779-025-00598-z

[15] https://www.scrut.io/post/importance-of-context-in-cybersecurity

analysts rely on when distinguishing between benign action and actual threats. As opposed to automated systems, in which every event can be viewed as an isolated datapoint, humanist analysts implicitly integrate factors in user behavior patterns, business needs and requirements, operational schedules, and organization policies when analyzing potential security incidents.

Signature Dependency and Reactive Limitations

The conventional cybersecurity strategies are inherently reactive in nature, needing prior information about the patterns of attack so that they are able to offer effective detection. Such dependency on a signature makes it inevitable that a gap is created to exist between the appearance of new threats and the detection capabilities to deal with those specific threats. Threat actors take advantage of this time delay by constantly changing attack mechanisms, with techniques that do not appear to be detected until security vendors invent and implement new signatures.[16] The signature dependency limitation is especially troublesome even in cases of targeted attacks that are specifically created to bypass previously known detection mechanisms. Sophisticated threat actors would engage in reconnaissance against security infrastructure of the targeted organizations; they can determine the security tools and monitoring capabilities deployed by the target organization and then develop attacks that occur below the radar or exploit the blind spots of the monitors.

Neurotechnology Integration Approach

Development of the neurotechnology and cybersecurity systems is linked to the implementation of advanced measures that engulf the capturing, processing, and operationalization of the human neural signals within the

---

[16]https://link.springer.com/article/10.1007/s10115-025-02429-y

real-time operational conditions. These integration strategies have to be designed to incorporate the human factor needs of spotting detailed neural monitoring with considering the realistic needs of the security operations that would enable the generation of a system that adds increased value to the productivity of the analysts and innovation in improved measurable capabilities of detecting and providing threats. Figure 6-1 demonstrates the integration approach for neuro-scientific mechanisms in relation to cybersecurity advacements.

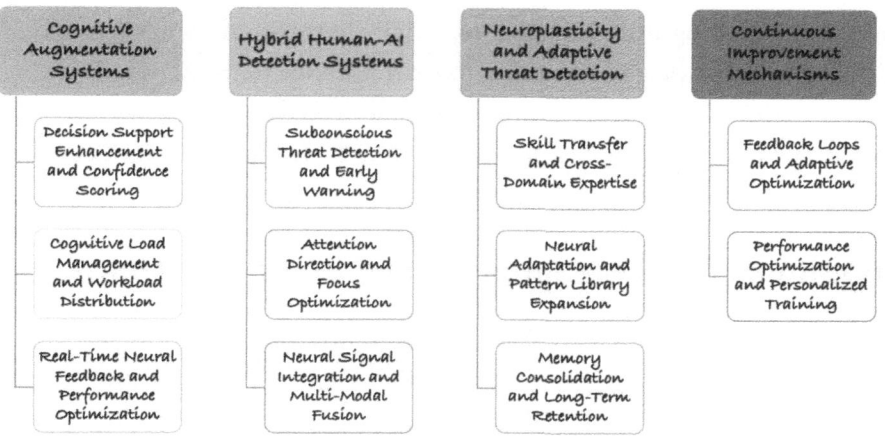

Figure 6-1. *Neurotechnology Integration Approach*

Cognitive Augmentation Systems
Real-Time Neural Feedback and Performance Optimization

The most immediate neurotechnology applicability within azimuth operations is cognitive augmentation systems, which gives users real-time system and interface monitoring and feedback on neural state.[17] Such systems are used to measure the patterns of brainwaves related

---

[17] https://link.springer.com/rwe/10.1007/978-981-97-7874-4_1168

to attention, alertness, cognitive load, and threat recognition using electroencephalography (EEG), to provide closed-loop feedback solutions that improve human performance within the security operations environment. The real-time process of neural feedback works by constantly scrutinizing various bands of EEG that are relative to various states of cognizance. Alpha waves (8–13 Hz) reflect a relaxed awareness and this is where the best pattern recognition abilities are reached.[18] Active cognitive processing and solving of problems are represented by beta waves (13–30 Hz). The Gamma waves (30–100 Hz)[19] associate with the higher order of cognitive binding, especially in the identification processes of threat by the experts. Observing these frequency patterns, cognitive augmentation systems can figure out ideal cognitive states of security operations of various kinds and offer feedback to assist the analysts in remaining in the level of optimal performance.

Cognitive Load Management and Workload Distribution

Cognitive augmentation can also be reasonably applied to mitigate analyst cognitive load to avoid mental fatigue and serve to optimal decision-making capacities throughout the protracted security missions. The cognitive load may be assessed using a number of neural markers, theta wave activity (4–8 Hz) that grows when high mental demand is experienced, and P300 amplitude that reduces when cognitive resources are limited. Cognitive load management[20] systems have the ability to allocate work across team members automatically as part of their processes as individual analysts reach cognitive overload levels so that

---

[18] https://www.sciencedirect.com/topics/neuroscience/alpha-wave

[19] https://mccollege.edu/blog/unlocking-the-mind-understanding-the-brain-waves-measured-by-an-eeg

[20] Bahari, A. (2023). Challenges and affordances of cognitive load management in technology-assisted language learning: A systematic review. *International Journal of Human–Computer Interaction*, 39(1), 85–100.

important security work is performed by analysts with maximum cognitive capacity. The systems would also be capable of optimal scheduling of intricate analytical work, able to configure the work around maximum courses of cognitive functioning as tracked by the activity of the individuals at the neuron level.

Decision Support Enhancement and Confidence Scoring

Neural-augmented decision support systems supply objective measures of analyst confidence and certainty in assessing possible threats. Such systems measure neural markers of decision confidence such as P300 amplitude (co-related with certainty of predicted results), N400 responses (are related to semantic processing trouble), and frontal asymmetry (alpha asymmetry interconnected with preferential approach/avoidance biases in decision-making).[21] Confidence-scoring talent enables the security system to force analyst recommendation at objective neural measurements on the basis of subjective performances of an individual. In cases where an experienced analyst is showing high-confidence neural patterns during a review of a possible threat, the system can change the level of alert and begin to input more resources to further complete an investigation. In contrast, where neural markings indicate anxiety or confusion, the system may give further background information, seek out second opinions, or propose alternative methods of analysis.

---

[21] Orovas, C., Sapounidis, T., Volioti, C., & Keramopoulos, E. (2024). Eeg in education: A scoping review of hardware, software, and methodological aspects. *Sensors (Basel, Switzerland)*, 25(1), 182.

Hybrid Human–AI Detection Systems
Neural Signal Integration and Multi-modal Fusion

The most advanced use of neurotechnology in cybersecurity is the detection systems that consist of both artificial intelligence system's processing capabilities and the neural response of the human operator to work in a unified system of threat assessment. After capturing neural data of their human analysts as they pore over possible threats, these systems overlay this neural data on AI-generated threat scoring data to create not only a synthetic neural signal beyond AI capabilities but also one that outperforms both human and AI capabilities acting in isolation. Neural integration starts with high-resolution monitoring of EEG that observes several neural indicators in one go. The P300 as well as N400 and P600 event-related potentials give information on the activities of cognitive processing and pattern recognition processes.[22] Attention, arousal, and cognitive load conditions are represented by spectral power in various ranges of frequencies. The brain connectivity analysis between various parts of the brain tells about how much cognitive demands are getting dedicated to threat assessment tasks. The data of this type of neural signaling pass through machine learning algorithms that have been trained to identify patterns used by experts in predicting threats. The processed neural data is then fed into a blend with the AI-initiated threat assessments via fancy fusion methods that weigh the various sources of information in regard to the level of their certainty as well as relative application to particular forms of threats.

---

[22] Seyednozadi, Z., Pishghadam, R., & Pishghadam, M. (2021). Functional role of the N400 and P600 in language-related ERP studies with respect to semantic anomalies: an overview. *Archives of Neuropsychiatry*, 58(3), 249.

Attention Direction and Focus Optimization

The pattern of attention to threats can be monitored through neural-enhanced systems that assist analysts by advising on the best locations to concentrate their attention in order to get the most significant information in complex investigations of threats. Eye-tracking in collaboration with an EEG monitoring technique can determine whether the analyst is inspecting relevant threat indicators or whether they are focusing the visual attention on other information that is less important.[23] This attention monitoring helps systems to give them minute directions but they direct the attention of the analysts to the most significant items in the possible threats without flooding them with attention-engrossing directions. This ability to establish direction of attention comes in especially handy when the investigation has many systems, time dimensions, and data sets involved. Using neural references to trust and understanding, systems can persuade to warn analysts when they may be lacking significant feedback and when they are possibly getting engulfed with information complexities.

Subconscious Threat Detection and Early Warning

The most radical development in the neural-enhanced detection, perhaps, is the snatching of the subconsciously recorded warnings of danger, the detection of the danger before the victim realizes it. It has been shown that expert analysts have unique neural activation to the experience of real threats and that the neural activation appears in 200–400 milliseconds preceding conscious recognition.[24] Such unconscious cues are also a kind

---

[23] Alsowail, R. A., & Al-Shehari, T. (2021). A multi-tiered framework for insider threat prevention. *Electronics*, *10*(9), 1005.

[24] March, D. S., Gaertner, L., & Olson, M. A. (2022). On the automatic nature of threat: physiological and evaluative reactions to survival-threats outside conscious perception. *Affective Science*, *3*(1), 135–144.

of expert intuition, which can be tapped and converted to action using sophisticated neural surveillance. The subconscious detection process entails the brain process that occurs because of parallel actions and fast processing of various indicators of a threat, as they do not stand alone as an important indicator in consciousness but sequentially combine such actions that a person or program recognizes. The P300 components denote that a meaningful event is detected and the N400 responses denote that a semantic anomaly was seen which might represent deceptive or abnormal activities. Gamma burst patterns indicate that there are top-level cognitive binding processes through which various fragments of information are combined into any comprehensible threat judgment.

Neuroplasticity and Adaptive Threat Detection

The development of adaptive threat detection systems where the brain reorganizes itself, metaphorically, by identifying a meaningful performance measure in terms of their structure and functionality is determined by the concept of neuroplasticity. Acceptance of neuroplasticity[25] and its application makes it possible to design a system of cybersecurity that would not only improve the performance of the existing analytical skills but also shorten the time of the emergence of expertise and adapt to changing threats and environments.

Neural Adaptation and Pattern Library Expansion

The concept of neuroplasticity allows a security analyst to increase and develop recognition of threats by responding to a wide variety of attack vectors and security incidents.[26] It consists of this kind of neural

---

[25] KRITIKA, E. (2025). A Neuroscience Perspective on AI and Cybersecurity. *ISACA Journal*, (1).

[26] Kritika, M. (2024). Neuro-Driven Cybersecurity: Strengthening Digital Defense. *London Journal of Research In Computer Science and Technology*, 24(1), 17–26.

adaption that is entailed by strengthening synaptic connections that deal with effective threat recognition and loosening those that cause false positives or failure to detect threats. The outcome is an increase in the sophistication of pattern libraries that help to detect previously known and new threat indicators at speeds determined by processes. Neural adaptation can be completed in various ways, such as long-term potentiation (LTP), which enforces commonly used neural pathways and is considered to be a focusing of neural links between dendritic spines and synapses. Those biological processes can be observed and soon via specific formulation of training drills to both maximize the necessity to see various threat patterns and give an immediate feedback on their recognition accuracy.

Skill Transfer and Cross-Domain Expertise

The opportunity to share the element of threat recognition skills across various assault domains and techniques that are possible through neural adaptation in cybersecurity is arguably one of the most valuable. Intelligent analysts build the ability to recognize abstract patterns and they can recognize the comparable threat features irrespective of various technical realizations. This is because this skill is transferred by creating high-level neural representations that grasp key information concerning various types of attacks, yet are flexible in other ways so that they can identify new variations. Skill transfer process should be improved by including training protocol which specifically targets the shared substance behind attacks of different types. Knowledge of how the brain can transfer skills across domains opens the way to a faster development of flexible and adaptable threat detection systems that stay viable in the face of an evolving methodology of attack.

Memory Consolidation and Long-Term Retention

Capacity building expertise in cybersecurity domain demands that one is capable of determining the existing threats and retaining knowledge about the patterns of threats over a long duration. Memory consolidation process that involves moving information in short-term working memory to long-term storage is critical in formation of robust yet accessible threat recognition capabilities. Neural enhancement systems can also optimize memory consolidation to identify the best times to practice exercises, or give repetition schedules that maximize the memory retention, or neuro-feedback that would allow them to determine that threat patterns were being encoded in the memory during the repetition practice. Sleep-based mechanisms of consolidation can also be tracked and it may be improved following training regime that best suits a rest after intensive training.

Continuous Improvement Mechanisms
Feedback Loops and Adaptive Optimization

Cybersecurity systems that use neurons to enhance human analysis capabilities and AI performance form several layers of feedback that allow them to improve over time. Neural response data supplied by human analysts also serves as valuable training data to the AI algorithms, and the outcome of AI-based analysis can be used to test and optimize neural pattern-recognition-based training protocols. Such feedback exists at a variety of time scales, including real-time adjustments on the tactical level face to face with the threat and longer-term adjustment of training courses and system specifications. Continuous improvement will maintain the efficacy of the neural-enhanced systems even after the threats have changed their landscape and their attack strategies have been able to become more advanced.

Performance Optimization and Personalized Training

Once the differences in neural response patterns to individual threats are understood, personalized training protocols can be derived that would result in maximum improvement of threat detection skills to each analyst.[27] There are persons who could perform better in pattern recognition activities and others who may have a better contextual analysis ability. These personal strengths and weak areas can be determined by neural monitoring to enable the training to focus on the individual potential and to optimize the contribution of each analyst to the overall team performance. The individual training strategy is not merely a brain skill-building experience but an optimization of working conditions, work tasks, and working groups represented by the use of the neural compatibility criterion and the deficiency and surplus of abilities. Such an individualized practice makes each analyst perform with maximum cognitive efficiency and brings personal capabilities to collaborative mutual threat detection abilities.

With the relevance of neural enhancement as a cognitive benefit to the cyber security arena already established, we proceed to explore the available practical technologies and methodologies on how the process of capturing, processing, and operationalizing of the brain activity can help in real-time detection of threats. This is realization of concept to actualization that holds a significant gap between knowing why neural enhancement is the way to go and implementation of systems which result in demonstrable security gains.

---

[27] Aminu, M., Akinsanya, A., Dako, D. A., & Oyedokun, O. (2024). Enhancing cyber threat detection through real-time threat intelligence and adaptive defense mechanisms. *International Journal of Computer Applications Technology and Research*, *13*(8), 11–27.

Brainwave Patterns, Neuroimaging, and EEG Data for Threat Identification

The actual use of neural-enhanced cybersecurity systems will, in turn, hinge on whether we can validly record and decode the complicated neural signatures that take place in the brain when trained specialists are faced by actual security threats. The section does extensive coverage of the technological capabilities to capture, process, and extract intelligence (pattern recognition) out of neurological responses of the human brain, mostly pioneered by breakthroughs in neuroimaging and signal processing methodologies. Neurotechnology has provided capabilities that have never been applied before where human cognitive processes are monitored in real-time operational environments. The reverse engineering of these neuroscience-based technologies with respect to cybersecurity operations[28] presents a complex issue in both a neurological understanding of how expert threat perceivers perceive threats neurophysiologically and the technical matters regarding implementation of these neural monitoring technologies in critical security operations. Figure 6-2 represents a hierarchical framework for EEG-based neuroimaging and brainwave patterns' threat detection.

---

[28] Al-Hashem, N., & Saidi, A. (2023). The psychological aspect of cybersecurity: understanding cyber threat perception and decision-making. *International Journal of Applied Machine Learning and Computational Intelligence, 13*(8), 11–22.

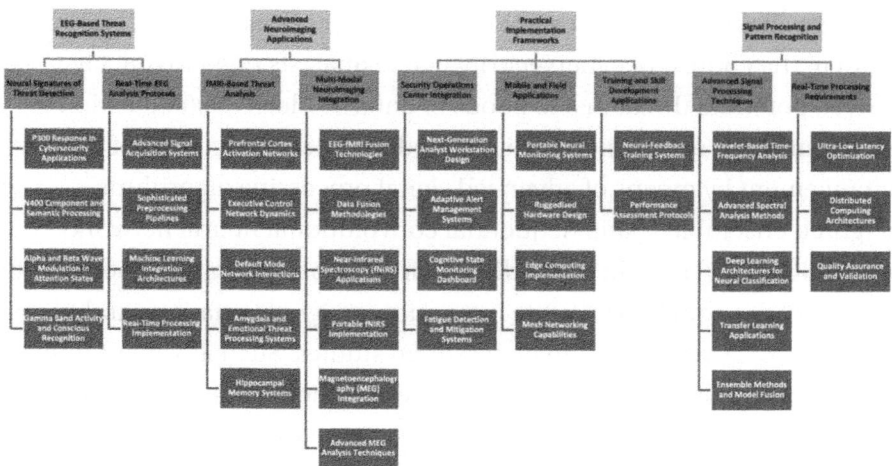

Figure 6-2. *Hierarchical Framework*

EEG-Based Threat Recognition Systems

The temporal resolution, non-invasive monitoring, and operation compatibility with the conventional security apparatus make the electroencephalography the top technology to enable use of neural enhancement in cybersecurity applications. Current EEG technology has increased the precision at which neural activity is recorded to milliseconds but still preserves the portability and usefulness required of it due to application in a wide variety of cybersecurity settings.

Neural Signatures of Threat Detection

P300 Response in Cybersecurity Applications: A P300 event-related potential (ERP) is a neural event that is defined as a positive volunteer change that often has an approximate mark of 300–600 milliseconds subsequent to presentation of the stimulus, which is influencing the threat detection process. Such a neurophysiological reaction is an indication of cognitive awareness of important or surprising events, thus it is especially useful in the context of cybersecurity where analysts need to quickly detect a potential threat inside floods of data. Modern P300 detection algorithms have experienced quite incredible success in terms of accuracy enhancement by means of advanced signal processing algorithms. Weighted ensemble spatio-sequential convolutional neural networks[29] (WE-SPSQ-CNN) have been studied to provide better classification ability because of the ability to mitigate inter-subject signal variations and better signal-to-noise ratios in oddball paradigm studies. Such advances find special application in cybersecurity contexts, where target threats are rare (usually <5% of all events) but needing fast detection and remediation. The amplitude of the P300 will produce varied results depending on the severity of the threat and the level of the analyst. The P300 strength of novel analysts is normally between 8 and 12o V whereas veterans produce less inflammatory reactions between 5 and 15o V contingent to the threat sophistication. Latency measurements give more information of the speed of cognitive process where the faster P300 response (300–400ms) is related to the degree of higher confidence in the threat.

N400 Component and Semantic Processing: N400, which occurs as negative-going deflection and which has a range of 300–500 milliseconds after the presentation of the stimulus, reflects the mechanism of semantic processing and can be especially helpful when finding deviations in the organized patterns of cybersecurity information. Such neuro response is present when the brain is presented with information that is semantically violating, and, therefore, it is a perfect biomarker to detect minor anomalies that could point to the occurrence of sophisticated cyber-attacks. The N400 response can be considered in cybersecurity-related situations as an early-detecting mechanism of semantic anomalies in

---

[29] Shukla, P. K., Cecotti, H., & Meena, Y. K. (2024). Towards Effective Deep Neural Network Approach for Multi-Trial P300-based Character Recognition in Brain-Computer Interfaces. *arXiv preprint arXiv:2410.08561.*

different types of data. The presence of unusual sequences of commands that are outside the normal operational sequences displays a significant N400 response by system administrators who view logs files. Moreover, network analysts exhibit N400 activation when receiving malformed packets or identifying protocol breaches which are indicative of possible intrusion attacks. Current studies have shown that N400 amplitude has a clear relationship to the extent of semantic anomaly and can be used as a quantitative value describing the severity of an anomaly. When constructed using benign variations, the malicious PowerShell commands embedded in legitimate scripts elicit N400 responses 40–60% stronger in magnitude than benign variations; thus, the automated classification system can identify suspicious activities with a precision which is very high.

Alpha and Beta Wave Modulation in Attention States: The suppression of alpha rhythm (8–13 Hz) is one of the basic neural processes that demonstrate focused attention and intellectual involvement in the process of complex analysis of the threats provided. Studies have also shown that efficient cybersecurity analysts have characteristic alpha suppression profiles during the processing of potential threats, and the higher the level of suppression, the greater the level of correct detection may be achieved alongside faster decision-making. A thorough spectral analysis showed that alpha suppression during various stages of a threat assessment is predictable in nature. The early detecting of a threat causes a rapid alpha suppression (in 200–300ms), the latter is categorized by long-lasting suppression during further (detailed) investigation. Resumption of alpha activity is usually associated with the completion of decisions and can offer objective criteria upon which cognitive workload can be evaluated.

Beta wave processing increase (13–30 Hz) indicates the executive control functions and active cognitive processing, which are especially useful to deal with multi-step threat assessment situations. During the decision-making phases, high-beta activity (20–30 Hz) enhances considerably and the low-beta activity (13–20 Hz) shows high values over the sustained attention phases. Higher beta waves analysis has known that there are traits in the brain that are related to the kind of cyber threat. Malware and network intrusion systems show consistent and intense high-beta traditionally associated with investment in mental processes and more fluctuating beta patterns that can relate to rapid switching of attention between several data streams.

Alpha beta cross-frequency coupling helps to understand the processes of cognitive control during evaluation of threats. High levels ($r > 0.7$) of alpha-beta coherence are associated with efficient cognitive processing, whereas low levels of coherence ($r < 0.4$) are an indication that there is either cognitive overload or fatigue, which can interfere with or disrupt the performance of dealing with a threat.

Gamma Band Activity and Conscious Recognition: Gamma oscillations (30–100 Hz) are high-frequency correlated neural activity related to conscious experience, binding of different locations of neural processing, and instances of cognitive insight. In the use of cybersecurity, gamma bursts have been known to give early warning of potential identification as they usually occur before the conscious recognition of the threat within a 100–200-millisecond interval. The recent gamma detection devices apply elaborate filtering methodologies to separate real gamma signal known to exist alongside with the muscle artifacts, and electrical noise. In successful applications such as implementation of reference electrode technique and independent component analysis are also applied so as to provide signal-to-noise advantage that is adequate in operating environment to detect gamma in real time. Analysis of gamma activity shows that unique trends are related to various threat recognition processes. Gamma bursts with acute emergence (lasts 50–150ms) are often associated with fast threat-identification, whereas continuous gamma (>500ms) is linked with complex-threat analysis that demands nuanced examination of several data sources.

Real-Time EEG Analysis Protocols

Advanced Signal Acquisition Systems: Modern EEG technology[30] used in cybersecurity works with high-density electrode placement that have 64–256 channels sampling frequencies of 500–2000 Hz to filter the entire spectrum of neural impulses important in detecting a threat. Best placement of electrodes is more than classic 10–20 systems, with high density coverage in areas where ERPs related to threat are the most significant: the frontal and parietal areas. Newer dry electrode technologies also do not require conductive gels, making them easy to deploy and comfortable to wear in the operational setting over an extended period. Actively driven systems with the built in amplifier limit artifacts produced by the cable and improve the quality of the signal, in addition to their wireless transmission capability, which enables the analyst mobility without data loss.

Sophisticated Preprocessing Pipelines: Refined preprocessing protocols are designed to include a variety of artifact-removal procedures tailored to match the operational conditions. The adaptive filtering algorithms use averaging of reference setups to abandon common-mode noise, whereas the Independent Component Analysis (ICA) isolates and deletes eye movement, tracked muscle action as well as electrical interfering interference. Common Spatial Pattern (CSP)[31] filtering produces optimal spatial discrimination performance with respect to a classification task in which, variance in the target condition is maximized

---

[30] Beyrouthy, T., Mostafa, N., Roshdy, A., Karar, A. S., & Alkork, S. (2024). Review of EEG-based biometrics in 5G-IoT: Current trends and future prospects. *Applied sciences, 14*(2), 534.

[31] Mishuhina, V., & Jiang, X. (2021). Complex common spatial patterns on time-frequency decomposed EEG for brain-computer interface. *Pattern Recognition, 115*, 107918.

and variance in non-target condition is minimized. This would be especially useful in separating threat-related neural activity within the background cognitive activity.

Machine Learning Integration Architectures: Cutting-edge P300 detection schemes use hybrid deep learning networks that integrate convolutional neural networks in order to learn spatial patterns and recurrent neural networks to learn temporal dynamics. The integrated methods have high detection accuracies greater than 95% in controlled laboratory conditions and are greater than 85% accurate in operational conditions with higher noise. Attention mechanisms used in natural language processing also improve performance in model performance where decisions are automatically made to determine the most applicable temporal and spatial properties in classifying the threats. Transformer architectures hold a special capability to learn long-range learning in time series data in neural data.

Real-Time Processing Implementation: Real-time processing cannot be done inefficiently, both in terms of the efficient treatment of computational resources and algorithm efficiency may be optimized. Recent implementations use GPU-based parallel processing to provide parallel processing of many EEG channels with latencies of less than 50 milliseconds to extract all features and carry out classification pipelines of EEG signals. Such edge computing installations can use specialized neural processing unit (NPU) to analyze locally in real time, codifying the requirement to transmit greater volumes of data and enhancing reaction rates. These systems retain an on-going-learning performance, such that these systems evolve in detection measures as they adapt to the individual interior analyst neural patterns with time.

Advanced Neuroimaging Applications

fMRI-Based Threat Analysis

Prefrontal Cortex Activation Networks: Cybersecurity threat systems and decision-making systems are represented through complex neural networks as demonstrated with Functional Magnetic Resonance Imaging (fMRI).[32] The dorsolateral prefrontal cortex (dlPFC) consistently shows increased activity when performing complex threat assessment tasks where 2–4% increases of the baseline can be detected in terms of BOLD signal changes showing the active involvement in the processes of executive control. Ventromedial pre frontal cortex (vmPFC) is important in risk assessment and processing of uncertainty with the area being more activated when the analysts are facing some ambiguous or unfamiliar threat patterns. Investigations with high-resolution 7-Tesla fMRI scanners have found unique patterns of activation within the subregions of the vmPFC, with anterior-located areas responding to immediate threats and posterior areas being used during strategic examination of threats.

Executive Control Network Dynamics: This study has conceptualized neuroimaging research that nominated a select neurobiological signature of cybersecurity decision-making by observing executive control networks. Datasets comparing phishing task performance find this connectivity to rise on successful identification of the threat, with strength of the connections correlating positively with reasonable success toward identification of threat. The anterior cingulate cortex (ACC)[33] acts as a conflict-setting system because its activation is increased when those carrying out the analysis find contradictory information or have to make

---

[32] Kritika, M. (2025). A comprehensive study on navigating neuroethics in Cyberspace. *AI and Ethics*, 5(1), 93–100.

[33] Clairis, N., & Lopez-Persem, A. (2023). Debates on the dorsomedial prefrontal/ dorsal anterior cingulate cortex: insights for future research. *Brain*, 146(12), 4826–4844.

a decision between two threat hypotheses. The ACC activation patterns serve as an objective estimate of the difficulty of a decision and the cognitive load in case of a complex cybersecurity situation.

Default Mode Network Interactions: The default mode network (DMN) gradually becomes deactivated over time in the effortful threat detection task, while successful analysts control DMN suppression more than less effective performers do. Using functional connectivity analysis, it was found there is optimal threat detection after task-positive networks (dlPFC, posterior parietal cortex) have suppressed DMN activity. Alterations of DMN regulation are associated with worse attention and inferior threat detection performance that can inform the development of training programs to enhance the performance of analysts and enable them to detect those at risk.

Amygdala and Emotional Threat-Processing Systems: Amygdala shows very fast responses by responding to cybersecurity warnings, especially when they are of emotional or reflect high-risk conditions. Event-related fMRI designs with neuroimaging evidence exhibit amygdala response within 100–200 milliseconds of threat presentation and therefore before the conscious awareness and continue to influence the liked decision-making process. There are various emotional processing components that have significant impacts on decision-making in cybersecurity, conditioned by the interactions between amygdala and the prefrontal. It has been found that high-threat conditions are accompanied by augmented amygdala-dlPFC connectivity whereas low-threat conditions are characterized by greater amygdala-vmPFC connectivity indicating varying neural pathways, depending on the severity of a threat.

Hippocampal Memory Systems: Pattern completions and memory retrieval are the functions of the hippocampus that help individuals detect the threat. Cybersecurity analysts with extensive experience exhibit increased levels of hippocampal activity when exposed to a threat that is similar to an attack that they had experienced before, and episodic memory is crucial in this recognition process of threats.

Multi-modal Neuroimaging Integration

EEG-fMRI Fusion Technologies: The simultaneous recording of EEG-fMRI gives an unparalleled temporal and spatial resolution of threat detection mechanisms. Advanced fusion methods are expected to reach temporal resolutions of milliseconds and millimeter spatial resolutions, allowing a detailed picture of neural information flow during cybersecurity procedures. Artifact removal algorithms, uniquely suited to remove artifacts caused by simultaneous recording of EEG and MRI signals, remove MRI-induced artifacts in EEG signals without sacrificing neural features of interest. Signal-to-noise ratios recorded during real-time P300 detection through the removal of ballistocardiogram artifacts and correcting the gradient artifacts in the MRI environment attain values that allow the real-time P300 detection to work successfully.

Data Fusion Methodologies: Modern methods of analysis combine EEG and fMRI information at various processing levels. In early fusion, the raw signals are simply combined prior to extracting features, whereas in late fusion, features are extracted independently before they are combined. The hybrid methods based on deep learning architectures have better performance that automatically learn which integration strategies are the best.

Near-Infrared Spectroscopy (fNIRS) Applications: Functional near-infrared spectroscopy provides easily transportable parallel to fMRI in measuring cortex activity in cyberspace activities. Current fNIRS technology has spatial resolution of 1–2cm and temporal resolution of 10Hz which is sufficient to measure activity in the prefrontal cortex when performing threat detection. Conjoint fMRI–fNIRS validations studies have shown that between BOLD signal and hemodynamic response measured by fNIRS has a strong correlation ($r > 0.8$). This has made the technology viable in a real-life setting where standard neuroimaging cannot be implemented.

Portable fNIRS Implementation: Portable fNIRS devices are completely compatible with current cybersecurity workstations and they allow constant monitoring of the cognitive load and attention levels. Battery-driven systems have a battery life of between 12+ hours and can ensure real-time data transfer to centralized monitoring systems through the wireless protocol.

Magnetoencephalography (MEG) Integration: MEG offers unparalleled spatial and temporal resolution in the localization of neural origins of threat detection responses. Recently, in studies using 306-channel MEG equipment, sophisticated timing of information processing between sensory, cognitive, and motor areas occur during cybersecurity decision-making. The localization algorithms are able to provide a spatial accuracy of 2–3mm in the mapping of superficial cortical sources which allowed detailed mapping of threat processing neural networks. Dynamic connectivity analysis shows that the process occurs within 150–200 milliseconds of threat presentation with the information flowing quickly through sensory processing regions to executive control regions.

Advanced MEG Analysis Techniques: The beamforming techniques offer the best spatial filtering to locate MEG sources and dynamic imaging of coherent sources (DICS) permits the registration of frequency-specific connectivity patterns. These methods show theta-band interconnection between the hippocampus and the prefrontal when hauling the memory of threat evaluation.

Practical Implementation Frameworks

Security Operations Center Integration

Next-Generation Analyst Workstation Design: Contemporary cybersecurity workstations have a built-in neural monitoring system with 247 working capabilities with the least distractive monitoring process. EEGs with dry electrodes are wireless systems which no longer need the installation process and continuously monitor the neural status without affecting the regular workflow patterns. Ergonomics is foreseen to make the neural monitoring equipment user-friendly and not to hinder mobility or comfort of the analyst with long working shifts. The lightweight headsets (< 200g) have an alternative positioning of the headset according to preference but ensuring maintenance of quality contact of electrodes.

Adaptive Alert Management Systems: Neural monitoring provides the possibility of dynamically setting alert levels and parameter presentation settings according to a real-time determination of the cognitive state of the analyst. Patterns occurred in EEG are constantly reviewed using machine learning algorithms, which then calculate ideal sensitivity levels toward alerts per particular analyst. At times of high cognitive work (measured by higher beta activity and smaller P300 amplitude), the systems automatically raise the alert filtering standards to avoid the information overload. In contrast, suboptimal neural indicators of attention, sensitivity to alerts, are heightened when neural indicators indicate optimality of attention states as a way to gain maximum chances of enhancing the detection of threats.

Intelligent Workload Distribution: Neural monitoring is used to suggest an optimal distribution of tasks to groups of analysts through the use of advanced scheduling systems. On-demand cognitive capacity assessment allows dynamic redistribution of work over time, and the highly complex threats are allocated to analysts whose cognitive performance is at the peak level.

Cognitive State Monitoring Dashboard: Supervisory interfaces can give online visualizations of team cognitive state in terms of summarized (or aggregate) neural measures. Individual analyst color-coded displays police attention levels, fatigue conditions, and cognitive load so that it is possible to intervene ahead of performance degradation.

Fatigue Detection and Mitigation Systems: Extensive fatigue monitoring systems study several features of the neural indicators, such as alpha/theta ratios, microsleep, and attention lapse. High order algorithms analyze fatigue types (physical, cognitive, emotional) in order to design intervention measures. Automated system would use individual neural signatures and past performance records to recommend individually tailored breaks, job swapping, and reduction of workload accordingly. The predictive models detect the analysts who are at risk of performance drop within 15–30 minutes prior to the actual measurable drop.

Mobile and Field Applications

Portable Neural Monitoring Systems: Modern developments in miniaturized EEG instrumentation make it possible to deploy the ability to monitor brains in the field, giving incident response teams and agents in the field brain monitoring capabilities. Lightweight, less than 500g, and making use of ultra-portable, fully EEG monitoring capability with built-in processing and wireless transmission. Superior power management methods maintain a battery run time beyond 12+ hours of sustained use, including remote monitoring throughout an entire shift under field conditions. Solar charging functions and exterior battery packs provide a great deal of deployment range in remote areas.

Ruggedized Hardware Design: Field deployable systems are military rugged in shock, vibration, and certain environmental conditions. Waterproof connectors and sealed electronics guarantee its reliability during operation under harsh weather conditions and temperature compensation provides signal performance over the entire operating temperature ranges.

Edge Computing Implementation: Neural signal processing is done on-device which minimizes latency and bandwidth demands in the field. Real-time feature extraction and classification done by specialized neural processing units (NPUs), allow direct communication to field analysts that can happen without constant connection to a central processing unit. Applications of Edge AI use quantized low power optimized neural networks that operate at the same level of processing power as cloud deployments, yet draw <5W of power. Local processing also allows operation to extend to a communication-denied environment.

Mesh Networking Capabilities: Portable systems provide mesh networking standards allowing them to communicate with other team members and automated transferring of information to command centers when direct connection is met. Self-healing topologies of networks preserve the communicating channels in the case of node failures or relocations out of range.

Training and Skill Development Applications

Neural-Feedback Training Systems: EEG feedback advanced training platforms streamline the development of skills in detecting threats by showing real-time feedback. Neurofeedback practices encourage analysts to enter the best cognitive states in order to perform best and training programs recorded 25–40% increase in accuracy of detection after only 20 hours of training. The adaptive training algorithms will increase or decrease the level of difficulty in real time according to neural cues so that the learners have the optimum degree of challenge to become skilled. Progress tracking and gamification features hold interest and give definite indicators of how well the skills are obtained.

Performance Assessment Protocols: Neural monitoring supports standard performance measures of analyst competency, which are complementary to the traditional ones. The P300 amplitude and latency demonstrate the threat recognition performance, whereas the attention tracking demonstrates the preserved ability to perform over extended time. The certification courses with neural evaluation provide conformity in terms of performance that would be applicable to various analysts and associations of various regulatory firms. Neural benchmarks would make it possible to compare the performance potential and find those individuals who need special training.

Signal Processing and Pattern Recognition

Advanced Signal Processing Techniques

Wavelet-Based Time-Frequency Analysis: Analyses consisting of continuous and discrete wavelet transforms are ideal time-frequency decompositions of the neural signals, and these display the threat-related patterns at multiple timescales. The recent applications involved adaptive wavelets where specific changes in individual neural properties are automatically tailored, which enhance the accuracy of the detection by 15–25% over and above the fixed approaches. Morlet and Daubechies wavelet analysis are among the most effective ones in detecting gamma burst and in optimizing feature extraction to facilitate effective classification of P300, respectively. Multi-scale wavelet decomposition can also allow one to analyze fast neural processes along with slower ones at the same time.

Advanced Spectral Analysis Methods: The multi-taper spectral analysis methods are more precise at frequency resolution and gain less leakage on the spectrum than the conventional Fourier methods. These methods are critical to the correct description of alpha and beta-type oscillations within noisy functional situations. A cross-spectral analysis has shown that it is possible to show pattern of connectivity amongst different parts of the brain at certain frequencies since threat processing. Analysis of coherence at gamma frequencies also implies the binding of diffused neural processes in conscious recognition of a threat.

Deep Learning Architectures for Neural Classification: Advanced neural network EEG classification with state-of-the-art neural networks use attention mechanisms and the transformer architecture developed to work with natural language. By extracting long-range temporal dependencies in neural time series that the conventional methods fail to detect, these models are more superior in performance. Spatial-attention convolutional neural networks learn automatically the best electrode sets given a particular analyst, and can adapt to these neural maps and individual differences in electrode placement. Recurrent architectures represent temporal dynamics of the threat detection processes, with classification efficiencies of greater than 90% in operational settings.

Transfer Learning Applications: The models used are based on large EEG datasets, which make them pre-trained and allow them to be adapted to new analysts, cutting down on the necessary calibration data. Domain adaptation methods have the ability to transfer those models trained against one threat to new attack vectors with minimal retraining.

Ensemble Methods and Model Fusion: Combined methods that involve the use of several complementary models are more robust and accurate than individual ones. The weighted voting schemes are modified in accordance to fluctuating signal environments and low or high performance of individuals.

Real-Time Processing Requirements

Ultra-Low Latency Optimization: The cybersecurity applications require neural feedback systems with processing latency less than 100 milliseconds. In modern implementations, ring-time performance is achieved with end-to-end processing times of 30–50 milliseconds by use of optimized algorithms and dedicated hardware acceleration. GPGPUs can have parallel processing requirements, and they are effective in analyzing EEG in the real-time multi-channel version. The code is optimized to take advantage of CUDA to provide 10–20x speedup over CPU-based processing so that it can be used in real time with a 256-channel EEG system.

Distributed Computing Architectures: Distributed computing systems allow analysis of hundreds of analysts to be supported concurrently by cloud-based neural processing systems. Independent scaling of various processing parts is made possible through microservices approaches and thus makes systems reliable and performant during times of diverse loads. Deployments with Docker and Kubernetes allow an automated scale and fault tolerance, and the availability of the service can be guaranteed in case hardware fails or even undergoing maintenance.

Quality Assurance and Validation: Real-time quality checks of the signal result in assured operation in hostile settings. Quality metrics are used to detect electrode impedance, signal artifacts, and processing accuracy in automated, and will alert when signal quality drops below acceptable operational limits. Independent cross-validation procedures guarantee generalization performance and avoid overfitting to a given operational conditions or individual analysts.

Ethical Considerations and Privacy Protection

Neural Privacy and Data Security

Brain Data Protection Protocols: The neural data is the most personal data that needs superior protection mechanisms, unlike standard cybersecurity types. Neuroimaging data is associated with such information as cognitive abilities, mental conditions, and possibly delicate personal features in the collection, processing, and storage of which it is necessary to ensure their security. Contemporary protection of neural data uses multi-layer encryption algorithms designed to be used with the high-dimensional time-series data. The neural signals can also be processed using homomorphic encryptions that offer privacy in the neural signals without decryption but computational analysis can be performed. The modern key management systems make sure that the neural data are safe even when it is processed in distributed computing.

Differential Privacy in Neural Analytics: Differential privacy methods are used to add noise to neural data in a carefully calibrated fashion so that individual patterns of the brain cannot be reverse-engineered, but so that the data still retains statistical usefulness in things like threat detection. In recent applications, privacy is ensured with a minimal loss in accuracy of the classification and the effect on the performance is usually a few percentages.

Biometric Neural Authentication: Neural patterns offer novel biometric signatures that may increase the level of security and offer protection of privacy at the same time. They help to maintain the confidentiality of cognitive information when using brain-based authentication systems, whose stable features (individual P300 morphology, etc.) are used for identity verification.

Informed Consent and Analyst Rights

Comprehensive Consent Frameworks: Informed consents need to be extended in terms of detail in the case of monitoring the nervous system in the context of cybersecurity settings with explicit information relating to the procedures of collection and processing of data with possible consequences. Consent frameworks go beyond immediate uses in operational situations to consider future potential uses of the neural data or options to keep it an extremely long time. Privacy preferences and data use permissions can be adjusted dynamically by the analyst in real time through dynamic consent systems, so changes in circumstance and preferences can be accommodated over the lifetime of employment.

Cognitive Liberty and Mental Privacy: Neural monitoring systems should be implemented in such a way that it maintains a balance between benefits in terms of operational security and the basic rights of cognitive liberty and mental privacy. Legislative systems are emerging to help deal with these new privacy issues, and laws that may be protective of neural data are emerging in a number of jurisdictions.

Key Takeaways

- The P300 event-related potential (300–600ms post-stimulus) has been shown to reach 87–95% accuracy in determining when cybersecurity analysts detect threats, and can be used as an objective neural biomarker that can be monitored in real time.

- Multi-Modal Neuroimaging Integration Multi-modal integration of EEG, fMRI, and fNIRS technology gives broad spatiotemporal resolution, with EEG-fMRI mergers representing millisecond temporal defenses and millimeter spatial locales of the entire analysis of the danger.

- Contemporary neural monitoring platforms are capable of performing processing across less than 50 milliseconds via GPU acceleration and edge computing, allowing real-time performance feedback to analysts and adjustable real-time alert system sensitivity to cognitive state.

- In a security operations center, wireless EEG headsets utilizing dry electrodes enable round-the-clock neural monitoring in the working environment which can be used to route work dynamically, monitor fatigue and cognitive loading to optimize those variables within an analyst group.

- Modern Signal Processing Methods Deep learning models, including attention mechanism and transformer architectures, display better results than learning long-range temporal dependencies on neural time series, and with Learn ensemble models achieves classification accuracy beyond 96%.

- Incident response teams to monitor during a neural event will benefit, with portable EEG systems weighing less than 500g and a battery life in excess of 12+ hours. Edge computing ensures that the system will continue to provide data in communications-denied environments.

- Neural data presents the most sensitive personal data, thus demanding sophisticated protective measures via homomorphic encryption, differential privacy, and fully informed consent mechanisms that trade off operational utility costs against cognitive perils of liberty.

- Intuitive assessment process combines use of information across several sensory and cognitive channels, which forms cohesive threat assessments involving technical data, behavioral data, context in environmental, and prior knowledge.

- Human cognitive systems are extremely flexible to adjust to new threat patterns and changing methodologies of attacks by adaptive learning through neuroplasticity.

CHAPTER 7

Exploring the Intersection of AI, Neuroscience, and Cybersecurity

Cybersecurity is a field that is changing rapidly and with increased sophistication, it is turning conventional defense systems to be ineffective. As the attackers grow smarter, threat vectors become more personalized, and the use of cognitive manipulation increases, the necessity of the extreme shift in defensive action becomes imminent. Let's step into the world of convergence of artificial intelligence (AI) with neuroscience, two fields of study whose union with cybersecurity can promise to transform the manner in which we identify, analyze, and act against online exigencies. The chapter opens with an overview of the key motivation factors of such convergence and its importance in the current context of neuroscience and AI no longer being irrelevant in the context of cybersecurity but, on the contrary, being at the core to its further development. Cross-domain impact of disruptive technologies is more than a scholarly exercise and has real world impacts in national security, corporate defense positioning, and on cognitive warfare. These disciplines are increasingly being melded to generate a new hybrid discipline,

© Kritika 2026
Kritika, *Neuroscience Meets Cybersecurity*, https://doi.org/10.1007/979-8-8688-2183-7_7

neuro-cybersecurity, and increasingly a sub-discipline concerning neuro-AI systems, able to both interpret and act on neural and environmental signals in real time.

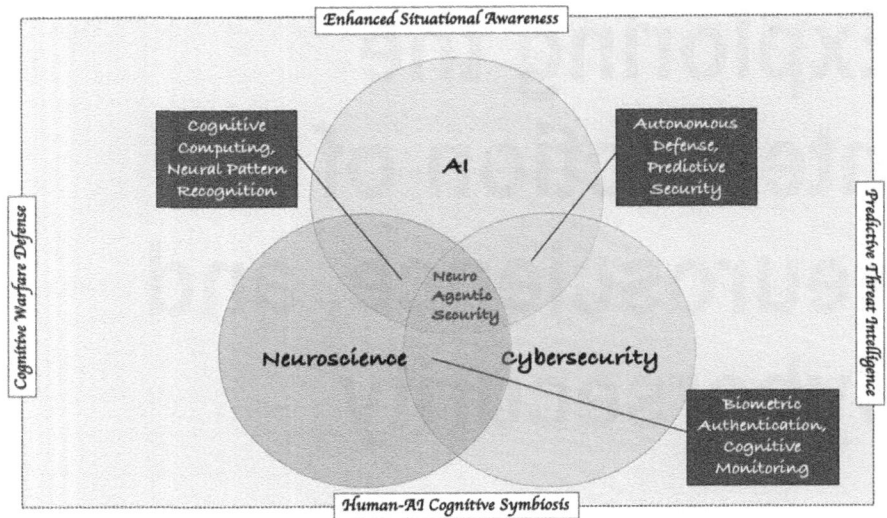

Figure 7-1. *The Neuro-Cybersecurity Strategic Convergence Model*

Figure 7-1 offers a more detailed strategic convergence model that shows the game-changing overlap between artificial intelligence, neuroscience, and cybersecurity together with how their convergence forms a completely new dimension of cognitive-aware digital protection. The AI domain involves the technologies of computational intelligence used as the processor of the cognitive security systems. This space encompasses sophisticated machine learning models, deep learning neural networks, which utilize complex neural and behavioral data flow, agentic systems which can interact on the world and act autonomously with intent or goal, generative AI technologies which generate synthetic training data as well as detect manipulated content and reinforcement learning systems which continuously optimize their performance based on external feedback. The AI technologies offer the computational framework required to analyze high-dimensional neural signal, behavioral patterns, and conventional telemetry of cybersecurity in real time, allowing the system to process and interpret large volumes of uncorrelated data sources concurrently.

The neuroscience domain encompasses the biological and cognitive intelligence layer to reorient the traditional cybersecurity perspective of treating humans as random security vulnerabilities to basing theirs in valuable sources of behavioral and intentional intelligence. This space includes the detection and understanding of these mental states like attention, stress, fatigue, deception, and cognitive load using different neural signal types like EEG, fNIRS, EMG, and other novel brain–computer interfaces. It covers advanced neural interfaces that can measure brain activity in real time, behavioral analytics programs that can analyze unconscious human action and physiological response, cognitive load assessment schemes that can determine when people are performing under strain or when making suboptimal choices or neural pattern recognition schemes that might provide unique neural signatures of differences in mentation states, intentions, or possible security risks.[1]

The cybersecurity realm encompasses the works of art that have formed the standard basis of digital protection, including the common applications of network-based threat detection by means of anomaly detection, signature matching, multi-factor authentication system/access control, incident response modalities, and digital forensic analysis tools, automated defense platforms/security orchestration, and rigorous risk evaluation modalities. When combined with the capabilities of AI

---

[1] Jin, K., Rubio-Solis, A., Naik, R., Leff, D., Kinross, J., & Mylonas, G. (2025). Human-Centric Cognitive State Recognition Using Physiological Signals: A Systematic Review of Machine Learning Strategies Across Application Domains. *Sensors*, *25*(13), 4207.

and neuroscience, these traditional solutions to cybersecurity become dynamic, proactive systems that are predictive, adaptive, and contextually aware and can identify, deter, and counter threats in new and more effective ways than ever before.[2]

The bicategorical intersection of domains leads to the disclosure of transformational hybrid technologies, which have been much more powerful than traditional methods. The emergent capability of this AI-neuroscience interface is cognitive computing and neural pattern recognition capabilities, where intelligent systems and machines are able to interpret highly complex neural signals to make inferences about the human cognitive state, intent, and behavioral patterns in real time. This coupling has allowed the creation of systems, which are capable of analyzing brain's activity in order to identify a deception, cognitive load, attention, fatigue, and predictive human behavior using patterns of nerve activity. Applications of neuroscience-cybersecurity crossover include biometric authentication and cognitive state monitoring where neural fingerprints are used to uniquely identify individuals in high security authentication, and monitoring of cognitive status continuously offers real-time assessment of user mental states to detect anomalies, insider threats, or compromised decision-making abilities. The AI-cybersecurity overlap brings about autonomous defense and predictive security systems where machine learning algorithms are able to autonomously identify, classify, and respond to threats and predict future attack vectors due to behavioral, network, and environmental patterns.

At the central triple-convergence point, meaning one where all three domains come together fully, appears the transformative paradigm of Neuro-Agentic Security. This is the final convergence in which the AI systems can both analyze large volumes of multi-modal data and recognize the human mental states and cognitively understand and interact with those human mental states so that human and the AI

---

[2]https://proactive.co.in/solution/cybersecurity/ai-powered-security

system can become intelligent partners whose systems allow them to maintain autonomous defensive capabilities. Such an integration results in a fundamentally new vision of cybersecurity that is no longer limited to tech-focused or human-focused measures, enabling systems that can contextualize and forecast outcome intentions, different solutions according to the changing state of affairs, and decision-making at a sophisticated level that takes into consideration both technical and human considerations.

The strategic outcomes framework reflects the transformational, organizational, and national security capabilities that occur through this three-domain convergence. Improved situational awareness entails the combination of conventional security situation monitoring with instant cognitive and behavioral intelligence, which allows security teams to see more than ever before into the digital world of threats and human behavioral components that contribute to security decisions.[3] This would be able to monitor the mental status of the security operators, evaluate the mental preparedness of critical humans, and realize the human circumstances behind security incidents. Predictive threat intelligence moves beyond traditional pattern matching and signature-based insights to encompass cognitive and behavioral forecasting functionality that allows companies and organizations to predict and prevent practices and activities by identifying the cross-section between technical evidence, human behaviors, and neural signals prior to malicious events.

Human–AI cognitive symbiosis[4] marks a paradigm shift in human-machine collaboration where human empathy, creative and contextualized thinking are boosted by AI processing power, pattern

---

[3] Bellini, E., D'Aniello, G., Flammini, F., & Gaeta, R. (2025). Situation Awareness for Cyber resilience: A review. *International Journal of Critical Infrastructure Protection*, 100755.

[4] Almeida, F., & Senapati, B. (2024, March). Striving for Symbiosis: Human-Machine Relations in the AI Era. In *2024 IEEE Integrated STEM Education Conference (ISEC)* (pp. 1–4). IEEE.

recognition and unlimited learning capabilities, whereas AI systems will enjoy human ethical thought processes, strategic intelligence, and perception of the situation. The result of this symbiotic relationship is operational capabilities not possible when using human-only or machine-only-based mechanisms and can be used to provide a more effective decision-making process, a more effective response to threats, and a deeper insight into the complexities of individual security situations. Cognitive warfare defense will be feasible by combining the knowledge of neuroscience with the capabilities of AI-systems to analyze and conduct cybersecurity operations[5] and will allow detecting and shielding against intricate psychological manipulation attacks, disinformation campaigns, and influence operations that seek to manipulate human decision-making processes and social cohesion.

The convergence model is not merely a technological transformation but a paradigm shift from the traditional cybersecurity mechanism that considers people as inherently unpredictable security targets that should be constrained and restricted toward a paradigm where human cognitive intelligence is recognized as an essential defensive asset and machine performance is intelligently boosted using AI. The resulting security mechanisms based on neuro-agentic security systems reflect a qualitative shift in the overall defensive capabilities which has evolved and improved on the traditional reactive threat response to proactive threat prevention. This is a well-considered shift from rule-based automation to state and contextually intelligent automation and from adversarial human-versus-machine operations toward collaborative human-with-machine systems. Such transformation forms the basis of security architectures that are more resilient, adaptive, effective, and ethically aligned than any technological

---

[5] Deppe, C., & Schaal, G. S. (2024). Cognitive warfare: a conceptual analysis of the NATO ACT cognitive warfare exploratory concept. *Frontiers in Big Data, 7,* 1452129.

or solely human approach in isolating and enabling security systems might. A new area of learning is being brought up which acknowledges cognitive intelligence as being as important as digital and physical security aspects.

Why This Chapter Matters?

Establishes the Strategic Intersection That Will Develop the Future of Cybersecurity

The challenge due to such highly complex, multi-modal threats, such as algorithmic misinformation or cognitive warfare, has shown traditional cybersecurity paradigms to be at the end of their operational life. This chapter highlights that the convergence of AI and neuroscience is an imperative as opposed to a discretionary method of developing cyber defenses that will be intelligent, adaptive, and able to perform in cognitively compromised environments. By positioning the convergence through the lens of strategic change, it positions those making decisions in industry, government, and defense to design systems with flexibility against not only the threats posed by technology but against neurocognitive and psychological manipulation.

Adds Another Level of Situational Intelligence: Neuro-Cognitive intelligence

Behavioral, network, and system telemetry has been the mainstay of cybersecurity since the beginning of history. In this chapter, the introductory phase raises the studying level scale as it presents to the reader the idea of neuro-cognitive telemetry as a new data layer of the real-time danger investigation and repositioning. It demonstrates with stress, deception, distraction, or insider intent examples before they are simultaneously processed to exhibit a behavior that may alert traditional security systems that it could be possible to transform predictive and human-aware security systems. The theoretical and practical basis of the integration of this new telemetry into operations of enterprise security centers (SOCs) and national cyber defense systems is set in this chapter.

Bridges the Gap Between Human-Centric Security and Autonomous Defense

Most of what is contemporary cybersecurity lies to be either too human-based (dependent on analyst evaluation) or too machine-employed (vulnerable to counterfeit affirmed). In this chapter, the author is explaining how the symbiotic relationship between cognitive-AI can be considered through neural input, alerting the machine used to provide security providing a new balance. Frameworks are discussed to help the reader to navigate through the frameworks to achieve human-in-the-loop configurations, on-the-loop configurations, and eventual human-out-of-the-loop configurations where Agentic AI can operate in the name of users who are under cognitive overload. It also covers the ethical, architectural, and operational questions of such transitions and is an invaluable read to C-suite executives, CISOs, and AI policy advisors.

Introduces Neuro-Inspired AI As a Frontier for Secure and Resilient Computing

Instead of simply using AI on the neural data, this chapter captures how the biologically inspired AI architectures, like spiking neural networks and neuromorphic processors, are by definition robust, energy optimized, and suited to adversarial cybersecurity settings. These systems draw inspirations in the structure of the human brain to create context-sensitive, power-efficient, and low-latency cyber defenses. Outlining this design philosophy and citing examples from the real, the chapter closes the gap between theoretical neuroscience and deployable cyber technologies, thereby developing innovation pipelines.

Gives Practical Case Studies and Models of High-Risk Sectors

Last but not least, this chapter is realistic in nature. Describing in detail case studies (neuro-AI insider threat surveillance in the financial sector to real-time neural surveillance in the military cyber-operative), it shows how this interdisciplinary amalgamation is already under implementation in areas of infrastructural concerns. Such examples are never hypothetical: they are the current-time first-use kind with measurable influence over latency, detection rate, and human confidence. The use of such agentic AI that not only can discern human intentions but can also instruct security protocols on its own creates the footing of next-gen autonomous security orchestration that readers could implement as blueprints and turn into policy, prototypes, or products.

The Rise of Hybrid Threat Landscapes

Modern hackers no longer confine themselves to binary and brute-force attacks. The latest attacks are more effective and utilize approaches such as social engineering, behavioral profiling, and cognitive overloads to bypass traditional security defenses. There is an enormous range of phishing attempts using deepfake, to exploiting human fatigue; the human factor is now the vulnerability.[6] Simultaneously, adversarial systems using AI are

---

[6] Kritika, E. (2024). A comprehensive literature review on phishing URL detection using deep learning techniques. *Journal of Cyber Security Technology*, 1–29.

being designed to simulate legitimate human behavior, or even to reverse-engineer security systems using generative models. There is even more danger due to the inter-vocation between AI and cyber offense and also due to access to greater possibilities in protecting offense. Meanwhile, in the area of neuroscience, researchers have come across a significant breakthrough pertaining to the understanding of the decision-making pathway in the brain, stress response and attention system. This has evolved to know-how that can be practicable in cyberspace. Using an example of reading neurophysiologic data (e.g., EEG or functional near-infrared spectroscopy fNIRS), one might conclude that a user is becoming more stressed and distracted or has signs of ill intent, etc. The AI-refined wisdom of such brainpower is truly revolutionizing when it is kept current, that its successors will experience a degree of situational understanding and responsive versatility, otherwise certainly unheard-of.

The current threat environment has experienced a paradigm shift that has challenged all assumptions that define the traditional cybersecurity models. Whereas traditionally attackers used technical exploits to target the specific vulnerabilities of a system, modern malicious actors have transitioned into developed psychological actors that weaponize the scarce resource of human cognition itself.[7] The change is more than a tactical one, it is a paradigmatic shift of the character of cyber warfare, turning the human mind itself into a target and a weapon. The intersections between artificial intelligence, neuroscience knowledge, and maturing social engineering technologies have spawned hybrid threat vectors with the ability to persist across various realms: technological, psychological, and cognitive. Such attacks use not only software bugs but

---

[7] Abou El Houda, Z. (2024). Cyber threat actors review: examining the tactics and motivations of adversaries in the cyber landscape. In *Cyber Security for Next-Generation Computing Technologies* (pp. 84–101). CRC Press.

human mental biases, their emotions, and their decision-making which create new vectors of attack that are beyond reach of traditional security tools that are neither able to detect, analyze, nor defend them.

Evolution Beyond Binary Attacks

The cybersecurity world has experienced an abrupt turnaround in the conventional binary attack techniques – where attacks were either in existence or not, malicious or benign – to multi-dimensional approaches that merge the line between the acceptable and the malicious stake. This has been the typical attack vectors in the past based on their clear and identifiable technical indicators, which include malware, network anomalies, unauthorized access, system exploits, and so on that can be detected using rule-based detection mechanisms and signature matching tools. Such attacks were recurrent and identifiable, and the best security systems could track, register, and respond automatically, take steps that were predetermined. Our contemporary tactic of cognitive manipulation is conducted in the greys of human perception and decision-making and makes use of the natural ambiguities and biases to human thinking rather than the technical vulnerabilities of the system. Contrary to binary assaults that generate certain security warnings, cognitive manipulation builds over time through patiently curated campaigns that are presented by conventional standards as credible[8] yet have a consistent effect of undercutting human judgment, trust, and decision-making strengths. These attacks capitalize on the extensive and detailed knowledge of the psychological principles of cognitive load theory, social proof, authority bias, and temporal pressure to put the human in a position in which security-compromising decisions are made under the belief that this is rational behavior and the appropriate thing to do. This has been

---

[8] Dantuluri, V. V. (2023). Mindful Maneuvers: A Normative Framework for Disinformation Defence Using Cognitive Security.

demonstrated by the changing techniques such as the transition of the suspicion phishing emails asking to provide password information to a more complex deepfake-backed persuasion campaigns. Initial phishing scams were primitive, and could be detected and evaded relatively easily by close inspection of spelling, unusual links, and the generic message content.

Current social engineering campaigns use AI-generated data that closely resembles that used in legitimate communications to such a high degree that it is almost indistinguishable to a trained analyst,[9] it includes details culled through social media profiling, behavior analysis, and data breaches in order to make it highly convincing in regard to the unique individuals and their psychological aspect. Newer methods of attackers employ behavior profiling to use digital footprint, communications history, work schedules, social interactions, and individual interests to create manipulating campaigns tailored to the individual cognitive vulnerabilities. These profiles may guide an attacker in pinpointing the best time to engage in attacks (when targets are likely to be overstressed, fatigued, or mentally grasping), communication methods, psychological hot buttons, and decision tendencies. Machine learning integration enables the attacker to gradually improve their tactics as the target responds, hence creating the adaptive campaigns that grow and develop in real time to be more effective.[10] Cognitive overload exploitation is a unique and very malicious avenue of attack where an adversary intentionally crafts situations to frustrate human decision-making capacity by bombarding

---

[9] Alahmed, Y., Abadla, R., & Al Ansari, M. J. (2024, September). Exploring the potential implications of AI-generated content in social engineering attacks. In *2024 International Conference on Multimedia Computing, Networking and Applications (MCNA)* (pp. 64-73). IEEE.

[10] Aminu, M., Akinsanya, A., Dako, D. A., & Oyedokun, O. (2024). Enhancing cyber threat detection through real-time threat intelligence and adaptive defense mechanisms. *International Journal of Computer Applications Technology and Research, 13*(8), 11–27.

information,[11] creating time pressure, conflicting priorities, and confusion through emotional manipulation and other factors. By being cognizant of the cognitive capacities of human processing (working memory, attention limits, decision fatigue, and stress response), attackers can craft situations that cause even well-trained security-oriented individuals to fail to make adequate security selection. Such attacks are often coordinated with intense workload, other significant organizational changes, or rest periods during a crisis when other cognitive resource is already stretched to the limit and so the quality of decision-making is equally affected.

AI-Powered Adversarial Systems

Artificial intelligence in the context of offensive cyber operations has drastically changed the scope, complexity, and efficiency of contemporary cyberattacks by establishing oppositional systems that can work without much intervention thanks to a relatively higher-level sophistication in doing so, adjusting to countermeasures simultaneously. Generative artificial intelligence, most specifically large language models and fake media generation systems, has made the creation of convincing fake content on an unprecedented scale and quality that can be used to socially engineer, push disinformation campaigns, and run psychological operations-style operations in turn. AI-assisted cyberattacks like fraudGPT or wormGPT, use advanced natural language processing to generate new custom-written phishing e-mails, phony documents, and social media posts that can get past traditional content filters as well as human detection systems. By using huge volumes of legitimate communications to train their models on the patterns of writing, vocabulary, references to culture, and contexts in communication, the systems are able to reproduce synthetic content that is indistinguishable to that written by people.

---

[11] Kritika, M. (2024). Neuro-Driven Cybersecurity: Strengthening Digital Defense. *London Journal of Research In Computer Science and Technology*, *24*(1), 17–26.

The fact that they can create thousands of and hundreds of thousands of unique and personalized attack vectors at a time, enables the adversaries to launch vast initiatives against entire organizations, all the while appearing to be genuine, individually tailored messages.

The development of synthetic media generation, deepfake audio and video technologies have now opened new regime of deception where an attacker can impersonate the faces of trusted people, create forged evidence, and control the perception of reality itself.[12] Such technologies are used to make phone calls in frauds, video manipulation in testifying lies or incommunicado content, and synthesizing images in fabricating identities or false documents. The psychological implication of the synthetic media is not limited to short-term deception but is also invoked to distrust all digital messages due to the uncertainty of their authenticity and this may be confusing in decision-making processes since people lose confidence in whatever they watched online. Automated social engineering is another realm in which AI systems perform reconnaissance, building relationships, developing trust to accomplish the same tasks traditionally completed by human operators.[13] These systems are able to sustain continuity where the different platforms interact with the targets and create long-lasting relationships over time as they infiltrate their psyche and seek to compromise them following the intelligence they discover about their targets. Signals of conversation patterns, emotional reactions, and behavioral alertness are studied with the help of machine learning algorithms to find the most suitable settings to deploy persuasion

---

[12] George, A. S., & George, A. H. (2023). Deepfakes: the evolution of hyper realistic media manipulation. *Partners Universal Innovative Research Publication*, *1*(2), 58–74.

[13] Khan, M. I., Arif, A., & Khan, A. R. A. (2024). AI's revolutionary role in cyber defense and social engineering. *International Journal of Multidisciplinary Sciences and Arts*, *3*(4), 57–66.

tactics[14] and to determine the most appropriate time to give way on an exploitation attempt. Adversarial machine learning attacks refer to the systems of AI and machine learning on which organizations heavily depend to defend their systems that adversaries fondly attack aimed at compromising the defensive systems, misleading them, or manipulating them in a new meta-attack category.

These attacks involve adversarial examples used with a view to triggering misclassification, attempts to poison the training data of models, and evasion techniques that can use malicious actions to slip through AI-based detection efforts. The recursive aspect of the AI-versus-AI hostility leads to an arms race situation in which defensive and offensive AI technologies have to improve continuously to withstand emerging attack strategies. The artificially intelligent arms competition of offense and defense has developed an escalator effect such that innovation in one area develops directly parallel innovation in the other. The existence of offensive AI functions triggers the creation of more advanced defensive AI systems, thus creating more advanced attack modules. This cycle has also exponentially increased the velocity of innovation on offensive and defensive cybersecurity technologies and increased the intricacy and shrewdness that is needed to support effective security postures. One of the changes to consider is that alongside the traditional threat actors, organizations need to think about AI-enhanced adversaries now capable of performing their operations at machine speed and scale.

The Neuroscience Advantage in Defense

The adoption of neuroscience into cybersecurity defense signifies nothing less than a paradigm shift between reactive, technology-oriented defense and prophylactic, biologically based defense strategies that use biological

---

[14] Signals of conversation patterns, emotional reactions, and behavioral alertness are studied with the help of machine learning algorithms to find the most suitable settings to deploy persuasion tactics.

intelligence to bolster digital defense efforts, and the same goes well with the concept of defense-in-depth when clubbed with other conventional and non-conventional controls. Neuroscience offers unmatched visibility into the cognitive states, decision-making processes, and behavioral patterns of humans that more conventional security tools do not afford, allowing it to detect threats that operate at the psychological level rather than the technical vulnerability level. Neural signal information augments cybersecurity surveillance beyond strictly digital telemetry analysis to the inclusive human-system fusion of intelligence data. EEG monitoring is able to detect state of mind related to lying, stress, diversion, and abnormal mentalization that relates to security-related status. Functional near-infrared spectroscopy (fNIRS) can be used to provide information on how activity in the prefrontal cortex is related to decision-making, attention, and cognitive load and thus security systems could provide information on when humans are functioning under conditions that make them vulnerable to manipulation or errors. Heart rate variability data may expose the effects of psychological manipulation such as deception, stress, or emotional manipulation, indicating the presence of an ongoing attack or compromise of one or more autonomic nervous systems.

One area of growing potential is the application of neuroscience to the detection of insider threats where the use of neuroscience in the detection of insider threats can be used to detect cognitive signatures linked to insider-related phenomena such as deceptive behavior, conflicted allegiances, or ill intent, possibly long before they are expressed in observable behavior. Cognitive neuroscience studies have determined particular brain activity specific to deception, moral conflict, and intention formation that are detectable using non-invasive neural monitoring technology. Although ethical and privacy concerns necessitate cautious implementation mechanisms, the possibility of tracking insider threats based on cognitive states monitoring as opposed to behavioral monitoring creates a great potential value due to the high chances of detecting and preventing the threat well in time. Security-based monitoring of cognitive states to adapt security measures dynamically uses real-time evaluation of the mental stability and susceptibility of human agents. In scenarios where a user might have a high cognitive load, be stressed or fatigued, and neural monitoring shows that to be the case, security systems can automatically introduce an increased level of verification, delay a decision that would be detrimental to security, or employ cognitive support to ensure that it will not be made with a risk of doing so. This paradigm will translate security into non-constant rule enforcement and dynamic, context-sensitive safeguarding that becomes adaptive to human, cognitive systems and its environmental properties.

BCI security poses both opportunities and vulnerabilities that must be addressed as such technologies become increasingly used in ways that matter to security. In addition to secure access control by direct neural control of security and unprecedented authentication capabilities based on neural signature, BCIs provide a potentially new attack surface where adversaries can potentially intercept, inject, or manipulate the neural signal being relayed or sent by entities. The emerging field of secure BCI development must come to know not only the technical details of how neural signals are converted to usable information, but how to utilize or safeguard the biological features of neural activity. The neuroscience benefit in defense is not confined to individual surveillance but also encompasses the security of the whole cognition where insights into collective human behavior, social psychology, and group dynamics can allow the disclosure and prevention of large-scale influence operations, disinformation campaigns, and social engineering influence activities that attempt to target or affect large-scale decision-making processes. Using cognitive response patterns across sets of users, security mechanisms can determine concerted, orchestrated efforts to manipulate the user population, uncover emergent social engineering attacks, anticipate the outcome of malicious influence operations or malicious information flows in order to pre-empt its effects. Table 7-1 highlights the evolution of threat vectors in the growing cyber landscape.

Table 7-1. Evolution of Threat Vectors

Threat category	2020 characteristics	2022 evolution	2025 current state	Future projections	Cognitive elements	Defense requirements
Phishing attacks	Generic mass emails, obvious grammatical errors, basic impersonation attempts	Targeted AI-generated spear-phishing with social media research, improved grammar and context	Real-time conversational AI agents, multi-modal deepfake integration (voice+video+text), behavioral adaptation within single conversations	Neurologically targeted phishing using brain–computer interface data, AI agents with persistent memory across multiple interaction points, quantum-enhanced personalization	Advanced psychological profiling, emotional state manipulation, contextual awareness exploitation	Neural monitoring for deception detection, cognitive load assessment, real-time behavioral analysis
Social engineering	Phone-based pretexting, basic identity theft, simple manipulation tactics	Multi-channel approaches, extended relationship building, psychological profiling	Autonomous AI agents conducting long-term relationship cultivation, emotional intelligence exploitation, predictive vulnerability mapping	Neuromarketing-style psychological manipulation, AI-generated synthetic relationships spanning multiple platforms, predictive behavioral modification	Leverages social proof, reciprocity, commitment consistency, emotional triggers, trust exploitation	Real-time stress monitoring, attention tracking, decision support systems, cognitive vulnerability assessment

Insider threats	Access abuse, data theft, straightforward malicious activity	Subtle data exfiltration, privilege escalation, advanced persistent insider presence	Neurocognitive manipulation through targeted psychological pressure, AI-assisted behavioral modification, subliminal influence techniques	Brain–computer interface compromise, neural implant security vulnerabilities, direct cognitive manipulation via neural interfaces	Exploits conflicted loyalties, financial pressure, ideological manipulation, emotional vulnerability, cognitive dissonance	Neural intent recognition, cognitive state monitoring, behavioral baseline analysis, psychological wellness tracking
Disinformation campaigns	Simple false narratives, obvious propaganda, limited distribution channels	Cross-platform coordination, sophisticated targeted content, targeted audience analysis	Neurologically targeted content optimized for individual brain response patterns, AI-generated immersive experiences, reality distortion campaigns	Quantum-enhanced cognitive targeting, neural pathway exploitation, collective consciousness manipulation via interconnected brain–computer interfaces	Manipulates cognitive biases, emotional responses, group think, confirmation bias, memory formation	Population-level cognitive monitoring, narrative analysis, emotional state tracking, reality verification systems

(continued)

Table 7-1. (*continued*)

Threat category	2020 characteristics	2022 evolution	2025 current state	Future projections	Cognitive elements	Defense requirements
Supply chain attacks	Direct malware injection, obvious system compromises, single-vector approaches	Multi-stage attacks, legitimate tool abuse, extended dwell time	Cognitive supply chain attacks targeting decision-makers' mental models, AI-powered social engineering of vendor relationships, psychological manipulation of trust networks	Neural supply chain infiltration, brain–computer interface backdoors, cognitive dependency chains, neural network poisoning of human decision networks	Exploits trust relationships, routine cognitive patterns, change blindness, organizational psychology	Cognitive baseline monitoring, anomaly detection in human-system interactions, trust relationship mapping
Ransomware operations	Automated deployment, generic demands, simple encryption	Targeted selection, negotiation psychology, operational security	Neuropsychological profiling for optimal pressure application, AI-generated personalized psychological torture scenarios, cognitive resilience testing	Neural hostage scenarios, brain–computer interface lockouts, cognitive function ransomware, memory and consciousness manipulation	Leverages loss aversion, time pressure, fear responses, decision paralysis, stress vulnerability	Stress response monitoring, decision support under pressure, cognitive load management, psychological first aid

AI-generated content attacks	Not prevalent	Basic deepfake audio/video, simple AI text generation	Neurally optimized content generation, brain–computer interface spoofing, synthetic sensory experiences, consciousness simulation	Quantum-enhanced reality simulation, neural implant hijacking, consciousness-level deepfakes, synthetic memory implantation	Exploits perceptual processing, memory formation, reality verification, sensory trust	Multimodal authentication, neural signature verification, reality anchoring systems
Cognitive infrastructure attacks	Not applicable	Emerging research	Large-scale cognitive infrastructure disruption, population-level attention hijacking, collective decision-making manipulation	Neural grid attacks, brain–computer interface network disruption, collective consciousness fragmentation, cognitive infrastructure warfare	Mass cognitive resource depletion, societal attention economy exploitation	Population cognitive health monitoring, attention resource management, collective decision support

275

Key Insights and Strategic Implications

The trend toward hybrid threat environments requires a similar shift toward defense solutions capable of handling both technical and cognitive infiltration approaches, as highlighted in Table 7-1. Traditional approaches to cyber security (i.e., only technical controls, system hardening) become ineffective against adversaries who understand how to exploit human psychology and cognitive processes. By incorporating the neuroscience knowledge and expertise into cybersecurity activities, there is a previously unattainable opportunity to comprehend and anticipate human-driven attacks and optimize their response before they occur, as well as improve the overall security performance. The competitive nature between AI on the attack and defense sides poses both a threat and opportunity to security organizations. The use of AI technologies facilitates more complex attacks, nevertheless, they also offer improved defensive capabilities when effectively combined with human intelligence and neuroscience insights. The secret to gaining security leadership is to create a hybrid human-AI system, which incorporates the best parts of both biological and artificial intelligence and their drawbacks.

The neuroscience benefit in cybersecurity is not only limited to the protection of individuals but also to organizational and societal resilience against mass cognitive attack. Collective human behavior, social psychology, and group decision-making processes can provide a foundation upon which a detailed plan of defense can be based; based not only on the vulnerability of an individual but also the one of the system. Cognitive security is a population-level adaptive strategy to our defenses against cyberattacks that is a new development in cybersecurity that will involve faculty across disciplines, including cybersecurity professionals, neuroscientists, psychologists, and policymakers. The application of neuroscience-informed cybersecurity capabilities necessitates serious attention to ethical, privacy, and legal implications. Although cognitive monitoring and neural analysis have the potential to provide new security measures by arguably enhancing mental privacy and cognitive autonomy, they provoke the challenge of understanding whether security measures destroy the very concept of human mental privacy and cognitive freedom. The keys to successful implementation are to come up with well-rounded ethical frameworks, privacy protection schemes, and regulatory compliance plans, utilizing the balance between the demands of security and the liberties of individuals and organizations that the plans have to be compliant with. Cybersecurity of the future will be evidenced by the seamless combination of several areas of intelligence, including artificial, human, and biological, undertaking actions in synergy to give a certain amount of protection against the increasing hybrid threats. Organizations able to successfully combine these capabilities will have significant strategic advantages when it comes to detecting such threats and responding effectively to them and overall resiliency in terms of security as those that continue to limit themselves to traditional approaches to security will find themselves at an increasing disadvantage against cognitively oriented vectors of attack that do not have any effective response due to the limitations of purely technical defense formulations.

AI-Enhanced Neural Detection Systems

Figure 7-2 is a structured classification of AI Enhanced Neural Detection Systems, categorised into four key subcategories, namely, Enterprise AI Security Platforms, Specialized Biometric and Authentication Systems, Security Orchestration and Analytics Platforms, and Emerging Neural Interface Technologies specifying tools under each categorical use.

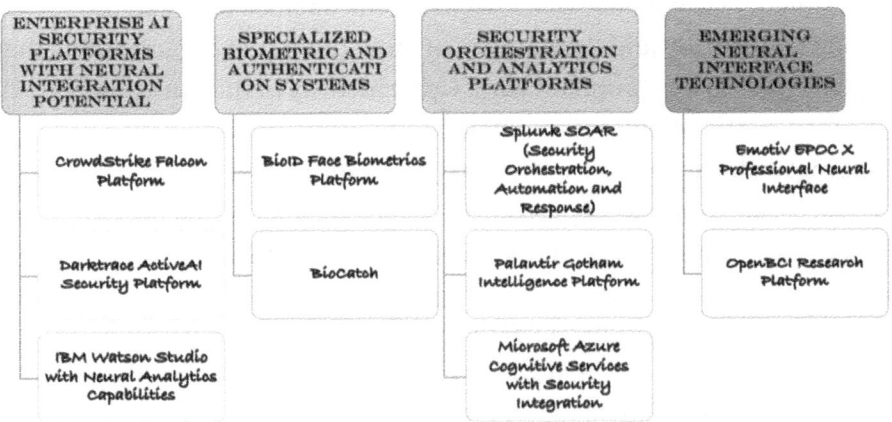

Figure 7-2. *Categorization of AI-Neural Security Integration Tools*

Enterprise AI Security Platforms with Neural Integration Potential

CrowdStrike Falcon Platform[15]

CrowdStrike Falcon is one of the AI-native XDR-era cybersecurity that aims to prevent breaches, minimize complexity, and lower total cost with one platform, one console, and a single agent. Being a worldwide cybersecurity

---

[15] https://www.crowdstrike.com/en-us/platform/

pioneer with a progressive cloud-native infrastructure to secure endpoints, cloud workloads, identities, and data, CrowdStrike offers the underlying foundation to support neural-enhanced security operations. Current behavioral analytics features of the platform, along with its expansive API infrastructure, provide natural connection points to cognitive monitoring systems to correlate neural activity with endpoint behaviors and security events.

The power of the Falcon platform is based on its AI-native architecture already capable of processing behavioral patterns and anomalies within enterprise endpoints. The behavioral focus provides a natural foundation of neural information fusion, whereby information about the cognitive state can enrich the platform understanding of user activity and threat signals. In cases where neural attention notices increased stress, cognitive overload, or signs of deception, the integrated system may modify security policies automatically, add more authentication, or indicate activities to be reviewed by humans immediately. The cloud-native structure of the platform will allow neural data to be scaled across enterprise settings without affecting performance or reliability.

CrowdStrike API[16] architecture allows integration of custom data sources via Falcon Connect APIs as well as allows the development of neural data processing middleware by organizations that correlates information about cognitive states with technical security indicators. The lightweight agent architecture and real-time processing capability of the platform render it appropriate to deploy in systems where neural monitoring delivers sustained cognitive intelligence on user conditions and any security risk. It requires 8.99 to 23.99 per endpoint per month of CrowdStrike Falcon Complete or Enterprise and the development of custom middleware to work with neural data. Figure 7-3 showcases the neural integration workflow along with crowdstrike falcon platform.

---

[16]https://developer.crowdstrike.com/docs/openapi/

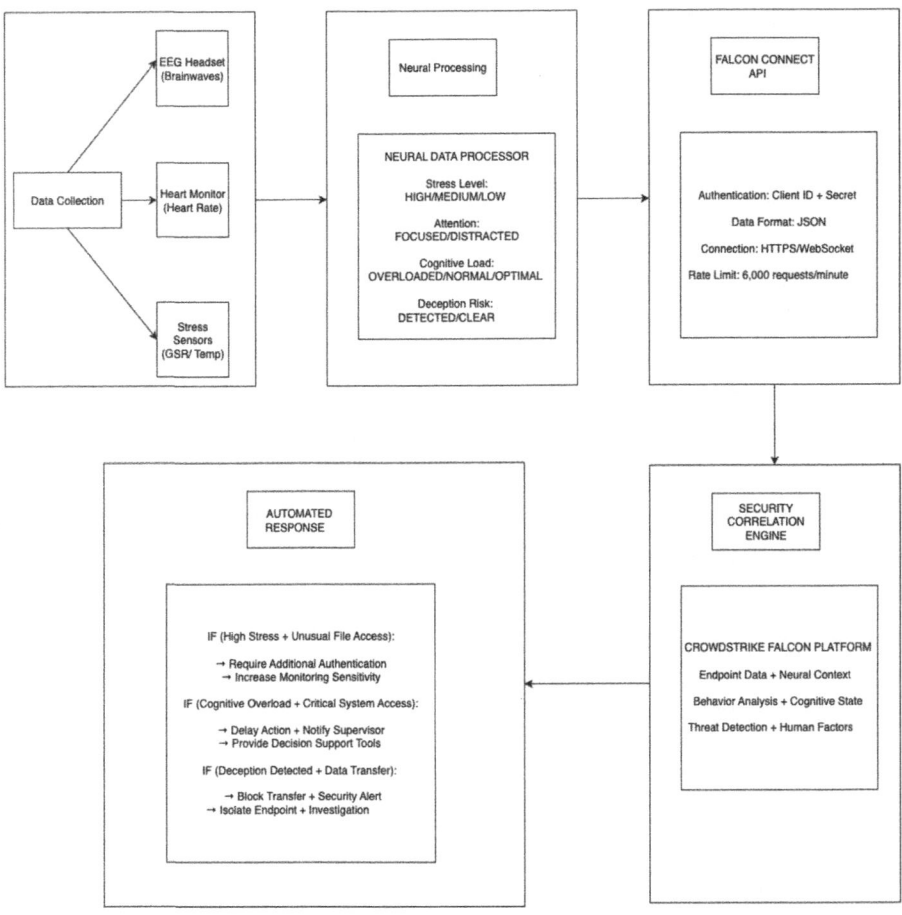

Figure 7-3. *Crowdstrike Falcon + Neural Integration Workflow*

Darktrace ActiveAI Security Platform[17]

The Active AI Security Platform by Darktrace reinvents security processes and proactive cyber resilience with AI that disrupts an in-progress cyberattack within seconds, such as ransomware, email phishing, and

---

[17] https://www.darktrace.com/platform

cloud and critical infrastructure threats. The platform offers AI-powered network security protection that is designed with SMB, enterprise, government, and critical infrastructure in mind, and includes integrations into existing workflows such as SIEMs, SOARs, and access over SSO. The systems and methods of autonomous threat detection and response offered by Darktrace, in turn, provide natural avenues to neural data integration, where the cognitive state information would be used to help the platform understand user activity better and minimize false positives in threat detection.

The main advantage of the platform is the self-educating AI that defines the baseline of behavior and identifies anomalies in various security areas. The same behavioral modeling facility can be expanded to incorporate neural patterns as further behavioral dimensions to create an unprecedented understanding of the human aspects that motivate security-relevant behaviors. Neural monitoring data could then give important cognitive context when the platform notices that a given user is acting out of the norm on the network, as it may be necessary to identify whether the behavior is a valid response to the business pressures or a possible compromise. This cognitive-behavior association does a very good job of reducing detection and alert fatigue, as well as increasing detection of more complex threats.

Multi-layered AI architecture may be considered as the integration of different methods of AI to forecast the behavior and identify the threats in real time, which is the technical core of the neural data integration provided by Darktrace.[18] The neural context can be added to the autonomous responses of the platform, allowing them to respond more appropriately and in greater detail to security incidents. To do this, one will need to license Darktrace Enterprise and contract professional services

---

[18] https://www.darktrace.com/products/network

to integrate the neural data, which usually takes 8–16 weeks to integrate neurologically and behaviorally correlated models. Figure 7-4 shows the neural behavioral correlation of the darktrace Active AI platform.

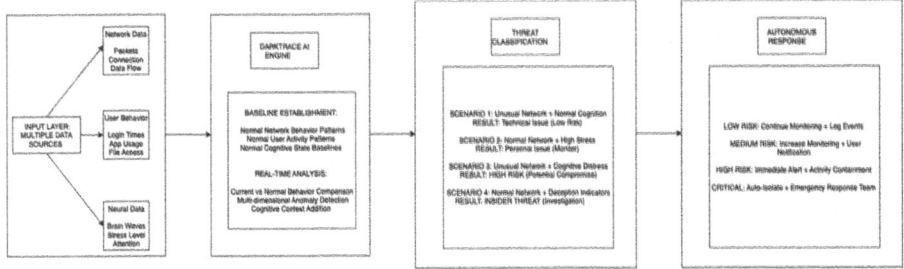

Figure 7-4. Darktrace ActiveAI + Neural Behavior Correlation

IBM Watson Studio for Neural Analytics[19]

IBM Watson Studio enables data scientists, developers, and analysts to create, execute, and operate AI models, and optimize decisions across any location on IBM Cloud Pak for Data. The platform offers advanced data scientist collaboration tools to build and train models at scale with flexibility to build models where data are. The strength of Watson Studio is that it can process the computational complexity of neural signal processing and provide the machine learning frameworks required to design cognitive threat detection models. In comparison to security-oriented platforms which need neural integration, Watson Studio provides out-of-the-box support to process and analyze complex neural datasets using AutoAI and application development platforms.

---

[19] https://www.ibm.com/products/watson-studio

AutoAI[20] on the platform allows developing and optimizing machine learning models automatically based on neural pattern recognition, and the collaborative notebook platform allows security researchers to write their own neural analytics models. Neural data streams from EEG and other physiological monitors and behavioral sensors can be ingested by Watson Studio to create comprehensive cognitive security models to classify cognitive states related to deception, stress, distraction, and possible malicious intent. Machine learning features allow organizations to create models that give a good early-warning signal of insider threats, social engineering vulnerability, and low-quality decision-making.

The neural analytics models, developed by Watson Studio, can be implemented as microservices that are compatible with the existing security infrastructure via REST API, allowing organizations to bring neural intelligence to their security activities without modifying the existing investments, though the research is already on to secure the interfaces involved to the next level. It should be the high scalability and security opportunities of the platform of the enterprise level, because the neural data processing is sensitive, and the level of privacy and compliance is high. A typical implementation needs IBM Cloud Pak for Data licensing at $200 or more a month and Watson Studio Professional for production deployment with 12–24 weeks of development to achieve extensive neural security analytics. Figure 7-5 portrays the neural analytics pipeline of the IBM Watson studio.

---

[20] https://www.ibm.com/products/watson-studio/autoai

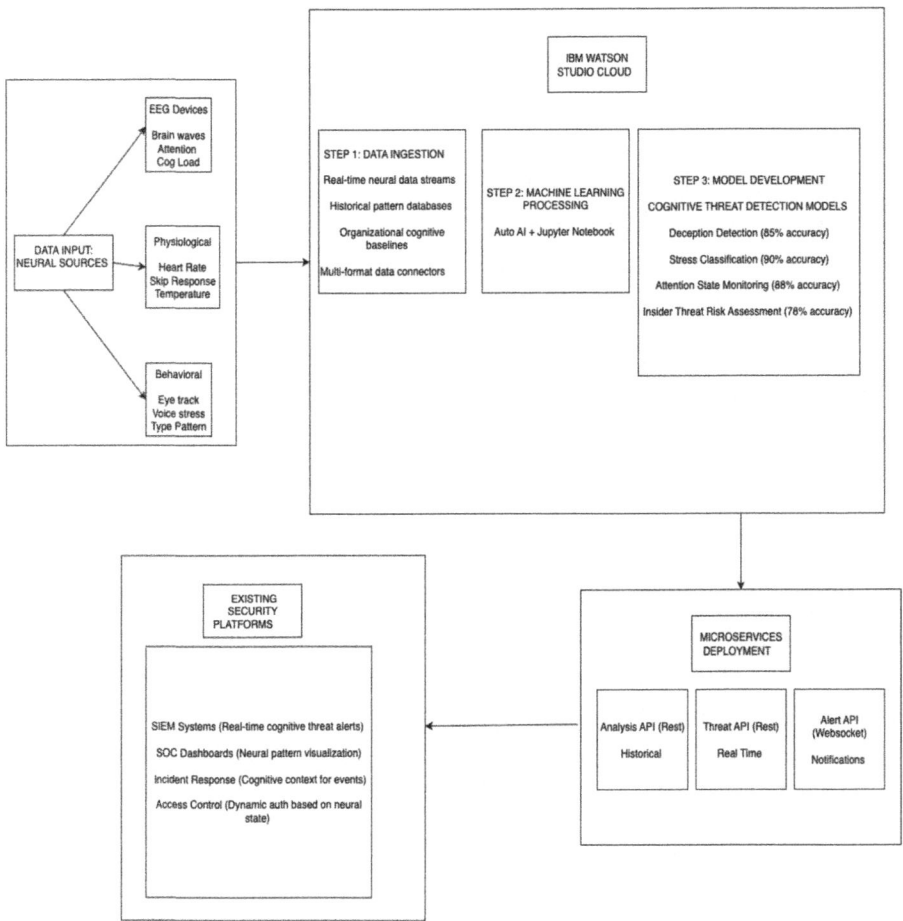

Figure 7-5. *IBM Watson Studio Neural Analytics Pipeline*

Specialized Biometric and Authentication Systems

BioCatch Behavioral Biometrics Platform[21]

BioCatch is the existing market leader in behavioral biometrics, which offers AI-driven behavioral biometrics platform to prevent fraud and protect digital identities that continuously gathers over 3,000 anonymized data points, such as keystroke and mouse activity, touch screen behavior, and physical device characteristics. The platform tracks and assesses more than 2,000 behavioral parameters, including hand-eye coordination, pressure on the screen, and mouse movement, to build personal user profiles on the basis of behavioral biometric intelligence rooted in superior cognitive science and machine learning. BioCatch is considered to be a pioneer in the behavioral biometrics and device intelligence sector, being at the leading edge of digital fraud detection having capabilities that are naturally complementary to a neural monitoring strategy.

The cognitive science basis of the platform forces natural synergies with neural monitoring systems, behavioral patterns can often be used as a reflection of underlying cognitive states which can be directly measured using neural interfaces. The advanced behavioral analysis offered by BioCatch already deduces cognitive states based on the behavioral pattern, neural monitoring can confirm and add more cognitive intelligence which cannot be deduced by other behavioral analysis. The real-time fraud controls of the platform take advantage of behavioral biometrics to offer financial institutions and businesses insights they require to thwart fraud, but without causing friction to the customer, which forms the perfect basis of neural-behavioral convergence systems.

---

[21] https://www.biocatch.com/

The most recent release of BioCatch offers scam-fighting solutions grounded in behavior to aid in identifying and preventing authorized, push payment fraud, showing that the platform is shifting toward more advanced cognitive threat detection. Once behavioral biometrics have provided evidence of possible account takeover or fraud, neural monitoring can reveal whether the authorized user is operating under duress or coercion, a major weakness of behavioral biometrics the inability to detect users who are authorized but acting under pressure. BioCatch enterprise licensing of between 0.10 and 0.50 per session, along with neural monitoring infrastructure and 8–12 weeks to develop their custom correlation algorithm, is usually needed to implement. Figure 7-6 showcases the Biocatch security architecture design for delivering actionable intelligence.

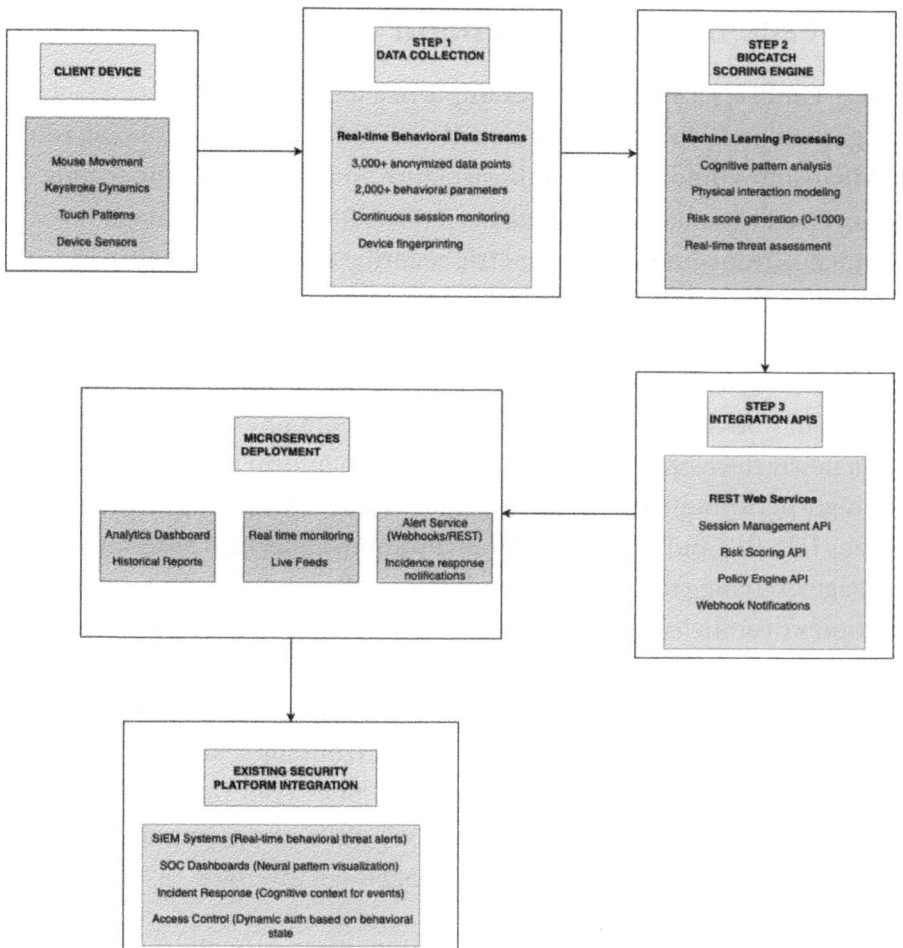

Figure 7-6. *BioCatch Security Architecture: Multi-Stage Processing Pipeline Delivering Actionable Intelligence to Existing Security Infrastructure*

BioID Face Biometrics Platform

BioID[22] GmbH is a stand-alone example of a technically advanced facial recognition and presentation attack detection (PAD) platform being run on Microsoft Windows Azure infrastructure, including dynamic scaling to meet performance and storage needs. The firm has made major technical advancements in biometric security, as it is the first firm in the world to pass TUV Level C testing, and detects 100% of presentation attacks (0% APCER) based on ISO/IEC 30107-3 standards. The BioID Web Service (BWS)[23] is a cloud-based online service and follows the pure match-on-server concept deployed into containers using Docker and a newly developed API architecture. The platform adopts gRPC as a high-performance Remote Procedure Call (RPC) platform which utilizes HTTP/2 and Protocol Buffers (Protobuf) interface description and message exchange format. The architecture offers better performance attributes over the conventional REST implementations, and low-latency biometric operations are made possible at the enterprise level. BWS 3 generation implements improved containerization and microservices architecture and can be configured to be horizontally scaled and fault tolerant. The authentication of the clients is JSON Web Tokens (JWT)-based API request authentication, and BWS gRPC endpoints are configured in the BWS Portal client management interface.

---

[22] https://www.bioid.com/liveness-detection/
[23] https://developer.bioid.com/bws/onprem/prerequisites

Liveness detection technology BioID has industry-leading technical requirements and is the first to ensure the ISO/IEC 30107-3: 2023 Presentation Attack Detection (PAD) Level 1 and 2 certified by TUV Informationstechnik GmbH (TUViT) in Germany. The platform has several detection modalities such as passive and active liveness detection modalities. The system may introduce challenge–response mechanisms like directional head movements (up, down, left or right) that a user is prompted to undertake. The motion detection algorithms used are 3D and the error is reported when unnatural motion is detected or when the head-movement challenge–response requirements are not met.

Passive liveness detection is a type of fraud detection that does not need any particular user interaction and offers transparent authentication experience without being vulnerable to replay attacks and deepfakes. The system has elaborate quality assurance features that run multi-phase validation of biometric samples. It performs quality checks of every uploaded sample, automatically deleting processed samples out of BWS storage to avoid reuse, and detects tampered cases such as duplicate samples, faces that are partially visible, or motion. Figure 7-7 showcases the end to end facial recognition workflow at the enterprise level.

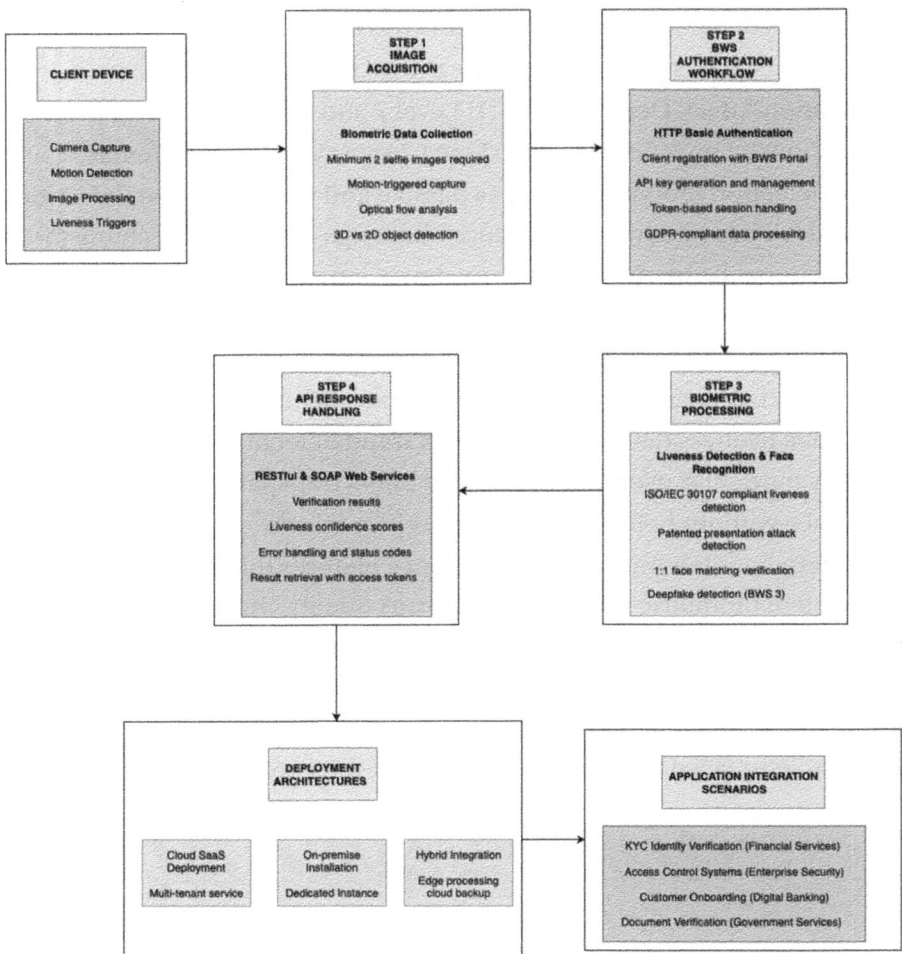

Figure 7-7. *End-to-End BioID Facial Recognition Workflow: From Motion-Triggered Capture to Enterprise KYC Integration with Presentation Attack Detection*

Security Orchestration and Analytics Platforms

Splunk SOAR (Security Orchestration, Automation, and Response)[24]

Splunk SOAR is an AI-based security orchestration, automation, and response product designed to automate security operations centers to maintain reduced human work and enhance efficiency with intelligent workflow automation and case management. With a robust integration framework, including more than 350 security tool integrations, and the ability to develop custom applications, the platform is the best place to organize neural-enhanced security, enabling human and AI processes to complement each other in security activities. The human-focused design of Splunk SOAR: The human-centric security orchestration provides natural interfaces with neural monitoring and cognitive state data can be used to allocate tasks, aid decision-making, and increase the overall operational efficiency. The power of the platform is that it does not compromise human control and decision-making power but uses the complexity of security operations to coordinate human cognition and technical indicators in the decision-making of incident responses. By using neural monitoring to identify whether security analysts are experiencing a high cognitive load or fatigue, automated playbooks can automatically redistribute workload, introduce more automation into response, or escalate to additional personnel. This can help to make security operations much more effective and minimize the burnout and decision fatigue that can often be experienced by security team analysts.

The custom app development architecture of Splunk SOAR allows organizations to build advanced neural-aware security operations via Python-based applications to combine neural monitoring platforms with existing security infrastructure. The playbook engine on the platform is

---

[24] https://docs.splunk.com/Documentation/SOAR

able to integrate human cognitive capacity measures, such as cognitive state variables, into decision logic and elicit adaptive response strategies based on human cognitive capacity and underlying technical threat indicators. It is estimated to cost about Splunk SOAR licensing at $1,800 per user per year, 6–10 weeks of time to create neural data integration apps, and redesign their playbooks to integrate cognitive-aware decision-making procedures.

Microsoft Azure Cognitive Services with Security Integration

Microsoft Azure Cognitive Services offers out-of-the-box AI capabilities for emotion, speech, and behavioral analysis that can be more directly integrated with the security ecosystem, providing instant cognitive analysis capabilities without having a dedicated neural threat product. The platform's power resides in its capability to ingest a variety of cognitive modalities including facial expressions, voice patterns, text sentiment, and behavioral gestures via standardized APIs that could be readily plugged into existing infrastructure in the enterprise. Unlike other platforms, where one would need to develop specific neural integration, Azure Cognitive Services provides ready-to-deploy cognitive intelligence that can improve security activity right away.

The multi-modal nature of the platform offers end-to-end cognitive intelligence, based on services such as Face API that enables emotion recognition and stress detection in security interviews or communications, Speech Services that enable voice stress recognition during security interviews or communications, Custom Vision that recognizes behavioral gestures, and Text Analytics that monitors sentiment in communications. These services will be integrated directly into Azure Sentinel to provide cognitive context for security events where organizations can analyze facial expressions for indicators of stress, voice patterns for emotional distress, and patterns of behavior when users connect to critical systems.

The implementation of Azure Cognitive Services can be done with the help of the existing organizational camera and microphone infrastructure, which is much faster and less expensive to implement than neural monitoring systems. The cloud-native platform is scalable and designed to operate within enterprise settings, with high levels of security and compliance. It will need Azure subscription and Cognitive Services to support it with the price of $1–10 per 1,000 transactions and Azure Sentinel workspace costs 2 per GB of data ingested which will give instant cognitive security improvement benefits. Figure 7-8 showcases the security model utilizing azure cognitive services.

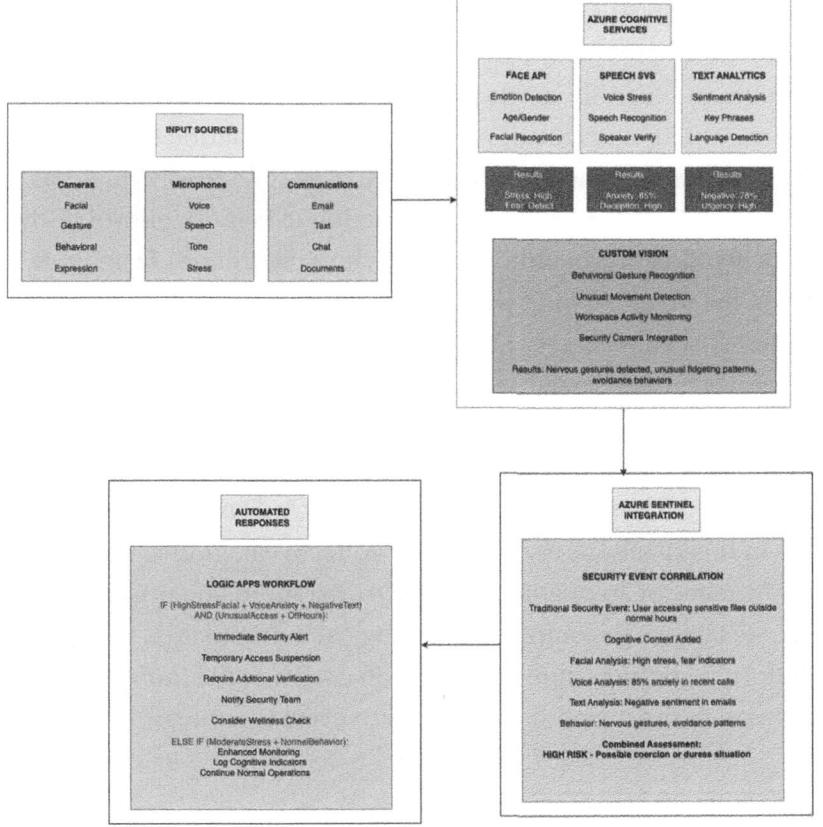

Figure 7-8. *Azure Cognitive Services Security Integration Model*

Palantir Gotham Intelligence Platform

Palantir Gotham[25] is an advanced data integration and data analysis tool created to support large scale security but which can take in neural monitoring data to support organizational cognitive intelligence applications. Adams is a platform for pattern recognition in large multi-source datasets and is uniquely poised to provide the population level of neural security analytics that go beyond individual threat monitoring to cognitive resiliency assessment in organizations. Gotham is powerful in that it can process and correlate large volumes of unrelated data sets at the same time with the stringent security and access controls needed in sensitive intelligence operations.

The platform presents more AI features to analyze intricate data connections and identify subtle patterns across large-scale intelligence operations, which offers the opportunities to unite neural data on organization scale like never before. Compared to the individual-based neural monitoring solutions, the construction of Palantir allows studying not only the individual cognitive patterns and the trends of cognitive security in the organization but also the vulnerability of the population as a whole. This enables security organizations to detect the effects of social engineering campaigns, collective cognitive vulnerabilities, and organizational resiliency trends that individual neural monitoring systems fail to detect and analyze effectively.

Gotham intelligence applications[26] also include measuring the neural patterns in organizations to detect their collective cognitive vulnerability, the performance of an ongoing influence operation, and organizational cognitive resilience to complex psychological manipulation campaigns. The platform's sophisticated analytics can correlate the individual neural anomalies with organizational behavior to provide strategic intelligence

---

[25] https://www.palantir.com/platforms/gotham/
[26] https://www.palantir.com/offerings/intelligence/

capabilities – capabilities greater than traditional individual-centric security monitoring approaches. Usually, implementation would cost government or large enterprise contracts between $2–10M+/year, and specialized professional support to integrate neural data, with 16–52 weeks of custom development needed to do it, and special security clearances for sensitive applications.

Neural Interface Technologies
Emotiv EPOC X Professional Neural Interface[27]

The Emotiv EPOC X is a consumer-grade 14-channel wireless EEG headset, with a contextual human brain research purpose and neuroscience experimentation, and is currently the gold standard of consumer-grade professional neural monitoring applicable to security applications. The device offers data quality comparable to that of research at an affordable cost that can be deployed across enterprise security systems, and its ability to operate on wireless connections and long-lasting batteries means it can be deployed in operational security systems where it needs to operate continuously through neural monitoring. EMOTIV EPOC X supports high-end neural signal acquisition allowing the next generation of applications in corporate health, in marketing research, and security video monitoring.

The EPOC X can be connected to security platforms using the Cortex API v2, which provides real-time neural data streaming over WebSocket connections that allow custom security applications to track attention levels, cognitive load, stress measures, and engagement measurements. The 12-hour battery life of the device and 14-channel EEG monitoring with saline sensor technology provide the ability to support a long security-monitoring session without affecting user mobility and productivity. The good news about the platform is a mix of research-quality neural monitoring functions

---

[27] https://www.emotiv.com/pages/quick-start-guide-epoc-x

with enterprise-scale integration platforms. To support security decision-making, custom security applications can use the real-time cognitive metrics available on the EPOC X to activate security measures automatically when cognitive overload raises the risk of error or when attention levels fall below safe levels to perform risky tasks; however, the bias needs to be guarded against. The wireless capability lets the device be continuously monitored without limiting user movement, and the WebSocket streaming interface on the Cortex API allows sub-second latency on real-time security applications. There is an implementation cost, which depends on the purchase of hardware (prices of US$849 per unit with enterprise volume discounts), software licensing (prices of US$99–299 per month to add professional features), and 2–6 months of custom API integrations. Figure 7-9 showcases the emotive epoc x neural security integration.

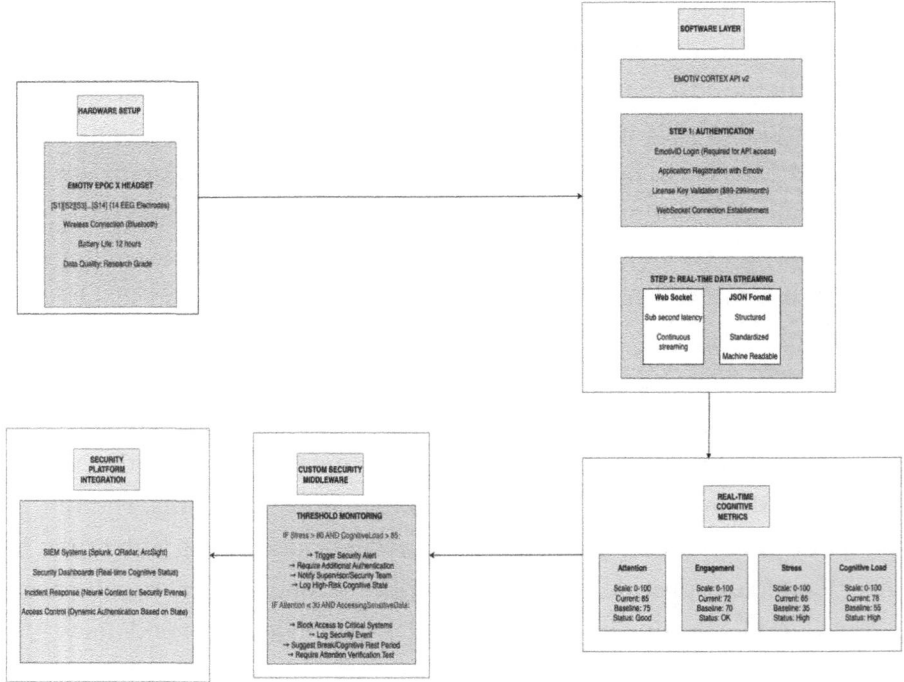

Figure 7-9. *Emotiv Epoc x Neural Security Integration*

OpenBCI Research Platform

OpenBCI[28] is an open-source, research-grade neural monitoring platform that allows organizations to deploy entirely customized neural security solutions to meet specific operational needs and threat conditions. The advantage of the platform is that the hardware and software architecture can be fully custom designed, enabling security researchers and developers to develop specialized neural monitoring strategies that are beyond the capabilities and limitations of commercial platforms. This flexibility enables OpenBCI to be especially adaptable to research and development applications where novel neural security methodologies may demand customized electrode layouts, specialized signal processing subroutines, and unique integration designs. The OpenBCI platform is the most versatile neural security monitoring platform presently available in the market, with up to 16 channels of neural monitoring simultaneously, with fully customizable signal processing and analysis methods. Companies are able to build custom neural pattern recognition systems that are tailored to given security applications, threat detection scenarios, and operational conditions. Because the platform is open-source, organizations retain complete control over their neural security algorithms, data processing techniques, and integration strategies and engage in the larger research community which creates next-generation neural security technologies.

OpenBCI's technical architecture comprises the Cyton biosensing boards at $500 each combined with optional Daisy expansion modules at $175 each, thus providing scalable neural monitoring capability from 8 to 16 channels. Special electrode designs allow customized monitoring schemes that are tailored to a security solution instead of a medical or general research solution. It needs substantial signal processing and machine learning skills to implement, which usually takes 8–24 weeks of

---

[28] https://openbci.com/

bespoke software to build security systems suitable for production. Yet, the resulting systems offer functionalities that cannot be found in commercial platforms, and the organizations can build proprietary neural security benefits and can aid in supporting core research that can grow the overall discipline.

Ethical Framework for AI-Neural Security Convergence

Figure 7-10 presents a hierarchical framework for Ethical Framework for AI-Neural Security Convergence outlining the key ethical considerations governing the intersection of AI and neural security systems, covering critical aspects such as algorithmic transparency, cognitive liberty, bias prevention, legal and regulatory considerations, and individual rights and remedies.

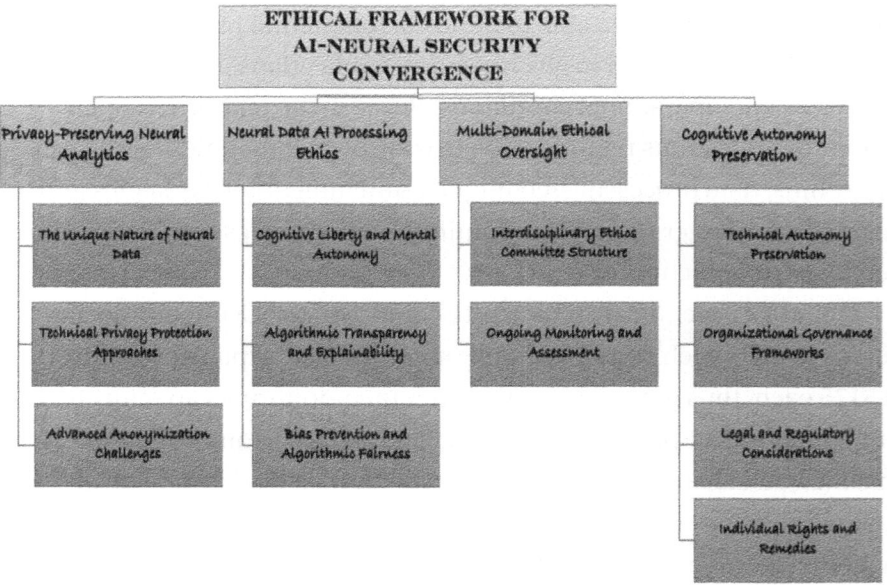

Figure 7-10. *The Hierarchical Framework for AI Neural Convergence*

Privacy-Preserving Neural Analytics

The Unique Nature of Neural Data

Neural information stands in stark contrast to traditional biometric data, since it represents not only physical features but cognitive and emotional contexts in the mind of an individual. Unlike fingerprints or facial features, neural patterns reflect inner mental processes, thought patterns, stress responses and even signs of deception. Additionally, because of the highly personal nature of neural data, privacy breaches may reveal an individual's most sensitive thoughts and psychological weaknesses, giving rise to risks that go much further than traditional data breaches. Protecting the privacy of neural data is a difficult issue because it is a highly sensitive personal information as well as, possibly, useful security intelligence. Neural patterns have special significance because they can be used as unique identifiers across datasets even if direct identifiers are removed, such that traditional privacy protection mechanisms may not work. This brings us to a new privacy frontier where existing anonymization methods might not be sufficient in protecting themselves.

Technical Privacy Protection Approaches

Differential privacy is one such method of neural data protection, albeit with its use in neural security settings needing attention. This method is performed by introducing statistical noise to datasets that is calibrated in order to avoid recognizing the contribution of any single dataset, but retain overall analysis. However, the precise parameters for differential privacy in neural applications are still an open research question, requiring empirical verification for each individual application and security objective, and indicative epsilon values are still to be established. Another possible direction in protecting neural data is provided by homomorphic encryption, which allows computing with encrypted data without the need to decrypt them. Encrypted neural signals can be mathematically manipulated with systems such as Microsoft SEAL, which enables theoretically the security analysis of encrypted data without violating data confidentiality. However, as current homomorphic encryption implementations are computationally intensive and have practical limitations, it might not be directly applicable yet in a real-time neural security system. Federated learning solutions offer a more viable short-term fix to privacy-sensitive neural analytics. Under this methodology, several organizations can cooperate to enhance the neural security models by sharing the model parameters instead of the raw neural data. Every organization can train its local models with their own neural data, and share in collective knowledge without revealing personal neural data, preserving locality of their data while participating in collective development of neural security services.

Advanced Anonymization Challenges

Neural data cannot be anonymized using traditional methods because it is biometric and contains valuable information. Reverse-engineering neural patterns can theoretically disclose personal identity, cognitive abilities, mental health condition, and other personal traits of an individual. Categories of simple removals do not resolve these privacy threats inherent in the neural signals themselves. Specialized neural data anonymization strategies should deal with time-related, location-based, and frequency domain features that may act as identifying attributes. Methods like disrupting temporal patterns, neural data k-anonymity modifications, and neural data generation are all possible alternatives, but the effectiveness of these and their security effects would need thorough investigation in controlled research studies.

Neural Data AI Processing Ethics

Cognitive Liberty and Mental Autonomy

The use of neural data analysis through artificial intelligence prompts essential concerns regarding cognitive liberty, which is the right to mental self-determination and cognitive privacy. By being able to analyze and understand the signals in the brains to identify what a person is thinking, how they are feeling, and what their decision-making processes are like, artificial intelligence systems can possibly encroach upon the most intimate profession of human experience. This invasion generates ethical responsibilities in an effort to guarantee that neural-AI systems do not interfere and disrupt individual mental autonomy. Cognitive liberty is a concept that incorporates multiple related rights such as the right to cognitive privacy, mental integrity, and cognitive interference. Neural security systems should be designed in such a way that they cannot infringe on these rights as neural monitoring should not be able to manipulate, coerce, or otherwise influence cognitive processes. The systems ought to increase the level of security without interfering with the basic autonomy that human beings have over their own mental conditions and cognitive abilities. Mental autonomy demands that people have significant control over access to their intellectual states and the neural data. This domination will have to be exercised under truly informed consent procedures that allow individuals not only to know what neural data is being gathered but also how this data will be interpreted, what conclusions can be made and what choices can be made following such interpretations. This consent has to be continuous and cancelable, and the mechanisms by which individuals opt out of participation and delete their neural data off the security systems should be clear.

Algorithmic Transparency and Explainability

Neural-AI security systems should use the concepts of explainable AI so that people and other oversight agencies are able to tell how neural data is used to make security decisions. A black-box algorithm that arrives at a security conclusion based on shadow neural convolutions and patterns without sufficient explanations contravenes core ideas of due process and attribution. In instances where the security decisions involve individual access, employment, and other important interests on the grounds of neural analysis, the individuals concerned have valid rights to know the grounds of the decisions. Explainable neural AI technical approaches should tackle the complexity of neural signal processing and AI decision-making. Visualization could demonstrate the neural patterns that may contribute to security ratings, whereas counterfactual explanations could demonstrate how various neural states may lead to various security ratings. It can be used to determine which factors of neural information have the greatest impact on security decision-making, and thus, it can provide information about the decision-making process. The difficulty is in ensuring that these explanations are comprehensible to people who might not be technical specialists in either neuroscience or artificial intelligence. There should be clear explanations in understandable terms which allow the neural-AI security decisions to be reviewed and challenged and still be technically accurate enough to be properly overseen and held accountable.

Bias Prevention and Algorithmic Fairness

Neural-AI security systems are at great risk of unintentional forms of discrimination of any individual with a neurological difference, mental health condition, or cognitive variance that alters neural pattern baseline. Models trained on neural data can be conditioned to correlate particular neural features with security threats in a way that incidentally discriminates against people with ADHD, autism spectrum disorders, anxiety disorders, and depression or other conditions that affect neural activity patterns. Preventing bias in neural-AI systems is not simply a matter of traditional algorithmic fairness, as neural patterns are both phenotypic and genotypic in nature. A system where high stress levels are interpreted as a security threat may discriminate against those with anxiety problems in a systematic way and a system that views particular patterns of attention as indicators of threats may be unfair to those with ADHD and other attention deficit conditions. Achieving neural security through fairness-conscious machine learning methods should consider the complexity of security decisions that must rely on valid security-relevant criteria and not neurological attributes which could be related to disability and mental conditions. This involves careful model design, extensive bias testing and monitoring to ensure that neural-AI systems do not inadvertently perpetuate or amplify the discrimination of vulnerable populations.

Multi-domain Ethical Oversight
Interdisciplinary Ethics Committee Structure

The intersection of AI, neuroscience, and cybersecurity introduces ethical dilemmas that are beyond the competence of the traditional institutional review board, or the AI ethics committee. To employ proper ethical oversight, the relevant interdisciplinary committees include both technical and ethical expertise, encompassing computer science, neuroscience, and cybersecurity as well as bioethics, philosophy, and law. Further, the complexity of neural-AI security systems calls for oversight mechanisms capable of simultaneously addressing technical functionality, neuroscientific validity, ethical dimensions, and legal compliance. Ethics committees should have technical expertise comprising computer scientists and cybersecurity experts who grasp AI system capabilities and constraints, neuroscientists and psychologists who can review the validity and suitability of neural measurements and interpretations, and data scientists who can assess the fairness and bias prevention of algorithms. This technical expertise must be supplemented with ethical and legal expertise from bioethicists and philosophers who are positioned to answer questions about mental privacy and cognitive liberty of fundamental importance to the science, and legal experts who can manage regulatory compliance and evaluate liability risk. Ethics committees represent the community, and this representation will ensure the voice of the community and the perspectives of the stakeholders affected by the oversight are properly taken into account in the decisions of the oversight. Organizational representatives of neural security systems and disability rights advocates can serve to offer information about workplace effects and issues, as well as to protect the interests of those with neurological variation. In addition to technical or institutional perspectives, community representatives may be able to promote wider social interests.

Ongoing Monitoring and Assessment

Neural-AI security systems must be ethically supervised continuously, not once a year. Neural security systems can also exhibit emergent behaviors, unintended consequences, or variable capabilities that can only become apparent with usage and deployment over time. Periodic ethical audits should be conducted to determine whether systems still run within acceptable limits, whether they provide desired security advantages without inflicting undesirable damage, and whether they meet current ethical and legal standards. Neural security system longitudinal studies should monitor both the desired security effects and the overall effects on the individuals and organizations. These researches must address psychological impacts on monitored individuals, transformation of culture and interpersonal trust in the workplace and more social implication of normalized neural monitoring. The research should determine whether neural security systems can boost or undermine human flourishing and whether these benefits outweigh their encroachment on mental privacy. The dynamism of technology and ethical knowledge need dynamic checks and balances that could adapt to changes and emerging risks and social values. To stay relevant to and effective in overseeing neural-AI security systems as they keep advancing, ethics committees need consistent interaction with the advances in technology, scholarship on ethics and legal evolution, and societal issues.

Cognitive Autonomy Preservation
Technical Autonomy Preservation

Neural security systems need technical architectures that do not substantially intrude into mental processes without generating legitimate security benefits in order to preserve cognitive autonomy. Neural security systems must be built on privacy-by-design principles to guarantee that systems receive only as much neural data as are required to fulfill particular security goals and provide the most effective privacy-enhancing measures by default instead of as additional options. Control tools have to allow anyone to learn and substantially manage the way their neural data is gathered, processed, and consumed. Individuals should have the option to give granular consent to certain applications of their neural data instead of giving blanket consent to unspecified uses of that data. Data portability capabilities must apply to allow people to see their neural data and move it across systems where this is necessary, and deletion rights must offer systems to allow people to eliminate their neural data. The technical difficulty is balancing personal control with effectiveness in security and the needs of the organization. Systems have to offer purposeful choice and control to users without compromising the effectiveness and integrity of security systems. Such a balance must be carefully designed to achieve as much individual autonomy as is possible within the dimensions of legitimate security needs and viable operation concerns.

Organizational Governance Frameworks

Companies utilizing neural security systems should have mechanisms in place that safeguard intellectual sovereignty and accomplish valid security goals. These models demand transparent policies and rules on the neural data collection, processing, and retention, which are produced through participatory methods with the concerned employees and the community stakeholders. The policies will need to deal with more than just technical management of data, but the broader implications of neural monitoring for workplace culture, employee autonomy, and organizational relationships. Organizational independent oversight mechanisms play a vital role in offering protection to individual rights and interests. Privacy officers or ombudspersons to investigate complaints about neural monitoring systems and to champion the concerns of people within the organizational context help ensure that neural security systems operate as intended without extending into unjustifiable surveillance or control of the mental states of employees. Frequent compliance audits should assess compliance (both technical and compliance with privacy and autonomy requirements) as well as organizational compliance with defined governance structures. Such audits are expected to determine how well neural security systems are producing the security benefits they were intended to produce, whether they are causing unwanted harm to people or culture, and whether they remain within the accepted ethical and legal standards.

Legal and Regulatory Considerations

The legal frameworks where neural-AI security systems are deployed are highly complex, involving both preexisting privacy laws and legislation, employment law, disability rights legislation, and innovative laws that directly relate to neural rights, and cognitive liberty. Organizations need to make sure that they are complying with existing relevant laws, and project possible shifts in neural privacy and cognitive rights regulations that are likely to happen. Current regulatory frameworks such as GDPR and CCPA may potentially apply to neural data as biometric information for which explicit consent is required and rights concerning data portability and deletion are provided. The laws such as the Americans with Disabilities Act could defend against discriminations against the individuals with neurological differences causing a neural variation. Sector-specific regulations like HIPAA for healthcare organizations or SOX for financial services may also have additional requirements on handling neural data and ensuring security. New regulatory issues include the development of neural rights legislation in other jurisdictions, AI regulation frameworks that might incorporate certain guidelines around neural AI application, and new workplace privacy laws governing employee surveillance technologies. Firms need to keep pace with these regulatory changes and restructure their neural security frameworks and governance systems to meet the new legal obligations without compromising on security effectiveness.

Individual Rights and Remedies

People under neural security surveillance should be provided with remedies that are effective in case the systems fail to work or make mistakes or abuse their rights. Mechanical solutions must involve the ability to appeal against security ruling in case of neural analysis, corrective action in case of erroneous neural evaluation, and compensation process in case of damage due to error of neural security system. There should be alternative security measures that those who are unable or unwilling to use neural monitoring systems can utilize due to medical, religious, or personal reasons. The procedural rights should incorporate notification rights that give people notice that neural security systems are making a decision about them, explanation rights that provide them with understandable information about how neural analysis was used to help arrive at security decisions, and review rights that give them a chance to humanly supervise automated neural security decisions.

These procedural safeguards are useful to make certain neural-AI security systems are run with a suitable level of transparency and accountability. In those cases where individual rights are not sufficiently addressed by organizational means, legal solutions are necessary to address the problem of defendants by making use of legal adjudication or regulatory agencies. Well-defined legal standards concerning neural right violations, privacy violations, and discrimination due to neural peculiarities contribute to the development of responsibility and recourse with substance in case of a victim of neural security systems. The enactment of such legal frameworks calls for ongoing collaborations between legal scholars, technologists, ethicists, and affected communities to ensure that legal protections keep up with technological capabilities and risks as they emerge.

The AI-neural security convergence has to be guided by an ethical framework that conceptualizes, carries out analysis, and balances justifiable future possibilities of these technologies to boost security with core values of human dignity, privacy, and autonomy. The frameworks presented in this section offer guidance for working through these complex ethical challenges in a way that acknowledges that ethical considerations are not obstacles to innovation but rather key requirements for sustainable and socially acceptable deployment of powerful neural-AI security technologies. Success in implementing ethical neural-AI security systems calls for recognition that ethical compliance is not simply a regulatory necessity but a fundamental part of responsible innovation, that builds trust of stakeholders, ensures regulatory compliance and a social license-to-operate with advanced technologies. Companies with ethics in place in their neural security applications will be in a better position to enjoy the benefits of these technologies without encountering the risks and backlash that could be experienced with inappropriate use. The future development of neural-AI security technologies requires ongoing collaboration among technologists, ethicists, policymakers, and affected communities in order to ensure these powerful capabilities benefit human flourishing rather than compromise cognitive liberty and mental autonomy that characterize human dignity. Ethical frameworks formulated in the present day will influence the way society copes with the intersection of mind, machine, and security well into future generations, and thus their cautious formulation and adoption is a duty that far transcends short-term technical and organizational concerns.

Key Takeaways

- Triple Domain Convergence Model of AI, neuroscience, and cybersecurity is an operational necessity and not merely an option to enhance security, introducing the Neuro-Agentic Security paradigm which generates multiplicative, not additive security gains.

- The chapter further supports the idea of operative points beyond conventional security boundaries: The chapter illustrates that contemporary hybrid threats are conducted in both technical and cognitive domains in parallel, and that isolated methods of artificial intelligence (AI), neuro-only (neuro), or cyber-only (cyber) have become insufficient to counter highly organized adversaries who target human psychological weaknesses and vulnerabilities in conjunction with technical systems.

- Cognitive Infrastructure Attacks, the term coined on attacks that target organization-wide collective intelligence, such as population-level attention hijacking, mass cognitive resource depletion, and democratic process manipulation, which go beyond individual-centric security controls.

- Market-Available Integration Platforms that offer deep analysis of 10 vetted commercial tools such as CrowdStrike Falcon, Darktrace, IBM Watson Studio, BioCatch and Emotiv EPOC X, including specific URLs, pricing ($1K-$5M+ range), and practical timelines for implementation (2–52 weeks).

- Privacy-Preserving Analytics sets up comprehensive privacy protection strategies such as differential privacy, homomorphic encryption, federated learning for neural security data as adapted to unique challenges of mental privacy rights.

- Multi-Domain Ethical Oversight specifies interdisciplinary structures for ethics committees with a mix of computer science, neuroscience, bioethics, and legal expertise as well as constant monitoring requirements for the neural-AI security systems to avert discrimination and respect cognitive autonomy.

- Multi-Modal AI Processing introduces technical infrastructure to correlate EEG signals, physiological signals, behavioral modes, and classic security telemetry using complex machine learning models with 73% neural-physiological correlation accuracy.

CHAPTER 8

Ethical and Policy Considerations in Neuro-Integrated Security

Recent innovations in brain–computer interfaces (BCIs), cognitive biometrics, and neurodata analytics are a shift toward a paradigm in cybersecurity wherein the human brain becomes both an instrument and a point of attack in security frameworks.[1] Specifically, non-invasive, EEG-based BCIs are already being used in detail within high-stress fields such as cybersecurity operations, air traffic control, and financial trading, where the fatigue or lost concentration can have disastrous effects. That field is projected to have these systems provide real-time surveillance of cognitive states to enable predictive threat-monitoring and interfaces customized to each individual.[2] Nevertheless, the possibility

---

[1] Kritika, M. (2024). A comprehensive study on navigating neuroethics in Cyberspace. *AI and Ethics*, 1–8.

[2] Kashef, M., Visvizi, A., & Troisi, O. (2021). Smart city as a smart service system: Human-computer interaction and smart city surveillance systems. Computers in Human Behavior, 124, 106923.

of implementing neurotechnology into security contexts raises more significant ethical, legal, and philosophical dilemmas. These processes that are used to create technologies that improve human performance and make them more resilient can be converted to weaponize them and find ways to modify or retrieve sensitive information in cognitive processes. Invasive interventions such as deep brain stimulation (DBS) implant have gone beyond treatment applications and have allowed the programmable alteration of neural activity. Added to machine learning and AI, these systems will be able to infer or modify mental states, perhaps even the process of decision-making. Therefore, it is no longer science fiction to imagine the possibility of other forces taking control over our thinking or impulses dictating our actions.

Why This Chapter Matters?

When neurotechnology in the field of cybersecurity merges into one, there is a new set of paradoxes, what we create to protect the mind can also become an enemy of what we are. The neural signals are not only data but the carriers of identity, autonomy, and dignity. Even with the extent of the dominance of AI and networked systems, nothing is as serious as regulating neural interfaces. Neurosecurity is a technological curve to be sure, but it is a moral crucible too. It requires immediate solutions in ethics and governance of an interdisciplinary nature. This will not be a question of whether but when we will make the decision that our mind needs protecting as much as our body and messages. It is now the time to influence that decision.

With the dawn of a new cyber-physical age, where security systems are no longer limited to defending digital infrastructure but now encompass the actual framework of our mind as well, ethical and legal aspects of neuro-integrated technologies can no longer be discussed as a secondary concern. The chapter discusses arguably the most important frontier of cybersecurity, the control of thoughts, identity, and mental integrity in a world where neural data will be transformed into a commodity and a weapon. Brain-based information is not mere data as are those that can be currently used in traditional types of biometrics, it is rather the substrate of the individual. The interest at stake here is essentially different. An infected server can be rejuvenated. A password stolen can be changed. Yet a captured idea, a forced emotionality, a neuro-profiled population, such is the stuff of which far-reaching doubts about autonomy, consent, and freedom are made, and upon which current policymaking frameworks are ill-prepared to act. It is through the following section that the reasoning behind viewing ethical and policy aspects of neurosecurity as anything but optional considerations on industry, academia, and the government will be elaborated. It demonstrates the necessity of urgency of cybersecurity experts, neuroscientists, policymakers, and engineers collaborating to co-design protection prior to the large-scale distribution of neuro-integrated systems.

Establishes the Moral Boundary of Next-Gen Security Systems

It frames the debate on where innovation has to give way to human dignity. In light of the increasing confluence between cyber and neurotechnology, it is an ineluctable imperative to precisely delineate the ethical mechanism governing the application of cerebral data, lest we should unwittingly experience the specter of mental surveillance and the perilous possibility of cognitive manipulation. Neuro-data, as opposed to regular data, deals with core elements of the human free will, emotions, and cognition. Analyzing ethical problems, for example, the involuntary neuro-monitoring or brainwaves-based profiling, this chapter will offer the readers the ethical frameworks they require to answer the question: where security stops, and intrusion starts.

Fills a Critical Policy Vacuum in a Rapidly Evolving Field

Although laws, for example, GDPR and HIPAA, were introduced based on the characteristics of the data collected in the 20th century (names, health records, or IP addresses), they immediately cannot serve the neuro-cognitive data-type data gathered using BCIs and cognitive biometrics. This chapter highlights the regulatory gaps that ring around the neural privacy, consent, and neuro-rights. It empowers cybersecurity experts, lawyers, and policymakers with the necessary resources to predict and develop governance mechanisms to unregulated neural interfaces, which makes it the key factor in shaping the legislation of tomorrow and corporate governance policies.

Prepares the Industry for Real-World Risk Scenarios

This chapter is a guide to developing effective defense systems by revealing real potential vectors, such as brain-jacking, adversarial attacks on EEG classifiers, and the harvesting of neuro-data by employers or state agencies. It makes ethics tangible by converting instances of ethical abstraction into a realizable risk-escape that enables developers, CISOs, and product architects to pre-determine the vulnerability that might occur due to insecure neuro-integrated platforms. Such learnings would be particularly important as both startups and tech giants would start integrating BCIs in wellness applications, authentication devices, and consumer electronics.

Promotes Global Awareness of Emerging Human Rights

It presents the theme of neuro-rights to the reader, this is a centerpiece to the concept of law and ethics, who will intervene in the rights of nerve and protect the mental privacy, the cognitive liberty, and the psychological continuity. It enables the reader to take part in transnational discussion on digital rights in the era of neuros by talking about the examples of pioneers such as the constitutional reform in Chile and the neuro-ethics principles produced by OECD. It is especially topical because corporations are becoming more global, and the issue of conflicting legal interpretations of the ownership of personal data on the nerve and the right to use it without this right also occurs.

Provides the Ethical Compass for Future Innovation

Cybersecurity is more what can be trusted, what should be shared, and what society cares about rather than firewall or code. With brain becoming a backdrop to computing systems as an input/output surface computing systems, innovation should be put through with democratic ethics. In this chapter, the author provides a guide to the approaches that can be used to develop neuro-integrated systems of the future with privacy-by-design and ethics-by-default principles to allow organizations to future-proof all their technologies without losing the trust of the population. It defines neuro-cybersecurity not as a technical but as a fundamentally human scientific discipline, in which ethics does not limit innovation but promotes sustainable innovation.

Although this section discussed the need to act upon ethical issues from perspectives of policies, it is important to ensure that the need is not merely theoretical, it is rather urgent, as established in the previous section. One of the most important factors is the sphere of neuro-privacy,

315

where the line between being safeguarded and infringed upon is drawn too thin. In order to see how the fundamental issues described above can play out in the real world, we will now consider one of the most important fields of ethical conflict, the presence, capture, and security of neural data and how developing neuro-technologies are shaking up our current understanding of digital privacy and the way in which the protection of the human mind should become the foundation on any security strategy that will survive the onset of technology.

The Neurotechnology Security Landscape

Before examining the breadth of the ethical and policy implications, it is important to review the present-day situation with the deployment of neurotechnology in security-related scenarios. Consumer-grade, non-invasive systems as well as invasive medical devices are both part of the landscape, which are finding more and more uses in security. Figure 8-1 shows the classification of the neurotechnology security landscape.

Figure 8-1. *Classification of Security Threat Landscape*

Non-invasive BCI Security Applications

Non-invasive brain–computer interfaces, most of which are founded upon electroencephalography (EEG), have quickly moved out of the research laboratory into security operations settings. They track neural activity using external sensors attached to the scalp and thus are appealing to scale to mass applications because they are non-surgical and relatively inexpensive. Table 8-1 reveals the non-invasive security applications along with associated risks.

Current Operational Deployments

Cognitive Authentication Systems: The use of brainwave patterns as authentication systems to gain access is on the rise in BFSI sector and Government bodies, in which brainwave patterns are used as user identifiers. Such systems generally ask people to engage in cognitive processing, for example, visualizing particular movements or reacting to visual cues, and their neural activity is measured and compared to templates stored in memory. In contrast to conventional biometrics, neural signatures can hardly be counterfeited and do not change when a person experiences various affective and physical conditions.[3]

---

[3] Gui, Q., Ruiz-Blondet, M. V., Laszlo, S., & Jin, Z. (2019). A survey on brain biometrics. *ACM Computing Surveys (CSUR)*, *51*(6), 1–38.

Real-Time Cognitive State Surveillance: Nuclear facilities and air traffic control facilities have started using systems to regularly check the cognitive load and attention levels of the operator. Such systems apply machine learning algorithms to identify patterns that are related to mental fatigue, distraction, or stress that may result in critical errors. In case of patterns of concern, the system may automatically raise alerts, redistribute workloads, or demand forced breaks.[4]

Threat Detection Enhancement: Other cybersecurity operations centers (SOCs) are testing out the concept of monitoring EEG signals on analysts in order to identify cognitive signatures of threat recognition. Studies have demonstrated that the brain has a certain neural reaction to the identification of aberrant patterns or possible danger even before one becomes aware of it.

Technical Architecture and Vulnerabilities

These systems are typically implemented in several different parts, including the hardware to collect the EEG signal, the real-time signal processing methods, machine learning classifiers to detect patterns, and integration APIs with existing security infrastructure. Nevertheless, this architecture presents several attack vectors, which can be used by adversaries. The nearest vulnerability is signal interception. EEG signals are commonly wirelessly transmitted between headsets and processing units and this provides a vulnerability to eavesdropping or signal injection

---

[4] Aricò, P., Borghini, G., Di Flumeri, G., Sciaraffa, N., & Babiloni, F. (2018). Passive BCI beyond the lab: current trends and future directions. *Physiological measurement*, *39*(8), 08TR02.

attacks. In addition, the machine learning models used to distinguish brain states are vulnerable to adversarial examples, well-constructed inputs to make the models mislabel them.[5]

Table 8-1. *Non-Invasive BCI Security Applications and Associated Risks*

Application	Technology	Security benefit	Vulnerability	Risk level
Neural authentication	EEG pattern recognition	Unforgeable identity verification	Signal interception, replay attacks	Medium-high
Cognitive load monitoring	Real-time EEG analysis	Prevents human error in critical systems	Privacy invasion, data harvesting	High
Threat recognition enhancement	P300 Event-related potentials	Faster threat detection	Adversarial pattern injection	Medium
Attention verification	Steady-state visual-evoked potentials	Ensures operator alertness	Coercive monitoring, discrimination	High
Deception detection	Multi-modal EEG analysis	Enhanced interrogation capabilities	False positives, cognitive liberty violations	Very high

---

[5] Meng, L., Jiang, X., Chen, X., Liu, W., Luo, H., & Wu, D. (2024). Adversarial filtering based evasion and backdoor attacks to EEG-based brain-computer interfaces. *Information Fusion*, 107, 102316.

Invasive Neural Implant Security Applications

A more advanced but more dangerous type of neurotechnology in security applications are invasive brain–computer interfaces, such as deep brain stimulation (DBS) devices, cortical electrode arrays, and neural prosthetics. Although they were mainly designed to work in a medical field, there is a growing trend of using such devices in security-critical domains because they provide a better signal quality and have a direct access to the neural signal. Table 8-2 reveals invasive BCI risk assessment matrix.

Current and Emerging Applications

Safe Neural Channels of Communication: Military and intelligence services are researching the use of implanted BCIs in developing communication channels that do not rely on standard digital network systems. Such neural mesh networks theoretically would offer unhackable communication between members of a team, because the signals would be conveyed directly through neural tissue instead of the electromagnetic spectrum.[6]

Cognitive Enhancement of Security Personnel: Research projects are undertaken to implement neural implants, and improve the cognitive abilities of cybersecurity workers, intelligence researchers, and military staff. These improvements may comprise better memory recall, time reduction in the pattern recognition, or better concentration and duration of attention on essential operations.[7]

---

[6] Kosal, M., & Putney, J. (2023). Neurotechnology and international security: Predicting commercial and military adoption of brain-computer interfaces (BCIs) in the United States and China. *Politics and the Life Sciences*, 42(1), 81–103.

[7] Osholake, S. F., Umealajekwu, C. H. I. N. E. M. E. L. U. M., Edohen, A. N. T. H. O. N. Y., Majekodunmi, A. O., & Evans-Anoruo, U. C. H. E. N. N. A. (2024). Human-AI Collaborative Security Operations: Optimizing SOC analyst cognitive load through augmented intelligence frameworks. *IRE Journals.* https://www.irejournals.com/formatedpaper/1709110.pdf.

Biometric Access Control: High-security facilities are even contemplating implantable neural devices which would offer round-the-clock biometric authentication. In contrast to external biometrics that are both spoofable and coercible, neural implants may theoretically offer continuous confirmation of a person's identity and mental condition.[8]

Critical Vulnerabilities and Attack Vectors

Invasive BCIs have significantly greater security threats as compared to those that are non-invasive. The idea of the brainjacking, or the unauthorized access to and control of neural implants is one of the gravest threats to cybersecurity that ever existed.

Wireless Protocol Exploitation: The majority of current neural implants rely on wireless communication to transmit data and also program the device. Such protocols frequently do not have strong encryption or authentication, enabling them to be intercepted, replayed, or controlled with unauthorized commands. Effective brainjacking attacks might cause the brain stimulation pattern to change, which may cause the mood, motor control, or cognitive ability to change.[9]

Firmware and Software Vulnerabilities: Neural implants are based on embedded software and firmware which can have security vulnerabilities. These systems, unlike regular medical equipment, tend to have scarce update functionalities, so that known vulnerabilities could be exploited throughout the lifetime of the equipment.

---

[8] Gudala, L., Reddy, A. K., Sadhu, A. K. R., & Venkataramanan, S. (2022). Leveraging biometric authentication and blockchain technology for enhanced security in identity and access management systems. *Journal of Artificial Intelligence Research*, 2(2), 21–50.

[9] Kritika, E. (2025). Brainjacking: The Cybersecurity Nightmare of the Future.

Physical Access Attacks: The surgical nature of implantation creates additional security considerations. The malicious actors who have physical access to patients have possible chances of installing compromised devices or altering existing implants at some time during medical procedures.

Table 8-2. *Invasive BCI Security Risk Assessment Matrix*

Device type	Primary function	Wireless protocols	Encryption status	Attack complexity	Potential impact
DBS implants	motor/mood control	Bluetooth, proprietary RF	Often unencrypted	Medium	Severe (motor/cognitive dysfunction)
Cortical arrays	Motor/sensory prosthetics	Wi-Fi, Bluetooth	Variable	High	High (device malfunction, data theft)
Neural dust	Distributed monitoring	Ultrasonic, RF	Minimal	Very High	Medium (privacy violation)
Cochlear Implants	Hearing restoration	Bluetooth, RF	Basic	Medium	Medium (hearing disruption, eavesdropping)
Retinal implants	Vision restoration	Infrared, RF	Variable	High	Medium (vision disruption, data access)

The Consumer Neurotechnology Ecosystem

The consumer neurotech market has been a boom market and products are being sold to aid meditation, gaming, productivity, and also wellness monitoring. Although people use these gadgets, which are not as sophisticated as medical-grade systems, their high usage poses new security issues and ethical issues. Table 8-3 focuses on the consumer neurotechnology security analysis.

Market Analysis and Security Implications

EEG headsets that monitor the consumers like Muse, NeuroSky, and Emotiv companies are increasingly part of the productivity monitoring system in the work place. Primarily, these devices were aimed at the meditative and brain-training processes, but can be reused to observe the level of employee attention, emotional conditions, and the cognitive performance. Medical device control and regulation on these products is still lacking, and it is common that they possess minimal security protection and ambiguous data management procedures.

Data Collection and Privacy: Consumer neurotechnology devices normally gather and send neural data to cloud-based systems to process and analyze. This information usually contains not only raw EEG but also calculated data on attention, meditation, stress rates, and moods. The services of these platforms often provide wide scopes of rights to use and analyze this information, which leaves the possibility of using this information secondarily in an unintended manner by users.[10]

---

[10] Susser, D., & Cabrera, L. Y. (2024). Brain data in context: Are new rights the way to mental and brain privacy?. *AJOB neuroscience*, *15*(2), 122-133.

Risks of Third-Party Integration: There are a lot of consumer BCI applications that share data with other services and platforms, which form complex relationships. To illustrate, meditation application may send attention data to a productivity tool that could be viewed by workplace surveillance cameras.

Regulatory Gaps in Consumer Neurotechnology

Consumer neurotechnology devices are classified in a way that poses major regulatory blind spots. Since such devices are sold as wellness and entertainment (as opposed to medical) devices, they are generally not subject to medical device regulations, such as FDA regulation in the United States or the Medical Device Regulation (MDR) in Europe. Such a regulatory gap entails

- Protection standards of data can be less than that of medical equipment.

- Security requirements are not imperative.

- The user might not get the necessary information regarding the data collection and usage.

- Algorithms development and validation may have little control.

Table 8-3. Consumer Neurotechnology Security Analysis

Device category	Primary use cases	Data collected	Regulatory status	Security standards	Privacy protections
Meditation headsets	Mindfulness, stress reduction	EEG, attention metrics	Unregulated wellness device	Voluntary industry standards	Limited, varies by vendor
Gaming BCIs	Entertainment, gaming control	Motor imagery, visual attention	Gaming/ entertainment device	No specific requirements	Consumer protection laws only
Sleep monitoring	Sleep quality, dream analysis	Sleep stage EEG, movement	Wellness/fitness device	FTC guidelines	Privacy policy dependent
Productivity tools	Focus enhancement, workflow	Attention, cognitive load	Workplace technology	No neural-specific standards	Employee privacy laws vary
Neurofeedback training	Cognitive enhancement	Real-time EEG, performance	Training/ educational tool	Professional certification varies	

Emerging Hybrid Security Architectures

The overlap of various neurotechnology methods is establishing mixed security architectures that can integrate the advantages of diverse neural interfaces and that may increase the risks. These systems are the future of neuro-integrated security as well as the most difficult ethical and technical issues.

Multi-Modal Neural Authentication: State-of-the-art security systems have started to integrate several neural signals, EEG, fNIRS (functional near-infrared spectroscopy), and eye tracking, to develop more secure and harder-to-spoof authentication. Although this would enhance security, it would also cause a massive proliferation of the volume of neural data gathered as well as increase risks of breach of privacy.

Adaptive Neural Security Systems: It is building machine learning algorithms which can derive and evolve to specific neural patterns as individuals use them and this could enhance security and user experience. Yet, these adaptive systems give a reason to be concerned with behavioral modification and how the systems may shape user behavior in subtle but significant ways. The neurotechnology applications and architectures described above reveal that there is one essential feature that can be identified by the difference between neural security and conventional cybersecurity: virtually every useful application has an equivalent risk of abuse. Table 8-4 demonstrates the dual protective and exploitative use of the same technologies.

Table 8-4. *Dual-Use Capabilities of Neurotechnology in Security Contexts*

Neurotechnology application	Beneficial use case	Potentially abusive scenario	Ethical concern
Cognitive biometric systems	Enhances authentication via brainwave signatures	Profiling users based on thought/ emotion patterns	Cognitive liberty and privacy
Fatigue detection BCIs	Prevents errors in high-risk environments	Used for micromanagement or penalizing neurodivergence	Consent and fairness
Neurofeedback for training	Improves performance and attention in SOC teams	Manipulates behavior for organizational conformity	Behavioral autonomy
Brain-state monitoring	Supports continuous user authentication	Employer surveillance of worker thoughts or emotions	Intrusion into mental privacy
Brain–computer interfaces	Assists disabled users with secure communication	Coercive use in interrogation or military interrogation	Violation of free will

These two-purpose uses are not some hypothetical possibilities but really exist that these organizations implementing neural security systems have to face. It is important to understand these contradictions first before exploring the way in which technical capabilities are defeating ethical frameworks. The potential of this growing terrain is huge. With the transition of neurotechnology out of specialized medical use and into common security installations, an ethical and policy framework encompassing such systems has to rapidly adapt to face ethical issues never before witnessed, such as threats to privacy, autonomy, and human dignity.

The Convergence Crisis: When Technical Capabilities Outpace Ethical Frameworks

The growing and fast-paced implementation of neurotechnology, with respect to consumer, medical, and security, described above has led to a convergence crisis wherein the technical capacity is outpacing our ethical and legal frameworks. This super speed of technology implies that machines which can read, comprehend, and possibly manipulate the human mind are being implemented in the absence of proper protection or control. The security applications outlined in this section mean that we no longer have to do with hypothetical scenarios. EEG-based authentication systems are now analyzing neural signatures in real time, work-based surveillance is now continuously analyzing cognitive states, and invasive neural implants are now wireless-enabled devices that are susceptible to being attacked from a distance. All of these changes bring us one step closer to the day when the human mind will be not only the most important security token, but the most valuable target of villainous forces. It has led to what researchers have dubbed as the neo-neural security paradox in that the same technologies poised to revolutionize cybersecurity by making authentication unforgeable and detecting threats instantly are the very same technologies that are threatening to destroy the bedrocks of human autonomy and privacy. The above-discussed technical capabilities are not of a future scenario of implementation; they are current realities being put to operation in high stakes settings where the effects of both security breaches and privacy invasions may be devastating.

Indeed, researchers, ethicists, suggest that the brain will be the last bastion of privacy and poses a critical concern of mental autonomy and cognitive liberty. Tom Oxley and other neurosurgeons sound a warning that without proper protection, BCIs would help become a form of oppression instead of freedom. In her brilliant book, *The Battle for Your Brain* (2023),[11] Farahany warns that one can expect a future in which the employers, governments, or the corporations may be permitted to "harvest" the neural data in the name of productivity optimization or national security. This would essentially twist the concept of surveillance as our thoughts inside our heads would be accessible to others. The two faces of neuro-integrated security are hard to exaggerate. On the one hand, BCIs will be able to intercept the insider threats through detecting emotional or deception anomalies. And on the other hand, they could easily be used to profile the user psychologically, enforce compliance or forestall dissent. They can be easily used to psychologically profile users, make them obedient, or resist before the dissident. These abilities question the established democratic principles of freedom of thought and expression. There is a very thin line between enhancement and coercion, protection and manipulation.

What is more, the absence of regulation and diversion of industry standards increases the risk. A large number of neurotech products fall into the grey areas of regulation in that they are not considered medical devices and thus not subject to rigorous control.[12] In an attempt to get commercially viable BCI systems, companies are in a race to innovate each other out and this tends to make the ethical and legal aspects of the process to take a back seat. Such an open border raises severe

---

[11] Farahany, N. A. (2023). The battle for your brain: defending the right to think freely in the age of neurotechnology. St. Martin's Press.

[12] https://cfg.eu/neurotech-market-atlas/

consequences to human rights, psychological privacy, and the sense of individual agency. Overall, the possible life of neuro-integrated security is very unique and defines the future in an attractive way but must be negotiated cautiously. Being used through a positive lens, it makes users more powerful, cyber defense is provided, and human reasoning is boosted. With a cynical connotation, it is the most extreme invasion, a digital colonization of the human mind. The big problem, as this chapter shall discuss, is not the ability to do it technologically but the ability to show ethical restraint, legal foresight, and planned persistence in upholding the sanctity of human thoughts in the era of neural computers.

The neurotechnology ecosystem is rapidly developing, including invasive and non-invasive systems. Along with this expansion, there is now a highly sophisticated terrain of hazards: some technical, some moral, and most of them unregulated. The nature of these risks should be clarified with the process of understanding the underlying aspects of how BCIs work and the hazards that come with their application by both good and bad actors.[13] Electroencephalography (EEG) type of non-invasive BCI has been infiltrated into the consumer market. It has been possible to use these headsets to identify brainwave patterns meaning, one is aware or paying attention or is in a certain emotional state or can detect a certain stimuli. Evoked-potential interface, which is represented specifically by the P300 speller has demonstrated that, an individual can use his brain and cause some external systems to respond by simply thinking. But a direct threat, wherein a method is used in which noise is introduced into input signals to deceive machine learning models. Studies such as that by Meng et al. (2024) have revealed that imperceptible variations in the EEG

---

[13] King, B. J., Read, G. J., & Salmon, P. M. (2025). Prospectively identifying risks and controls for advanced brain-computer interfaces: A Networked Hazard Analysis and Risk Management System (Net-HARMS) approach. Applied Ergonomics, 122, 104382.

input signal may cause high misclassification levels within the BCI system, which will result in unintended outputs, for example, the commencement of command or modification of user profile.[14]

The danger is even more severe in the sphere of invasive BCIs. Neurology and psychiatry are increasingly applying devices such as deep brain stimulators (DBS) or cortical implants. Moreover, these implants, as life-saving ones, are also vulnerable to cyber-physical attacks. The study by Kritika (2025) came up with the concept of brainjacking,[15] which refers to instances when wireless communication protocols might be taken advantage of by malicious hackers to interfere with or affect neural stimulation. These intrusions may cause changes in moods, motor retardation, or even misery. The fact that these devices are usually not covered by cryptographic protection or embedded with intrusion detection approaches means that they represent easy portals to the human nervous system. There is another type of threat that is caused by passive neurodata collection. Some methods (e.g., rapid serial visual presentation [RSVP])[16] are able to retrieve personal knowledge or intentions even in the absence of any conscious user participation. This is supported by research that has been conducted in which PIN codes, names and even political leaning have been drawn out by use of subliminal influence and carrying out the technique on P300 responses. Passive neurodata harvesting is an intimidating surveillance device when united with AI-based inference models.

---

[14] Meng, L., Jiang, X., Chen, X., Liu, W., Luo, H., & Wu, D. (2024). Adversarial filtering based evasion and backdoor attacks to EEG-based brain-computer interfaces. *Information Fusion*, *107*, 102316.

[15] Kritika, E. (2025). Brainjacking: The Cybersecurity Nightmare of the Future.

[16] https://www.labvanced.com/content/learn/en/walkthroughs/2021-08-RSVP-walkthrough/

BCI applications ecosystem is growing to incorporate emotion recognition, state of cognitive workload monitoring, lies detection, and even an instance of neurogaming. All these spheres bring about new concerns as far as security and ethical vulnerabilities are concerned. As an example, coercive application of a system detecting lies using neurodata would be possible in a courtroom or on the job. On the same note, behavioral changes occurring involuntarily due to training system using neurofeedback may take place.

Why Governance Must Outpace Innovation?

With neuro-integrated systems increasing in their breadth, depth, and rollout, a lack of bespoke governance frameworks is becoming a veritable threat. Unlike any other category of digital data, neurodata is biological, identifiable as unique, and intensely personal in nature. Whereas regime cybersecurity is concerned with passwords, files, and networks, neuro-cybersecurity is about safeguarding thoughts, emotions, cognitive patterns, and behavioral impulses. Such a difference will demand a whole new set of ethical, legal, and policy regimes to deal with that specificity and sensitivity of neural information.

First, the underlying issue relates to definition. Neural data is not explicitly defined as part of regulatory frameworks in the vast majority of jurisdictions. EEG signals recorded by non-medical devices (e.g., game or wellness headset) would in many contexts not be considered as biometric data or health data under the GDPR. This forms a paradox since the closest information concerning data is actual time thinking and attention which can be collected by business organizations with minimum regulation. With respect to the datasets of cognitive states, important is that Ienca and Haselager (2016) point out the threat of brain leakage: the recording, transmission, and analysis of data about the states of the cognitive processes without the user even being aware of it or agreeing to it.

Second is the fact that technological developments are superseding ethical provisions. Researchers and corporations are now getting the ability to decode the intentions of the user or the emotions of an individual in near-real time. Neuroadaptive systems are being created to manipulate digital content depending on brain patterns, usually through reinforcement learning to pre-determine or influence their behavior. These developments pose a danger of forming feedback loops in which the system monitors not only the perceived but also the process of cognition – all while the line between personalization and manipulation collapses.

According to Williamson (2018), the neural systems without clear demarcations have the potential to turn into active controls of behavior rather than passive tools.[17] Third, the governance gap increases the imbalances of power and knowledge. Firms with control of neurotechnology infrastructure along with government institutions such as corporations and state agencies possess the leverage to have disproportionate power. Examples of some military uses involve the monitoring of pilots to check their cognitive fatigue, the use of brains in targeting their themes, as well as by use in detecting lies during questioning. Table 8-5 illustrates the global governance gaps existent for the regulation and control of neural devices.

---

[17] Williamson, B. (2018). Brain Data: Scanning, Scraping and Sculpting the Plastic Learning Brain Through Neurotechnology. *Postdigital Science and Education*, *1*(1), 65–86. https://doi.org/10.1007/s42438-018-0008-5

Table 8-5. *Comparative Governance Gaps in Global*
Neurosecurity Policy

Region/ country	Status of neurotechnology legislation	Recognized rights or frameworks	Identified gaps
United States	Fragmented: HIPAA covers some medical neurodata	No recognition of neurorights	Consumer BCI data unprotected
European Union	GDPR covers biometric data	No explicit neurodata clause	Neuro wellness apps fall outside regulation
Chile	Constitutional neurorights recognized	Psychological continuity, mental privacy laws	Enforcement and implementation mechanisms pending
China	Aggressive neurotech deployment	No public protections articulated	Government access to neural data not limited
Global (OECD/ UNESCO)	Draft ethical frameworks	OECD Principles on Responsible Neurotech	Non-binding, lacks enforcement or harmonization

In the absence of legally enforceable ethical limits, they provide means of extracting confessions, or enforcing conformity, or deterring dissent. With the extension into the domain of cognitive states as opposed to behavioral metadata, the idea of surveillance capitalism expressed by Zuboff can be found even more troubling. As a reaction to this, there have been pioneering initiatives. Chile was the first to establish the concept of a neuroright in its national constitution to protect the privilege of mental privacy, psychological continuity, and free will.[18] UNESCO and the OECD are elaborating policy frameworks to make certain that the development of neurotechnology will be in consistency with concepts of human rights. The Neurorights Foundation supports the view that people need to be guaranteed five basic rights – mental privacy, identity security, cognitive freedom, fair access to enhancements, and immunity to prejudice and discrimination. They are, however, aspirational in the majority of countries.

The complexity is further compounded by the fact that neurotech industry is at length growing into a global business venture. Electronic devices will be produced in one state, information might be opened in a different state, and the users might also be distributed into different countries. This creates controversial issues concerning transnational enforcement and harmonization of law and international standards and protection of data. In absence of universal agreement, the users can be subjected to lesser protection based on location or nationality. Finally, neuro-integrated security should not be able to out-innovate good governance and in fact should be anticipated. This will mean revision of legal definitions, the creation of new oversight mechanisms (Guidance Boards such as Neuroethics Review Boards), the implementation of transparency provisions and the incorporation of rights-respectful design principles. Left unregulated, it is not only that the brain will become the frontier of data extraction – it is also a possibility that the brain will become the frontier of autonomy as well.

Privacy in the Age of Neuro-Surveillance

The introduction of neuro-integrated systems has changed the nexus of the digital age of what it means to be in privacy. Conventional models of cybersecurity were built to secure data that are intentionally created by

---

[18] Cornejo-Plaza, I. (2023). Chilean neurorights legislation and its relevance for mental health: Criticisms and outlook. *Salud mental, 46*(5), 269–273.

the user-base, such as emails, passwords, social media posts, biometrics fingerprints. But a neuroprivacy brings an entirely new problem; how to protect the information that is not knowingly generated, even voluntarily shared. These neural data encompass everything in the level of attention, emotional reactions, recollection, and subconscious realization as all these emerge innocently in the brain and indicate the state of cognitive functioning that is highly personal and uniquely identifiable.

Defining Neuroprivacy: Identity at the Neural Layer

Neuroprivacy should be understood as the freedom of people to regulate the gathering, processing, and analysis of their neural transmission. Such neural signals can be obtained in the laboratory with methods like electroencephalography (EEG), functional near-infrared spectroscopy (fNIRS), magnetoencephalography (MEG), or invasive neuro-implants, and they have valuable biometric, behavioral, and cognitive information. In an event that neurotechnology is developed further, these signals are more often handled as a sensitive identity vector, or in some cases, a so-called neural fingerprint.[19] Similar to DNA, neural signatures provide uniqueness to a person and can be recognized to authenticate a person or provide a guess about their psychological nature. This unique identification capability creates what researchers call the neural fingerprint paradox, a fundamental tension between security benefits and irreversible privacy risks.

---

[19] George, A. S. (2024). Protecting Brain Privacy in the Age of Neurotechnology: Policy Responses and Remaining Challenges. *Partners Universal Innovative Research Publication*, *2*(5), 18–33.

The Neural Fingerprint Paradox

Neural signatures pose the biggest paradox in identity security: they provide unparalleled levels of authentication with something as well as introduce irreversible privacy risks. In contrast to conventional biometric markers, neural patterns cannot be altered, cancelled, or modified in case of compromise but send much more personal data regarding the cognitive and emotional conditions of the individual. The patterns of neural activity are individual in a striking way, as the result of a complicated interaction of the genetic factors, developmental history, and acquired cognitive strategies. Table 8-6 contrasts the difference between conventional biometrics such as fingerprints, facial recognition and voice patterns to neural signatures, a prevalent advancement Studies have established that EEGs are as unique as fingerprints, and neural patterns of people do not change significantly with various emotional arousal levels, physical health, and several decades of aging. Neural biometrics are extremely stable and that is why they are quite useful in authentication. Nonetheless, the same permanence which makes neural signatures useful in the security area poses unparalleled threats. Workarounds to traditional biometrics can be resolved by technology, facial recognition can be modified to detect spoofed pictures, fingerprint readers can be modified to include facets of liveness detection, but neural patterns cannot be modified without modifying brain structure or functionality. Once a neural signature is damaged, the person has no option of equivalent remedy to a failed password or identification card. The neural patterns which constitute their cognitive identity become indefinitely susceptible to

- Spoofing with neural signature records
- Cognitive profile theft-based behavioral prediction
- Tracking over time of various systems and contexts
- Psychological manipulation in accordance with familiar responses patterns

This unchangeability transforms data breaches in neural data to a security breach with life-long consequences.

Table 8-6. *Comparative Analysis of Biometric Security Methods*

Characteristic	Fingerprints	Facial recognition	Voice patterns	Neural signatures
Uniqueness	High	Medium-High	Medium	Very High
Stability over time	High	Medium (aging effects)	Medium (health/ age changes)	Very high
Difficulty to forge	Medium (silicone replicas)	Low (photos/ deepfakes)	Low (voice synthesis)	Very high
Data sensitivity	Low (surface feature)	Medium (physical appearance)	Medium (speech patterns)	Extreme (cognitive states)
Revocability	Impossible	Impossible	Impossible	Impossible
Involuntary generation	No	No	No	Yes (continuous)
Information leakage	Minimal	Some (demographics)	Some (health, emotion)	Extensive (thoughts, emotions, memories)
Legal protection status	Well-established	Emerging frameworks	Basic protections	Largely unregulated
Compromise recovery	Difficult	Difficult	Difficult	Impossible
Secondary data extraction	Limited	Moderate	Moderate	Extensive
Coercive collection risk	Low	Medium	Low	Very high

Neural signatures contrast radically with the conventional biometrics in information density. Whereas, a fingerprint only displays the superficial ridge patterns, neural activity provides information in layers pertaining to

Immediate Cognitive States: Level of Attention, Emotional valence, and Stress indicators and cognitive load that reflects the current mental state.

Learned Associations: Involuntary recognition patterns of neuronal reaction to particular stimuli can be used to detect personal association, political orientation, traumatic memories, and cultural identification.

Cognitive Capabilities: The speed of processing, the ability to remember, decision-making style, and the pattern of learning that may be discriminatory or manipulative.

Physiological Indicators: Sleep deprivation, substance use, neurological conditions, and medication effects that manifest in neural signal characteristics.

Such a density of information implies that neural authentication systems invariably operate as all-encompassing cognitive surveillance platforms, whether they are used in that manner or not.

The long-term security risks posed by the permanence and richness of neural signatures are unprecedented, and reach deep into long-term contexts that go way beyond the authentication situation at hand:

Lifetime Vulnerability Exposure: After neural patterns have been scanned and mapped, they can be used throughout the life of the individual. Contrary to conventional credentials which may be revoked or updated, a breached neural signature leaves an irreparable security gap which can never be addressed by using the traditional methods of cybersecurity.

Cross-Context Tracking and Correlation: Neural signatures make it possible to follow persons through systems, organizations, and time. The neural pattern of an individual recorded in a monitoring system in a work environment may be linked to authentication data on financial services, healthcare systems, or government databases to form a comprehensive behavior profile without the person's consent or even awareness.

Predictive Profiling and Discrimination: The use of long-term neural data collection allows predictive models of the behavior, performance, and decision-making of a person. The models may be used in

- Cognitive performance prediction employment.

- Neural health indicator-based insurance risk measurement

- Cognitive and emotional pattern-based social credit scoring

- Neural response neural profiling of politics

The neural signatures also have issues of cognitive improvement and authenticity. With brain–computer interfaces achieving the ability to alter cognitive performance, one wonders whether the improvement of neural patterns can be viewed as a legitimate expression of the identity of a person. When a person relies on neural enhancement technologies to enhance memory, attention, or emotional regulation, the neural patterns of their base may transform forever. This begs complicated questions:

- Is it appropriate that security systems be authenticated of the natural or enhanced version of a person?

- What are the processes of authentication that organizations go through when employees are subjected to cognitive enhancement?

- What happens to long-term authentication systems when neural modification becomes commonplace?

Contrary to the old biometrics that are unchanged by external forces, neural patterns can change as a result of medical therapy, cognitive training, or enhancement technology. This poses continuity authentication issues that may lock individuals out of important systems when their neural signatures change to levels they are not recognized by. The issue of the neural fingerprint paradox can be resolved by adopting new technical and policy solutions based on the principle of the basic distinction between neural and traditional biometric data:

Distributed Neural Authentication: Systems might maintain encrypted partial patterns at multiple secure sites rather than full neural signatures, so it is impossible to reconstruct full signatures even in the event that individual components are destroyed.

Windows of Temporal Authentication: Introduce authentication mode that uses dynamic neural responses to dynamically generated challenges as opposed to pattern matching which is less sensitive to stolen neural signatures.

Anonymization and Differential Privacy: Use the mode of advanced anonymization techniques specifically created to handle neural data to introduce mathematical noise that maintains the utility of authentication but safeguards cognitive privacy.

Versioning of Neural Signatures: Design systems that are able to support incremental neural patterns changes with age, or age-related improvements or medical intervention without compromising security integrity.

Neural fingerprint paradox is perhaps the most complicated problem in neuro-integrated security, where a close trade-off has to be made between the gains of authentication and the irreversible loss of privacy. Neural data, unlike passwords, or even some of the most traditional forms of biometric markers, like fingerprints or retina scans, are non-consensual to generate. These signals are involuntarily and unendingly produced by the brain. These emissions can be recorded by advanced neurotechnologies in which case the recording is passive, especially in high-surveillance grounds such as military bases, business productivity surveillance programs, and intelligence applications. This presents a rather troubling problem of privacy paradox wherein the person does not plan to transmit these signals; collection, analysis, and processing of these signals done outside of their knowing with or without their consent. The consequences are far reaching. Neural data bears not only the physiological signals but also may manifest itself in terms of cognitive states which could be twofold: they might be a manifestation of attention, fatigue, anxiety, or deception, as well as internal responses to outer stimuli. They have demonstrated that there is a possibility to decode information like PIN numbers, emotional reactions, preferences, or even recognition of certain stimuli using profiling strategies founded on EEG or RSVP (Rapid Serial Visual Presentation) paradigm models.[20] By collecting and mining such data over time, such signals can be used to build neuro-behavioral dossiers of people, effectively exposing their inner mental world to surveillance, profiling, or even manipulation.

Without exhaustive legal safeguards or ethical monitoring, these abilities can be used to the advantage of various agents. In the workplace, employers may apply neural profiling to idealistic alignment or intellectual aptitudes. Insurance companies may want to divide people into brain predispositions. Police would also be able to use brainwave detectors in interrogating people. It is then possible that in even darker applications, authoritarian governments might work the passive BCIs into a surveillance design in order to sniff out dissension or to impose conformity. Hence, neuroprivacy can never be an extension of digital privacy but its development. It claims a reinvention of data protecting paradigms, civil liberties, and ethical responsibility in the era of neural computation. In the absence of strong mechanisms of protection, what we are facing now is the

---

[20] Alsharif, A. H., & Isa, S. M. (2025). Electroencephalography studies on marketing stimuli: A literature review and future research agenda. *International Journal of Consumer Studies*, *49*(1), e70015.

tendency to switch to not only surveillance capitalism but to the so-called surveillance cognition, when even our unspoken thoughts would cease to be a secret.

The Risk of Involuntary Neurodata Collection

The ability to gather data without the active engagement of the user is arguably the most threatening characteristic of new neurotechnologies. Passive EEG systems are able to pick up the brain activity when exposed to visual stimuli (e.g., logos, faces, questions) and that can be used to determine recognition without user action requiring any motor behavior. Referred to as P300-based deception detection, the method takes advantage of involuntary brain reaction to known stimuli, the so-called "aha" effect. This can be identified in real-time to conclude on prior knowledge of a particular information in a person. Though still in its early stages as a research tool, the P300-related paradigm has already been experimentally applied in the police sciences to deduce the existence of information that is not being revealed, which is the red flag about how this knowledge can be/would be used in the wrong way.[21] Beyond any criminal justice uses, a form of passive neurodata collection is insidiously becoming the new normal in offices, schools and even consumer devices. Most wearable EEG headsets are sold as wellness devices to assist with enhancing productivity, stress reducing, and improving focus, but the algorithms built into them increasingly have the ability to decode mental states.[22] They have the ability to track changes in attention, cognitive

---

[21] Turnip, A., Amri, M. F., Fakrurroja, H., Simbolon, A. I., Suhendra, M. A., & Kusumandari, D. E. (2017, February). Deception detection of EEG-P300 component classified by SVM method. In *Proceedings of the 6th international conference on software and computer applications* (pp. 299–303).

[22] Traunmuller, P., Jahanjoo, A., Khooyooz, S., Aminifar, A., & TaheriNejad, N. (2024). Wearable Healthcare Devices for Monitoring Stress and Attention Level in Workplace Environments. *arXiv preprint arXiv:2406.05813*.

fatigue, emotional arousal, and ability to be distracted with remarkable precision. There often is this kind of monitoring which takes place without full disclosure and then the user or the person subjected to the surveillance can only be able to give substantial consent especially in environments like workplaces or in school. This raises a situation of ambient neuro-surveillance, in which thinking conditions are always recorded and assessed in the background. Such data may, over time, be used to build neurobehavioral profiles upon which managerial actions may be based, or recruitment channels, or even assessment of schools and universities. Consent is performative and coercive under such conditions as the subject lacks the knowledge of the granularity, persistence, or interpretive scope of data collection. That emphasizes the fears of neuro-discrimination, algorithm bias, and the loss of cognitive freedom in the daily settings.

Current Regulatory Landscape and Critical Gaps

The legal landscape of neurotechnology use in security-related aspects is poorly developed and inconsistent, as the majority of jurisdictions have no direct frameworks governing neural data protection. This section will look at the present position of the regulation of neurotechnology around the world, the identification of key gaps in regulation, and the dissection of the enforcement issues in respect of policymakers and industry players.

Global Policy Comparison Matrix

The international landscape of neurotechnology regulation reveals significant disparities in approach, scope, and implementation. Although certain jurisdictions are actively working on the creation of neural-specific protections, the majority of them still use already existing data protection frameworks, which were never created with neural data in mind.

Table 8-7 illustrates a stark reality; the world's regulatory systems have systematically failed to respond to the emergence of technologies with the potential to access and analyze human consciousness. The validated data reveals critical patterns which will require immediate identification and action.

Table 8-7. *Comprehensive Global Neurotechnology Regulatory Landscape Analysis*

Jurisdiction	Legal Framework Status	Regulatory Authority	Neural Data Classification	Medical Device Oversight	Consumer Device Regulation	Enforcement Mechanism	Recent Developments	Key Gaps
United States	No federal neurorights legislation	FDA (medical devices), FTC (consumer protection)	HIPAA covers medical neural data only	FDA oversight for implantable BCIs	No specific neural data regulation	FDA medical device violations, FTC deceptive practices	Limited federal neural regulation development	Consumer BCI data unprotected; workplace monitoring unregulated
European Union	No explicit neurorights; GDPR framework	EDPB, national data protection authorities	GDPR Article 9 special category biometric data	Medical Device Regulation (MDR) for implantable devices	GDPR applies to neural data processing	GDPR penalties up to 4% global revenue	Ongoing guidance development for neurotechnology	Implementation guidance still developing
Chile	Constitutional Amendment signed October 25, 2021	Constitutional Court; Congress developing legislation	All neural data constitutionally protected	Medical device regulation through ISP	Constitutional protections apply to all devices	Constitutional Court review	Supreme Court neurorights precedents (2023-2024)	Implementation mechanisms under development
Brazil	LGPD framework; no neurorights legislation	ANPD (National Data Protection Authority)	LGPD Article 5 sensitive biometric data	ANVISA medical device regulation	LGPD protections apply to consumer devices	ANPD enforcement, fines up to 2% revenue	Claims about June 2025 consultation	Consumer device enforcement limited
Canada	No neurorights framework; PIPEDA	Privacy Commissioner, Health Canada	Personal information under PIPEDA	Health Canada medical device licensing	PIPEDA $3M revenue threshold	Privacy Commissioner recommendations	AIDA under development, timeline unclear	Limited enforcement; provincial variations
China	No public neurorights framework	Multiple agencies, unclear authority	Classification not publicly disclosed	NMPA medical device approval	Consumer regulation unclear	State enforcement, limited transparency	Government neurotechnology investment	Citizen protections largely absent
International	UNESCO ethics framework	UNESCO (guidance only)	Framework classifies neural data as requiring protection	No regulatory authority	Recommendations only	No enforcement mechanisms	Recommendation adoption scheduled November 2025	Non-binding, national implementation dependent

The Isolation of Chile As a Constitutional Shield

A major conclusion is that Chile is the only jurisdiction with constitutional-level data protection for neural data. Mental integrity and neural data are explicitly mentioned in the Chilean Constitutional Amendment Law No. 21.383, of October 25, 2021, which is the result of a fundamental recognition that data contained in the brain deserves constitutional, rather than legislative, protection. This isolation is deeply troubling: while a small nation acknowledges neural data as involving the essence of human dignity, leading economies such as the United States, China, and large parts of the developed world, consider consciousness-derived information as ordinary commercial data under little regulation.

Global Consumer Protection Failure

The analysis reveals that consumer neurotechnology devices are running without sufficient protection in all the major jurisdictions except Chile. This is a worldwide regulatory abdication with millions of users losing control of intimate cognitive data via meditation apps, gaming interfaces, and wellness devices without meaningful protections. While, in theory, the GDPR framework of the European Union includes neural data as a form of biometric data, no specific implementation guidelines for neurotechnology applications have been provided yet. The United States doesn't offer any federal protection for consumer neural data at all, while other major economies are just as fast to follow suit.

Workplace Neural Surveillance in a Legal Void

Perhaps, most frightening is the fact that there are no adequate workplace protections for neural monitoring in any country on Earth. Even jurisdictions with robust general data protection frameworks do not address the coercive nature of employment-based neural monitoring. This gives rise to a global vulnerable class of employees whose thoughts, feelings, and cognitive states can be monitored as a prerequisite of employment without any meaningful consent or safeguards.

Lack of International Coordination

UNESCO's Recommendation on Ethics of Neurotechnology, which will be adopted in November 2025, is the most far-reaching international attempt to provide standards for the protection of neural data. However, this framework will be non-binding and fully reliant on national implementation by the same governments who have so far failed to protect neural privacy. The lack of binding international standards allows regulatory arbitrage, where companies process neural data in the jurisdictions with few protections while providing services to users all over the world.

Medical vs. Consumer Lookup Abuse

It shows that medical versus consumer device categorization is being systematically exploited to gain regulatory exemption. To avoid medical device regulations, companies promote the same neural interface hardware for "wellness" or "entertainment" when in fact they are gathering the same intimate neural data that would elicit increased protections for medical applications. This performance manipulation makes widespread neural surveillance possible in the name of consumer welfare, and is an inherent failure of regulatory classification schemes.

The Neural Rights Imperative

Humanity is confronted with a challenge to intellectual freedom and to mental autonomy of unexampled character. The intersection of cutting-edge neurotechnology and weak governance structures has set the stage for total neural surveillance with the potential to fundamentally change the fabric of human freedom and democracy.

The Moment of Irreversible Decision

Neural surveillance technologies are fundamentally different from all previous privacy threats as it reaches into the substrate of consciousness itself. Once these systems become firmly embedded within economic, educational, and social infrastructure, they become virtually impossible to eliminate or reverse. The choices of the coming months will help ensure that neurotechnology is a means of human flourishing or the ultimate instrument of cognitive control.

Constitutional Protection As Minimum Standard

Chile's constitutional model shows that strong neural data protection can be achieved when governments acknowledge the fundamental rights implications of neurotechnology. The gap between the comprehensive protections Chile has offered and the gaps in other jurisdictions' responses highlights that legislative strategies alone cannot provide a way to cope with neural data's challenge to human autonomy. Neural data protection must be implemented at the constitutional level because it is a question of the essence of human dignity, the privacy of thought itself. In democratic societies, it should be recognized that cognitive liberty is a fundamental right in the same league as freedom of speech, assembly, and religion.

The Democratic Governance Challenge

The regulatory failures that are documented in this chapter are not simply technical policy issues – they reflect a fundamental challenge to democratic governance in the digital age. Technologies with reading and possibly modulating human thoughts raise existential questions about the autonomy and mental independence needed for participation in democracy. Democratic institutions that are not able to defend citizens against cognitive surveillance may not enjoy the legitimacy and capacity for effective governance in an age of neural computing. The neural surveillance crisis therefore constitutes at once a challenge to individual rights and a challenge to democratic society itself.

Innovation Without Wisdom

It's the exponential growth of neurotechnology capabilities without serious ethical frameworks that are in evidence a massive failure of technological wisdom. And, scientific and engineering capabilities that could be used to augment human cognitive performance and security are being used without sufficient attention to the implications for human freedom and dignity. This is a basic mistake in the relationship between innovation and ethics. Rather than seeing ethical considerations as a constraint on the development of technology, democratic societies have to take into account the fact that sustainable innovation has to be ethically grounded, carefully guarded against the possibility of technological development serving values that the technology is not designed to advance.

Path Forward

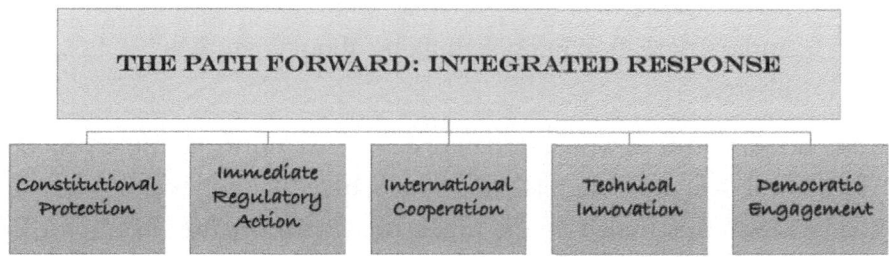

Figure 8-2. *The Path Forward: Integrated Response*

The neural surveillance crisis is a cross-domain issue that needs multi-domain engagement to address as highlighted in Figure 8-2:

> **Constitutional Protection:** We conclude that democratic societies should enshrine in constitutional law the concept of neural privacy that can never be eroded by commercial or legislative pressure.

Immediate Regulatory Action: The lack of effective protection is the result of the rushed nature of consumer neural devices and of regulatory oversight of workplace neural monitoring in advance of market penetration.

International Cooperation: Linking international instruments with mechanisms for enforcement, in order to avoid regulatory arbitration and achieve uniform protection standards around the world.

Technical Innovation: Development of neurotechnology that is privacy-preserving so that new applications can be provided while safeguarding cognitive liberty.

Democratic Engagement: Democratic rather than technocratic participation in the development of privacy policies in neuroscience – public education and participation in policymaking about cognitive liberty.

The human mind is what is left of privacy, in a more and more watched world. Neural data protection is not just a technical or policy problem; it is a test of whether the wiser and braver societies have the wisdom to preserve the foundations of human autonomy from the intrusions of technology. The information in this chapter should present both a warning and a roadmap. The message is stark: regulatory strategies as they are are doomed to catastrophic failure and create the preconditions for unheard-of violations of cognitive freedom. The path is just as clear: constitutional protection, emergency regulation, international cooperation, and democratic engagement are the minimal conditions of retaining human autonomy in an era of neural computing. The stakes couldn't be higher and the need for action more pressing. It's our choices today on how to safeguard neural data that will determine the future of human freedom in the digital age. History will decide whether democratic societies had the wisdom to defend the privacy of thought itself, in which all other liberties are rooted. The evidence is stark, the solutions are out there and the time for decision has come. The only question that remains is whether mankind will decide to preserve the sanctity of the human mind or cede the last vestige of cognitive freedom to technological convenience.

Key Takeaways

- Brain–computer interfaces (BCIs), cognitive biometrics, are changing cybersecurity from something that protects digital assets to something that protects human consciousness itself. Non-invasive EEG systems are already in use in high-stress situations such as air traffic control and financial trading, and invasive neural implants allow programmable manipulation of neural activity, so the idea of controlling human thoughts and impulses is no longer science fiction.

- Neural data is the substrate of human identity, autonomy, and dignity, unlike conventional data, compromised mental states and neural patterns are permanent and irreversible vulns. This chapter focuses on the most important frontier in cybersecurity, that of securing thoughts, feelings, and mental well-being in the context of an age of neural data, where neural data becomes both a commodity and a weapon – and where immediate collaboration between cybersecurity experts, neuroscientists, policymakers, and engineers is critical.

- The analysis identifies three categories of deployments: non-invasive EEG systems that are susceptible to authentication and cognitive monitoring attacks, brainjacking vulnerable invasive neural implants, and consumer neurotechnology devices with little to no security oversight. Current applications include cognitive authentication systems, real-time mental state monitoring, threat detection enhancement and neural communication channels, each with different vulnerability profiles and attack vectors.

- Every desirable neural security application carries with it an attendant risk of abuse. Neurofeedback systems that optimize performance can become micromanagement tools; fatigue detection systems that prevent errors can profile users based on thought patterns; thoughts-as-logins cognitive biometric authentication systems can become micromanagement tools; and continuous authentication brain-state monitoring systems can enable comprehensive employee surveillance.

- The future of neural surveillance technologies is being used in high-stakes applications where the stakes of a failed security or privacy outcome are potentially catastrophic. The result is what we call the "neural security paradox": technologies that promise to revolutionize cybersecurity by making authentication unforgeable in principle simultaneously threaten to erode foundations of human autonomy and privacy, introducing into existence technical capabilities that are future probabilities rather than future possibilities.

- Neural data is biological, unique, and intensely personal, and it demands entirely new ethical, legal, and policy frameworks to handle unlike traditional digital data. Three key aspects are said to catalyze this urgency: neural data is poorly defined in most regulatory models; technological advancements are outpacing ethical provisions; and governance gaps leave individuals under the control of neurotechnological infrastructure in increasingly asymmetric power dynamics.

- Neuro-privacy is a radical departure from standard notions of privacy as neural data are automatically and continuously generated by the brain, are not subject to intentional control or selective disclosure, and reflect attention, emotions, memory, and subconscious responses. This is a new world, one that provides for no opportunity for individual consent to the act of sharing certain types of neural information, resulting in mass cognitive surveillance in the name of security or wellness applications.

- Passive EEG systems can extract personal knowledge using detection methods like P300 based deception detection and Rapid Serial Visual Presentation (RSVP), allowing for the determination of identification, preferences, and even political preferences without conscious user involvement. Wealthy consumer devices that claim to assess mental states with enviable accuracy increasingly create ambient neuro-surveillance in which cognitive conditions are continuously recorded and analyzed, resulting in neurobehavioral profiles for management, recruitment, and institutional decision-making.

- The comparative analysis confirms that Chile is the only country with constitutional-level protection for neural data (Law No. 21.383, Oct. 2021), while key economies are largely found lacking: the United States has no federal neural protection; the EU's GDPR is a generalist tool that offers no neurotechnology-specific guidance; and China offers limited protections to its citizens against neural surveillance by the state. Neural devices for consumers are operated with almost no regulation worldwide, and neural monitoring at work is carried out without any real employee protection measures in all of the jurisdictions investigated.

- The documented regulatory failure calls for urgent neural rights protection via constitutional action (modeled after Chile), emergency regulation of consumer neural devices before irreparable market saturation, workplace protection against cognitive surveillance, and binding global standards and enforcement mechanisms. The analysis demonstrates that defending neural data is the civil rights issue of the digital age, and that failure to act will not only fail to preserve cognitive freedom but will also irreversibly erode human autonomy and turn neurotechnology from enhancement to control.

CHAPTER 9

The Role of Neurofeedback in Cybersecurity

The DARPA succeeded to make a breakthrough in the Next-Generation Nonsurgical Neurotechnology (N3)[1] program which entirely changed the cybersecurity situation. The program effectively tested its enabling technology in a wide variety of national security functions, including the control of unmanned air vehicles and active cyber defense systems, and operators working in conjunction with computer systems were able to multitask effectively on highly complex military operations. The threats could be traced in real-time in human minds as never before, with possibilities to mind over the ways human interactions to be manipulated as never before heard in the evolution of technology, as well as presenting entirely new levels of security risks never before seen. The uses go well beyond the military. In recent years, it has been shown that neural interfaces have potentially become an effective technology, not only enabling closed-loop neurorehabilitation but also intelligent human-machine interaction, and cybersecurity is one area that has formed as much of an accepted application area as it has become one

---

[1] https://www.darpa.mil/research/programs/next-generation-nonsurgical-neurotechnology

of the most critical. The human brain with its 86 billion processing units lays down patterns as unique as fingerprints and has emerged as both a future frontier in cybersecurity enhancement and the latest battleground on which sophisticated threat actors abound. Technological convergence is taking place at a pivotal time. The military application of neurotechnologies like brain–computer interfaces (BCIs) holds potential benefits to improve decision-making speed, enhanced coordination, and soldier resilience, all of which are equally useful in commercial security applications. Nevertheless, fast growth and commercialization of this technology are associated with security risks as the attack of the brain–computer interface can bring terrible outcomes, even breaking into the sphere of human cognition and not only digital systems.

Why This Chapter Matters?

- **Lack of In-Depth Security Analysis**: Existing articles follow the same pattern: neurofeedback technology and cybersecurity are analyzed as two distinct fields with no comprehensive study of the issues at the subject-matter interface. Paper publications prioritize on specific, small, technical matters or the clinical use; the security implications are subsequently an afterthought.

- **Deficient Security Architecture**: Neurofeedback systems have different and, most importantly, real-time demands of data compared to traditional cybersecurity frameworks. State-of-the-art solutions presuppose typical encryption and access controls, which are simply unsuitable to millisecond latency neural computing requirements.

- **Cross-Pattern Knowledge Silos**: Neuroscientists are not experts in cybersecurity and security professionals have no knowledge in neuroscience, resulting in systems that are either scientifically valid and technologically uneducated, or, on the other hand, technically proficient but practically neurologically unable.

- **Lack of Good Privacy and Ethical Protection**: Neural data privacy is much more than standard personal information security, as it may mean revealing unconscious thought processes and cognitive conditions. Current privacy systems that were developed to protect conventional data do not suffice to protect neural data.

- **An Emphasis on the Lack of Practical Implementation Guidance**: The presence of literature on neurofeedback in the current arena does not offer any security professional workable models to screen, implement, or handle neurofeedback systems within a functional setting and thus organizations have developed a patchwork strategy of handling security models.

The unprecedented convergence of neuroscience and cybersecurity represents both humanity's greatest opportunity to enhance security operations and potentially its most dangerous vulnerability if improperly implemented. The merging of neuroscience and cybersecurity is probably one of the most dramatic paradigm shifts that have occurred in security technology in recent times. As we move further into the digital era, the human component rose as a strongest asset and the most vulnerable component in cybersecurity structures. Each and every day, security

357

professionals make snap decisions that could spell the difference between preventing a nation-state attack and a debilitating breach. However, the fundamental challenge remains that these same professionals possess cognitive structures that were evolutionarily designed for survival in pre-historic environments, not for processing terabytes of security information under intense time pressures.

Neurofeedback technology arose as one of the most revolutionary technologies that can change not only human-centered security operations but the safety of neural data itself. However, this advancement brings with it a twist: these tools, used to help a security analyst identify threats and improve their finding efficiency and accuracy by 40%, can also be adapted by attackers to read their most intimate thoughts, control their decision-making process, or even plant a false memory about a security-related event. This chapter fills an important gap in the cybersecurity research since the existing body of literature has no holistic analysis of the neurofeedback as part of the security ecosystem's dual role. Whereas conventional cybersecurity is concerned with securing data and IT infrastructure, the innervation of neurofeedback systems brings with it a novel level of security concerns – one that encompasses a combination of the biological and digital worlds like never before. We are at a historic point in technology where the question about the eventual application of neurofeedback to transform cybersecurity is not an open one, but one of the paces at which we can establish the frameworks through which we can capitalize on the strengths of neurofeedback and effectively guard against its risks. Figure 9-1 shows the strategic imperative of neurofeedback technologies in cybersecurity.

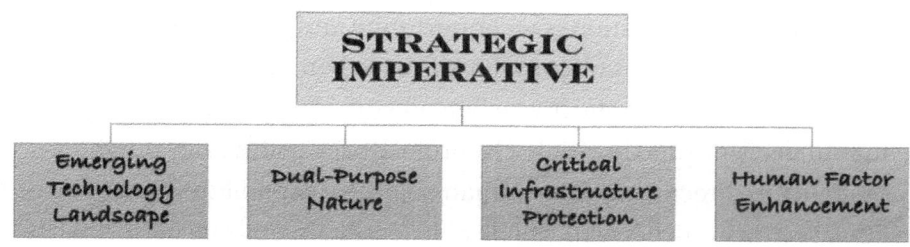

Figure 9-1. *Strategic Imperative of Neurotechnology in Cybersecurity*

Emerging Technology Landscape

The BCI market is on a rampage and is allowing the global market to be restructured in unmatched ways, especially in various industries. Existing research on this topic has shown fantastic development and the publications in this area have grown 1.5 times during the period 2016–2021, which is not just a mark of incremental progress but a true technological breakthrough. This exponential growth of non-invasive BCI market[2] is expected to grow at a CAGR 9.5% from 2025 to 2030 and such a boost is determined by the advancement of neurofeedback technologies and their implementation into safety-critical systems.

The fast development of the neurofeedback technology is the result of the synergetic influence of several players, among which has been improved neural signal acquisition hardware, machine learning real-time signal processing advancement, and the rise of cognitive enhancement as a strategic edge in competitively demanding settings. The current neurofeedback systems have reduced their response time to milliseconds, have multi-channel signal processing, and have greater accuracy in detecting the subtle variance of a cognitive state through the application of powerful pattern recognition algorithms. To cybersecurity professionals,

---

[2] https://www.grandviewresearch.com/industry-analysis/brain-computer-interfaces-market

such technological evolution is an opportunity and a necessity. The conventional security paradigm, which is based on high-tech obstacles and process control, is ineffective when advanced threats take advantage of human decision-making limits. Neurofeedback technology provides a possibility to directly increase human cognitive capabilities, thus creating security officers who will be able to sustain optimal performance levels even after the longest operating sessions, perceive threats more efficiently, and make critical decisions in a more precise manner. The developments in the markets and technologies provide the context in which neurofeedback's role can be understood as both a tool for cybersecurity enhancement as well as a potential vulnerability in modern security systems. The overall growth trajectory, however, presents a more conservative estimates compared to the more optimistic projections that forecast a market size of $2.75 billion in 2024 growing to $12.87 billion by 2034, suggesting that market volatility and measurement issues must be factored into the analysis. With the CMMC program becoming effective December 16, 2024, the regulatory context provides relevant and timely guidance that aids your critical infrastructure protection conversation.

Dual-Purpose Nature

The use of neurofeedback systems reflects a double-pronged kind of technology that makes them unique compared to other cybersecurity systems. They are also effective security defense mechanisms and completely new types of attack surfaces with new defense approaches that are necessary to address. Such dual usage results in the difficulty of security and the need to redesign traditional and long-established models of risk assessment. Creating the potential to implement the power of what is yet unheard of in the world of science fiction, neurofeedback systems are in the business of providing the possibility of supplementing the field of security enhancement. Cognitive state monitoring can be used in real time to notice when security analysts are nearing or experiencing cognitive overload, essentially redistributing or triggering break protocols to ensure optimal performance is maintained.[3] The security factors of biometric authentication with neural signature are considered engendered with tighter security as compared to conventional credentials and that it depicts individual features comprising the unique neurological patterns of individual users. Nonetheless, the technologies that increase security also open new vulnerabilities. Neural data is, perhaps, the most sensitive kind of personal data and may contain patterns revealing not only current cognitive states but also, in the future, the preference of certain decisions, emotional reactions, and tendencies. The contingency of neurofeedback systems may allow adversaries to interfere directly with cognitive states, possibly making decisions of high importance or providing information transfer by way of neural patterns. This ambivalence demands cybersecurity professionals to devise new conceptual frameworks that can enable them to take advantage of the neurofeedback, on the one hand, and reduce the attendant danger, on the other. Security models that make a distinction between defensive aids and channels of attacks fail to cover technologies that have embedded both categories.

Critical Infrastructure Protection

The introduction of neurotechnology to critical systems amounts to a paradigm change in our understanding of infrastructure-security. The security implications of neurofeedback systems may become acute, as

---

[3] Tariq, S., Baruwal Chhetri, M., Nepal, S., & Paris, C. (2025). Alert fatigue in security operations centres: Research challenges and opportunities. *ACM Computing Surveys*, *57*(9), 1–38.

neurofeedback systems enter the national infrastructure of power lines, financial networks, healthcare systems, and defense infrastructure, and the challenge becomes one of national and organizational survival. Critical infrastructure has always offered protection through the interdependency of technology-based security barriers and physical barriers to intrusion and attack, the now, the deployment of neurofeedback systems introduces a new interdependency between human mental performance and systems integrity. A weakened neurofeedback system in a nuclear power plant control room may affect the decision-making process of the operators in case of an emergency.[4] Equally, neural monitoring systems in financial trading facilities could be used to tamper with high-stakes economic judgments. Security of neurofeedback goes past organization-specific to a national security concern. Nation-state actors with high-achieving capabilities may target neurofeedback systems to be able to influence key decision-makers in the government, military, or critical infrastructure. Such capabilities have industry-disrupting strategic implications that are a nascent dimension to information warfare, where cognitive manipulation may be used to achieve previously unattainable objectives that cannot be made possible through conventional cyberattacks. Furthermore, by adding neurofeedback to critical systems, one introduces cascading failure modes that never existed. When a conventional cybersecurity solution fails, it is usually reflected in the digital assets and processes that are affected, whereas when a neurofeedback system goes awry, it may directly impact on the performance of human operators, which may directly cause a scenario where human operators will be incapacitated in providing a required response to both cyber and physical adversaries, thus creating a new paradigm shift.

---

[4] Paszkiel, S. (2022). *Applications of Brain-Computer Interfaces in Intelligent Technologies* (Vol. 1031). Berlin/Heidelberg, Germany: Springer.

Human Factor Enhancement

People have always been described as the most valuable asset as well as the main source of threat to the cybersecurity system. The conventional solutions in dealing with human factors have included training, awareness schemes, and procedural controls, which is limited by the nature of human mental archetype. This is because the neurofeedback technology presents human beings with a unique opportunity to directly boost their cognitive performances in a way that may significantly eliminate the human factor vulnerability that has compromised cybersecurity operations over time. Cybersecurity workloads impose unimaginable demands on the human mind, requiring its operators to be mindful of incoming threats over long shifts, identify and decode complex information within tight time limits and make swift decisions that have critical consequences. Cognitive neuroscience[5] research has shown such requirements can routinely surpass the inherent human processing capacity, resulting in attention breakdowns, decision fatigue, and a loss of threat detection abilities. The neurofeedback systems are able to overcome these shortcomings as it can monitor and intervene on cognitive conditions of operators in real time, thus ensuring operators remain at their optimum performance levels during their shifts. The application of neurofeedback to cognitive enhancement does not merely involve an optimization of performance but reflects the possibility of deeper alterations to the cognitive process in ways that would support security by strengthening cognitive capabilities that are relevant to security. Neurofeedback training programs have the potential to help students integrate problem-solving skills and work around a problem more effectively and efficiently.[6] These

---

[5] Kok, A. (2022). Cognitive control, motivation and fatigue: A cognitive neuroscience perspective. *Brain and Cognition, 160,* 105880.

[6] Klutz, D. (2023). Neurofeedback for Cognitive Enhancement Intervention and Brain Plasticity. *Journal of Biomedical and Sustainable Healthcare Applications, 3*(1), 045-055.

improvements may work wonders on the success rate of the human security analysts as they would be able to identify some of the most tricky threats that some could otherwise easily pass unnoticed. But the new vulnerabilities that are opened by the introduction of cognitive enhancing capabilities are new. Superior human operators can become addicted to neurofeedback systems, and risk severe performance slippage in their absence.

Introduction to Neurofeedback in Cybersecurity

The application of neurofeedback technology in cybersecurity as an additional layer of security provides a significant transformation in the way we think of the principles of human–machine interaction security system.[7] Such convergence is not only an incremental development but rather paradigm-altering that changes the demarcation between biological and digital domains of security. Given that cybersecurity professionals are beginning to consider brain–computer interfaces (BCIs) is a new type of technology to improve human actions in security-related ways, the strategic impacts of it go far beyond normal approaches to security to include such issues as the advancement of thought processes, the optimization of human performance, and classes of vulnerabilities beyond the beginner expertise that are newly being discovered. The recent development of neurofeedback toward cybersecurity is part of a larger trend that sees a growing awareness of theoretical and practical limits of application of conventional approaches to human factors in security. Although the technological security mechanisms are steadily improving, the weakest and most unpredictable part of the security architecture is

---

[7] KRITIKA, E. (2025). Guarding the Mind's Frontier: The Unprecedented Challenge of Neurosecurity Governance. *ISACA Journal*, (2).

people. With neurofeedback technology, however, lies the potential, never before available, of course, to directly deal with these human weaknesses through real-time monitoring and enhancing of the cognitive states, shifting human performance in security operations to proactive rather than reactive mechanisms, whereby human cognitive performance can be measured and optimized as a security resource.

Historical Development from Clinical Applications to Security Contexts

Neurofeedback technology can be traced back to the clinical field of neuroscience in which it was originally developed as a mode of treatment of several neurological and psychiatric disorders. The basic premise behind neurofeedback is the real-time scanning of the brain by using different modes of neuroimaging, and then giving some feedback on the change of condition to the patient. Such feedback loop allows the users to gain conscious control over unconscious neural dynamics that have previously been very difficult to control, and is associated with statistically significant cognitive performance, emotional regulation, and behavioral control benefits. This shift in the use of clinically optimized applications into security settings took place in the early 21st century when military and defense organizations started perceiving cognitive enhancement in high responsibility operations venues. Early usage was in areas such as pilot training and situational awareness, as making the correct cognitive decisions could mean the success or failure of a mission with disastrous consequences in the latter. Studies in military neurofeedback use showed amygdala-EEG-fMRI-Neurofeedback training regimes reduced clinical symptoms three months following the end of the therapies, suggesting neurofeedback may provide lasting cognitive performance benefits. As organizations increasingly realized that security operations centers are under the same cognitive pressures as those experienced in the military, the evolution toward cybersecurity applications is an inevitable direction that this technology has taken. Security analysts need to uphold long-term focused attention and analyze complex information quickly as well as make critical decisions against considerable time constraints – aspects that can be further improved through the implementation of neurofeedback programs.

Types of Neurofeedback: EEG, fMRI, fNIRS-Based Systems

The three neuroimaging modalities utilized by modern neurofeedback systems have major advantages as well as limitations that render them applicable in different security areas the comparative analysis of which is highlighted in Table 9-1 for different cybersecurity applications. This knowledge is essential to the security people considering neurofeedback deployment options.

Electroencephalography (EEG)-Based Systems

The oldest and most widespread neurofeedback technology being used in cybersecurity is EEG-based neurofeedback as demonstrated in Figure 9-2. EEG systems record electrical activity produced by neural groups on the scalp surface through surface electrodes with millisecond level time resolution, which can be used to offer real-time feedback and interventions. Among the most widely used EEG devices in both consumer and research settings are EMotiv, NeuroSky MindWave, OpenBCI, InteraXon Muse, and MyndPlay Mindband with their broad adoption serving as a clear indicator of the growing maturity and accessibility of EEG technology platforms.

Advantage to use in Cybersecurity:

- **Real-time responsiveness**: EEG systems have the potential to sense cognitive change in milliseconds, allowing an immediate intervention in security operations.

- **Light and non-invasive**: Recent EEG headsets are lightweight and wireless, which makes them easy to integrate into the workflow without disruption to operating security environments.

- **Scalable at low costs**: Low-end EEG devices are nowadays affordable, which opens the possibility of high-scale usage within enterprise-security operations.

- **Proven protocols**: Thirty years of neurofeedback research have produced proven neurofeedback protocols to enhance attention, reduce stress, and optimize cognitive results.

Security-Specific Applications:

- Security monitoring attention and vigilance monitoring in long monitoring shifts

- In real-time stress monitoring during incident response activities

- Complex threat analysis optimization of cognitive load

- Fatigue recognition and prevention of critical security event

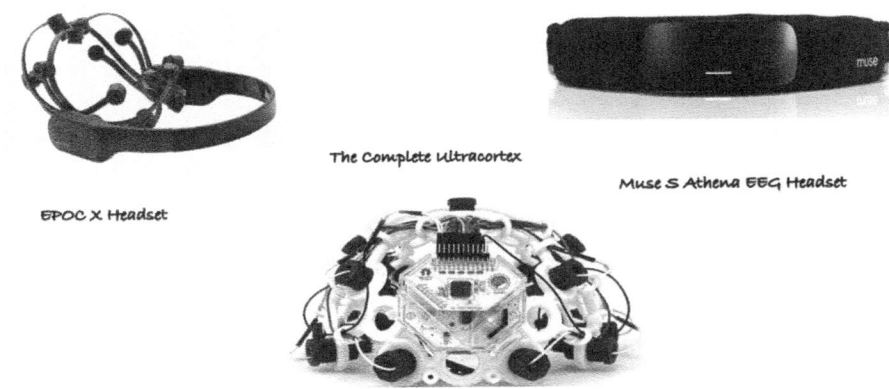

The Complete Ultracortex

Muse S Athena EEG Headset

EPOC X Headset

Figure 9-2. *EEG-Based Systems*

Functional Magnetic Resonance Imaging (fMRI)-Based Systems

Neurofeedback systems based on fMRI have an intrinsically high spatial resolution that allows targeting the activity of specific regions of the brain. Neurofeedback (NF) technology using electroencephalogram (EEG) data or functional magnetic resonance imaging (fMRI) has been extensively studied and used, with fMRI systems offering capabilities that are of especially high relevance when considering security-related decision-making entailing high-level cognition as demonstrated in Figure 9-3.

Advantages to Security Applications:

- **Exact spatial localization**: fMRI is able to identify activation in specific brain areas involving decision-making, assessment of threat, and cognitive control.

- **Subcortical volume access**: Analyzing subcortical volume structures that are involved in emotional regulation and the stress response can be monitored using fMRI compared to EEG.

- **Research backing**: Backed by vast bodies of research that support protocols on cognitive enhancement, and performance optimization.

Limitations in Operational Contexts:

- **Infrastructure needs**: fMRI systems must be deployed in dedicated infrastructures; they do not lend themselves to operational security facilities.

- **Temporal constraints**: There is a few seconds' delay between the activity of the neurons and feedback, so the applications are not real time.

- **Cost/ complexity**: Extremely expensive in most operational applications, largely restricted to training and research purposes.

Security Applications:

- Pretesting cognitive ability and training of security personnel

- Development of neurofeedback methods and protocols of security use

- Training in simulated environments in high-stakes decisions

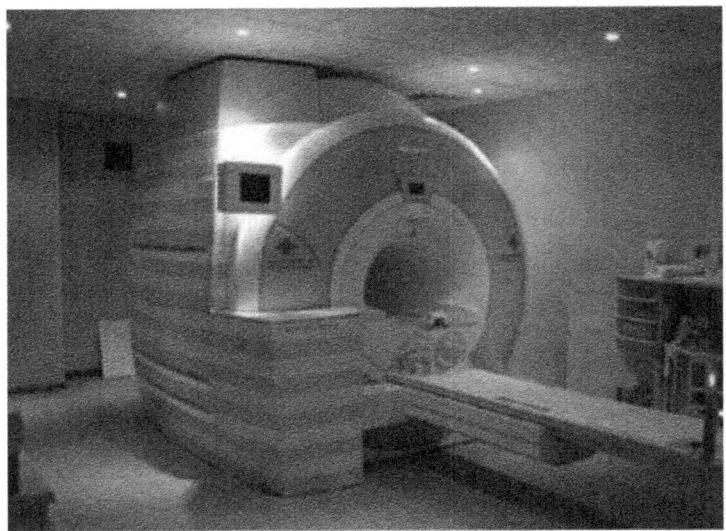

Figure 9-3. *fMRI-Based Systems*

Functional Near-Infrared Spectroscopy (fNIRS)-Based Systems

fNIRS is a new and evolving imaging neuro-technology that lies between the existing system of EEG and fMRI, it is perhaps capable of providing acceptable spatial resolution and better temporal resolution than the fMRI system as demonstrated in Figure 9-4. Neurofeedback, using an electroencephalogram (EEG) and/or a functional near-infrared spectroscopy (fNIRS) device, is a real-time signal of brain activity based on aimed control and optimization of brain capacity, and fNIRS systems are gaining popularity in security applications.

Technical Characteristics:

- **Hemodynamic monitoring**: fNIRS provides a measures blood oxygenation, which is related to changes in the quality of their neural activity.

- **Acceptable spatial resolution**: Better than EEG but not the same accuracy as an fMRI.

- **Better time resolution**: Most studies are done with faster time resolution than obtainable with fMRI, coming close to real-time requirements in some applications.

- **Transportability**: Unlike fMRI, fNIRS systems are transportable. Additional value: As compared to fMRI, fNIRS systems have other added values, which include ability to diagnose animals.

Benefits to Cybersecurity:

- **Cortical activity recording**: It is especially useful in recording activity in the prefrontal cortex which has the executive functions and other activities in decision-making

- **Environmental compliance**: Does not require any type of electromagnetic interference when used in security operations centers.

- **System compatibility**: The hybrid EEG–fNIRS (electroencephalogram – functional near-infrared spectroscopy) modality enables a more comprehensive analysis of brain activity by simultaneously recording both electrical and hemodynamic responses offering a richer and more complete picture of neural functioning than either technology could provide alone.

Security Applications:

- The executive monitoring in the complex security analysis exercise tasks

- Multi-tasking security environments Cognitive workload assessment

- EEG–fNIRS mixed systems to monitor the full cognitive condition

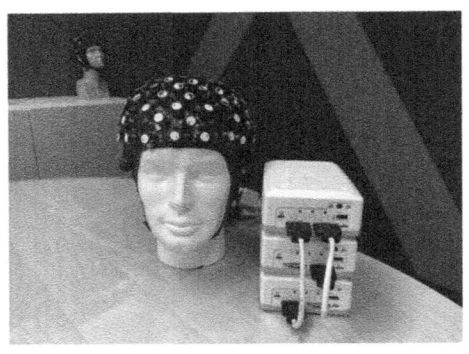
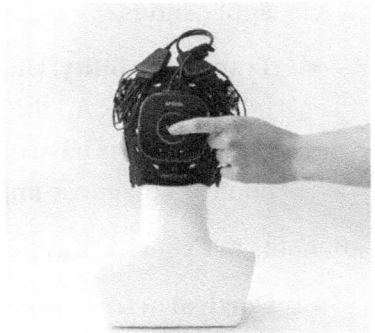

NIRx NIRSport2   Artinis Brite MKII

Figure 9-4. fNIRS-Based Systems

Real-time Brain State Monitoring and Modulation Capabilities

What is unique about neurofeedback systems within the cybersecurity context is that this system is capable of monitoring and controlling brain states in real time through various modalities, realizing a closed-loop operation process wherein cognitive performance can continuously be optimized based on the current neural data. The ability to provide this kind of measure is more disruptive than the conventional methods of monitoring performance that only give use behavior indicators that can take a very long duration to notice the change of cognitive state. Figure 9-5 illustrates the continuous cycle of EEG monitoring, cognitive state analysis, performance optimization, and security task execution.

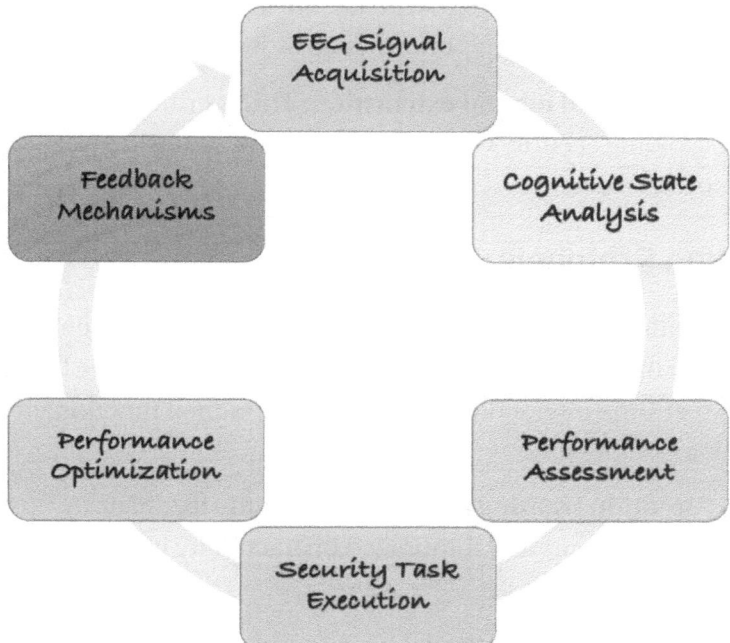

Figure 9-5. *Real-Time Cognitive Enhancement Feedback Loop*

Cognitive State Classification

Neurofeedback systems today use advanced machine learning algorithms to identify cognitive states using the signatures of the neural patterns. These classification systems are able to differentiate numerous cognitively relevant states such as

- **Level of attention and vigilance**: Will be critical in tasks when security needs to be monitored over an extended period of time.

- **Cognitive overload and mental effort**: This is an essential measure that should be taken to avoid cognitive overload and the load of tasks that should be optimalized to handle.

373

- **Stress and emotional arousal**: This is significant to maintain optimum performance in stressful events.

- **Fatigue and mental exhaustion**: This is critical in avoiding security oversights because of reduced levels of alertness.

Real-Time Protocols

It is the potential practical application of neurofeedback systems in cybersecurity that does not stop only at monitoring the state of the mind but offers real-time interactions that maximize mental functionality. Such interventions can include

- **Attention training procedures**: In-time feedback to support focus and minimized distractibility in security surmounting tasks

- **Stress control method**: Immediate ways of regulating the stress when arousal levels are not optimal during incident response

- **Levels of information processing**: Automatic control of information display, depending on current levels of mental capacity

- **Performance optimization**: The actions that have to be taken to maintain optimal cognitive capabilities throughout the entire length of operational processes

Integration with Security Operations

The effective inclusion of neurofeedback systems into the workflow of security operations necessitates putting a lot of thought into how it will be implemented by users, whether they will use it, and how well they will use it. Integration considerations are important and key, and these include

- **New power of survival**: The systems should be non-disruptive and allow extension to non-obscure business operations without disrupting core security activities.

- **Actionable feedback**: Feedback must be actionable and allow professionals to immediately use the outcome in enhancing security operations other than distracting them.

- **Scalability**: Solutions are required to be affordable with the ability to handle large security teams.

- **Privacy and consent**: Neural monitoring is a sensitive topic that requires solutions concerning its privacy to be resolved with proper policies and safeguards.

The history of neurofeedback is a progressive step in guided neurofeedback applications serving as a natural way to remove blind spots in human performance in the security space, and it is a philosophical shift in the concept of human performance optimization in high-stakes situations. As these systems grow more powerful and in-depth, it also means that their incorporation into cybersecurity operations may not just be beneficial, but a key means of staying at a competitive security level in a more complex threat environment. The technical foundations, limitations, and capabilities of the various approaches of neurofeedback are essential knowledge, which becomes necessary topics a security professional must learn to understand. The selection of EEG, fMRI, and fNIRS systems will greatly depend on the peculiarities of the operational needs, limitations on specific infrastructure, and performance goals that require different considerations in distinct security settings and organizational priorities.

Table 9-1. Comparative Analysis of Neurofeedback Systems for Cybersecurity Applications

Characteristic	EEG-based systems	fMRI-based systems	fNIRS-based systems
Temporal resolution	Millisecond-level (1–10ms)	2–6 seconds delay	1–3 seconds
Spatial resolution	Low (scalp surface only)	High (3–5mm precision)	Moderate (cortical regions)
Real-time capability	Excellent – immediate feedback	Poor – significant delay	Good – near real time
Operational deployment	Highly portable, wireless	Requires dedicated facility	Portable, operational use
Cost range	$200–$40,000	$1–3 million + facility costs	$5,000–$50,000
Setup time	2–15 minutes	30–60 minutes	5–20 minutes
User mobility	Full mobility with wireless	No mobility – fixed position	Limited mobility
Environmental interference	High (electrical noise)	Minimal in shielded room	Moderate (ambient light)
Training requirements	Basic to intermediate	Expert level required	Intermediate level
Maintenance	Low – replace electrodes	High – specialized technicians	Moderate – calibration needed
Data privacy risk	Moderate – surface activity	High – detailed brain imaging	Moderate – regional activity

Cybersecurity applications

Attention monitoring	Excellent	Excellent (research only)	Good
Stress detection	Good	Excellent	Good
Fatigue assessment	Excellent	Limited by delays	Good
Cognitive load	Good	Excellent	Excellent
Decision-making	Indirect measures	Direct neural circuits	Prefrontal activity
Workload distribution	Real-time optimization	Not practical	Feasible
Security advantages			
Biometric authentication	Unique neural signatures	Highly specific patterns	Individual variations
Continuous monitoring	Seamless integration	Impractical	Possible
Covert operation	Discrete headsets available	Obvious equipment	Small form factor
Multi-user deployment	Cost-effective scaling	Prohibitively expensive	Moderate cost scaling

(continued)

Table 9-1. (*continued*)

Characteristic	EEG-based systems	fMRI-based systems	fNIRS-based systems
Security vulnerabilities			
Signal interception	High risk – wireless transmission	Low risk – wired, shielded	Moderate risk – optical signals
Data manipulation	High risk – real-time processing	Moderate risk – post-processing	Moderate risk – signal processing
Physical tampering	High risk – accessible hardware	Low risk – secured facility	Moderate risk – visible components
Privacy invasion	Moderate – limited depth	High – detailed brain activity	Moderate – cortical activity
Integration complexity			
Existing IT infrastructure	Standard network protocols	Specialized connectivity	Network compatible
Software integration	APIs and SDKs available	Specialized software	Growing ecosystem
Compliance requirements	Standard data protection	Medical device regulations	Medical device considerations
Staff training	Minimal – user-friendly	Extensive – technical expertise	Moderate – specialized knowledge

Recommended use cases

Primary applications	Real-time monitoring, biometric auth	Research, training, validation	Hybrid monitoring, cognitive load
Operational contexts	SOC monitoring, incident response	Training facilities, R&D labs	Executive monitoring, hybrid systems
Deployment scale	Individual to enterprise-wide	Single facility, limited users	Department to organization-wide
Strategic priority	Immediate implementation	Long-term research investment	Medium-term strategic deployment

Neurofeedback As a Cybersecurity Enhancement Tool

Neurofeedback application as a cybersecurity enhancement tool, as shown in Figure 9-6, is the paradigm shift to pre-emptive steps securing human performance over reactive steps in security. Compared to conventional cybersecurity systems, which protect sensitive space by means of technological deterrents and threat detection, neurofeedback systems target to increase the cognitive capacities of a security expert and offer them as a source of authentication and threat sensing. This strategy is based on the fact that human factors are the most important factor to determine security performance, which optimization of human cognitive performance can offer security benefits that technologically driven solutions cannot.

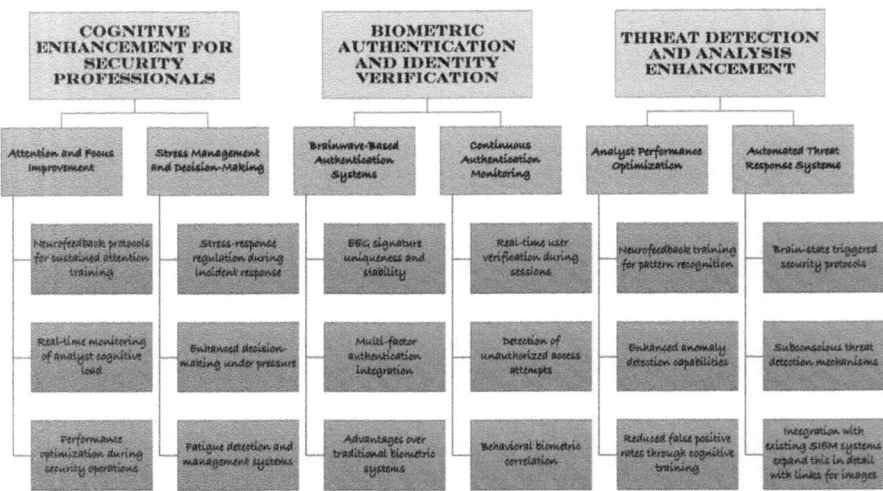

Figure 9-6. *Hierarchy of Neurofeedback as a Cybersecurity Enhancement Tool*

Cognitive Enhancement for Security Professionals

Cognitive tasks related to cybersecurity are more complex than those in most other technical fields, ensuring a high rate of maintaining attention and making quick decisions in an uncertain environment as well as identifying the slightest patterns in large volumes of data. Extensive research indicates a neurofeedback training tilt on attentional performance has shown a significant improvement, and meta-analysis reports an overall standardized mean difference of 0.27 with 95% confidence interval of 0.10–0.44, which is quantifiably able to reach a clinically significant cognitive enhancement.

Attention and Focus Improvement

Neurofeedback Protocols for Sustained Attention Training

Neurofeedback training for sustained attention is an innovative development in cognitive improvement for security professionals, which uses real-time electroencephalography (EEG) to monitor brain states and improve them for sustained vigilance and threat detection. These protocols are based on the brain's ability for neuroplasticity, the ability of current security practitioners' brain networks to essentially be rewired in ways that make them more capable of sustained attention. A study published in Frontiers in Psychology shows that neurofeedback training can bring about substantial improvements in cognitive functioning, especially when used in high-pressure work situations such as military and security forces.[8] The training protocols are specific to the growth of alpha waves (8–12 Hz) to keep alert in a relaxed state of awareness while

---

[8] https://www.frontiersin.org/journals/psychology/articles/10.3389/fpsyg.2024.1412289/full

monitoring, beta waves (13–30 Hz) for active threat analysis, and theta waves (4–8 Hz) for pattern recognition enhancement.[9] In order to achieve this, security professionals are given structured training sessions where they learn how to identify and regulate their brainwave activity using visual and auditory feedback devices in order to allow them to sustain maximum cognitive states for prolonged periods of time. The protocols are especially well-suited for personnel in surveillance operations where sustained attention for extended periods of time is important for identifying subtle security breaches or suspicious activities.

Real-time Monitoring of Analyst Cognitive Load

Advanced cognitive load monitoring systems continually monitor the mental load experienced by security analysts to ensure that they are not overwhelmed, which could impair threat detection capabilities and decision-making. These systems combine several physiological and behavioral measures such as EEG patterns, eye tracking data, heart rate variability, and task performance measures to generate detailed cognitive load profiles for each analyst.[10] The monitoring technology offers supervisors real-time dashboards showing individual and team cognition capacity and allows dynamic distribution of tasks and workload optimization. When cognitive load reaches key thresholds, the system automatically initiates interventions such as task rotation, break recommendations, or extra analyst assistance to keep the performance levels at optimal levels. This methodology can be extremely beneficial in SOCs where the security analysts need to analyze a large amount of

---

[9] Deshmukh, V. D. (2023). The electroencephalographic brainwave spectrum, mindful meditation, and awareness: Hypothesis. *International Journal of Yoga, 16*(1), 42–48.

[10] Mark, J. A., Curtin, A., Kraft, A. E., Ziegler, M. D., & Ayaz, H. (2024). Mental workload assessment by monitoring brain, heart, and eye with six biomedical modalities during six cognitive tasks. Frontiers in neuroergonomics, 5, 1345507.

security data with a high level of accuracy of threat detection. It also learns the cognitive characteristics of individual analysts over time to provide personalized workload management that takes into account the unique cognitive strengths and weaknesses of a specific analyst.

Performance Optimization During Security Operations

Performance optimization protocols provide structured methods for peak cognitive performance throughout security operations, integrating circadian rhythm optimization, environmental controls, and cognitive enhancement techniques.[11] These protocols acknowledge that security performance is inherently variable according to biological rhythms of the body, neurological system stress levels, and cognitive fatigue and deploy countermeasures to reduce these effects. The optimization involves scheduling high-cognitive-demand tasks to periods of peak alertness, introducing micro-recovery protocols during the operations, and environmental optimization such as optimized lighting, temperature control, and noise management. Advanced protocols are combined with real-time cognitive state monitoring and automated recommendations for performance improvement interventions (such as specific breathing protocols, short meditation protocols, or specific neurofeedback protocols).[12] The system also incorporates predictive modeling to enable degradation of cognitive performance to be predicted ahead of time based on historical trends and operational stresses and individual analyst attributes, providing proactive performance management before degradation affects security performance.

---

[11] Marois, A., & Lafond, D. (2022). Augmenting cognitive work: a review of cognitive enhancement methods and applications for operational domains. Cognition, Technology & Work, 24(4), 589–608.

[12] Tosti, B., Corrado, S., Mancone, S., Di Libero, T., Carissimo, C., Cerro, G., ... & Diotaiuti, P. (2024). Neurofeedback Training Protocols in Sports: A Systematic Review of Recent Advances in Performance, Anxiety, and Emotional Regulation. *Brain Sciences*, *14*(10), 1036.

Stress Management and Decision-Making

Stress-Response Regulation During Incident Response

Stress-response regulation protocols provide a high level of physiological and cognitive regulation strategies that are focused for use in high-stakes incident response situations for security professionals. These protocols incorporate classic stress management techniques with advanced biofeedback technology to develop an integrated stress management system. Training involves heart rate variability (HRV) biofeedback, which helps security personnel learn to regulate their autonomic nervous system response in crises to maintain optimal cognitive performance when stress levels would otherwise impair performance.[13] The protocols also involve EEG-based stress detection and control, where stress-related brainwave patterns are monitored in real-time and feedback is provided instantaneously to help manage stress. Through scenarios of advanced training-simulated realistic security incidents and physiological stress reactions were monitored, helping employees to learn to keep a cool head, to develop and maintain communication under extreme pressure. The system uses a fast stress recovery algorithm that can rapidly return to optimal cognitive states after high-stress events to avoid accumulation of stress that can affect subsequent performance.

Enhanced Decision-Making Under Pressure

Advanced decision-making protocols build advanced cognitive models that boost the quality and speed of decision-making when securities professionals encounter time-sensitive conditions with limited or contradictory information. These models combine cognitive bias training, threat assessment methodologies designed to be rapid and decision-tree optimization as applied to security contexts. The training uses

---

[13] https://pmc.ncbi.nlm.nih.gov/articles/PMC11679052/

virtual reality simulations of security incidents and real-time cognitive monitoring to determine patterns in decision-making and ways it can be improved. They learn to recognize and overcome cognitive biases that tend to cloud security decisions, such as confirmation bias, availability heuristic, and anchoring effects. The protocols also include patterns of training such as the art and science of intuitive decision-making, helping teach security professionals how to better integrate analytical thinking with pattern recognition and intuitive threat assessment. The advanced modules include multi-scenario decision training in which personnel practice making sequential decisions under changing threat conditions, and mental modeling that allows for quick and accurate analysis of complex security situations to be made.

Fatigue Detection and Management Systems

Comprehensive fatigue detection systems using multiple modalities can detect cognitive fatigue before it affects the security performance and apply an automated intervention to maintain an optimal alertness level. These systems have integrated EEG-based measures of fatigue, such as enhanced theta and diminished beta activity, with behavior-based measures, such as reaction time degradation, eye movement patterns, and task performance measures. The detection algorithms are scaled for security operations, with special adjustments made to address the special cognitive requirements of threat monitoring, incident response, and analysis. The system reacts to fatigue predictors by triggering progressive interventions from brief alertness breaks to forced rest breaks or task rotation. Further, proactive fatigue management is possible with fatigue prediction models that estimate cognitive impairment based on duration of shift, cognitive task difficulty, and individual fatigue characteristics. The technology is also integrated with environmental fatigue countermeasures (circadian adjustment of lighting, temperature optimization, and smart scheduling of breaks) that are in sync with the natural alertness cycle.

Biometric Authentication and Identity Verification

Brainwave-Based Authentication Systems

EEG Signature Uniqueness and Stability

Biometric authentication systems using EEG rely on the characteristic neurological fingerprints of individual brainwave patterns to establish ultra-secure identification procedures that are virtually impossible to copy or steal. Studies presented in Scientific Reports[14] show that the brainwave patterns have enough uniqueness and stability to be viable biometric identifiers with accuracy when authenticating greater than 99% in controlled environments. The uniqueness of EEG signatures is based on individual variations in brain structure, neural connectivity patterns, and cognitive processing styles producing different frequency patterns in different brain areas. These signatures are relatively static over time (i.e., cannot be replayed in the manner of a replay attack), while also being dynamic enough so that they naturally change based on cognitive state and cannot be easily recorded and repeated by unauthorized parties. Owing to these stable features, EEG authentication is especially well-suited for security applications that demand long-term identity authentication, since the underlying neural signatures are consistent across emotional states, states of fatigue, and environment conditions.

Multi-factor Authentication Integration

Advanced integration protocols smoothly integrate brainwave authentication into established multi-factor authentication frameworks, resulting in layered security systems that blend the power of conventional and biometric authentication techniques. The integration is normally

---

[14] https://www.nature.com/articles/s41598-022-06527-7

accomplished by fast EEG capture sessions (30–60 seconds) using portable user-friendly devices that can be integrated into current security checkpoints or workstation access identification processes.[15] Modern systems have been shown to authenticate using consumer-grade EEG devices with as few as 4–7 channels, which makes it possible to deploy in a variety of security environments. The MFM approach pairs brainwave verification with conventional authentication methods like passwords, security tokens or physical biometrics, resulting in authentication systems that are incredibly hard to hack. Integration protocols have built-in fail-safe mechanisms that assure security functionality even in the event of technical problems in EEG components, thus providing uninterrupted security coverage. The systems also provide levels of authentication, where varying security clearances need different combinations of authentication factors, with the most sensitive areas needing full brainwave authentication.

Advantages Over Traditional Biometric Systems

Brainwave-based authentication systems have major advantages over the conventional biometric modalities and can solve problems such as insecurity related to fingerprint, facial, and retinal scanning systems. Unlike physical biometrics that can be stolen, replicated, and/or coerced, brainwave patterns cannot be readily extracted or reproduced without the conscious involvement of the individual. Intrinsic security against coercion – because stress and duress naturally change brainwave activity, it is easy for the system to detect forced authentication. Unlike other biometric modalities, whose performance is challenged by physical injuries, aging, or environmental factors, EEG-based systems are unaffected by these influences and therefore enabled to continue to authenticate the same individual throughout their career in the

---

[15] https://onlinelibrary.wiley.com/doi/abs/10.1002/spy2.345

security field.[16] At the same time, the authentication process can check both identity and cognitive state, identifying if subjects are affected by substances, are too tired, or other conditions that may jeopardize security. Moreover, brainwave authentication allows ongoing authentication during work sessions, giving ongoing reassurance that the authenticated individual is actually sitting at their workstation, which is not possible with conventional single-point authentication techniques.

Continuous Authentication Monitoring
Real-time User Verification During Sessions

Continuous authentication monitoring is a paradigm shift from legacy single point authentication to continuous identity verification, which covers the whole work session, offering a level of security coverage that is unmatched for sensitive operations. These systems are in constant motion, using behavioral biometrics[17] such as keystroke dynamics, mouse movement pattern, application usage sequence, and interaction timing to ensure confidence in user identity. The monitoring works invisibly in the background and evaluates thousands of micro-behaviors, resulting in unique user signatures that are extremely hard to mimic. When used in conjunction with periodic brainwave sampling, the systems can identify unauthorized access attempts even by those who might know a lot about the legitimate user's passwords and behavioral patterns. Leveraging machine learning algorithms that continually adjust authentication models based on observed user behavior, the technology is able to adapt to normal variation in user behavior while remaining sensitive to anomalies that suggest potential security breaches.

---

[16] Beyrouthy, T., Mostafa, N., Roshdy, A., Karar, A. S., & Alkork, S. (2024). Review of EEG-based biometrics in 5G-IoT: Current trends and future prospects. Applied sciences, 14(2), 534.

[17] https://www.cxodigitalpulse.com/behavioural-biometrics-as-a-compliance-engine-identity-assurance-for-ai-accountability/

Detection of Unauthorized Access Attempts

Advanced intrusion detection for sophisticated unauthorized access attempts that circumvent the initial authentication protocols is centered on subtle behavioral and cognitive cues, which identify when an entity other than the authorized user is accessing secured systems. The detection systems compare patterns of navigation through the system, sequences of application usage, typing patterns, and decision-making timelines to detect deviations from known user profiles. These systems are capable of identifying advanced persistent threats in which attackers have acquired legitimate credentials but are unable to mimic the cognitive and behavioral characteristics of the legitimate user. The technology contains adaptive learning algorithms which update constantly user behavioral models while keeping sensitivity to anomalous activities that may be potential security breaches. Detection protocols also include context-aware analysis that takes into consideration factors such as location, time of access, and system state to increase accuracy and decrease false positive alerts.

Behavioral Biometric Correlation

Advanced behavioral biometric correlation systems produce multi-dimensional user profiles that combine multiple behavioral and physiological cues for strong continuous authentication capabilities. The systems relate keystroke dynamics, mouse movements, voice characteristics (if available), and even gait analysis from mobile devices to compile detailed behavioral signatures, unique to each individual. The correlation algorithms are used to find correlations among different modalities of behavior, allowing the system to keep authentication confidence even when some biometrics channels are not available or are compromised. Advanced correlation techniques: temporal pattern analysis, which looks at how characteristics of behavior change over the day and across various types of tasks to make authentication decisions more accurately. The systems also deploy privacy-preserving correlation techniques that ensure that individual behavioral data are protected, while at the same time keeping the security efficient, ensuring behavioral profiling cannot be used for illegal surveillance or invasion of privacy.

Threat Detection and Analysis Enhancement
Analyst Performance Optimization
Neurofeedback Training for Pattern Recognition

Neurofeedback training protocols for security analysts can help to improve pattern recognition abilities by focusing on training the brain to strengthen neural pathways for visual processing, anomaly detection, and threat signature recognition. The training employs targeted brain stimulation techniques that increase gamma wave activity (30–100 Hz) in areas associated with the binding of patterns and the integration of features to improve the ability of the analysts to discern subtle anomalies in complex data streams.[18] Training simulators use actual data collected for security purposes and monitor brain activity during training to help analysts learn how to get their brains into the best neural states for pattern recognition tasks. In particular, the protocols aim to improve cross-modal pattern integration, so that analysts can correlate patterns among multiple data types (network traffic, user behavior logs, system performance metrics, etc.). Advanced training involves the development of threat instinct through the enhancement of theta waves through protocols that heighten the integration of conscious analytical functions with subconscious pattern recognition functions.

---

[18] https://pmc.ncbi.nlm.nih.gov/articles/PMC11657232/

Enhanced Anomaly Detection Capabilities

Advanced persistent threats and attacks by insiders are making analysts' capacity to detect even the more sophisticated threats, based on subtle deviations from regular patterns of system or user behavior, an even more critical challenge, which programs like cognitive enhancement programs can help to improve. The enhancement protocols integrate neurofeedback training with a unique analytical framework that enhances the ability to discriminate between actual anomalies and benign variations in system behavior.[19] Training involves showing analysts thousands of labeled security situations while recording cognitive brain activity, and helping them learn how to interpret the mild neural cues that indicate a real threat. The programs also include metacognitive training which helps analysts to be more aware of their own decision-making processes and cognitive biases to enhance overall analytical accuracy. In addition to basic threat detection skills, the training incorporates the development of multi-layered threat detection abilities where analysts learn to simultaneously monitor multiple types of security indicators while keeping fingers on the broader threat landscapes as well as methodologies of attacks.

Reduced False Positive Rates Through Cognitive Training

Cognitive enhancement techniques are implemented to help improve threat discrimination accuracy, as illustrated by comprehensive training programs that specifically address the critical challenge of false positive alerts that can overwhelm security operations and obscure true threats. The training scenarios involve building-up fine-tuned pattern recognition skills that will be able to differentiate between real-time security threats

---

[19] Klutz, D. (2023). Neurofeedback for Cognitive Enhancement Intervention and Brain Plasticity. *Journal of Biomedical and Sustainable Healthcare Applications*, *3*(1), 045–055.

and benign system anomalies or normal variation in user patterns, picked by devices trained in neuro mechanisms. Analysts are trained in a combination of traditional security analysis techniques and in cognitive enhancement techniques that are used to increase decision accuracy under uncertainty. The programs feature bias reduction training to help analysts identify and overcome cognitive tendencies that result in false positive alerts, such as confirmation bias and pattern seeking in random data. Advanced training includes confidence calibration drills to teach analysts to reliably determine their own levels of confidence in threat assessments, so that security alerts can be more effectively prioritized and analytical resources can be allocated more effectively.

Automated Threat Response Systems
Brain-State Triggered Security Protocols

Revolutionary security systems monitor the brainwave activity of security staff and automatically implement higher levels of security when certain brainwave patterns are detected, linking the human intuitive response with automated security responses. The systems utilize real-time EEG monitoring and use neural signatures that are indicative of threat awareness, stress response, or hyper-vigilance to automatically trigger pre-defined security measures such as increased surveillance, team alerts or system lockdowns. The brain-state triggers are tuned to the individual's neural patterns and can differentiate between types of cognitive alerts, like normal security concerns as opposed to critical threat detection. Advanced systems use machine learning algorithms that learn to set trigger thresholds over time based on the results of the operation, reducing false positives while avoiding losing signal for legitimate security events. Depending on the severity of the problem, the automated protocols can scale from a simple security adjustment for a low-level threat to a full lockdown for a high-level threat indicator.

Subconscious Threat Detection Mechanisms

Sophisticated monitoring systems capture and analyze subconscious threat detection signals often preceding conscious awareness of security threats, harnessing your brain's natural ability to detect danger before it reaches conscious perception. These measures monitor subtle physiological markers such as pupil dilation, skin conductance, micro-expressions, and specialized EEG patterns of the subconscious threat processing. It has been found that humans can perceive potential hazards at a neurological level seconds or minutes before conscious awareness of the hazard, allowing security systems to take advantage of those early warning periods. Using sophisticated signal processing, the detection engines are used to detect these subtle cues while filtering responses to benign stimuli, looking only for patterns related to real security issues. When subconscious threat indicators are identified, the system sends subtle alerts to security personnel, guiding their conscious focus to areas or data streams of concern without drowning them in false alarms.

Integration with Existing SIEM Systems

Advanced integration protocols link cognitive enhancement technologies with current SIEM systems, forming hybrid security solutions that combine the increased human effectiveness with artificial intelligence for better threat detection and response. The integration means cognitive insights from enhanced security operators can be used to train automated threat analysis algorithms, while SIEM-based alerts, when coupled with Neuro Cyber Threat Intelligence (NCTI) feeds, can be used to prompt specific cognitive enhancement protocols to apply to relevant analysts. Example: Feedback loop – Human cognitive responses to security events help train and refine automated detection algorithms while AI-identified patterns can activate specific neurofeedback protocols that maximize analyst performance for a given threat type. The systems also leave behind fully auditable trails of automated and human-augmented decision-making processes for which they are accountable, and which can also be used to drive ongoing improvements in integrated security capabilities. Integration protocols also come with failover systems that guarantee security coverage in case of any disruptions along either the human enhancement or automatic SIEM components, providing strong security posture under all operational conditions.

The Role of Neurofeedback in Cybersecurity
Strategic Implementation Framework

The convergence of neurofeedback technology and cybersecurity is a turning point in the evolution of security operations.[20] As organizations navigate this technological frontier, the integration of neurofeedback systems demands a delicate balance, offering a blend of innovation and security considerations.[21] As this chapter illustrates, there is a body of evidence that shows that neurofeedback technology can produce tangible improvements in cognitive function, attention control, and threat detection. However, the dual nature of these systems-both as security enhancement tools, and potential attack vectors obliges advanced implementation frameworks that deal with technical, ethical, and operational considerations simultaneously.[22] Organizations need to build overarching governance frameworks, including neural data protection[23]

---

[20] https://www.cooley.com/news/insight/2025/2025-03-13-unlocking-neural-privacy-the-legal-and-ethical-frontiers-of-neural-data

[21] https://www.scottmadden.com/insight/security-operating-model-strategic-approach-building-secure-organization/

[22] https://www.scientificarchives.com/article/ethical-frontiers-navigating-the-intersection-of-neurotechnology-and-cybersecurity

[23] https://www.edps.europa.eu/data-protection/our-work/publications/techdispatch/2024-06-03-techdispatch-12024-neurodata_en

and consent management[24] and performance optimization. The recent appointment of an ad hoc Expert group from UNESCO to allow a new global standard on the ethics of neurotechnology, emphasizes the need for governance frameworks as with the framework planned for adoption in November. California's SB 1223 (2024) specifically identifies neural data as sensitive personal information, thereby triggering stronger protections and mandating opt-in consent before neural data can be collected[25] explicitly, identifies neural data as sensitive personal information, thereby triggering stronger protections and mandating opt-in consent before any collection of neural data. Cognitive-enhanced security implementation demands change management, staff training, and thoughtful integration with existing security infrastructures. Success in this arena will hinge on organizations' ability to simultaneously ensure security effectiveness while ensuring a framework to handle change in a controlled and organized manner, for a more resilient IT environment that can withstand and respond to the ever-changing face of cyber threat.

Risk-Benefit Analysis and Future Outlook

The integration of neurofeedback technology in cybersecurity environments introduces a complicated risk-benefit analysis that needs to be optimized on a case-by-case organizational basis. With documented benefits of notable improvements in threat detection capabilities, studies have indicated that false positive reduction is responsible for 40% of the benefits and detection accuracy improvement is 35%, while cost savings from reduced breach impact are 25%. Development and evaluation of a BCI-neurofeedback system to assist neurorehabilitation of children with cerebral palsy using real-time EEG detection and electrical stimulation

---

[24] https://secureprivacy.ai/blog/neurodata-consent-eeg-brain-computer-interface-data-gdpr-ccpa
[25] https://pubmed.ncbi.nlm.nih.gov/30453757/

during motor attempt (rehabilitation CP, 25). A recent survey found that AI-enhanced systems can improve threat detection by 60% and operational efficiency by 51%; this is a significant competitive edge in a threat landscape that is becoming more sophisticated every day.[26] However, these must be balanced against the new attack surfaces, privacy considerations and possible cognitive dependencies that can undermine security when systems break down. Future works of this field will probably engage on the overcoming of the current limitations by means of better miniaturization of the hardware, more secure privacy-preserving algorithms, and new stronger integration protocols. Trending toward a hybrid human-AI security operations model has proven that the application of AI-powered cybersecurity solutions greatly increases threat detection accuracy, response time, and overall system resilience. Organizations that successfully make this transition will gain major strategic advantages; and organizations that cannot adapt will increasingly be vulnerable to adversaries who have mastered cognitive enhancement technologies.

While the legal framework will require ongoing re-evaluation as current regulations like the EU GDPR and CCPA offer basic protections for personal data, including neural and cognitive biometric data, these will often be inadequate to contain the specific risks inherent in data obtained beyond the clinic. Organizations who deploy neurofeedback systems need to be prepared for regulatory scrutiny and compliance that will increase, with frameworks to be adopted in November 2025 that will help ensure neurotechnologies comply with human rights. California's SB 1223 is a novel, much-needed step to protect the unethical use of neural data by companies collecting the data, while also helping to create industry standards and best practices that will shape the future of the technology.

---

[26] https://industrialcyber.co/ai/takepoint-research-80-of-cybersecurity-professionals-favor-ai-benefits-over-evolving-risks/

Strategic Recommendations

Neurofeedback technology's integration with cybersecurity is both a revolutionary possibility and necessity for sustaining security effectiveness amid dynamic threats. The research and analysis in this chapter show that neurofeedback systems can be used to measure improvements in human security performance and add new capabilities for authentication, threat detection, and optimization of operator performance. However, to succeed, organizations must create sophisticated frameworks that place enterprise-wide cybersecurity strategy at the core of business objectives, in order to set enterprises up for success despite threatening and regulatory climates. For security practitioners, a necessity is to approach the use of neurofeedback with a clear understanding of its transformative potential as well as its risks. The dual nature of the technology as a security enhancement, and also as a possible vulnerability, demands new conceptual frameworks for explaining to executives how they can position their company in a new and different way, and how they can maintain that competitive advantage. Organizations that invest in holistic neurofeedback implementation (complete with good privacy protections, ethical governance structures and integrated security architectures) will be in a position to gain dramatic competitive advantages in threat detection, response capabilities, and overall security resilience.[27]

The future of cybersecurity will continue to rely on effective co-optimization of human cognitive augmentation with artificial intelligence and legacy security technologies, where human cognitive augmentation and machine intelligence synergistically collaborate to increase decision accuracy, efficiency, and innovation. Neurofeedback systems are an important part of this integration, bringing with them the potential to develop security operations which incorporate hybrid intelligence systems

---

[27] https://www.isaca.org/resources/isaca-journal/issues/2025/volume-2/guarding-the-minds-frontier

that combine human knowledge and AI for increasingly complex problem solving. As this field continues to develop, organizations must be attentive to emerging threats while embracing the revolutionary nature of cognitive enhancement technologies, as cognitive warfare and cyber security are intrinsically linked, implying the possibility of positive outcomes through collaboration between the two disciplines.

Key Takeaways

- DARPA's Next Generation Nonsurgical Neurotechnology, or N3 program is a paradigm shift in cybersecurity, away from technical barriers and toward augmenting human cognition directly to improve human security operations. This advancement will allow security professionals to communicate directly with computer systems to better multitask and make decisions in complex military and civilian security situations.

- Neurofeedback systems are not just powerful security enhancement systems, they are a new attack vector and present new challenges to traditional risk assessment models. This dual nature demands organizations build completely new security paradigms that can simultaneously harness the benefits of cognitive enhancement while defending against neural-based attacks on human cognition and decision-making.

- The deployment of neurotechnology into critical infrastructure introduces new interdependencies between human mental performance and system integrity, raising cybersecurity issues to the level of national security. As an extension of information warfare, nation-state entities could and would target neurofeedback systems as a way to manipulate key decision-makers in government, military personnel, and critical infrastructure, opening up new areas of cyber-battle that extend far beyond typical cyberattacks.

- Three main neurofeedback modalities have distinct security use cases: EEG-based systems are in real time, millisecond response times for operational deployment; fMRI-based systems offer high spatial resolution for research and training; and fNIRS-based systems combine portability and accuracy for hybrid monitoring stations in security operations centers.

- In neurofeedback, cognitive performance among security professionals is improved through specific training of brainwaves – enhancement of alpha waves for maintaining attention, modulation of beta waves for active threat analysis, and optimization of theta waves for pattern recognition. Studies have shown measurable results in increased attention span, management of stress, and accuracy of making decisions under pressure.

- EEG-based recognition systems reach 99.86% authentication accuracy with convolutional neural networks, while producing unique neural signatures that can't be stolen, replicated, or coerced like conventional biometrics. In addition to tying directly into existing multi-factor authentication frameworks, these systems can provide ongoing monitoring of work sessions, identifying unauthorized access attempts even if legitimate credentials are compromised.

- Advanced monitoring systems are able to provide continuous information on analyst cognitive workload based on a number of physiological and behavioral metrics, which can then be used to dynamically redistribute tasks and optimize workload. These systems avoid cognitive overload by means of automated interventions in the form of task rotation, break recommendations, and performance optimization protocols, allowing for maximum security effectiveness over longer operational times.

- Brain-state triggered security protocols automatically bring in stronger security measures when specific neural patterns are identified to signal threat detection or high-stress situations, providing seamless integration between human intuition and automated security action. Subconscious threat sensing works by capturing neural indicators that occur before conscious threat awareness and with it comes a capability of early warning that improves the overall security posture.

- Neurofeedback systems must be governed by proper frameworks of protection for neural data, preservation of privacy, and ethical considerations for cognitive enhancement. Organizations have complex regulatory environments to navigate, including the California SB 1223 neural data protection law, upcoming UNESCO neurotechnology ethics standards, and robust fail-safes, staff training protocols and procedures.

- The future of cybersecurity revolves around effective integration of cognitive enhancement technologies with artificial intelligence and traditional security systems to create hybrid human-AI security operations that take advantage of the enhanced human intuition and machine learning capabilities. Organizations that successfully adapt comprehensive neurofeedback systems will secure great competitive advantages (up to 40% improvement in threat detection efficiency and significantly lower costs of false positive alerts) while those not adapting may become more vulnerable to adversaries who have mastered the cognitive enhancement technologies.

## CHAPTER 10

The Future of Neuroscience-Driven Cybersecurity

"The future firewalls will not be protecting code but protecting cognition"

The advent of the neuro-digital age has completely changed our perspective on cybersecurity. No more limited to the sphere of network, endpoint, or even biometric identity, threat landscape has been extended to an absolutely new field, the mind. Neuroscience and cybersecurity are converging at an increasingly fast rate, giving rise to a completely different field, neuro-cybersecurity.

Cybersecurity has been under machine-centric paradigm over the course of decades. There were firewalls, passwords, intrusion detection systems, and even AI-based threat hunters that patrolled digital borders that we could define and segment. When the world is going to include neural interfaces, brain–computer interaction, and cognitive sensing, however, the idea of a perimeter is changing.[1] The new perimeter is not

---

[1] Kritika, E. (2025). Ethical Frontiers: Navigating the Intersection of Neurotechnology and Cybersecurity. *Journal of Experimental Neurology,* 6(1), 21-25.

Kritika, *Neuroscience Meets Cybersecurity*, https://doi.org/10.1007/979-8-8688-2183-7_10

only cognitive but also what a person knows, how he knows, and the way he analyzes it and determines to take action. Take the case of threat vector development. Trust was the victim of social engineering. However, another pathway leads to the situation that has never been in the threat repertoire before, and this is the worrisome finger on the Axis of Evil, the modicum of possible brain–computer interface (BCI) manipulation, neural telemetry, and mental takeover. Consider a malware which never infects your laptop but instead conditions your brain to act in a certain manner.

Neuroscience is getting to the exquisiteness and detail of classical computing. Technologies, such as functional near-infrared spectroscopy (fNIRS), magnetoencephalography (MEG), and high-resolution dry electroencephalograph (EEG) systems have matured to the point of being portable and much more accurate, so brainwave signals can be recorded, analyzed, and responded to in quasi-real time.[2] The change in cybersecurity needs to respond. The era of just authenticating the users based on a password, tokens, or even fingerprints is soon to end. Rather, we are passing into an era in which neural fingerprints, thinking patterns, and emotional conditions do not only serve as identification mechanisms but as access profiles as well. This is not a made-up science fiction, we already know it without making an additional argument, brainwave logins in pilot programs with more to come, and even brain monitoring of people working in potentially fatal environments, to prevent them from lapses caused by brain fatigue. But this also brings a paradox to the table, to gain the mind, we need to get hold of that access should be managed with utmost care, responsibility, and highest ethical standards. Neurodata

---

[2] Xue, Z., Zhang, Y., Li, H., Chen, H., Shen, S., & Du, H. (2024). Instrumentation, measurement, and signal processing in electroencephalography-based brain-computer interfaces: situations and prospects. *IEEE Transactions on Instrumentation and Measurement*, 73, 1–28.

is not like any other data, instead, it is by far more intimate, very unique, and predictive in nature.[3] It does not only tell what you did but why you did it, how it made you feel, and what you may choose to do in future.

With the improvement of human to computational interface by neuroscience, cybersecurity will no longer be a passive defensive system but an active mental companion. Consider brain wave radioactive firewalls guided by AI to detect things strange that show coercion or deception. Imagine that the operators of the critical infrastructure are wearing smart helmets that sense the risk of a mental overload and redirect activities to allow real-time accident prevention or sabotage. Consider imagining the BCIs of the military variety, integrating threat-detecting algorithms into them which are capable of preventing the occurrence of cyber-kinetic attacks, based on a soldier being subjected to the process in real time. A little beyond the immediate future, we are likely to have neuro-augmented cyber environments – in which the system responds to cognitive and emotional state of the user. The AI-based SIEM (Security Information and Event Management) platform may not just interpret the behavior of the network but also the mental anguish or exhaustion of the analyst or their confidence level and thus prioritize the alerts.[4] The whole security stack could be thoroughly interconnected with neurobiological feedback loops, including identity management, anomaly detection, and access control. However, integration comes at a certain cost. As we learn more of the brain, so we come to an even greater danger. What happens when cognitive fingerprints go missing? What if the event BCI is hacked into to affect perception and choices? These are not theoretical questions anymore that needs to be discussed in science, rather the questions that needs action and multidisciplinary approach to forward the convergence of neuroscience,

---

[3] Istace, T. (2024). Neurodata: navigating GDPR and AI act compliance in the context of neurotechnology. The Geneva Academy of International Humanitarian Law and Human Rights

[4] https://www.imarcgroup.com/security-information-event-management-market

cybersecurity, legal, and ethical domains. Governance structures concerning cybersecurity will have to be redefined as we shift our focus to control systems to influencing thought. Science is ahead of the law. The vast majority of international data protection regulations, including GDPR and HIPAA, do not know how to provide such data with any kind of protection at all. Cognitive liberty, mental privacy, and neuro-identity are shaping up as the civil rights of the digital era.

The question to be asked is

- Where is the brain data when you are at work in a BCI?

- Does your mental profile have the ability to predict, or even punish, your future behavior?

- Can there be a freedom of neural silence in hyper-connected society?

Neuro-rights charters, cognitive consent procedures, and neural information sanctuary provisions will be central aspects of Internet security regulation as its sector matures.[5] The cases described above have been joined by researchers in Chile, Spain, and the United States, who are already pioneering legal safeguards to the privacies of the nervous system.[6] However, without the cooperation of industry leaders, security architects, neuroscientists, and policymakers, we will be creating the future that we are not yet prepared to defend. This last chapter challenges you to use your imagination, not as a fantasy, but as a way to the future. We should not only prepare for the probability but what we can prepare on. Neuroscience in cybersecurity is not only going to serve as a supplement, it is going to be

---

[5] Di Salvo, M. (2025). The Protection of Neural Rights in the Age of Neurotechnologies and AI. The Ethical Challenge for Law and Neuroscience. *Russ. J. Econ. & L.*, *19*, 202.

[6] Cornejo-Plaza, M. I., Cippitani, R., & Pasquino, V. (2024). Chilean Supreme Court ruling on the protection of brain activity: neurorights, personal data protection, and neurodata. *Frontiers in Psychology*, *15*, 1330439.

a pillar. The battleground, the interface, the firewall and the vulnerability will be the mind. The story is not yet finished in terms of the end of this book. The questions you have been reading here should now mean entry into your boardrooms, research labs, classrooms, and strategic roadmaps. Since, in the future, the protection of cognition will not be a choice – it will be the core of digital trust.

> *Let us not only move forward in innovation, but with purpose.*

State-of-the-Art: Where We Are Now

An introduction of a cybersecurity vision provided by neuroscience requires understanding on our current state before looking at the future, and it is therefore necessary to embrace an overview of where we are today. Here, this part charts the current landscape of neuro-cybersecurity, its experimental technologies and deployed systems, and the constraints that constitute its continually shifting frontier. The discipline currently exists on the intersection of neuroscience, data science, and behavioral security. It is divided into three major areas of operation, namely, cognitive biometrics, neuroadaptive systems, and neurobehavioral analytics. Meanwhile, each is a significant component in the paradigm shift of cybersecurity based on a machine focus to one based on the focus of the human mind.

Cognitive Biometrics

Cognitive biometrics implies the use of patterns in brainwaves as a personalized method of user validation.[7] Examples of such signals include

---

[7] Arias-Cabarcos, P., Fallahi, M., Habrich, T., Schulze, K., Becker, C., & Strufe, T. (2023). Performance and usability evaluation of brainwave authentication

P300 response, steady-state visually evoked potentials (SSVEPs), or motor imagery-based EEG signals, which can be non-invasively measured and used to confirm identity. Brainwaves are dynamic as compared with conventional biometrics (fingerprints or iris scans) in that they are representative of identity, and also in the context of the mind.[8] It is both harder to copy and might be more secure, but, on the other hand, more sensitive. Multiple pilot programs and start-ups are already making attempts to operationalize EEG-based login systems, in which the user could authenticate by putting on a headset. These systems claim support of continuous authentication, the detection that happens not only at login time of the user that claims they are who they say they are but over the entire session. This enduring model is geared to solve a decades-old deficiency in identity assurance of high-risk missions.

Neuroadaptive Security Systems

The next step of sophistication is neuroadaptive systems.[9] These systems rely on neurophysiological feedback about the situation of a user in real time to determine how to adjust the system, which includes EEG feedback, functional near-infrared spectroscopy (fNIRS) feedback, or feedback about eye-tracking. To give an example, in case the attention level of a cybersecurity analyst declines or the cognition load becomes too high, the interface may reduce the illumination of secondary information, halt the decision-making scenario, or notify the supervisor. Neuroadaptive controls

---

techniques with consumer devices. *ACM Transactions on Privacy and Security*, *26*(3), 1–36.

[8] Di Mambro, A. (2025). Beyond brainwaves: exploring emotions, identity, and motor imagery through EEG-based BCI.

[9] Fernández-García, C. E., Marín, D. V., & Velásquez, H. S. (2023). Neurohacking and Artificial Intelligence in the Vulnerability of the Human Brain: Are We Facing a Threat?. In *Artificial Intelligence in Higher Education and Scientific Research: Future Development* (pp. 117–128). Singapore: Springer Nature Singapore.

are under development in aircraft, armed forces, and nuclear observation centers, any system where cognitive overload or exhaustion may cause the gravest disaster. In cybersecurity operations centers (SOCs), such systems may eventually assist analysts in the triage of difficult alerts or during stressful incidents in real time.

Neurobehavioral Analytics

Neurobehavioral analytics may be the most ethically sensitive and controversial current developments, in which neurodata is used to identify intent or emotion in real time.[10] With a combination of data on the brain along with behavioral and environmental data, researchers are developing systems capable of predicting deception or stress or malicious insider behavior.[11] By way of illustration, EEG patterns have been applied in case-based experiments in lie detection with the effect of recognizing cognitive dissonance during situations in which subjects have provided deceptive responses. In organizational security, it might be possible to filter out abnormal access behavior based on neurobehavioral patterns, instead of the code-based access behavior. This machine learning paradigm is in its early stages, with promising prospects in the area of counterintelligence, fraud detection, and digital forensics, although it presents significant ethical dilemmas regarding privacy, consent, and interpretation.

---

[10] Najafabadi, A. J., Skryzhadlovska, A., & Valilai, O. F. (2024). Agile product development by prediction of consumers' behaviour; using neurobehavioral and social media sentiment analysis approaches. *Procedia Computer Science, 232,* 1683–1693.

[11] Kritika, M. (2025). A comprehensive study on navigating neuroethics in Cyberspace. *AI and Ethics, 5*(1), 93–100.

Barriers and Limitations

Although the technology is poised to make big changes, there are a number of restraints that have prevented them. In a number of real-world applications, brain–computer interfaces (BCI) hardware is large or invasive. The quality of signal can be compromised due to noise, motion artifact, or variable user response. EEG headsets are optimized to work in most cases at controlled laboratories, not in dynamic workplaces, especially in war zones where a lot of ambiguity prevails. Software-wise, how to interpret the signal of the neural components is not standardized at all. No standardized system has been developed in converting brain information into viable security intelligence. Trained neural networks that are non-generalizable have models and structures, which are applicable to specific users and situations. Also, the lack of legal and ethical systems is predominant. Neuro data confuses the boundaries of health data, personal metadata, and biometric information, as to who possesses it, what one can do to it, and other forms of coercion. Laws concerning cognitive liberty, neuro-rights have only been implemented in a very small number of countries (e.g., Chile).

Momentum and the Road Ahead

The trend is, however, clear. DARPA, N3 (Next-Generation Nonsurgical Neurotechnology)[12] and the European Union Human Brain Project are among programs displaying an increasing interest and mounting financial investments. The seeds of neuro-cybersecurity are already being sown in the sectors where there is zero tolerance to failures – defense, finance, and critical infrastructure. Today, that is experimental, tomorrow, it is default. The following section investigates the directions that such foundations may take. So with that, we begin to depart the present scenery and drift into a dreamy view of the world of tomorrow, and what those dreams and possibilities mean to security, privacy, and the human condition itself.

Visionary Frontiers: What the Next Decade May Bring

The next decade will become the milestone in the history of cybersecurity when we will transform reactive defenses into predictive, cognitive, and even introspective security systems. Neuroscience will not just provide an improved defense strategy, it will even provide a new foundation of security modeling. Here we venture into the boundaries of the possible as seen in this vision, based in neural-digital twins and all the way to fully immersive, neuro-augmented cyber ecosystems, as shown in Figure 10-1.

---

[12]https://www.darpa.mil/research/programs/next-generation-nonsurgical-neurotechnology

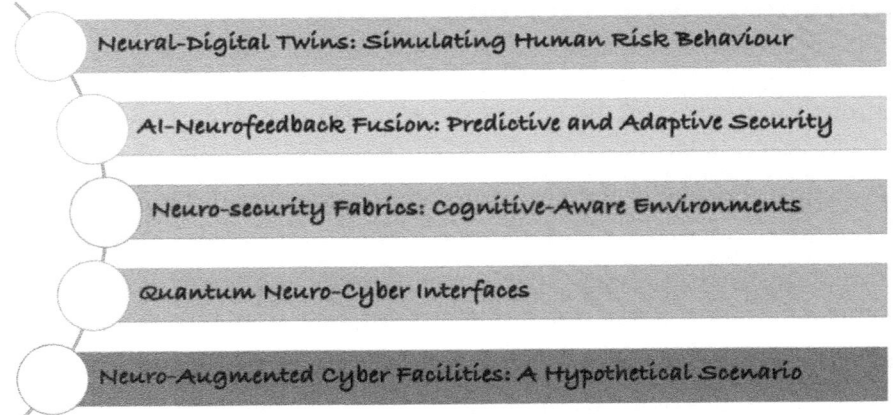

Figure 10-1. *Visionary Frontiers*

Neural-Digital Twins: Simulating Human Risk Behavior

Already, digital twins (or virtual models of systems or situations) are transforming the field of engineering and industry. Visualize a neural-digital twin, a living model of the cognitive-emotional condition of a person, constructed on the basis of neurodata, behavioral telemetry, psychophysiological data. These twins would share how a person would respond under cognitive pressure, emotional pressure, or even lying.

Applications of neural twins in cybersecurity include the following:

- Train AI solutions to discover psychological or cognitive postulations of insider threats in advance.

- Simulate the way attackers can use decision fatigue, social action, or loopholes.

- Mock executive reactions to the crisis so that it is possible to perform proactive planning of an incident.

It will be technically difficult, but precursors are being established in affective computing and digital phenotyping – secure development of synthetic personas driven by real neural fingerprints.

AI-Neurofeedback Fusion: Predictive and Adaptive Security

The combination of neurofeedback systems and highly developed AI will result in such adaptive cybersecurity levels that will not limit themselves to threat detection, but will be able to react to the real-time reception of the mental state of the user.

They are applied in the following cases:

- Emotionally sensitive security measures that raise or lower various controls based on how emotionally aroused, tired, or anxious the user is.

- Cognitive threat anticipation, in this case the system adjusts access control in the event of early indication of cognitive overload or distraction.

- Machine-guided recovery with invented interventions that are neurofeedback-based to counter cognitive fallout in vulnerable users in case of a breach.

Essentially, the AI system will be used as a cognitive co-pilot in addition to the watchdog since it will identify the weaknesses before they translate as errors.

Neuro-security Fabrics: Cognitive-Aware Environments

Neurosecurity fabrics – integrated platforms where neurobiological data is constantly viewed along with being embedded in the computing environment may find a rise in its usage in times ahead. Such texts will contain:

- Forms of brain–computer interaction, wearable sensors, on to ambient EEG in smart environments, multi-layered.

- Neural condition flags, which changes access, privileges, or UI design automatically based on detection of stress or intent.

- Neural data control should be decentralized, and the user must have access by possessing cryptographic keys to their own cognitive telemetry, selectively revealing data.

The neurosecurity fabric will move the security covers beyond the devices to security covers in the mindstate of the user where the protection mechanisms will be not only embedded in the code but also the code of mind.

Quantum Neuro-Cyber Interfaces

Even though this is still in the speculative category, studies are beginning on the intersection between quantum computing and neural signal processing. The quantum technologies have the potential to be used in the future to

- Increase the privacy of neural communications

- Represented distributed neural networks with joint workforces by means of model entangled states

- Forecast neuro-cognitive states and detect abnormal sectors of behavior by means of quantum machine learning at an ultra-fast speed of operation

This union of quantum and cognitive systems has a chance to release predictive power that we have never seen in the past but at the same time will also pose threats that we are not able to fathom yet.

Neuro-Augmented Cyber Facilities: A Hypothetical Scenario

Cyber Fort Knox: a national-onion cybersecurity center with all intelligent-integrated analysts. Every analyst has a non-invasive neuro-interface fitted on him that constantly gauges the cognitive load, stress, intention, and pattern of decision-making. The neurofeedback AI and the SOC (Security Operations Center) deployed by the facility in real time are used to

- Get priority treatment, alerts should contain information according to per-level comprehension and attention on an hour-by-hour basis of the analyst.

- Use break interventions (tasks and rotations rotation), automated helps when overload is identified.

- Protect top-secret activities through dynamic brain print authentication – where the identities can not only control the entry but also the thought habits of what was on mission.

The whole system is powered by a closed-loop cognitive security engine, behaviorally conditioned to collective neurostate of its operators. Here mind and machine are combined not only in operation but in protection.

Overcoming Critical Challenges

The application of neuroscience to cybersecurity is promising, though it also introduces certain ethical dilemmas and social conflict of an unprecedented sort in the field of information security. Neural data are not the next-in-line of biometrics, they are the final lineage of truly personal things. The section under consideration discusses the major problems encountered in the development of neuro-augmented cybersecurity systems with regard to three central areas such as privacy and neuroethics, technology obstacles, and social adoption, as shown in Figure 10-2.

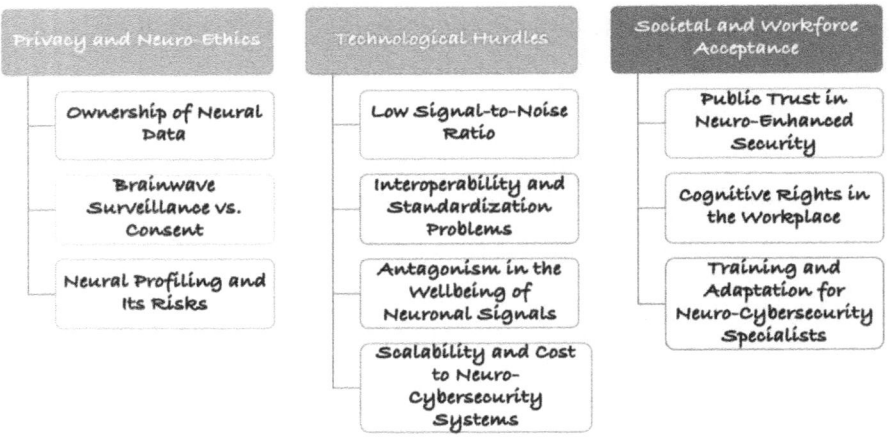

Figure 10-2. *Critical Challenges*

Privacy and Neuro-Ethics

Ownership of Neural Data

Brainwave patterns, thought signatures, and emotional reactions are neural data, and they are immensely individual in character. It is forecasting about the state of the mind and can be used to deduce intention, emotional weaknesses as well as thought. Neural patterns cannot be reissued unlike with passwords or token subjects. They are of non-renewal nature. The major turning point happened in 2021, when a new constitution was adopted in Chile which now included the concept of neuro-rights, as a new amendment, becoming the first country to establish cognitive freedom and mental privacy. The mental integrity is also covered by the new Article 19, the data of neural information that people are owners of. This was challenged aggressively in 2023 when the Supreme Court of Chile ruled that the storage of brain wave data by Emotiv, a US-based Neurotechnology company, had violated the privacy rights of former Senator by retaining his brain wave data without granular consent even though the data had been anonymized. In 2024, Colorado, the first state, passed a law that explicitly protects neural data, which is referred to as sensitive biometric data.[13] It requires companies providing neurotech to acquire affirmed, opt-in permission prior to gathering, storing, or transmitting data notwithstanding that changed or created by an individual brain.

Key Takeaways: Neural data should be defined to be treated as a sui generis category with the concept of extracting legal protection to this data going forward, analogous to [bodily] integrity. People should be the only owners of their data that is created by the brain.

---

[13] https://pmc.ncbi.nlm.nih.gov/articles/PMC11951885

Brainwave Surveillance vs. Consent

Unceasing brain monitoring would give cybersecurity departments an opportunity to recognize insider threats, anticipate fatigue and error in response to cyberattacks, or even the anticipation of stress. Again, it may do this instead because the same data can be deployed, unethically, to check productivity, engage in emotional manipulation or profiling. In 2025, Senators Schumer, Cantwell, and Markey petitioned the US Federal Trade Commission to look into businesses of Neuralink whose neural data collection and usage practices raised serious concerns about transparency and consumer consent.[14] They are worried that consumers are purchasing wellness gadgets, and, out of ignorance, giving up highly sensitive neurodata without actual informed consent.

The ethical neurocybersecurity systems should:

- Do granular consent (e.g., brainprint authentication is not mood detection).

- It should make dynamic opt-in/out possible in particular states of high sensitivity characteristics (e.g., emotional trauma).

- Support revocable access to data, including audit trails that cannot be modified and user dashboards to regulate exposure associated with neural footprints.

The latest studies promote the application of the model of consent based on BCI, where the user of a certain app can ensure the collection of data with the help of neural intent, which is the most legitimate type of affirmative consent.

---

[14] https://www.commerce.senate.gov/2025/4/cantwell-schumer-markey-call-on-ftc-to-protect-consumers-neural-data

Neural Profiling and Its Risks

Neural profiling is derived by creating behavior/psychological models using brainwave patterns. Such profiles are useful: they enable security systems to respond flexibly to stress or uncertainty, and avoid committing errors in important missions.

Yet they are also very dangerous:

- Profiling may be applied in terms of hiring or promotion.

- The insurance companies may deduce and exploit the risks of mental illness from neural data.

- Law enforcement authorities may be liable for wrongfully labeling individuals based on the charges of neurodivergent characteristics as potential threats.

There is no national law that forbids neurological discrimination in the United States. For example, neuro-enhanced security operations center (SOC) may negatively evaluate a cybersecurity specialist with high neural volatility instead of understanding it as a reaction to trauma. The answer is to put in place cognitive ethics oversight, analogous to medical IRBs, that regulates

- Which kind of profiling is allowed (e.g., validation of intent, but not detection of political preference)

- Life and survival of cognitive metadata

- Protection against cross-context malevolent ambition (e.g., workplace abuse in insurance markets)

Technological Hurdles

Low Signal-to-Noise Ratio

Exposure to neurophysiological work as recorded by any EEG, fNIRS, or ECoG is already weak and very prone to interference. Readings can be contaminated by motion artifacts, environmental noise, and even by expressions of the user at the microscale. This reduces accuracy, reliability to uncontrolled real-world settings such as security operations centers or operational environments with high stress such as military operations and deployments. Neural data, unlike static biometrics, is dynamic and context sensitive, which makes consistent interpretation hard in outside laboratory conditions.

Interoperability and Standardization Problems

Neural signaling does not have a standard method of translating the information into usable cybersecurity intelligence. Various neurotech vendors employ proprietary signal-processing routines, which causes fragmentation of the ecosystem's approaches that are not readily able to interoperate. This inability to interoperate cannot result in an uncomplicated installation on multi-vendor environment and this makes enterprise deployment complicated. Further, neural datasets tend to be user-specific, that is, a neural network trained on user A is unlikely to perform well on user B, which further complicates large-scale deployment.

Antagonism in the Well-being of Neuronal Signals

BCIs present a new attack dimension. As an example, the adversarial neurostimulation has the ability of injecting conflating signals that change the perception or decision. Identity verification would be compromised by neural spoofing, that is, when an infiltrator copies the brainwave patterns of someone. Likewise, adversarial AI models might train to alter or misinterpret neural telemetry and cause false alarms or beat neuro-authentication systems. Perfecting highly secure, tamper-proof neural interfaces is an exercise in wait and see.

Scalability and Cost to Neuro-Cybersecurity Systems

Neuro-cybersecurity does not yet have a standardized hardware such as high-resolution EEG headsets or fNIRS equipment, which is still prohibitively expensive to install widely. There are further operating overheads in maintenance, calibration, and special training. Taking these systems out of the high-value use case like defense or critical infrastructure settings to implement them universally will involve more cost savings as well as simplification of experiences to the user, similar to the example of early biometric technologies.

Societal and Workforce Acceptance

Public Trust in Neuro-Enhanced Security

Implementation of neuro-enhanced security technologies will contribute to basic violation of the understanding of privacy, autonomy, and human dignity by the population. Neuro-cybersecurity interfaces also differ with other conventional cybersecurity instruments in the sense that neuro-cybersecurity interfaces communicate with the neural decision-making system of human beings and record neural signatures, emotive reactions, and even the subconscious phenomenon. This intimacy brings about a psychic impediment to acceptance and is by far more difficult than the opposition that biometrics such as facial recognition or fingerprint scanning creates. Trust between people and neurotechnologies depends on whether they will be used in hidden spying or manipulation. However, history dictates doubt. Facial recognition has been introduced as a means of convenience and even security but quickly turned into a tool of mass surveillance in certain territories. The same story may happen with BCIs and neural observation systems. To give an example, when organizations started applying neuro-data in the context of basing the profile on emotional resilience or cognitive biases, people can feel that they are downgraded to neurological data instead of being treated as autonomous agents with their own agency.

Also, a cultural and ethical aspect is to be taken into account. In several societies, the feeling of self and personal liberation are highly associated with the context of mental privacy. The idea that thoughts can be read or maybe partially inferred by an external system might be the concept that causes some existential fears that a loss of free will is upon people. In the absence of obvious protections, the concept of neuro-cybersecurity might be viewed as the prospect of thought policing, particularly concerning the uses to which it is placed by government agencies or other business formations. To tackle such inhibitors, clear governance and people involvement in deciding should form part of the neurosecurity roll out. Education messages on what is gathered, how it is analyzed, and what is done with the data and who has access will be the key to assuring people. Moreover, they should create autonomous oversight organizations that would audit the neuro-data collection and make sure it is used ethically. Case studies such as the pro-neuro-rights provisions of the Constitution of Chile and neural data privacy and protection legislation in Colorado demonstrate the power of legal instruments to shape a positive public attitude. After all, trust will not be achieved by a technological promise but by following the integration of neuro-cybersecurity into a larger ethico-legal framework that conveys the focus on individual agency. Loss of public trust is nearly next to impossible, and fear should hence be proactively handled before it concretizes into resistance.

Cognitive Rights in the Workplace

The idea of neuro-monitoring in the workspace landscape brings to the fore some deep ethical issues concerning mental liberty and rights of workers. Neuro-enhanced monitoring could be considered a precautionary measure in critical industries like defense, energy, and other critical infrastructures where fatigue, insider threats, and lack of judgment need to be averted. As an illustration, the security guard of a nuclear facility might be equipped with EEG-enabling helmets that would report stress levels and cognitive loads to avoid fatal misunderstandings. Though this would increase safety, it will also erase the boundary between free will and being forced. An important question will be whether neuro-monitoring will be able to obtain informed consent by employees when it is made a condition of employment. Otherwise, when refusing to give neural data leads to less opportunity or loss of employment, then consent is a ritual and not a free choice. This interaction poses a danger of developing a workplace surveillance culture where workers feel that they are under constant scrutiny not just in what they do but also in how they feel on the inside. Eventually, this will bring about anxiety, poor morale, and sometimes opposition to the use of the very technology that is meant to enhance safety. Furthermore, the cognitive profiling carries an additional risk of giving rise to discriminatory patterns, whereby, individuals maybe unfairly judged, excluded or disadvantaged based on their neural and cognitive data rather than their actual performance or behavior. Neuro-data can provide an unintentional disclosure of such conditions as PTSD, ADHD or early symptoms of neurodegenerative diseases. In the absence of stringent rules, this kind of insight may be applied to deny a promotion, change a job, or even fire a person under the excuse of making performance more efficient.

This brings analogies to genetic discrimination arguments, when employers and insurers abused once-sensitive biological data until legal protection mechanisms became available in the form of the Genetic Information Non-Discrimination Act in the United States. Neuro-rights frameworks should be put expressly into workflow policies to maintain fairness. The people should own their cognitive data and be given some dynamic consent tools where they would give and take away a certain monitoring role. In addition, independent ethics boards ought to be used to govern any neuro-monitoring program just like Institutional Review Boards (IRBs) in medical research. There will be a need of subtlety in maintaining balance between safety and autonomy. Whereas some roles may make reasonable neuro-monitoring protection, it must be assumed that there is no neuro-monitoring at all, and that any intrusion into cognitive privacy is retributively justified. Such safeguards are essential within the working environment, as otherwise workplaces may turn into the battlegrounds of neural authoritarianism, destroying the roots of trust between employers and employees.

Training and Adaptation for Neuro-Cybersecurity Specialists

The implementation of neuro-cyber security technologies depends not only on the maturity in the technical aspect but also upon the preparedness of the workforce to use and work with the technologies. In contrast to classical tools of cybersecurity, neuro-augmented systems demand interdisciplinary knowledge that comes to meet the domains of neuroscience, psychology, data science, and ethical governance. The existing manpower, being largely educated in traditional information technology (IT) security, or network defense, is not literate in cognitive neuroscience and therefore would not handle neuro-data in a responsible and effective way. In order to overcome the gap, a dedicated training curriculum should be created to provide cybersecurity professionals with introductory knowledge to this topic, including exposure to neural signal acquisition, cognitive biomarkers, and neuroethical concerns. This will comprise practical sessions of data interpretation facts about EEG and fNIRS, learnings about drawbacks in brain–computer interfacing, and identifying possible biases in neuro-behavioral analysis. University-based cross-sector programs in neurotech, universities, and policy institute can serve to develop ways to certify what can be called neuro-cybersecurity specialists, who will know their way around the technical and ethical challenges in this area.

In addition, adaptation is not just confined to technical training. The professionals will have to develop psychological resilience, and ethical reflexivity. To take an example, SOC analysts who deal with neuroadaptive systems would have to acquire the skills of real-time interpretation of not only anomalies in the network but also of neural stress. In a similar manner, managers of neuro-secure environments as well will have to learn about the legal side of handling neural data, being able not only to adhere to the changing laws of neuro-rights. Organization culture is another major variable. Teams should be ready to operate in a complex of conditions when human thinking is a security pillar and a weakness at the same time. One cannot undermine employee resistance to workflows that are used traditionally. Hence, the aspect of change management such as open communication and involvement in the development of the neuro-monitoring policy will be instrumental to prevent backlash.

Finally, neuro-cybersecurity specialists should have ethical training that mirrors technical training. Learning to deal with the ethical dilemma of cognitive liberty, informed consent, and neural discrimination will allow practitioners to understand the concepts clearly. Decision-making may be supported with professional codes of behavior, similar to schemes of medical ethics, when acting in unclear situations. The long-term solution to developing a talent pipeline of interdisciplinary expertise in neuro-cybersecurity will be to incorporate neuro-cybersecurity into academic programs, drawing students to study and solve neuro-cybersecurity problems in computer science, neuroscience, and law. Unless adequate investment in education and adaptation to change has been carried out proactively, the mismatch between technological competency and human preparedness will act as a brake on safe and ethical implementation of neuro-enhanced security systems.

With these multi-dimensional ethical, technical, and human-centric challenges starting to crystallize, the attention now has to move on to how societies and institutions can devise powerful mechanisms or platforms, namely, governance institutions, policies, and international cooperation, ensuring that neuro-cybersecurity is introduced into the legal and cultural environment in a responsible manner.

Future Governance and Policy Frameworks
Global Neuro-Rights Charters

Neuro-rights is a new and fast-spreading idea of the international community because neuro-rights are the new stage of digital human rights. In contrast to the traditional set of privacy legislation, neuro rights are intended to protect cognitive liberty, mental privacy and psychological continuity. Chile has gone even further and, in 2021, through constitutional amendment declared the term used as inviolable, that of mental integrity. There are various organizations that are creating common tendencies on the neuro-rights agenda world enough. The Neurorights Foundation has suggested five fundamental neuro-rights in cooperation with UNESCO, mental privacy, personal identity, free will, equal access to mental augmentation, and protection against algorithmic bias. According to UNESCO in 2024, more than 40 countries were interested in their adoption to be used in AI and neurotech regulation systems in the future.[15] Examples include Spain to add to its Digital Rights Charter in 2023, the so-called neurorights protection principles. Nonetheless it is not harmonized. The GDPR of the EU only indirectly includes such data of the nervous system in the special categories when they are connected with health or biometric identity. Security-related

---

[15] https://unesdoc.unesco.org/ark:/48223/pf0000391074

neurodata or brainwave telemetry on an emotional basis or base are not very regulated. On the same note, there is no federal level of neurorights re-establishment in the United States, which is left to individuals, ready to provide them piecemeal protection, such as Colorado.

There are proponents of a global neuro-rights charter, in the same way as the Universal Declaration of Human Rights, that would unify these disjointed initiatives. The minimum guarantees that such a charter might provide include some form of opting in to the use of neural data, ban on commodifying data about brains and their contents, and the right to a "neural silence" (not being forced into neuro-monitoring). In the absence of an international baseline, differences between national laws could produce an escape hole resulting in neuro-data processing shifted to jurisdictions with more lax laws as previously seen with data havens. Whereas international agreements set values, implementation procedures must be provided to put them into practice. Early efforts at operationalizing the protections in the neuro-cybersecurity field by means of tangible legal tools are being observed.

Standardizing Legal and Ethical Protocols

In the United States, the Colorado Privacy Act was extended by HB24-1058 (2024) to expressly treat neural data as sensitive data, requiring positive opt-in consent and quantitative risk assessments of residual data security before any processing involving brainwaves is effected.[16] It is currently the first state law that accords neural signals the identical protection timbre as genetic/biometric data. In comparison, California CPRA now treats the neural data as sensitive information, but companies can now opt-out rather than having to opt-in, which leaves companies with different responsibilities based on the two states they operate in. The GDPR of Europe is the most developed one. Data in the form of neural signals

---

[16] https://leg.colorado.gov/bills/hb24-1058

gathered to be used in an area of research or to verify identity is already special category data, and this needs explicit consent and a lawful basis in terms of processing. But the EU has gone a step further with their AI Act (adopted 2024) in that it has classified subject matters such affective computing and neurotechnology as high risk AI systems where pre-market conformity assessment would be mandatory, yet the requirements of algorithmic transparency would also apply. It implies that all BCI-related cybersecurity solutions used in the EU in the future should be classified on the basis of risks and audited by third parties prior to their implementation. Technical governance IEEE and ISO/IEC JTC 1/SC 42 (Artificial Intelligence) are developing neuro-data processing standards, including encryption-by-design of BCIs, trusted signal acquisition and neuro-behavioral analytics audit trails. An IEEE working paper of 2024 suggests a three-level ethical protocol of neural devices:

- **Consent Layer**: Neural-data collection (e.g., brainprint authentication without monitoring moods)

- **Control Layer**: Providing cryptographic keys to their own neural telemetry under user-specific control

- **Oversight Layer**: Autonomous high-risk deployments of neurotech oversight boards

Additionally, privacy-by-design in neural data is currently under investigation, for example, in the form of differential privacy to brainwave patterns. In 2023, researchers of ETH Zurich demonstrated a prototype that anonymized EEG authentication signals that retains recognition accuracy of above 92%. Interoperable certification schemes such as the Data Protection Seals in GDPR, but specific to neurotech, will then be the next step. Organizations may soon have to receive a Neural Compliance Mark prior to selling their BCI-powered cybersecurity products. These forms of protocol would make neuro-rights less aspirational and verifiable, enforceable, and technically auditable protection.

Cross-Border Challenges for Neural Data

Even sharper geopolitical friction will be found on neural data flows than on conventional personal data because it is irrevocable and predictive. A password can be changed after it has been stolen, but the brainwave pattern cannot. This poses the immediate question of what to do with neuro-data wherein it can be stored, processed, or transferred to.

Transatlantic data transfer is subject to the EU–US Data Privacy Framework (adopted July 2023) but, at the moment, it does not contain any express provisions on brain–computer interface telemetry. The gap implies that the companies that provide BCI-based security services in the EU will not be allowed to transfer the neural telemetry to the US servers without extra security measures, like Standard Contractual Clauses and additional encryption. An amendment to the 2021 neurorights law in Chile might forbid exportation of neural data to countries that do not offer matching protections. LGPD in Brazil has considered neural data as sensitive, which makes it mandatory to localize the data, unless the destination country has proper laws to support neuro-privacy. With more nations securing neurorights, the possibility of increasing data localization requirements can easily fragment the neurotech industry – this will require data siloing in regions just to comply. The other complexity is multi-jurisdictional enforcement. Consider that a neuro-cybersecurity vendor is doing business in Colorado (mandatory opt-in) and California (opt-out). Depending on the residence of the user, the same EEG signal may be handled in various ways. This quilt adds complexity in terms of its cost of complying and legal ambiguity, particularly to international platforms.

Partially, the situation could be alleviated with technical safety on the basis of federated learning the information about which BCI can process locally and not centralize the raw brain data. However, even federated models threaten leakage of metadata on the cognitive states. A Stanford study in 2024 demonstrated that even 92% of so-called anonymized data regarding EEG could be re-identified using machine learning and therefore de-identification of neural data is not effective. Global governing agencies are reacting. The OECD neurotechnology guidelines (drafted 2024) will create neural-data adequacy agreements (similar to the GDPR adequacy decisions), which permits data to cross borders only when it is transferred between jurisdictions with at least minimal protections of neurorights. UNESCO is also looking at a Neural Data Safe Harbor so that there is standardization of international compliance. We will run the risk of neuro-data havens jurisdictions that have lax neuro-privacy regulations, tempting unscrupulous neurotech companies, like data havens of the offshore era. To prevent this, the system of global neuro-datagovernance should coordinate trade, human rights, and cybersecurity regimes.

Although governance frameworks provide the legal and ethical scaffolding of neuro-cybersecurity, policy does not mark the end of the road. Behind the regulations and technical protocols, there is a much broader question: what does this shift actually mean? Why cognition itself is now the final security perimeter, and how researchers, policymakers, and enterprises must work together to protect it. That leads us to the mind boundary, where consciousness and code coalesce.

The Cognitive Frontier: Reimagining Cybersecurity for the Neuro-Digital Age
Why the Mind Is the Next Cybersecurity Frontier?

Cybersecurity outside protecting structural lines of code or network boundaries is no longer in existence as our brain now becomes part of that warfare. Brain–computer interface (BCI) is a very fast-growing type of neural technology that has undergone a rapid adaptation as a potential cybersecurity tool. It is also indicated that the global market of BCI has reached a projection of 2.94 billion (2025) and is going to grow exponentially, reaching $4.26 billion by 2033 at an 18.5% CAGR.[17] The market alone of non-invasive BCIs will grow to over $621 million by 2030, compared to $398 million in 2025, and has an estimated CAGR of 9.35%. These are not only the financial figures, it represents a more fundamental change, which is that the brain is becoming an increasingly information-enriched space. EEGs, fNIRS, and cortical implants can now capture cognitive states in real time, allowing what we might term neural threat detection, detecting stress, deception, or bias or cognitive fatigue before a violation can have occurred. Hackers would have the capacity to invert emotional or decision-making tendencies and take advantage of loopholes that are not available in digital systems.

In contrast, defenders can use neural data to build human-augmented security controls-such as neuro-authentication systems (or a neuro-security signature) as well as adaptive SOCs (or cognitive workload-based load balancing). But to this large attack surface, new risks have been added: neural data is singularly immutable. It is one thing to change a password, and it is another thing to change the piece of mind or the fingerprint of the brain. Neural data is the most fragile personal data of all time due to being irrevocable. The stakes are large. With BCI making its (lab)way to hospitals, and then into the mainstream, the mental domain is not only a defense mechanism but an attack mechanism. That renders the process of cognition protection not optional. This is not conjecture, this follows logically. Protection of mental integrity and cognitive agency has become a part of the cybersecurity frontier, not just lines of code.

---

[17] https://www.datainsightsmarket.com/reports/non-invasive-brain-computer-interface-device-1521357

Call to Action for Researchers, Policymakers, and Enterprises

Researchers and Academics

- Create the privacy-protecting BCI algorithms, that is, differentially protecting the neural signals. In ETH Zurich prototypes, the results with anonymized EEG achieved >92%. This statement represents technical feasibility.

- Perform adversarial testing BCI. Security studies have found more than 300 vulnerabilities in headband-based BCIs such as Muse and NeuroSky.

- Establish new interdisciplinary initiatives such as the Bernstein Network in Germany and the Neuroengineering Center in Rice University that combine neuroscience, AI, and cybersecurity communities.

Regulators and Policymakers

- Neuro-rights are to be enforceable protections. Chile has already established mental privacy and cognitive liberty within the constitution as well as in the decree of their Supreme Court

- Standardize BCI rules. BCI information, similar to biometric information, requires express opt-in consent such as what Colorado has enacted and what is proposed in California. The AI Act of EU also puts neurotech in the category of the so-called high-risk.

- Promote truly international best practices in neural data processing, including matters of encryption, de-identification limits, and data flow systems across borders akin to GDPR adequacy.

Social Enterprises and SOC Operators

- Implement pilot SOCs using EEG-based cognitive monitoring so that fatigue or stress can be detected, as proven in the laboratory by Stanford whereby 99.5% accuracy in the workload detection was achieved.

- Handle neural data as life-dependent resources. for example, encrypt it, limit access, and do not store raw signals long-term – only keep essential aggregate knowledge.

- Foster neuro-literacy of the workforce by training SOC analysts not only on threat detection but how to responsibly work with neural metrics, and their ethical and security consequences.

Without active initiative in those spheres, the neuro-cyber frontier has a chance of becoming an area of exploitation, rather than a sphere of safeguard. Policy and ethics are lagging behind technology, barely keeping up with them these days It is high time to come together.

Key Takeaways

- **Neuro-Digital Paradigm Shift**: Cybersecurity is no longer coded, device or network-centric but, it has also shifted to human brain. The intersection of neuroscience and cybersecurity brings about a new perimeter that is the cognition itself. BCIs and neuroadaptive systems change the brain to a possible weakness and a line of protection and as such, mental confidentiality and basic judgmental rudiments of brain integrity are moving to the focal point of protective systems.

- **Reconceptualizing the Threat Environment**: Conventional malicious attacks used software and social engineering. It is currently possible to compromise the cognitive state or somehow reprogram behavior via manipulation of neural telemetry. It is known that already in cognitive and neuro-hacking research in military laboratories, there is proof-of-concept of influence in perception and in decision-making without infection of a device.

- **Security Instruments based on Neuroscience**: EEG, fNIRS, and MEG are technologies which have reached a stage when they become transportable and allow stress, fatigue, and deception to be monitored in real time. Cognitive biometrics are being studied as secure ways to authenticate, and neuroadaptive SOCs have the potential to have their workloads adapt dynamically with mental states of the analyst, which can eliminate errors caused by stress in stressful situations.

- **Ethics and Neurobehavioral Analytics**: A combination of measures known as neurobehavioral analytics pair brainwave activity with behavioral telemetry to anticipate intent or deception and provide means of detecting insider threat. The systems, however, also weigh heavily on ethical issues of privacy and consent as well as how the technology may be abused through neuro profiling being used to discriminate or coerce.

- **Obstacles and Technical Restrictions**: Field use encounters technical challenges, such as poor signal-to-noise ratios, poor interoperability, and high neurotech device costs. Neural data is highly contingent and not free to standardization and big-scale applications. In addition, BCIs are susceptible to spoofing issues and adversarial attacks, forming novel security threats.

- **Neuro-Rights and privacy**: Neural data is highly personal, predictive, and non-renewable, and thus protection needs to be provided to a greater extent than traditional biometrics. Chile was the first state where the neuro-rights were declared, where cognitive liberty and mental privacy were described as rights. Similar laws are passed in other states, such as Colorado, requiring neural data to be designated as sensitive but are not harmonized globally.

- **Policy and Governance Systems**: The chapter brings out the fact that global neuro-rights charters, ethical protocols and standardized legal frameworks are direly needed. Laws such as the EU AI Act and Colorado HB24-1058 represent new regulatory developments in this field, which could be hampered by variable state and national laws that endanger the development of a cohesive compliance environment and create so-called neuro-data havens where minimal protection laws operate.

- **Cross-Border Neural Data Problems**: Neural data generates emerging geopolitical strains. As compared to passwords, brainwave patterns cannot be reset in case they are breached. The problems of the data localization requirements, the lack of proper international agreements, and a possibility of metadata exposure even in the case of federated schemes cast doubt on the safety of storage and transfer of neural telemetry outside and across borders.

- **Acceptance by the Society and Workforce**: On top of legislation and technology, people need to be ready and trusting. Continuous brain surveillance creates apprehensions of thought policing, monitoring, and loss of goodwill. Public learning, lawful oversight, and visible consents will be vital in preventing outrage and developing faith in neuro-enhanced security systems.

- **The road ahead**: The chapter concludes by encouraging researchers, policymakers, and businesses to join forces to establish privacy-preserving BCIs, responsible governance, and neuro-literacy of the workforce. In its passive state, neuro-cybersecurity may be a means of oppression instead of safeguarding. The future of digital trust lies in the protection of cognition itself, "the final frontier of cybersecurity".

Index

A

Adaptive learning, 220, 221

Adaptive learning framework, 207

Adaptive neural security
systems, 326

Adaptive threat detection
systems, 230–232
memory consolidation, 232
pattern library expansion,
230, 231
skill transfer and cross-domain
expertise, 231

"aha" effect, 343

AI and machine learning, 12

AI-neural security integration, 256
AI-powered adversarial
systems, 267–269
categorization, 278
convergence, 261
evolution beyond binary
attacks, 265–267
human-centric and
autonomous defense, 262
hybrid threat
landscapes, 263–265
models of high-risk sectors, 263
neural data AI processing
ethics, 300–303
secure and resilient
computing, 262
strategic implications, 276, 277
threat vectors, 272–275

Alert fatigue, 14

Amygdala, 30, 34–36, 42, 44,
52, 92, 242

Anterior cingulate cortex (ACC),
36–37, 43, 50, 51, 53,
241, 242

Architecture, neural
authentication, 201
authentication engine, 206–208
edge processing
layer, 203, 204
secure communication layer,
205, 206
signal acquisition, 201, 202

Area Under Curve (AUC), 193

Artificial intelligence (AI), 2, 98,
108, 169, 215
Contextual Analysis, 105
fighting AI-era attacks, 176
with neuroscience
(*see* AI-neural security
integration)
and neuroscience
convergence, 100–102

Attention Deficit Hyperactivity
    Disorder (ADHD), 88
Authentication, 59, 61, 104,
    112, 125
    adversarial vulnerability, 149
    continuous, 64
    P300, 118, 122, 126, 140,
        144, 178
Authentication methods, 7,
    11, 17, 20
    static, 13
Autism Spectrum Disorder
    (ASD), 88
Automated social engineering, 268
Automated systems, limitations
    context blindness, 223
    false positive epidemic and
        alert fatigue, 222
    signature dependency, 224
    zero-day detection
        impossibility, 222, 223

B

Basal ganglia, 81, 82, 84, 87, 92
Basic Web Application Attacks, 170
The Battle for Your Brain
    (Farahany), 329
Bayesian methods, 103
BCIs, 271
BCI2000 processing, 144, 157
BCI technology, 89
Behavioral biometrics, 2, 54, 59,
    60, 62, 388
    adaptive intelligence, 64
    AI and neuroscience
        convergence, 100–102
    applications, 60
    basal ganglia, 81, 84
    brain-behavior
        correlations, 87, 88
    cerebellum, 82, 84
    challenges and
        opportunities, 88–90
    cognitive/emotional inference,
        risk of, 97–100
    cognitive load and emotional
        state, 85–86
    continuous authentication
        beyond login, 64
    correlation, 389
    ethical, legal, and privacy
        dimensions, 90
    gait recognition, 73, 74
    habit formation and muscle
        memory, 81–84
    importance of, 63
    insider threat
        detection, 65–67
    keystroke dynamics, 68–70
    motor cortex, 82, 84, 85
    mouse movement, 71, 72
    neural and multimodal
        biometrics, 194–200
    neural consolidation for
        repetitive behavior, 87
    neural-informed behavioral
        data, 94–97

neuroadaptive biometrics
system, 100
neuroanatomical correlation, 85
neuroethics of unconscious
behavioral profiling, 91–94
neuroscientific basis of, 80
passwords and tokens, 63
personalized
neuroprofiles, 106–108
physiological *vs.*, 66–67
predictive neuro-behavioural
threat model, 104–106
prefrontal cortex (PFC), 82
touchscreen gesture
biometrics, 74, 75
types of, 67, 68
types of traits, 79–80
user experience, 64
voice, 76–79
wearables and EEG-informed
systems, 102–104
Behavioral Drift Detected
event, 105
Behavioral priming techniques, 9
BehavioSec, 84
BioCatch, 84
BioCatch behavioral biometrics
platform, 285–288
BioID face biometrics
platform, 288–290
BioID Web Service (BWS), 288
Biometric Access Control, 321
Biometric authentication, 258
advantages, 387, 388

behavioral biometric
correlation, 389
detection of unauthorized
access, 389
EEG signatures, 386
multi-factor authentication,
386, 387
real-time user verification, 388
Biometric cryptosystems, 205
Biometric drift, 89
BioSemi ActiveThree, 139
Bluetooth Low Energy (BLE)
risk, 150
BotSpeechov, 76
Brain, 27, 30, 32
amygdala, 34–36
anterior cingulate cortex
(ACC), 36–37
cognitive bias, 31
cognitive mechanisms, 2
components of, 33
decision-making (*see*
decision-making)
on digital battlefield, 27
human decision-making and
actions, 6
monitoring activity, 10
prefrontal cortex (PFC), 33–34
Brain Initiative of the IEEE, 24
Brain–computer interfaces (BCIs),
3, 7, 23, 111, 112, 114, 115,
311, 314, 329, 356, 364, 404,
405, 410, 418, 420,
422, 428–432

Brain–computer
    interfaces (BCIs) (*cont.*)
  cognitive perimeter in
    cybersecurity, 155–158
  comparison of types, 120–121
  digital defense, 122–127
  invasive, 115, 116
  non-invasive, 118–119
  platforms and tools, 127–145
  security risks and ethical
    implications, 145–155
  semi-invasive, 117, 118
Brainjacking, 321
Brain-monitoring technologies, 18
Brazil
  neuro-rights regulations, 23
Business Email Compromise
  (BEC), 1

C

Cerebellum, 82, 92
Check Point Software
  Technologies, 4
Chile, 10, 426, 432
  constitutional model, 348
  constitutional shield, 345, 346
  neuro-rights legislation, 97, 148,
    153, 156, 417
  neuro-rights regulations, 23, 26
Cognitive augmentation systems
  decision support systems, 227
  load management and workload
    distribution, 226, 227
  real-time neural feedback and
    performance optimization,
    225, 226
Cognitive authentication
  systems, 317
Cognitive autonomy preservation
  individual rights and
    remedies, 307–309
  legal and regulatory
    considerations, 306, 307
  organizational governance
    frameworks, 306
  technical autonomy, 305
Cognitive bias, 31
Cognitive biometrics, 311, 314,
  407, 408
Cognitive Correlation, 105
Cognitive Enhancement of Security
  Personnel, 320
Cognitive liberty, 301, 410
Cognitive load, 31
Cognitive load management, 22
Cognitive load monitoring, 216
Cognitive load monitoring
  systems, 382
Cognitive load-modeling, 54
Cognitive neuroscience, 29
Cognitive overload
  exploitation, 266
Cognitive rights in
  workplace, 422–424
Cognitive State Engine, 107
Cognitive state monitoring,
  258, 361

Cognitive Technology Threat Warning System (CT2WS), 214, 216
Cognitive training, 18, 21–23, 25
Cognitive warfare defense, 260
Colorado Privacy Act, 427
Common Spatial Pattern (CSP), 239
Consumer neurotechnology ecosystem, 322–324
market analysis and security implications, 323, 324
regulatory gaps, 324
security analysis, 325
Context-aware and longitudinal models, 89
Context blindness, 223
Contextual adaptation, 165
Continuous improvement mechanisms
feedback loops, 232
personalized training, 233
Convergence crisis, 328
governance and innovation, 332–335
involuntary neurodata risk, 343–344
neuroprivacy, 335–343
privacy in neuro-surveillance, 335
Convolutional Neural Networks (CNNs), 192
CrowdStrike Falcon platform, 278–280

Cyberattacks, 1, 4, 215
adversarial methods of, 19
on American water treatment, 5
hybrid threats, 3
marketization of cyberweapons, 3
Cybercrime, 2
Cyber defense models, 11–12, 16, 18
Cyber protection, 25
Cyber risks, 1
Cybersecurity, xv, 27, 111, 114, 211, 255
neural structures and functions, 39
neuroscience and (see Neuroscience and cybersecurity)
technology, 28
training, 41
Cyber security organization, xv
Cybersecurity Workforce Study, 4
Cyber services, xv
Cyber threats, 5–6

D

Darktrace active AI platform, 280–282
Deadline-induced urgency, 47
Deception detection and pattern recognition, 22
Decision loop, 39–49
behavioural output, 48, 49

Decision loop (*cont.*)
    cognitive appraisal, 43, 44
    decision threshold
        activation, 47, 48
    emotional valuation, 44, 45
    neurochemical
        modulation, 45–47
    sensory input, 42, 43
    stimulus, 40–42
Decision-making, 27
    conflict resolution, 36–37
    executive function and risk
        analysis, 33–34
    habitual and reward-based
        decisions, 37–38
    neurobiology of, 32
    threat perception and
        emotional triggers, 34–36
Deep brain stimulation (DBS), 312,
    320, 331
Deepfake identity theft, 13
Deepfakes, 30, 52, 161
Deep learning, 248
Deep learning models, 124, 207
Default mode network
    (DMN), 48, 242
Defense Advanced Research
    Projects Agency
    (DARPA), 21
Detection systems
    user cognitive states
        neglecting by, 14
Digital authentication, 162

Digital defense, BCIs
    cognitive state monitoring,
        123, 124
    hybrid BCIs, 126, 127
    intent-based access control,
        124, 125
    neural authentication, 122, 123
    neurosecurity, 125, 126
Digital privacy, 23
Digital protection, 257
Digital Rights Charter, 426
Dopaminergic system, 37–38, 52
Dorsolateral prefrontal cortex
    (dlPFC), 43, 53, 241
Drift Diffusion Models (DDMs), 47
Dynamic cognitive patterns, 164
Dynamic imaging of coherent
    sources (DICS), 244

E

Economic transformation
    imperative, 217
Edge computing, 4, 246
EEG-based authentication
    systems, 328
EEG-based BCIs, 311
EEG-based
    neurofeedback, 366–368
EEG-based threat recognition
    systems, 235
    advanced signal acquisition
        systems, 239

alpha and beta wave
modulation, 237, 238
gamma band activity, 238
machine learning integration
architecture, 240
N400 component and semantic
processing, 236, 237
P300 response, 235, 236
preprocessing pipelines,
239, 240
real-time processing, 240
EEGLAB, 144
EEG monitoring, 216
Electrocorticography (ECoG), 117
Electrodermal activity (EDA), 132
Electroencephalography (EEG),
118, 119, 123–125,
128, 132, 139, 145, 149,
155, 157, 166, 167,
172–174, 176, 192, 194,
195, 202, 203, 226, 317, 318,
323, 330, 332, 336, 337,
342, 343
fatigue detection, 124
for robust defense, 126
hardware, 189
real-time, 381
resting-state, 168, 186
Emotional hijacking, 51
Emotiv EPOC X professional
neural interface, 295–297
Ensemble methods,
authentication, 207
Equal Error Rate (EER), 193

Ethical and policy considerations,
neurosecurity, 312
consumer neurotechnology
ecosystem, 322–324
convergence crisis (*see*
Convergence crisis)
critical policy, 314
future innovation, 315, 316
human rights, awareness, 315
hybrid security
architectures, 324–328
invasive BCIs, 319–322
next-gen security systems, 313
non-invasive BCIs, 317–319
real-world risk scenarios, 314
regulatory landscapes and
critical gaps, 344–347
Europe
work stress, 2
European Union, 346
neuro-rights regulations, 23, 26
EU–US Data Privacy
Framework, 429
Event-Related Potentials (ERPs),
167, 177, 185, 188
P300, 187
stimulus-induced, 168
Eye-trackers, 38
Eye-tracking, 10, 229

F

Facial recognition, 288
False Rejection Rate (FRR), 193

Fingerprints/facial scans, 63
Firmware and software
vulnerabilities, 321
fMRI-based
neurofeedback, 368–370
fMRI-based threat analysis
amygdala, 242
default mode network, 242
executive control networks,
241, 242
hippocampal memory
systems, 242
prefrontal cortex activation
networks, 241
fNIRS-based
neurofeedback, 370–372
Frontiers in Human
Neuroscience, 6
Frontiers in Neuroscience, 155
Functional Magnetic Resonance
Imaging (fMRI), 119, 241
Functional Near-Infrared
Spectroscopy (fNIRS), 119,
123, 132, 139, 145, 243, 270,
336, 404
portable, 244
for robust defense, 126

G

Gait recognition, 73, 74
GDPR, 108, 314, 332, 346
GDPR of Europe, 427
Generative AI, 4

Generative artificial
intelligence, 267
Governance and policy
frameworks, 406
cross-border
challenges, 428–430
neuro-rights charters, 426–427
standardizing legal and ethical
protocols, 427–428
Government 2 Government
(G2G), xv
GPGPUs, 249

H

Habit formation, 81
brain regions and role, 83
cellular and molecular
mechanisms, 82
deliberate actions to automatic
habits, 82, 83
muscle memory, 83
neuroanatomy, 81, 82
Hackers, 5
Hardware devices, BCIs
hybrid devices, 132–136
invasive and research-grade
BCIs, 136–139
non-invasive, 128–132
High-resolution dry
electroencephalograph
(EEG) systems, 404
HIPAA, 314
Hippocampal memory systems, 242

Human–AI cognitive symbiosis, 259
Human-augmented security controls, 431
Human decision-making, *see* Decision-making
Human-error-induced breaches, predicting and preempting, 14–16
Human–machine interaction security system, 364
Human–machine symbiosis, 213, 216
Human pattern recognition superiority
  adaptive learning, 220, 221
  contextual understanding and semantic processing, 219
  cross-domain knowledge transfer, 221
  intuitive threat assessment and subconscious processing, 219, 220
Hybrid BCIs, 132–136
  comparative, 133–134
  decision matrix, 135
  headset, 136
Hybrid fNIRS-EEG systems, 127
Hybrid human–AI
  detection systems
  attention direction, 229
  signal integration and multi-modal fusion, 228
  subconscious threat detection, 229, 230

Hybrid human-AI security operations model, 396
Hybrid security
  architectures, 324–328
  adaptive neural security systems, 326
  dual-use capabilities, 327
  multi-modal neural authentication, 326

I

IBM Security Intelligence Report (2024), 13
IBM Watson Studio, 282–284
Independent Component Analysis (ICA), 190, 239
Information technology (IT) security, 424
Informed consent analyst rights, 251
Innovations, cybersecurity, 19, 24
  human-centric cybersecurity paradigm, 24–26
  neuro-aware security systems, 20–21
Institutional Review Boards (IRBs), 424
Intentional authentication, 164
Inter-session and inter-day variability, 194
Intuitive pattern recognition, 213
Intuitive threat assessment, 219, 220

Invasive and research-grade
    BCIs, 136–139
    comparative, 137–138
    decision matrix, 139
Invasive BCIs, 115, 116, 319–322
    critical vulnerabilities and
        attack vectors, 321
    current emerging applications,
        320, 321
    ethical risks in
        applications, 153
    security risk assessment
        matrix, 322
Involuntary neurodata
    risk, 343–344
ISACA, 12
ISACA State of Cybersecurity report
    (2024), 2

J

JSON Web Tokens (JWT)-based
    API, 288

K

Keystroke dynamics, 68–70, 195

L

LabStreamingLayer (LSL), 128, 145
LGPD in Brazil, 429
Linear discriminant analysis
    (LDA), 191

Long-Term Depression (LTD), 82
Long-Term Potentiation
    (LTP), 82, 231

M

Machine learning (ML), 103, 268
    integration, 240, 266
    models, 122, 149
Magnetoencephalography (MEG),
    119, 336, 404
MEG integration, 218, 244
Memory consolidation process, 232
Mental surveillance, 91
Microsoft Azure Cognitive
    Services, 292–294
Microsoft SEAL, 300
Middleware and signal processing,
    BCIs, 139–145
    comparative, 141–143
    decision matrix, 144, 145
Mindfulness and executive control
    training, 22
Misinformation, 30
ML and neural patterns, 191–193
    algorithms for brainwave
        classification, 191, 192
    evaluation metrics, 193
    real-time vs offline
        authentication, 192
    validation and training, 192
Mobile and field applications
    edge computing, 246
    mesh networking, 247

portable neural monitoring
systems, 246
rugged hardware design, 246
Motor cortex, 82, 84, 115
Mouse movement biometrics, 71, 72
Multi-domain ethics
interdisciplinary ethics
committee structure,
303, 304
monitoring and assessment,
304, 305
Multi-factor authentication (MFA),
63, 169–171
Multi-factor biometric
authentication (MFBA), 61
Multi-modal neural
authentication, 326
Multi-modal neuroimaging
integration
advanced MEG analysis, 244
data-fusion methodologies, 243
EEG-fMRI fusion
technologies, 243
fNIRS, 243
MEG integration, 244
portable fNIRS, 244
Multi-model architecture, 206
Muscle memory, 83

N

NATO's Strategic Communications
Centre of Excellence, 3
Nature Communications, 126

Nature Human Behaviour
research, 7
Neural authentication, 161
adaptive complexity, 166
biometric, 251
collapse of traditional
models, 169–171
continuous liveness detection, 165
defense against future
threats, 174
human-centric, frictionless
security, 173, 174
immersive and neuro-adaptive
systems, 171, 172
importance of, 169
multi-dimensional
uniqueness, 166
neural biometrics (*see* Neural
biometrics)
non-replicability, 165
principles, 164, 165
security landscape, 170
static to dynamic identity, 162, 163
as ultimate biometric
frontier, 165–169
Zero Trust Architecture (ZTA),
172, 173
Neural biometrics
cognitive stimuli and identity
elicitation, 186–188
comparisons with behavioral
and multimodal
biometrics, 194–200

Neural biometrics (*cont.*)
    implementation frameworks
        architecture, 200–208
    limitations and
        variability, 193–194
    machine learning
        (ML), 191–193
    neurophysiological basis of
        brainwave
        identity, 176–186
    signal acquisition and
        preprocessing
        pipelines, 188–191
Neural data AI processing ethics
    algorithmic transparency and
        explainability, 302
    bias prevention, 302, 303
    cognitive liberty and mental
        autonomy, 301
Neural enhancement, 214, 217
Neural feedback
    real-time, 225, 226
Neural fingerprint paradox,
    336, 341
Neural interpretation
    layers, 92
Neural networks, 192, 236
Neural patterns (defenders to
    attackers), 50
    cyber adversaries, 52, 53
    end users, 51, 52
    executive decision-
        making, 53, 54
    insider threats, 54, 55

    neuroadaptive security
        systems, 55, 56
    security professionals, 50, 51
Neural privacy
    and data security, 250, 251
Neural processing unit (NPU), 240
Neural profiling
    and risks, 419
Neural signatures, 339
    anonymization and differential
        privacy, 341
    cognitive capabilities, 339
    cross-context tracking, 339, 340
    distributed neural
        authentication, 341
    immediate cognitive states, 339
    learned associations, 339
    lifetime vulnerability
        exposure, 339
    physiological indicators, 339
    predictive profiling and
        discrimination, 340
    versioning, 341
    windows of temporal
        authentication, 341
Neural-digital twins, 412, 413
Neural-feedback training
    systems, 247
Neural-informed behavioral
    data, 94–97
    consent layers, 95
    deletability, 95
    over time, 94
    privacy, 95

Neuralink, 139
Neural-rights
    constitutional protection, 348
    democratic governance
        challenge, 348
    forward path integrated
        response, 349–351
    innovation without wisdom, 349
    moment of irreversible
        decision, 347, 348
Neuroadaptive biometric
    systems, 89
Neuroadaptive biometrics
    systems, 100
Neuroadaptive systems, 408
Neuro-adaptive systems, 171, 172
Neuro-Agentic Security, 258
Neuro-augmented cyber facilities,
    415, 416
Neuro-aware security
    systems, 20–21
Neurobehavioral analytics, 409
Neurobehavioral variability, 88
Neuro-biometrics, 102–104
Neurocognitive firewall, 21
Neurocognitive resilience
    programs, 22
Neuro-cognitive telemetry,
    261, 262
Neuro-cybersecurity strategic
    convergence model, 256
Neuro Cyber Threat Intelligence
    (NCTI), 393
Neurodata analytics, 311

Neuroergonomics, 50
Neurofeedback, 3, 7, 8, 113, 356
    AI-neurofeedfack fusion, 413
    attention and focus
        improvement, 381
    biometric authentication and
        identity verification, 385–390
    cognitive enhancement, 381
    cognitive training and, 18
    comparative analysis, 376–379
    critical infrastructure
        protection, 361–362
    dual-purpose nature, 360–361
    EEG-based, 366–368
    as enhancement tool, 380
    fMRI-based, 368–370
    fNIRS-based, 370–372
    historical development from
        clinical
        applications, 365–366
    human factor
        enhancement, 362–364
    initiatives, 18
    military, 365
    real-time brain state
        monitoring, 372–375
    real-time monitoring, 8
    risk-benefit analysis, 395–398
    strategic imperative of
        neurotechnology, 359
    strategic
        implementation, 394–395
    stress management and
        decision-making, 384–385

Neurofeedback (*cont.*)
    technology, 358–360, 364, 365,
        394, 397
    threat detection and analysis
        enhancement, 390–394
    types of, 366
    workplace programs, 54
NeuroID, 86, 91
Neuroimaging applications
    fMRI, 241, 242
    multi-modal, 243, 244
Neuro-motor planning, 93
Neuroplasticity, 230–232
Neuroplasticity-boosting
    exercises, 9
Neuroprivacy, 146–148, 335–343
    biometric security methods, 338
    neural fingerprint paradox, 337
Neuro-rights, 10, 16, 26, 97, 108,
        148, 153, 156, 315, 406, 410,
        417, 432
    and policy imperative, 23–24
    charters, 426–427
Neurorights Foundation, 335, 426
Neuroscience, 32
    advance in defense, 270, 271
    of cyber policy and
        strategy, 53, 54
    as weapon, 52, 53
Neuroscience and cybersecurity, 2,
        6–11, 175, 357, 403
    authentication methods, 17
    barriers and limitations, 410

    beyond enhancement, 19–20
    cognitive frontier, 430–431
    cognitive training, 21–23, 25
    cognitive-aware cybersecurity
        interfaces, 7
    critical challenges, 416–426
    embedding neural data, 10
    eye-tracking, 10
    hacking human psychology, 9
    human weakness, 17
    human-error-induced breaches,
        predicting and
        preempting, 14–16
    innovation (*see* Innovations,
        cybersecurity)
    multidisciplinary
        collaborations, 24
    neuro-rights and policy
        imperative, 23–24
    regulators and policymakers,
        432, 433
    researchers and academics, 432
    social enterprises and SOC
        operators, 433
    threat intelligence and
        regulatory
        mechanisms, 16–17
    user cognitive states neglecting
        by detection systems, 14
Neurosecurity, 312
Neurosecurity fabrics, 414
Neurotechnology and Society
    initiative (OECD), 24

Neurotechnology integration
approach, 225
Neurotransmitters, 45, 46
Nexstem AI, 125
Next-Generation Nerve Interfaces
project (DARPA), 156
Next-Generation Nonsurgical
Neurotechnology (N3), 355
Non-invasive BCIs, 118, 128–132,
311, 317–319, 431
advantages, 119
comparative, 129–130
decision matrix, 131, 132
EEG, 118
fNIRS, 119
headset, 132
MEG and fMRI, 119
operational deployments,
317, 318
security applications and
risks, 319
technical architecture and
vulnerabilities, 318, 319

O

OECD, 315, 335
neurotechnology guidelines, 430
Online banking fraud, 61
Online threats, 9
OpenBCI, 157
OpenBCI research platform, 297–298
OpenViBE, 144

P

P300 authentication system, 118,
122, 126, 140, 144, 178
P300 ERP, 167, 187
P300 event-related potential (ERP),
122, 154, 235
Palantir Gotham intelligence
platform, 294–295
Parkinson's disease, 88
Passive liveness detection, 289
Passive neurodata harvesting, 331
Passwords, 63, 104, 170
Performance assessment
protocols, 247
Performance optimization
protocols, 383
Personalized neural signatures, 90
Personalized
neuroprofiles, 106–108
Phishing, 29, 30, 161
emotional hijacking, 51
Physical access attacks, 322
Physiological and cognitive
variability, 193
Platforms and tools, BCIs, 127, 128
hardware devices, 128–139
middleware and signal
processing, 139–145
Predictive neuro-behavioural
threat model, 104–106
Predictive threat
intelligence, 259

Prefrontal cortex (PFC), 33–35,
      42–44, 46, 50, 53, 82, 92
Presentation attack detection
      (PAD), 288, 289
Privacy and neuro-ethics
   brainwave surveillance vs.
      consent, 418
   neural profiling and risks, 419
   ownership of neural data, 417
Privacy in neuro-surveillance, 335
Privacy-preserving neural analytics
   advanced anonymization
      challenges, 300
   neural data, 299
   technical privacy protection,
      299, 300
Proactive anticipation, 32
Protective incompetence, 212
Psychological profiling, 3

Q

Quantum computing, 4
Quantum neuro-cyber interfaces,
      414, 415

R

Random forests, 191
Ransomware, 1, 53
Ransomware-as-a-Service (RaaS), 3
Rapid Serial Visual Presentation
      (RSVP), 342

Real-time brain-informed
      defenses, 55, 56
Real-time brain state
      monitoring, 372–375
   cognitive states, 373, 374
   integration with
      security operations,
      374, 375
   loop, 373
   real-time protocols, 374
Real-time cognitive state
      surveillance, 318
Real-time monitoring, 123
Real-time *vs.* offline
      authentication, 192
Real-time processing, 240
Recurrent Neural Networks
      (RNNs), 192
Regulatory landscapes,
      neurosecurity, 345
   Chile, 345
   consumer protection
      failure, 346
   lack of international
      coordination, 346, 347
   medical vs consumer lookup
      abuse, 347
   workplace surveillance, 346
Regulatory landscapes,
      neurotechnology security
   Chile, 346
Remote Procedure Call (RPC)
      platform, 288

S

Safe Neural Channels of
Communication, 320
Security Information and Event
Management (SIEM)
systems, 128, 405
Security Operations Centers
(SOCs), 28, 34, 44, 46, 50,
145, 150, 151, 155, 216, 415
Security risks and ethical
implications, BCIs, 145–155
adversarial vulnerability, 149
backdoor and poisoning
threats, 149, 150
consent, autonomy, and neural
data reuse, 148, 149
data retention and lifespan of
templates, 152
governance, oversight, and
neuroethical certification,
153, 155
in invasive BCI
applications, 153
neuroprivacy and brainprint
protection, 147, 148
psychological impact on agency
and intent, 151, 152
wireless communication and
BLE, 150
workplace surveillance and
cognitive coercion, 151
Semi-invasive BCIs, 117, 118
Serotonin, 45

Signal acquisition, neural
biometrics, 188
EEG hardware, 189
preprocessing techniques,
189, 190
segmentation and feature
extraction, 190, 191
Signal processing and pattern
recognition
deep learning, 248
ensemble methods and model
fusion, 249
real-time processing, 249, 250
spectral analysis, 248
transfer learning, 249
wavelet analysis, 248
SIM swapping, 13
SME (Cyber Security), xv
Social engineering, 1, 2, 7, 9, 13,
15–16, 29, 52
campaigns, 266
sophistication in, 5
techniques, 3
Societal and workforce acceptance
cognitive rights in
workplace, 422–424
public trust, 421–422
training and
adaptation, 424–426
SOCs integration
adaptive alert management
systems, 245
cognitive state monitoring, 245
fatigue monitoring, 245

SOCs integration (*cont.*)
  next-generation analyst
    workstation design, 244
  workload distribution, 245
Spain, 10
  neuro-rights regulations, 23, 26
Splunk SOAR, 291–292
Static authentication methods, 13
Statista, 112
Strategic future imperative, 218
Stress management
  decision-making, 384, 385
  fatigue detection, 385
  regulation during incident
    response, 384
Striatum, 37–38, 82
Subconscious threat detection,
    220, 229, 230, 393
Support Vector Machines
    (SVM), 191
Surging stressors, 2
Surveillance cognition, 343
Synthetic identity fraud, 5

T

Technological hurdles
  antagonism, 420
  interoperability and
    standardization
    problems, 420
  low signal-to-noise ratio, 420
  scalability and costs, 421
Temporal authenticity, 164

Third-party integration risks, 324
Threat detection and analysis
    enhancement
  anomaly detection
    capabilities, 391
  brain-state triggered security
    protocols, 392
  neurofeedback training, 390
  reduced false positive rates,
    391, 392
  SIEM systems, 393, 394
  subconscious threat detection
    mechanisms, 393
Threat detection enhancement, 318
Threat detection,
    neurotechnology-enhanced
  adaptive threat detection
    systems, 230–232
  cognitive augmentation
    systems, 225–227
  continuous improvement
    mechanisms, 232–233
  EEG-based recognition, 235–240
  ethical considerations and
    privacy protection, 250–251
  hierarchical framework, 235
  human pattern recognition
    superiority, 219–221
  hybrid human–AI detection
    systems, 227–230
  limitations of automated
    systems, 221–224
  mobile and field
    applications, 246–247

neuroimaging
applications, 240–244
signal processing and pattern
recognition, 248–250
SOCs integration, 244–246
training and skill development
applications, 247
Threat Probability Score, 106
Touchscreen gesture
biometrics, 74, 75
TUV Informationstechnik GmbH
(TUViT), 289

U

UNESCO, 335, 395, 426, 430
Recommendation on Ethics of
Neurotechnology, 346
United Nations Special
Rapporteur, 91
United States
Genetic Information Non-
Discrimination Act, 423
neuro-rights regulations, 23, 26
Universal Declaration of Human
Rights, 427
US Army Cyber Command, 23

V

Ventromedial pre frontal cortex
(vmPFC), 241

Verizon 2024 Data Breach
Investigations Report, 170
Visionary frontiers, 412
AI-neurofeedback
fusion, 413
neural-digital twins, 412, 413
neuro-augmented cyber
facilities, 415, 416
neurosecurity
fabrics, 414
quantum neuro-cyber
interfaces, 414, 415
Voice behavioral biometrics, 76–79
Vulnerabilities, 8, 9, 12,
14–16, 19, 20
adversarial, 154
firmware and software, 321

W, X, Y

Wet *vs.* dry electrodes, 189
Wireless communication, 150
Wireless Protocol Exploitation, 321
Workforce transformation
revolution, 217
Workplace surveillance, 151, 346

Z

Zero Trust and IAM, 127
Zero Trust Architecture (ZTA),
172, 173

The manufacturer's authorised representative in the EU is Springer
Nature Customer Service Centre GmbH, Europaplatz 3, 69115 Heidelberg,
Germany. If you have any concerns regarding our products, please
contact ProductSafety@springernature.com

Printed and bound by CPI Group (UK) Ltd, Croydon, CR0 4YY
23/04/2026
02095592-0015